SECOND EDITION

Exploring Christianity:
An Introduction

Robert C. Monk
Joseph D. Stamey

McMurry College

PRENTICE HALL, *Englewood Cliffs, New Jersey 07632*

Library of Congress Cataloging-in-Publication Data

Monk, Robert C.
  Exploring Christianity : an Introduction / Robert C. Monk, Joseph
D. Stamey. 2nd ed.
     p.   cm.
  Includes bibliographical references.
  ISBN 0-13-296153-9
  1. Christianity. I. Stamey, Joseph D. II. Title.
BR121.2.M583 1990
200—dc20   89-39174
                                               CIP

Editorial/production supervision and
  interior design: Patricia V. Amoroso
Cover design: Lundgren Graphics, Ltd.
Manufacturing buyer: Mike Woerner

 © 1990, 1984 by Prentice-Hall, Inc.
A Paramount Communications Company
Englewood Cliffs, New Jersey 07632

Scripture passages throughout the text have been reprinted
with permission from the *Revised Standard Version of the Bible*,
copyrighted © 1946, 1952, 1971, 1973.

Printed in the United States of America

10 9 8 7 6

ISBN 0-13-296153-9

PRENTICE-HALL INTERNATIONAL (UK) LIMITED, *London*
PRENTICE-HALL OF AUSTRALIA PTY. LIMITED, *Sydney*
PRENTICE-HALL CANADA INC., *Toronto*
PRENTICE-HALL HISPANOAMERICANA, S.A., *Mexico*
PRENTICE-HALL OF INDIA PRIVATE LIMITED, *New Delhi*
PRENTICE-HALL OF JAPAN, INC., *Tokyo*
SIMON & SCHUSTER ASIA PTE. LTD., *Singapore*
EDITORA PRENTICE-HALL DO BRASIL, LTDA., *Rio de Janeiro*

Contents

CHAPTER FIVE

The Foundations of Modern Christianity

Preface

Exploring Christianity has been designed as a comprehensive introductory text for use in studying Christianity, its history and development, and the variety and unity of its beliefs, traditions, practices, and organizational structures. It has grown from our experience, during the past twenty years, in teaching a number of rather different college-level courses in religion studies. One of these is a semester-long "Introduction to Christianity" course, the successor to a course called "Introduction to Religion." "Introduction to Religion" focused on several of the world's religions, usually allocating from three to five weeks to the study of Christianity. We believe that *Exploring Christianity* can be used for courses of either type. It was largely our sense of need for a text that can be used either as a main text for a semester-long study of Christian traditions or for a more concentrated shorter unit that influenced our attempt. We have also drawn on our experience in courses on "Religion and Society" and "Christianity and Human Problems," in each of which we felt the need for a brief, comprehensive introductory study of Christian groups and traditions.

There are a number of excellent works dealing with the history of Christianity. We have often found these useful, but too detailed or technical for the courses we were conducting. There are also a number of available introductory texts that treat Christianity. Most of these have strong points to recommend them. However, most of the ones we attempted to use seemed, like the works on church history, better suited for other kinds of courses; they were either too detailed or too specialized. We set ourselves the task of developing a text that can be used either as the principal text for an entire course dealing with Christian religious traditions or for a unit in a course dealing with comparative or world religions, religion and society, Western civilization, or religion and contemporary issues. We realize that our text will be vulnerable to the criticisms we have made of others and to some unique to it; however, we have aimed at producing a book that can be used flexibly and that will provide an adequate and comprehensive, but not overly technical or specialized, introduction to the study of Christianity.

The second edition of *Exploring Christianity* differs from its first edition in two major ways. The historical sections in Chapters Three, Four, and Five have been thoroughly revised, and the original Chapter Eight has been replaced by an entirely different chapter. Chapter Eight dealt with the life stories of a very large number of exemplary Christians from a large number of Christian traditions and historical contexts. In response to suggestions from many who have used the book, as well as to our own teaching experience using it, we decided that the stories were too brief to achieve their aim of allowing students to enter imaginatively the lives of the exemplary persons. In the new Chapter Eight, the number of exemplary Christians is reduced to thirteen. Their stories are told as brief biographies, long enough, we hope, to achieve the aim of the chapter. We also believe that, though the short biographies are heavily weighted toward recent times, they include a wide range of representative lives and experiences, so that the new chapter, supplementing the historical sections, genuinely adds to the reader's comprehension of the unities and diversities of Christian tradition.

Chapters Three, Four, and Five were rewritten in order to focus more directly on a smaller number of themes, episodes, and issues in Christian history. This approach replaces the more panoramic or survey approach of the first edition. Many users of the book reported that students frequently felt swamped by the amount of detail that the first edition attempted to incorporate. In the new edition there is use of narrative recreation to highlight ways in which significant developments of Christian tradition appeared to those who experienced them.

In addition to these major changes, *Exploring Christianity* has been updated and revised in a number of ways that we believe will make it a more useable and teachable text. Sections on recent trends in world Christianity have been added in Chapter Nine. The positions of the chapters "Christian Beliefs" (Chapter Seven in the first edition) and "Faith and Knowledge" (Chapter Six in the first edition) have been reversed, putting the emphasis where we think it more appropriately belongs, with discussion of the unity and content, the what of Christian belief, preceding the discussion of the more abstract ideas of its hows and whys.

Exploring Christianity is not a history of Christianity, though we believe it will give the student acquaintance with the major outlines of Christianity's historical development. Chapters One through Five follow essentially a chronological, or historical, outline from the Jewish backgrounds of Christianity to its emergence as a truly world religion in the nineteenth and twentieth centuries. They do not attempt historical completeness, which would be impossible in a book of this size. Rather, they attempt, through selective thematic emphasis, to give an adequate introduction to the configuration and variety of forms and groups within Christianity. Major developments in the evolution and diversification of Christian bodies, movements, and practices are sketched and traced; in fact, they are explored in terms of their overall significance and impact on Christian development. Other chapters (Six to Nine) deal with central issues and topics in other than historical orderings. Still, an understanding of the movements, persons, and ideas discussed in those chapters will be greatly enhanced by the historical framework of the earlier chapters.

Chapter One deals with Jewish religious history from its beginnings through the first and second centuries of the Roman Empire, especially as this history provides background for understanding the emergence and development of Christianity.

Chapter Two deals primarily with the mission and message of Jesus.

Chapter Three traces the emergence of Christianity from obscurity as a Jewish sect in the early Roman Empire to its commanding position as a spiritual, cultural, social, and political force in the late Roman and Byzantine civilizations.

Chapter Four continues the story of Christianity's development through its Western Renaissance and Reformation settings up to the present.

Chapter Five focuses on cultural, intellectual, and religious changes that helped mold Christianity.

Chapter Six characterizes the major Christian beliefs as they have been confessionally and theologically expressed. The chapter follows the traditional credal or confessional outline used in much of systematic theology. Here we attempt to be as nontechnical as possible, but do not avoid names and terms (e.g., "Christology," "modalism") that figure prominently in theological discussion. We must emphasize that this work is not intended to be a *history* or an *encyclopedia* of Christian thought. To take one example: although we characterize Trinitarian and Christological controversies, we do not attempt to characterize or trace the development of all, or even many, of the variant positions relative to these issues, many of which had great numbers of adherents.

Chapter Seven discusses a cluster of topics that are indispensable for understanding the content of Christian belief and the development and role of Christian institutions. First, the relationship of Christian approaches to "the knowledge of God," as discussed in Greek philosophical schools, and the basis of Christian approaches to knowledge of God in Judaism are examined. Five—or six, if Christian mysticism is considered a separate approach—Christian approaches to the question of revelation and reason are explored. Also, the relation of faith to scientific method and theorizing, recent and classical discussions of the nature of religious language, and questions concerning the sources and nature of authority in Christian traditions are presented and examined.

Chapter Eight presents a variety of creative figures and related movements from Christian history—reformers and renewers. Certain of these are dealt with to some extent in other parts of the book. Here, the emphasis is on the variety and diversity to be found in individual and group expression within Christian history.

Chapter Nine describes some of the major contemporary issues faced by Christian groups against the background of a characterization of contemporary society and its international setting. Here, too, we give interpretations of the major trends of Christian organizational and individual response to the contemporary issues and setting.

At the end of each chapter (with the exception of Chapter Eight) is a list of questions that systematically covers the materials discussed in the chapter. Possibly many instructors will find it useful to call these questions to the attention of students when making reading assignments. Some instructors may use them as written assignments or for class discussion or review sessions.

Each chapter also has a list of additional readings. These are not intended to be chapter bibliographies. They are given to provide guidance for readers who may wish to pursue topics discussed in the chapter and may be useful to instructors in assigning additional readings.

In using *Exploring Christianity*, one will find a certain overlapping of material. Albert Schweitzer is dealt with in Chapters Two, Four, and Nine. Other figures appear and reappear in various chapters. In a few cases our approach has resulted in a degree of repetition. What will ordinarily be found will—we hope—not be repetition but enrichment. Our fundamental approach is, for want of better terms to describe it, thematic and contextual. Each chapter is relatively self-contained.

We do not intend to evaluate the various positions or views of the Christian groups described in this book. Even when a position is referred to as "heretical," this should be taken by the readers to mean the leadership or majority of members of groups we are describing considers the position to be divergent from positions they consider orthodox. Similar considerations should be taken as applying to our characterization of various positions or beliefs as "orthodox" or otherwise.

We have attempted throughout *Exploring Christianity* to use language that will not be offensive to readers of various backgrounds and affiliations. Thus, we have not used the term "Old Testament" to characterize the Scriptures of Judaism, though we have used the term to characterize or describe a traditional *Christian* theological concept and use of the Jewish scriptures. This may seem almost to be a distinction without a difference, but we believe it is a distinction worth making. In the same spirit, we have used the descriptions B.C.E. (Before the Common Era) and C.E. (Common Era) to refer to the periods (roughly) before and after the birth of Jesus. A discussion of the Christian theological stance with respect to the appropriateness or inappropriateness of the use of sexual characteristics or gender specific pronouns when speaking of God is integral to the method and content of the book.

We must express our appreciation to colleagues at our own college and at other colleges and universities who have helped with criticism and encouragement. Particularly, thanks should go to Professors William Barrick and Johnnie Kahl of the faculty of McMurry College and to students who have used *Exploring Christianity* in the courses previously mentioned. We also thank the reviewers of our original proposal and of a preliminary version of our text, who, we hope, will be able to see that we have adopted the majority of their suggestions and have taken account of the others. In this connection, we must especially express gratitude to the four reviewers of the text of our second edition. We found their willingness to give frank and detailed responses concerning what they found to be the strengths and weaknesses of *Exploring Christianity* encouraging and especially valuable. We have incorporated many of their suggestions and are convinced that the new edition has been improved as a result.

Our participation in a seminar on early Christianity held at various universities and theological seminaries in the southwest during the past two decades has contributed probably much more than we realize to our ideas about many of the topics discussed herein. A generous grant from the Sam P. Taylor Foundation to one of the authors contributed to the development of some of the ideas expressed in Chapter Nine.

We would be seriously at fault if we failed to express gratitude and appreciation for splendid copyediting and for the excellent editorial assistance we received at every stage of our work.

CHAPTER ONE

Christianity: Its Jewish Context

Most Christians and Jews are aware that Christianity emerged from first-century Judaism. However, many have only vague ideas about the relationship of these two religious traditions either in their beginnings or throughout their continuing history. A common mistake made among Christians is to assume that at the formation of a Christian community in Jerusalem immediately following the death of Jesus there was a complete separation of the two traditions and that thereafter there was little significant contact between them. In fact, the separation was much slower, and interaction between Judaism and Christianity has been continuous—sometimes friendly, sometimes turbulent—since that time. Historically, an important part of Christianity's self-definition has been derived from its interpretation of its original and continuing relation to Judaism. This chapter investigates the kinship of these two major religious traditions. Because both are living traditions that have changed and continue to change, it is not possible to understand the relationship of one to the other by focusing only on the historical beginnings of Christianity within Judaism. Their relationship today affects our understanding of each tradition, both in the past and in the present.

THE JEWISH SETTING OF CHRISTIANITY

Jesus and his immediate followers were Jews living in the Palestinian homeland that had been identified with their forefathers from at least 1200 B.C.E.[1] Known as Hebrews, a name derived from nomads called *Habiru* or *Apiru*, they were originally part of a large group of nomadic wanderers that inhabited the fringes of the more "civilized," or agricultural, territories of the Mesopotamian, Egyptian, Syrian, and Canaanite regions. The Hebrews emerged as an identifiable community around 1200 B.C.E.

---

[1]C.E. (Common Era) in this text refers to the common era shared by Christians and Jews. B.C.E. (Before the Common Era) refers to the time before the origin of Christianity.

During the next several centuries they developed beliefs and practices that separated them from the societies surrounding them. Central among these beliefs was the affirmation of *one* God who had chosen the Hebrews to be a special people. In a world where polytheism was common, the identification of one God with a specific people was not unusual. However, the claim that this God, Yahweh, was the *only* God, that he possessed transcendent power over all reality, and that he had chosen Israel to be *his* people to represent him to all other nations was significantly different. The Hebrews further saw themselves as subject to Yahweh's demand for exemplary conduct, which emphasized a distinctive pattern of moral and ritual holiness. This code incorporated prescribed religious rites, dietary taboos, and moral commandments. By the time of Jesus, the code had been formulated in minute detail, with exacting standards defining every aspect of behavior. The Hebrews also believed that Yahweh actively participated in history to guide, discipline, and sustain them. Continuously active in human history, Yahweh became for the Hebrews a personal God with whom each individual could have a direct relationship and from whom they derived value and meaning for their lives. The history of Yahweh's participation in the life of the ancient Hebrews, along with the ritual-ethical codes derived from this involvement, is interwoven into what became the Hebrew Torah (the first five books of what Christians know as the Old Testament). To these materials were added the words of Hebrew prophets and other writings.[2] These sacred writings were a central source of religious belief and ethical practice. Confident that Yahweh is a God of history, the Hebrews believed that this God had guided their destiny and would always do so. By the first century this belief had crystallized into the expectation that Yahweh would, through the sending of a Messiah (an anointed deliverer), bring the Hebrews and the world into a new day.

Those who followed Jesus and his teachings shared these central Jewish beliefs and built upon them. Over the centuries, however, the Christian superstructure built on Jewish history, tradition, and Scriptures came to differ significantly from Judaism.

JEWISH HERITAGE PRIOR
TO THE FIRST CENTURY C.E.

The beliefs and practices of the Hebrews developed from a long and complex history. Jews trace their origin to Abraham, although the biblical account begins with stories about the creation of the world and human life. Abraham, a native of Mesopotamia, migrated into Canaan around 1800 B.C.E. There, according to the Book of Genesis, he and his son Isaac and grandson Jacob lived as nomadic sheep and cattle herders. The same tradition states that Jacob—whose name was changed to "Israel" after an encounter with God—went with his sons into Egypt during a period of famine to live with one of his younger sons, Joseph, who had become a man of power among the Egyptians. They stayed for centuries but eventually were reduced to the status of slaves.

During this period a primary religious conviction emerged. Abraham had come into Canaan under the guidance and sustaining power of God. He left the gods of Mesopotamia to serve a God who had made him a promise—that Abraham would

[2]See Appendix I for a listing of Hebrew Scriptures.

be father of a great people, and that through him (and his descendants) "the families of the earth shall bless themselves" (Genesis 12:1–3). So the "children," or "sons," of Israel came to believe in their particular and unique relationship to God.

Their status as slaves in Egypt became the setting for a renewed relationship between God and Abraham's descendants. Moses, specifically called by God for a unique task and to whom God revealed the name Yahweh, led the Israelites out of their Egyptian bondage (ca. 1290 B.C.E.). After wandering in the Sinai for a generation, they entered Palestine, understanding it to be the Promised Land given to them by Yahweh. During this wilderness experience a decisive event occurred, ultimately perhaps more important than the escape from Egypt. The promise made by God to Abraham was renewed through a covenant (a contract) wherein Yahweh was to be the God of the descendants of Israel and they were to be his people. The covenant was God's promise to be their God forever and their promise to be his people. Their commitment meant following a specific religious and ethical code represented by the Ten Commandments, which were supplemented by a multitude of other moral and cultic regulations.

After a period during which the political organization of the descendants of Israel was a loosely structured confederacy of tribes, a nation, taking the name of Israel, emerged under the leadership of David in 1000 B.C.E. Under David, Israel reached its height of political ascendancy, occupying a position of importance among the nations of the eastern Mediterranean. After the reign of David's son Solomon, the Israelite state split into two kingdoms: Judah and Israel. For several centuries these kingdoms enjoyed political freedom, although for much of that time they were threatened by and often subservient to the "superpowers" of the period, Egypt and the kingdoms that successively controlled the Mesopotamian valleys.

From its beginning, Israel's relationship to God had been celebrated and reinforced through stories recounting its history, distinctive cultic patterns of worship, and elaborate codes of moral instruction. At first passed from generation to generation in oral traditions, some of these acquired written forms early. Together, these oral and written traditions formed the basis of the Torah (the body of Israelite law and covenant), which from the time of David was shaped into an organized pattern. As the nation consolidated its social and political structure, a written form of the Torah gained a significant place in the life of the people, reflecting the changing social patterns where trading and political activity depended on writing. Oral traditions continued, however, to supplement and interpret the written forms.

Distinctive religious concepts progressively developed among the Israelites. David and his successors were never deified, as many rulers were in ancient civilizations. God was understood to be ruler of Israel; the king of Israel was always God's servant but only a vice-regent for God.

In the southern kingdom, Judah, worship slowly became centralized in a temple in Jerusalem. This centralization of worship was one response to the constant temptation to conflate and intermix Israel's religion with the worship of the peoples among whom Israelites lived. Canaanite polytheistic worship of agricultural gods who promised fertility of the land was especially attractive to the Israelites as they settled from nomadic life to agriculture. These surrounding religions also claimed to provide political prowess and success to their adherents. Consequently, Israel's monotheistic faith was constantly challenged by the idolatry (worship of gods other than Yahweh) of its neighbors.

As the political fortunes of the Israelite kingdoms rose and fell, voices of prophets (messengers of God) rose, to remind Israel of the ancient covenant. According to the prophets, idolatry and the failure to adhere to the moral commandments were causing political chaos that could be corrected only by returning to the worship of Yahweh. These prophets, interpreting political events within the framework of religious allegiance and moral discipline, inserted into Israelite beliefs a principle that eventually became more important than participation in ritual observances of the temple cult. Prophetic tradition claimed that the relationship went beyond observance of ritual and external moral commandment: What Yahweh demanded was an inner commitment to justice, mercy, loving-kindness, and "humbly walking" with him (Micah 6:8).

Israel was conquered by Assyria in 722 B.C.E. and Judah by Babylon in 587 B.C.E. The dissolution of the kingdoms brought political and religious crises. The descendants of Israel were not to be a national entity or enjoy political freedom again until the modern period, except for a brief respite under the Maccabees (165–63 B.C.E.). Nevertheless, the religious crisis was more significant. After 722 B.C.E. the northern kingdom effectively disappeared from history. With the Jerusalem Temple's destruction (587 B.C.E.) and the removal of many of the southern nation's elite, including the priests, to Babylon, the meaning of Israel's relationship to God had to be reinterpreted.

Jerusalem continued to have a very important symbolic significance as the City of God. However, one especially significant reformulation of belief was the recognition that worship could take place wherever believing descendants of Israel gathered. In exile, the community's attention focused on the ancient tradition of the covenant and the laws that were derived from it. The patterns of worship and the moral conduct demanded by ancient tradition did not require a physical temple, even though many of the exiles fervently hoped for a return to Palestine and the rebuilding of God's Temple. Out of this new insight and the cultural realities of exile rose the *synagogue,* a setting for local worship outside Jerusalem and a place for the study of ancient tradition. Cut off from the Temple and its traditions in this exile, the Israelites came to a greater appreciation of the written portions of the Torah, which they continued to organize and elaborate.

A reinterpretation of Israel's destiny also became prominent during the exile. Prophetic voices, noting Yahweh's reliability and justice in punishment of Israel's unfaithfulness, emphasized the steadfastness and kindness of God's love that followed them into exile. The prophets anticipated a restoration of Israel in which it would have a new role. Israel would become as a "light to the nations" (Isaiah 49:6) revealing God's power and love to all peoples. In this way Israel would realize the completion of God's promise to Abraham. Often tied to this expectation of renewal and restoration in prophetic imagery was the expectation that this fulfillment would take place under the leadership and direction of God's anointed one, the Messiah. This Messiah would not only restore the Israelite nation, but, just as important, be the agent for the restoration of God's rule in the life of the people. In the Messianic age Israel would be obedient to God's law and as such serve as the light of God's love to all peoples.

The Persian emperor Cyrus, after conquering the Babylonians, released the Judeans to return to Jerusalem in 538 B.C.E. The return was made by only a portion of the Judean exiles, but these persons were convinced that the prophecy of restoration was taking place. After delay and the overcoming of many obstacles, the Second

Temple was built (ca. 520–515 B.C.E.). A new name was also attached to these returning exiles. Their designation as "Judeans," a title reflecting the geographical area from which they had come and to which they were returning, was shortened to "Jews."

Because the Jews remained politically subservient to the Persians, religion became more than ever the binding force among them. Ezra, a returning priest, brought about a renewal of interest in the Torah, now nearing its final written form as the first five books of the Hebrew Scripture. With the public reading of the Torah by Ezra (Nehemiah 8:2ff), the descendants of Israel renewed the ancient covenant, resolving again to live by its precepts.

The written Torah became a central focus of interest because it prescribed belief, worship patterns, and social as well as ethical behavior. Its laws extended to many details of daily life: Dietary taboos defined clean and unclean food, circumcision was required of all males to distinguish men of the covenant, marriage with non-Jews was forbidden, ethical instructions emphasized the sanctity of human life.

Focus on the written Torah called for a group of scribes responsible for its exact preservation. Such scribes were joined by other judiciously trained experts in the divine law contained in the Torah. Their task was the application of the Torah's insights and teachings to the ever-changing Jewish social and historical situation. This emphasis on the written Torah did not completely supercede the traditional "oral," or nonwritten Torah, which continued its interpretative function among many Jewish teachers and spiritual leaders. Prophetic writings and traditions also rose in prominence during the period, assuming a supplementary role to the Torah by offering additional interpretative insights as well as Messianic expectations.

The relatively brief interlude of political independence for Palestinian Jews won by the Maccabees resulted from Jewish insistence on the worship of no god but Yahweh. Antiochus IV, a Greek-Syrian king, insisted that all his vassal states, including Israel, should worship Zeus, the chief of the Greek Gods, of whom Antiochus claimed to be an earthly manifestation. This call to worship another god was accompanied in Judah by the active desecration of Jewish sacred places and books. A country priest, Mattathias, and his sons revolted, refusing to worship any god but Yahweh. Known as the Maccabees, they led their countrymen to a period of political independence. The motive for the revolution was religious—monotheism demanded the freedom to live as Jews without being compelled to worship non-Jewish gods or abandon the cultic and dietary practices that set them apart from other inhabitants of the Greek-Syrian empire.

In the postexilic period, Judaism also became geographically diverse. A portion of the Jews who were taken into captivity in Babylon chose to remain there, founding and maintaining a significant Jewish community. From there they scattered throughout the eastern Mediterranean world. By the time of Jesus, Jews of the dispersion, or Diaspora, as these non-Palestinian Jews came to be called by historians, outnumbered those in the homeland.

JEWISH RELIGIOUS PARTIES

While the Jewish community was bound together by its religious beliefs and practices, first-century Judaism was anything but a monolithic entity. The appeal to Rome for support by feuding factions of the Maccabean royal household brought Pompey in 63 B.C.E. to establish an uneasy Roman overlordship of Judah. Roman control allowed the continuation of a limited and subservient Jewish Monarchy, unified until after the reign of Herod the Great, then divided geographically among Herod's sons in 4 B.C.E. Political control was thereafter variously effected, with Rome sometimes exercising direct rule over parts of Palestine and sometimes ruling through Herod's descendants.

Sadducees.   The social and religious divisions that developed after the exile had a far-reaching effect on Judaism and the development of Christianity. Josephus, a Jewish historian writing at the close of the first century C.E., lists four major groups influential in the Jewish community. The priests related to the Temple in Jerusalem and the wealthy Jerusalem landowners constituted a group known as *Sadducees.* The Sadducees accepted only the written Torah as authentic spiritual authority, since it described Temple ritual and practice. To the extent they entertained Messianic beliefs at all, they held a conservative view of the "kingly" Messiah, who would guarantee proper Temple worship. It is possible that some of the early Sadducees identified the Messiah with Simon, the youngest of the Maccabean brothers, who had (ca. 140 B.C.E.) taken upon himself the offices of both king and high priest. Because of their position as spiritual and economic leaders of the community, the Sadducees were in greater contact with Greek and Roman culture. They tended to accept social and cultural changes brought by contact with Rome but continued to be conservative in worship.

Pharisees.   The *Pharisees* were a successor group to the Hasidim (the loyal, or pious, ones) who had emerged as early resisters to the Hellenization of Israel, brought about through contact with Greek culture after the exile. The Pharisees of the first century followed the Hasidim in their concern to interpret and apply the Torah to everyday life. For them Torah was not simply the written forms of the first books of the Bible, but included the commandments of the oral Torah handed down from generation to generation by the great teachers of Israel. The Pharisees also recognized as authentic teachings the works of the prophets and a group of materials probably written after the exile known as the "writings." Knowledge and instruction in these works, and their application to everyday life, fell to the rabbi, or teacher, among the Pharisees. Normally laymen, the Pharisees could be from any segment of society but were particularly drawn from craftsmen, artisans, and merchants. As a group they enjoyed religious prestige and influenced the understanding of the "law" among the general populace. They expected a Messiah who would institute a kingdom of righteous people—those who would assiduously follow the Torah, both written and oral.

Zealots.   The *Zealots* were, as the name has come to indicate, a radical group. They were dedicated to overthrowing Roman political control of the Jews by whatever means. Religiously, they probably were drawn from all segments of society, although they were most closely related to the Pharisees. Their Messianic expectations were for a king who would reestablish the Davidic kingdom.

Essenes.   Each of these groups is mentioned in the New Testament, and Jesus' teachings are often contrasted with these teachings and attitudes. The fourth party mentioned by Josephus was the *Essenes.* Until recently little was known about the group. Scrolls found hidden in Dead Sea caves in the twentieth century are thought by many scholars to give much information about the Essenes. This group formed an ascetic community usually living on the edges or actually withdrawn from the general Jewish society. The Essenes expected the reestablishment of "pure" Judaism only when the sinfulness of the community would be cleared away in a great holocaust allowing God's goodness to triumph over the evil of the world. This event would end the present world and establish a righteous and pure community. The new age instituted by this event would result from the coming of two Messiahs: the Messiah of Israel would lead the war against evil, and the Messiah of Aaron would establish the New Jerusalem and its new Temple. For the Essenes, one of the signs of the corruption of the age was that even the Jerusalem Temple had been desecrated. In their understanding, it was presided over by the line of false and unrighteous priests stemming from the Maccabean period.

While these identifiable religious groups held roles of leadership in the society, most first-century Jews belonged to none of them. By their very nature the parties limited their membership to relatively small percentages of the population. The common people followed the Torah commandments as best they could and worshipped at the Temple and the local synagogues. Undoubtedly, they were influenced and swayed by the opinions and practices of the religious parties. Typically, they obeyed the Sadducees, perhaps admired the Pharisees, sympathized with the Zealots, and held the Essenes in awe. Judaism at the time of Jesus provided a rich tapestry of religious ideas and expectations within a framework of central commitment to Yahweh, his covenant, and his commandments.

A central theme of Jewish life in the first century was the expectation of one who could renew Israel's relationship to Yahweh through the purification of the community and the fulfilling of the ancient promises made to Abraham and his descendants. Such expectations were part of the fabric of Jewish religion from the time of the prophets. This element of Jewish faith intensified during the political and social changes wrought by their postexilic encounter with Greek and Roman culture. For most Jews, some form of Messianic belief probably figured as an important part of their religious background. For some, perhaps many, it was a fervent hope. The identification of Jesus as the Messiah was a natural development for Jews who accepted his teachings.

JESUS AND THE JEWISH COMMUNITY

Jesus entered the Jewish scene as a public figure when he began a teaching ministry using methods similar to those of other Jewish teachers. He gathered a group of disciples and taught them by commenting on and interpreting ancient Jewish beliefs and laws. However, he claimed an authentication that did not depend on previous teachers, thereby questioning traditional interpretations of the Torah. His teachings emphasized doing the "will of God" rather than rigorous adherence to the commonly accepted Pharisaic and Sadducean interpretations of the Torah commandments. Accompanying Jesus' teaching was a healing ministry seen by the ordinary people as a sign of unusual spiritual powers. His images of the Messianic age suggested a servant role for the Messiah, whose kingdom would be found where the faithful followed God's will by selflessly serving others. These Messianic ideas contrasted with those of the Jewish parties and were not attractive to those who expected immediate deliverance from the power of evil experienced in the rule by Rome. Also, unlike the renowned rabbis of the time, Jesus took his teachings to the ordinary people rather than to the cultural and religious leaders. His teachings, and some of his actions, ultimately led to Jesus' death. Accused of blasphemy for appealing to the authority of God rather than that of tradition, and apparently for his attacks on the authority of the Pharisaic scribes and the Sadducean priesthood and Temple cult, he was crucified by the Romans for insurrection (on the basis of a supposed assertion that he was the king of the Jews).

At first disillusioned and scattered at Jesus' death, his followers quickly came to proclaim that they had witnessed the presence of a living, resurrected Jesus. They took his resurrection to be confirmation that Jesus' teachings and actions were those of God himself. Jesus was the anointed of God and, therefore, the long-expected Messiah. As such, he had inaugurated in his life, death, and resurrection the kingdom so anxiously awaited by the Jews. This Messiah was not one who brought political independence or ritual and moral righteousness, but one who brought a new expression of Yahweh's love centered in selfless giving.

The followers of Jesus, soon known as Christians for their proclamation that Jesus was the Christ (the Greek translation of Messiah), at first challenged the Jewish community at large to believe with them that Jesus was the Messiah— the anointed one of God. Early Christian writers went to great pains to show that Jesus fulfilled the ancient prophetic expectations (Matthew 1:22, 12:17; Acts 2:22–32).However, this proclamation was accepted by only a small minority of Jews. Most continued to believe a future Messiah would fulfill their dreams of restored political independence and religious purification.

Conflicts in the earliest Jewish Christian community.   Those who accepted Jesus as the Christ soon found their numbers increasing. Included in the expanding community were Hellenists (Acts 6:1). These were either Greek-speaking Jews of the dispersion who, in Jerusalem for the Passover, were attracted to Christianity; Jews who had acquired Greek customs; or perhaps Greek and Roman proselytes to Judaism who now accepted Christianity. In any case, they constituted a large enough group in the Jewish Christian community to be recognized and to complain about their treatment by "the Hebrews," or Jerusalem Jews. This distinction between the Jews of Palestine and the Jews or proselytes who reflected a broader exposure to the Greco-Roman culture expanded as Christian evangelism moved outside of Palestine. Since most of the first Christians were Jewish (Hebrews or Hellenists), the proclamation was taken into the Jewish synagogues of the dispersion (Acts 13:5, 17:1). Reception was mixed and often negative. The Christian message nevertheless found fertile soil among the *Gentiles*—non-Jewish neighbors in the Greco-Roman society, many of whom had admired Jewish monotheism and the Torah's moral code.

The Apostle Paul, a Hellenistic Jew who originally had bitterly opposed those who proclaimed Jesus to be the Messiah, after his conversion to Christianity took it as his special mission to preach to the Gentiles (Galatians 1:17). Because of Paul's and others' missions, by the late first century the majority of the Christians were Gentiles. This created a crisis in the church. If persons converted to Christianity were not Jews through birth or covenant, was it necessary for them to become practicing Jews, keeping the dietary and ritual laws of the Torah? Paul, appearing before a council of Christian elders in Jerusalem, argued that it was neither necessary nor wise. A decision was made that Gentiles did not have to follow the Jewish law in all its detail (Galatians 2:1ff; Acts 15:6–21). This decision, which perhaps only recognized accepted practice by that time, indicates the development of another early distinction among Christians. Two distinct groups existed side by side: Jewish Christians, who practiced the precepts of the Jewish law, and Gentiles, who did not. The tensions created by this situation lessened with the passing years, for the Christian mission found abundant fruit among the Gentiles and had limited success among the Jews. After the destruction of Jerusalem by the Romans in 70 C.E., there was no significant geographical center left for Jewish Christianity. Christianity, like Judaism, spread throughout the empire with no early central authority.

THE JEWISH WAR AGAINST THE ROMANS

The single most important event in Jewish history in the first century was the war fought to throw off the Roman yoke in 66–73 C.E. Zealot patriots dominated the political events of the latter part of the century and succeeded in fomenting a war that resulted in the destruction of Jerusalem and the Temple in 70 C.E. These Messianic patriots continued their influence until a final and catastrophic conflict (132–135 C.E.) under the leadership of Simon Ben Kosifa (Bar Kokhba). This conflict destroyed Jerusalem and effectively scattered the remaining Palestinian Jews. There was no significant Jewish political community in Palestine from that time until the events leading to establishment of modern Israel in 1948.

The political and religious consequences of the destruction of the Temple were revolutionary. The destruction eliminated the worship centered there and the role of those responsible for it—the priests. Their colleagues, the landowners, were also displaced, so that the influence of the traditional Sadducees was lost forever. The Zealots, having lost the war with Rome, were eliminated; their reason for existence was lost in the Jewish defeat. While the exact fate of the Essenes is unknown, their Dead Sea community was evidently destroyed during the war or its aftermath.

The Jewish group that survived the wars was the Pharisees. Their interests did not demand a Temple, for the Torah could be studied and applied anywhere. The concerns and methods of the Pharisees by this time already dominated the dispersion synagogues. Their chief emphasis centered on preservation of the Torah, knowledge of its teachings and application of these to everyday life. Such emphases gave stability and content to the Judaism that survived. It was around this Pharisaical leadership that post-Jerusalem Israel coalesced. Jacob Neusner suggests that the priestly interests also were not totally lost after the fall of Jerusalem. The synagogue already served as a place of worship as well as teaching. The priestly concern for regularity, order, and continuity survived in post-Jerusalem Judaism in synagogue and family worship.[3] The Judaism that emerged in the next few centuries welded together these interests into what became rabbinic Judaism: the classical pattern that has survived almost unchanged for eighteen centuries.

HEBREW SCRIPTURES

The patterns of pharisaical Judaism that developed before the destruction of the Temple allowed Judaism to survive repeated crises in the ensuing centuries. In the post-Jerusalem community, the pharisaical system of education and reformulation

---

[3]Jacob Neusner, *The Way of the Torah* (North Scituate, Mass.: Duxbury Press, 1979), pp. 12–13.

of the law assumed a central role in the preservation and systematization of the Hebrew law and its scriptures. Highly influential in the synagogues, where most male Jews learned to read and write through the study of the Torah, the Pharisees had by the time of Jesus established *academies* for advanced study of oral and written Scriptures. In these academies disciples gathered around renowned teachers (rabbis). The most famous of these institutions were the schools of Hillel and Shammai. In these academies ancient patterns of interpretation were expanded. Central to the method was refinement of traditional answers given to questions raised by the constant adjustment of the understanding of the Torah to changing social and historical conditions. Clarification of issues, debate about appropriate answers, and amplification by the teacher led to new interpretations and the rise of classical rabbinical learning, an expansion of the oral tradition. Different academies developed unique patterns of interpretation, giving a dynamic quality to the total endeavor.

After the destruction of Jerusalem, the Jews were anxious to stabilize their precarious situation. One concern of the period was the establishment of a "regular list," or "canon," of the ancient Scriptures. The Pharisees had from an early time accepted a broader group of Scriptures than the priests. For the Pharisees, the prophets clearly represented God's will and were interpreters of the Torah. Therefore, their writings were cherished as sacred. Over the centuries other writings also understood to speak for God had been added. These writings incorporated a variety of literature: devotional materials, stories, proverbs, and so on. While the Torah had taken its final form at the latest by 200 B.C.E., and the prophets by 100 B.C.E., the writings were a more fluid group of materials. The value and authenticity of many documents was heatedly disputed. Integral to the question of a proper canon of authentic Scriptures were questions about which writings were authoritative and therefore sacred.

In this context another question arose. Jews of the dispersion, particularly those who had lived for generations under the influence of Hellenistic culture, often lost their ability to read and understand Hebrew readily. Pious dispersion Jews, therefore, translated Hebrew scriptures into a number of Greek versions. The most influential of these was the Septuagint, a work of Jews living in Egypt. Some of the materials in the Septuagint were translated as early as 250 B.C.E. By the first century this work was broadly used among dispersion Jews. It included the traditional sections: Torah, Prophets, and Writings. However, the writings in the Septuagint included works not originally written in Hebrew, but written by Jews in Greek. Many of them reflected late postexilic times and were apocalyptic in interest. They were "original" rather than traditional works. What was to be the status of these works and others like them found in the several Greek translations?

It is not clear how it was decided which works were to be accepted as authentic, but the decision was evidently completed by the turn of the first century C.E. The decision appears to have been influenced by an academy that appeared at Jabneh (Jamnia) on the coast of Palestine after the destruction of Jerusalem. The confusion of the attack on Jerusalem in 70 C.E. led the then-current leader of the Hillel academy, Rabbi Ben Zakkai, after seeking permission from Vespasian, the Roman general, to move the academy to Jabneh. Along with the academy at Jabneh there came the court of the religious community—the successor to the Jerusalem Sanhedrin, or ruling religious court. Since the leaders of the old Sanhedrin were no longer in control, the new court was made up of scholars—essentially the members of the academy.[4] This academy/court appears to have determined which books among the various writings would be accepted as authentic Scriptures. Traditionally the date given for the decision is 90 C.E.

The criteria developed to determine authenticity must have included several principles, but the basic consideration seems to have been whether a work could be traced in some manner to the prophetic period or tradition. If it could, it was worthy of acceptance; if it could not, it was rejected. The result was to reduce substantially the number of writings included in the final canon to twenty-four books considered to be ancient "tradition."[5] This scripture came to be known as *Tanakh,* combining the Hebrew first letters of each of the sections: *Torah* (Pentateuch), *Nebi'im* (Prophets) and *Ketubin* (Writings).

The fate of the Septuagint among Jews and Christians is curious. From an early time, the Septuagint was regularly used as the Christian source of the Hebrew Scriptures. This is an understandable development, since Christianity expanded most rapidly among Gentiles and among dispersion Jews. The common language among the Christians scattered over the Roman Empire was Greek, so it was natural to use this familiar translation. It became the authentic form of the "Old Testament," or "Old Covenant" (the Christian designation of the Hebrew Scripture), for the church throughout its early centuries.

When the Scriptures were translated from Hebrew to Latin by Saint Jerome in the fourth century, the books incorporated were those found in the Septuagint. This Latin translation, the *Vulgate,* became the basis of Western Christian Scripture. Centuries later, Protestant reformers, noting the difference between the Hebrew versions and Greek versions, and anxious to return to the earliest tradition, omitted from their translations the extra works included from the Septuagint in the Vulgate. These materials were assigned to an Apocrypha, only recently included (and usually as secondary material) by Protestants in translations of the Jewish Scriptures.

Among the Jews, the Septuagint was rejected completely as the movement toward consolidating the tradition became stronger. Perhaps its popularity among Christians also contributed to its rejection by Jews.

The differing Jewish and Christian attitudes toward the Septuagint in the early centuries only reflect wider divergencies in attitudes toward the Jewish Scripture. Christians of the period, following Paul, spoke of the "New Covenant" that Jesus brought; therefore, the Jewish Scripture became for the Christians the Old Covenant, or testament. Justin Martyr, a Roman Christian writing in the second century, took the distinction further. In his "Dialogue with Trypho" (Trypho was a Hellenized Jew), Justin attempted to show that the Jews had misunderstood their own Scriptures when they turned them into "laws" for righteous living. He argued that the law had been given to the Jews as an instruction in moral integrity and purity of heart rather than a pattern to be observed in a legal fashion. Justin made extensive use of the prophets to show that Jesus was the anticipated Messiah and thereby the consummation and the true character of Judaism. He went so far as to claim that Christians who follow Jesus are really the true Israel—heirs

---

[4]Samuel Sandmel, *Judaism & Christian Beginnings* (New York: Oxford University Press, 1978), p. 138.

[5]In this calculation the twelve prophets are counted as one, as are the books of Samuel, Kings, Ezra-Nehemiah, and Chronicles.

to the promises and the true successors to the Jews.[6] Justin's claim had the effect of making the Hebrew Scriptures Christian at the expense of the traditional Jewish understanding of these same Scriptures. Clearly, in the second century, the two religious communities shared the same Scriptures, but interpreted them from radically differing viewpoints.

QUESTIONS

1. What were the particular beliefs of Jews that distinguished them from their neighbors? Which of these beliefs were later incorporated into Christianity?
2. Justin's understanding of Christianity as the true fulfillment of Judaism made Judaism only a "predecessor" religion to Christianity. Many Christians throughout history have shared this view. What effect does such an understanding have on the relationship between modern Jews and Christians?
3. What is the Jewish Torah? Comment on its role in the development of Jewish religion and its significance for modern Judaism.
4. Using a dialogue pattern, create a conversation between representatives of each of the Jewish parties that existed at the time of Jesus, showing their distinctive beliefs and social patterns.
5. What conflicts did Christianity have to resolve within its own community because of its foundations in a Jewish heritage?
6. Outline major phases in the development of Hebrew scriptures as we presently know them.
7. Comment on the relationship of the Septuagint to the development of modern forms of Christian scripture.

FURTHER READING

The following titles are offered as representative of a wide range of writings on Jews and their heritage.

ABRAHAMS, ISRAEL. *Jewish Life in the Middle Ages*. Philadelphia: Jewish Publication Society, 1958.

ARENDT, HANNAH. *Origins of Totalitarianism*. New York: Meridian, 1958.

DAVIES, W. D., ed. *The Cambridge History of Judaism*. 4 vols. Cambridge, Mass.: Cambridge University Press, 1979.

HESCHEL, ABRAHAM J. *God in Search of Man: A Philosophy of Judaism*. Philadelphia: Jewish Publication Society, 1956.

KEMELMAN, HARRY. *Conversations with Rabbi Small*. New York: William Morrow, 1981.

MARGOLIS, MAX, and MARX, ALEXANDER. *History of the Jewish People*. Philadelphia: Jewish Publication Society, 1953.

MICHENER, JAMES. *The Source*. New York: Random House, 1965.

---

[6]Justin Martyr, "Dialogue with Trypho," *Ante-Nicene Fathers*, Vol. I, chs. 122–25.

NEUSNER, JACOB.   *Between Time and Eternity: The Essentials of Judaism.* Encino, Calif.: Dickenson, 1976.

————.   *Formative Judaism: Religious, Historical and Literary Studies,* Third Series: *Torah, Pharisees and Rabbis.* Chico, Calif.: Scholars Press, 1983.

————.   *Judaism in the Beginning of Christianity.* Philadelphia: Fortress Press, 1984.

————.   *There We Sat Down: The Story of Classical Judaism in the Period in Which It Was Taking Shape.* Nashville, Tenn.: Abingdon Press, 1972.

————.   *The Way of the Torah.* 3rd ed. North Scituate, Mass.: Duxbury Press, 1979.

OESTERLEY, W. O. E., et al.   *Judaism and Christianity.* New York: KTAV Publishing House, 1969.

POTOK, CHAIM.   *Wanderings.* New York: Alfred A. Knopf, 1978.

ROTH, CECIL.   *Short History of the Jewish People.* London: East and West Library, 1953.

SACHAR, HOWARD.   *A History of Israel.* New York: Alfred A. Knopf, 1947.

————.   *The Course of Modern Jewish History.* New York: World Publishing Co., 1958.

SANDERS, E. P.   *Paul and Palestinian Judaism.* Philadelphia: Fortress Press, 1977.

SANDMEL, SAMUEL.   *Judaism and Christian Beginnings.* New York: Oxford University Press, 1978.

SPONG, JOHN SHELBY, and SPIRO, JACK DANIEL.   *Dialogue: In Search of Jewish Christian Understanding.* New York: Seabury Press, 1975.

STEINBERG, MILTON.   *The Making of the Modern Jew.* Indianapolis, Ind.: Bobbs-Merrill, 1934.

TREPP, LEO.   *Judaism: Development and Life.* Belmont, Calif.: Dickenson, 1966.

WOUK, HERMAN.   *This Is My God.* New York: Random House, 1965.

ZBOROWSKI, MARK, and HERZOG, ELIZABETH.   *Life Is with People.* New York: International Universities Press, 1952.

CHAPTER TWO

Jesus and the Beginning of Christianity

Imagine that at some time during the late sixties in the first century C.E., a reader of Jewish background, or a Gentile familiar with the Jewish Scriptures, possibly in their translation into Greek called the Septuagint, should by some means have acquired a copy of the short work that now appears in the Christian New Testament as the Gospel of Mark. Mark's gospel is the second and shortest of the four gospels—Matthew, Mark, Luke, and John—that give accounts of the preaching and teaching, the public ministry, and the arrest, trial, and crucifixion of Jesus of Nazareth. Imagine also that this reader has never before heard of Jesus or of the movement inspired by him within Palestinian Judaism, now rapidly spreading throughout Asia and into European parts of the Roman Empire, and rapidly becoming a gentile (non-Jewish) movement. The reader would not have had far to read in Mark's gospel before finding remarkable claims being made about Jesus. The very title of the book—it was not originally called the "Gospel According to Saint Mark"—given in its first line, announces that it is the "good news" (this is what "gospel" means) "of Jesus Christ, the Son of God." Then there are two quotations from the Jewish Scriptures, from the books of Malachi and Isaiah, most often held by Jewish leaders of the first century to be predictions of the coming Messiah. The passage from Malachi speaks of God's messenger coming to prepare the anticipated sudden appearance of the Lord to purify his temple. In its context in the book of Malachi, it is shortly followed by the assertion that the preexilic prophet Elijah will come to prepare the way for the Lord. The passage from Isaiah also speaks of "preparing the way" for a new exodus of the people of Israel, for a return from captivity through the wilderness to the land of fulfillment that God has promised them. Although most contemporary biblical scholars believe that the original context of the Isaiah passage was the hope for a joyous return of Jewish exiles from their Babylonian captivity (begun in 597–586 B.C.E.), during the first century it was usually applied to what must have seemed the promise of an even greater release—the time when the Messiah would establish God's rule over the whole world.

After these brief citations from the Jewish Scripture, Mark's gospel gives a brief account of John the Baptist (who in the ninth chapter is implicitly identified by Jesus with the prophet Elijah), who comes announcing the nearness-at-hand of the kingdom of God, calling his fellow Jews to repentance. Jesus is described as being one who comes to John for baptism and who receives a special acknowledgment from the Spirit of God, in the form of a dove, that he is "my well-beloved Son." These words suggest another passage from the Jewish Scriptures (Psalm 2) that could be interpreted by Jewish readers as a Messianic passage, since it is one of the "enthronement" hymns that probably had been used in connection with the coronation of the kings of Israel or Judah. The Messiah was looked forward to as one who would be king of a newly reunited Israel, a descendant of David who would be a greater David.

Then, according to Mark, Jesus is "driven" by the spirit of God into the wilderness, where he remains for forty days (a period reminiscent of the forty years spent by Israel in the wilderness, totally dependent on God, after the Exodus from Egypt and before the entry into the Promised Land of God's Kingdom in Palestine, where they were led by Joshua). Mark tells us that Jesus (whose name, Yeshua, is the same as Joshua), during his forty days in the wilderness, underwent a testing and, like the Israelites, was similarly provided for by God:

> And he was in the wilderness forty days, tempted by Satan; and he was with the wild beasts; and the angels ministered to him.
>
> (MARK 1:13 RSV)

After leaving the wilderness, Jesus begins his ministry in his native Galilee. He announces that God's Kingdom is at hand and calls for people to accept it with repentance and faith. He calls four disciples among the faithful people who (the reader knows) are looking forward to the Kingdom of God, since they immediately leave their work and follow him. Jesus heals many persons; the healing of four individuals is described in detail, the fourth being a "helpless" paralyzed man brought by four well men of faith. Jesus tells the paralyzed man that his sins are forgiven. This produces among some of the onlookers—Mark tells us that they are scribes (authorities on the interpretation of the Jewish Scriptures)—a shocked response: they accuse Jesus of blasphemy, since only God can forgive sins. Jesus then tells the paralyzed man to rise and take up the pallet his four friends have used to carry him,—and he does, healed. Soon afterwards, Jesus calls his fifth disciple, Levi, a tax collector (thus an outcast, or sinner, since he is working for the hated king Herod and thus, indirectly, for the Roman oppressors).

In the central part of Mark's gospel, in a pattern that the author highlights by having Jesus call it to his disciples' attention (Chapter 8, verses 14–21), Jesus engages in the threefold activity of announcing the coming, or the fulfillment, of God's Kingdom by calling disciples. In Chapter 3, verses 13–19, a list of the names of twelve is given (interestingly, the name of Levi is not given, though the name Matthew is). In another gospel, Matthew and Levi are said to be the same person. Mark's way of presenting the calling, with first five individuals called, then a list of twelve, results in a narrative in which—though Jesus has called twelve of his disciples to receive special training and carry out special missions—thirteen names are given, one the name of an outcast, an instrument of the gentile oppressors. Thirteen specific healings are recounted, one of them of a Gentile, the others Jews, including the four already cited. The number symbolism also appears in accounts of Jesus' teaching and feeding the multitudes who follow him in Galilee. Jesus twice feeds enormous crowds miraculously. On the first occasion he uses two fish and five loaves of bread to feed five thousand people, with twelve baskets of leftovers collected afterwards; on the second occasion, he uses seven loaves to feed four thousand people with seven baskets of leftovers collected. In a boat on the sea the disciples think that Jesus is reprimanding them because they have only one loaf of bread with them, but he calls their attention to the numbers of loaves and leftovers.

The reader of Mark in the sixties C.E., if that reader had been brought up in the traditions and trained in the Scriptures of Judaism, would see at once that the symbolism—after a period of wilderness testing lasting forty days, of five and seven loaves, twelve and seven baskets—is emphasized by Jesus to his disciples in Mark as a way of saying graphically that the Messianic Age, the Kingdom of God, has dawned. The five books of the Law, the twelve tribes of Israel, the seven days of creation, the seventy nations of the Gentiles, all are brought together symbolically in the feedings and healings. The imagined reader might have responded with incredulity or perplexity, with hope or certainty, but certainly would have realized that an amazing claim was being made concerning a man named Jesus who had lived in Palestine only a generation before. Such a reader may have decided to inquire further into the new movement to discover what truth there was to the message that seemed to be attracting so many. It was not long before the followers of Jesus were said by one of Rome's officials to be "turning the world upside down."

We have used Mark's gospel as our example, since Mark may well have been the earliest written of the four gospels. Each of the other gospels does something similar to what Mark does, using some of the same and some different literary methods and devices to proclaim the faith of the early followers of Jesus—faith that Jesus was indeed the expected Messiah and the Son of God raised miraculously from death after having been crucified. Matthew and Luke essentially follow Mark's outline but do not emphasize the number symbolism as Mark does. Matthew stresses Old Testament parallels, particularly from the first six books of the Jewish Scriptures, with incidents in the life of Jesus and gives numerous quotations from many parts of the Jewish Scriptures, which he interprets as specific prophecies that Jesus has fulfilled. Luke stresses that the prophetic passages from the Hebrew Scriptures about incorporating the poor, the weak, women, outcasts, sinners, and foreigners in God's Kingdom are being fulfilled. John's gospel, which follows a different outline of events in telling the story of Jesus' ministry, uses the number seven (always in Jewish religion symbolizing the fullness or perfection of God's creation), recounting seven signs or miracles performed by Jesus, each indicating the newness of life, a life called "eternal," that can be experienced fully and now by those who know God through Jesus Christ, his son. Interspersed with the seven signs is a series of interpretive spiritual discourses that the author has Jesus give to his hearers.

SOURCES OF KNOWLEDGE ABOUT JESUS

The Historical Jesus and the Christ of Faith

Christianity began as a result of the activity of Jesus during the latter years of the first third of the first century C.E. There is much important background information from first-century Judaism that provides vital historical knowledge about

Jesus. The Talmud, the works of the Jewish historian Josephus, and the Dead Sea Scrolls that belonged to the Qumran (probably Essene) community provide a wealth of material. By and large, however, the only direct sources about the life and teachings of Jesus are to be found in the New Testament, the Christian Scriptures. Some scholars have suggested that some of the noncanonical gospels, such as the Gospel of Thomas, found at Nag Hammadi in Egypt in the 1940s, may rest on a body of tradition independent of the sources utilized by the canonical gospels. (See Chapter Six for discussion of the Christian Gnosticism represented by many of the Nag Hammadi works.) What we certainly do not have is access to significant historical information about Jesus from non-Christian sources. Within the New Testament, though Jesus is quoted (rarely) and his actions are at times directly or indirectly mentioned in the epistles (I Corinthians), only the four gospels provide any extended information about him.

Because of the nature of the gospels as proclamations of the fulfillment of God's Kingdom through Jesus' life, death, and Resurrection, they do not easily lend themselves as sources for the construction of biographies of Jesus. Nevertheless, a contemporary Jewish historian, David Flusser, has written in a book intended as a purely historical (and theological) study of Jesus as a figure in first-century Judaism, the following:

> ...it is possible to write the story of Jesus' life. True, we have fuller records about the lives of contemporary emperors, and some of the Roman poets; but, with the exception of the historian Flavius Josephus, and possibly St. Paul, among the Jews of post–Old Testament times Jesus is the one about whom we know most.[1]

Almost any assertion made about Jesus on the basis of historical scholarship can be challenged and will be subject to qualification. The following account attempts to give an accurate, probable picture of the historical Jesus. The Christian churches have traditionally asserted most of what will be said here plus much more about the Christ of their faith. One of the beliefs of the New Testament Christians was that after the Resurrection of Jesus and the imparting by him of the Spirit of God to the community of his followers, much more knowledge about him and his mission was made known—revealed by him in his Resurrection appearances or by the Spirit of God to the churches—than had been communicated during his pre-Resurrection ministry (see Luke 24:49; John 16:12–15). Thus, to Jesus' followers the new material and new interpretations, added to material remembered and transmitted about Jesus and his teachings, did not involve invention or fabrication. It nevertheless was subject, in theory, to the test of coherence with what the earliest disciples of Jesus remembered and reported.

The Nature of the Gospel Accounts

All of the gospels relate Jesus' actions and the events of his life to various Old Testament prophecies. Typical are the second and third verses of Mark, which, in connecting the beginning of Jesus' ministry with the message of John the Baptist, quote parts of two Old Testament passages, Isaiah 40:3 and Malachi 3:1. Both were clearly understood by most Jews in Jesus' time to be prophecies concerning the coming of the Messiah. All of the gospels, Matthew at times more explicitly than

---

[1]David Flusser, *Jesus* (New York: Herder and Herder, 1969), p. 7.

the others, frequently cite Old Testament events or passages as foreshadowing and foretelling the episodes in Jesus' life. Also, each gospel uses symbols drawn from Israel's religion and history to make clear that Jesus is the Messiah, and that in him the promises made to the patriarchs and prophets are being fulfilled.

Matthew, Mark, and Luke are frequently called the Synoptic Gospels, since they follow a common outline. They also incorporate a great amount of common material, not just in subject matter but in language, with very many almost identical passages that differ only in slight variations in wording. Matthew and Luke also have similar common materials and wording (with rather large variations at times) not present in Mark. Matthew and Luke have unique materials not found in the other or in Mark or John.

Close study of the three Synoptic Gospels during the past two centuries has led a majority of biblical scholars to believe that Mark was the earliest written of the gospels and was used as a source by Matthew and by Luke. Matthew and Luke were believed to have drawn on another written (or possibly oral) source, often called Q (from the German word *Quelle,* meaning "source"), for their common material not present in Mark, mostly teachings of Jesus. This view became the accepted, or traditional, account of the sources of the Synoptic Gospels. It was called the Two-Source Hypothesis. Traditionally each of the gospels was attributed either to one of the original twelve disciples of Jesus (Matthew and John), or to a close associate of an original disciple (Mark), or to one who fulfilled an apostolic role in the early church (Luke, thought to be a travelling companion of the missionary apostle Paul). Although there is interesting material from very early Christian traditions that bears on the apostolic sources of authorship of the gospels, the great majority of biblical scholars are extremely cautious in evaluating such material. The consensus of opinion among biblical scholars is that the authorship of the gospels cannot be determined with certainty. Generally, all are held to have been written within the first two generations of the Christian movement. A recent New Testament scholar, J. A. T. Robinson, placed them all within the first generation, as being composed before 70 C.E. All of the New Testament writings, including the four gospels, are written in *koiné* Greek, the "international" language for business and other transactions for many in the eastern half of the Roman Empire. For our purposes, questions concerning authorship of the gospels are not of central concern.

John's gospel follows a completely different order of events than the Synoptics do. From an early period of Christian history it was referred to as the "spiritual gospel," with the implication, perhaps, that the major significance of the events reported in it—Jesus' turning water into wine or giving sight to a blind man—was to be sought in a spiritual interpretation of their meaning.

Two of the gospels, Matthew and Luke, have accounts of the birth of Jesus and the events preceding it. These accounts are very different from each other in detail. The role of Mary, the mother of Jesus, is highlighted in Luke's account, as is the fact that those who learn of the birth of the Savior—shepherds in the fields—are among the humble poor. Luke emphasizes throughout his gospel that it is a sign of the beginning of the Messianic Age that the good news of forgiveness, healing, and new life is being proclaimed to women, the poor, the outcast, sinners, foreigners, and those without prestige or influence. In Matthew's gospel, the role of Joseph, the supposed father of Jesus, is highlighted. Joseph is presented as a man of faith like the Old Testament patriarch Abraham, the birth of Jesus is treated as a miracle even more wonderful than the birth of Abraham's son Isaac, and the events surrounding the birth are implicitly related to other events of Israel's history, including the descent into Egypt and the Exodus, suggesting their repetition and fulfillment in Jesus. Later in Matthew's gospel, Jesus is presented as a new and greater lawgiver, who ascends the mountain to interpret in his Sermon on the Mount the law given to Israel through Moses on Mount Sinai.

Two of the gospels, Mark and John, begin with accounts of the baptizing activities of John the Baptist. Matthew and Luke contain accounts of these events too. All of them use several chapters detailing the ministry of Jesus. If one read only the Synoptic Gospels, one might believe that most of Jesus' ministry took place in Galilee. John's gospel has Jesus' ministry alternate between Galilee and Judea. The time span covered by the ministry seems much shorter in the Synoptics than in John.

After the chapters describing the ministry and message of Jesus—Mark has much less teaching material than the others—each of the gospels devotes several chapters to an account of the events of the last few days of Jesus' activity: his trip to Judea; his entry into Jerusalem to celebrate the Passover with his disciples; his conflict with the religious authorities, Sadducees and Pharisees; his last instructions to his disciples, including a celebration of the Passover with them (here there are very important differences between John and the Synoptics); his arrest and appearance before the Sanhedrin and the Roman governor Pilate; the determination that he should be put to death; and his crucifixion. (Crucifixion was the method used by the Roman *government* to punish noncitizens, including runaway slaves and persons guilty of insurrection.) There are a number of interesting differences in the accounts of these events from gospel to gospel.

This is even more true of the Resurrection accounts, although here, too, the gospels are in fundamental agreement. Shown as having lost hope at Jesus' arrest and crucifixion, his disciples are told afterwards—"on the third day"—that he has risen from the dead. Then each of the gospels except Mark, which apparently in its original form ended with an angel's announcement of the Resurrection and the promise that Jesus would soon meet the disciples in Galilee, recounts a number of appearances of the risen Jesus to his disciples. The disciples are told by Jesus, in a variety of ways, that they will be empowered by God and will take the message of salvation to others, even throughout the whole world.

THE MINISTRY OF JESUS

Jesus appears to have begun his ministry in Galilee, the northern part of Palestine. Galilee, where he conducted most of his activity, was governed by one of the sons of Herod the Great, Herod Antipas, who ruled at the pleasure of the Romans. The southern part of Palestine, Judea, with the holy city of Jerusalem and its Temple, was under the direct rule of a Roman official. The Sanhedrin, with a majority of its members being Sadducees and the remainder Pharisees, was the supreme Jewish religious council and served as a governing board for Jerusalem and its environs. Roman intervention was more frequent in Judea than in Galilee, since the Sanhedrin and Temple authorities had only a minimal number of troops at their disposal.

It is sometimes suggested that the Romans did not allow them to impose the death penalty. Because it was a center of religious pilgrimage for Jews throughout

Michelangelo, *Christ.*   (*Rome, S. Maria Sopra Minerva.*)

the world, Jerusalem frequently was the locale of explosive religious and cultural interaction. Roman rule, including the presence within the walls of the holy city of non-Jewish troops, was bitterly resented.

John the Baptist

We have seen in Chapter One and in the first section of this chapter that first-century Judaism was to a large degree apocalyptic in outlook. Devout Jews prayed that God would establish His Kingdom during their own times. They attempted to live in ways that would aid and speed the coming of God's Kingdom. To the Essenes (or Qumran community), living in a way that would hasten God's Kingdom meant to withdraw from contacts with non-Essenes, to repent of one's sins, to practice acts of ritual purification (such as frequent ceremonial washing), to live by the precepts of the Torah, and to wait in readiness for God's commands. To the Pharisees, it meant keeping all the commandments of the Torah with sincerity and to the last detail.

At some point before the beginning of the ministry of Jesus, a message concerning the coming of God's Kingdom began to be proclaimed by a man named John. Tradition soon gave John the title Baptist or Baptizer because he called on those responding to his message to be baptized by him in the Jordan River as a sign of repentance for past sins and of the intention to live with an attitude of inner readiness for God's Kingdom.

The Gospel of Luke recounts a tradition according to which John was a cousin of Jesus and was explicitly sent by God to be Jesus' forerunner. In all of the gospels, John is portrayed as the forerunner of Jesus. Contemporary New Testament scholars treat with caution both the traditions of John's kinship with Jesus, avowal of Jesus as Messiah, and his claim to be Jesus' forerunner. However, nearly all scholars are agreed that John's movement was decisive for the beginning of Jesus' ministry, that Jesus did see John's activity as a sign that God's Kingdom was at hand, and that Jesus was baptized by John at or prior to the beginning of his own ministry. New Testament evidence points to the continuation of John's movement after the work of both John and Jesus had been ended by their executions. It also points to tensions between the two movements and to the joining of Jesus' movement by some of John's disciples both before and after the crucifixion of Jesus (John 1:35–42; Acts 19:1–7).

The message of John was simple, although its interpretation is controversial. John announced that "the Kingdom of God is at hand" and called on people to respond by repentance (sorrow for sins and willingness to lead a new life in accordance with God's will). Repentance and willingness to lead a new life were to be indicated by baptism. It has sometimes been suggested that being baptized by John symbolized willingness to become a Jew all over again, signifying rededication, recommitment, even a kind of rebirth. Thus, John's baptism may have been partially analogous to the kind of ritual purification that a gentile convert to Judaism would undergo. For John, baptism was a once-for-all event. It was not like the repeated ceremonial washings of the Essenes. Some similarities between John and the Qumran community have been noted. However, John did not counsel withdrawal from society or the world, as the Essenes did. Rather, he told converts to await the kingdom's coming while maintaining their new attitude of repentant faith and abiding by the commandments of the Torah to treat others with justice and mercy:

> And the multitudes asked him, "What then shall we do?" And he answered them, "He who has two coats, let him share with him who has none; and he who has food, let him do likewise." Tax collectors also came to be baptized and said to him, "Teacher, what shall we do?" And he said, "Collect no more tax than is appointed to you." Soldiers also asked him. And he said to them, "Rob no one by violence or false accusation, and be content with your wages."
>
> (LUKE 3:10–14 RSV)

In these precepts John differed from the Pharisees. The Pharisees would have agreed with most of what he demanded, but would have added detailed instructions about keeping the ritual parts of the law, particularly the intricate regulations about Sabbath observance. For John, apparently the crucial commandments of the Torah could be reduced to great simplicity and involved one's attitudes and actions toward others.

John's message and activity aroused great excitement. Large numbers of people came to hear him in the rugged country near the Jordan River. Some, no doubt, came out of curiosity. Many received baptism. Many began to refer to John as a prophet. *Prophet* is used in the Old Testament to designate one who is sent by God to deliver a message. Usually the message is intended to bring its recipient to faith or repentance or both, to give a warning, or to give encouragement and guidance in a time of crisis. Sometimes the message is directed to the rulers of Israel, sometimes to the whole of God's people. Sometimes it is addressed to non-Israelites. It is significant that for Judaism in the first century there was a long-standing tradition that prophecy had ceased hundreds of years earlier and that there would be no new prophet until God sent "a prophet like Moses" (spoken of in Deuteronomy 18:15–18), or one who would represent or be the great Old Testament figure Elijah, as forerunner of the Messiah. Thus, the appearance of a prophet would be considered a Messianic sign. Early Christians, and possibly Jesus, identified John the Baptist with Elijah. Naturally the very existence of claims that John was a prophet would indicate to Herod Antipas and the Romans that a threatening Messianic movement was building; suspicions were therefore raised about John. John apparently compounded his difficulties by strongly criticizing Herod's life-style and activities. John was arrested and imprisoned by Herod, and eventually was put to death.

Jesus paid high tribute to John the Baptist. He saw John's work, as has been noted, as a clear indication of the nearness of God's Kingdom. In this sense there is no doubt that Jesus considered John to be his forerunner. Though it is difficult to characterize fully the content of John's message, and very difficult to see what he intended the full significance of baptism to be, his emphasis on the nearness-at-hand of the Kingdom of God connects his message very closely with that of Jesus. The major difference seems to have been a nuance, or what the philosopher Whitehead sometimes described as a small difference that makes all the difference. The central proclamation of both John and Jesus was the same: "The Kingdom is at hand; repent and believe." For John, this meant that the Kingdom was so close that there was nothing that people could appropriately do but wait for it with repentance and faith. For Jesus it meant that the Kingdom was already present, and that the New Age was breaking into the old and conquering it. One who repented and had faith did not need to wait for the Kingdom to come, but could already enter it—immediately.

The Message of Jesus

This was in fact the message of Jesus—that the hoped-for Kingdom of God was breaking in and available to those who could receive it by obedient faith.

Signs.   Jesus apparently began and largely carried out his ministry in Galilee, which was ruled by Herod Antipas, a son of Herod the Great. It was not until later, when Herod Agrippa ruled briefly over a reunited Palestine (still under Roman control), that the majority of Jews were willing to accept a member of the Herod family, originally of Idumean (non-Jewish) stock, as being Jewish. Herod Antipas was not a popular ruler, though there was a party of Herodians who depended on and supported him. Subject to Roman approval, he ruled Galilee and a part of the area across the Jordan River called Perea.

Jesus began his ministry by announcing the beginning of the New Age, the Kingdom of God. In one sense, the Kingdom was present in its fullness—in those who had received or entered it; in another, the Kingdom was not present in its fullness. It was not yet visible to all, it was visible only to those who had *faith,* but it *was* present and would come in its fullness. Its presence was entirely the gift of God. Its visible triumph would be the work of God. Nevertheless, now that it was present and available, all were invited to enter—to receive it in their lives as God's gift. All that was required was the ability to discern its presence by faith—a kind of trustful insight or openness—and repentance—a willingness to let one's life be shaped by it. Since technically *Kingdom of God* meant a condition or realm in which

God's will is accomplished, this meant that willingness to enter God's Kingdom implied willingness to let one's life be shaped by God's will.

Jesus addressed his message to all Jews, but especially those who for one reason or another would not have been qualified or fit to be received into the Kingdom. This group included social and religious outcasts. Galilee, with a much larger gentile population than other parts of Palestine, offered large opportunities for ritual and ideological contamination. Also, many ordinary working people, even if they avoided contacts with foreigners, might not be trained in the intricacies of Pharisaic Torah interpretation, or might find keeping the detailed Pharisaic laws virtually impossible or impractical. Women, who were not trained in the intricacies of Pharisaic Torah interpretation, or might find keeping the detailed Pharisaic laws virtually impossible or impractical. Women, who were not trained in the Hebrew Scriptures, were segregated from men both in Temple and synagogue services. Then there were those persons who were outcasts because they collaborated with the Romans or Herod—tax collectors, for instance. There were also moral outcasts like prostitutes, and those who were religiously unclean because of spiritual or physical conditions like the insane, thought to be possessed by evil spirits, and lepers.

To all these, Jesus announced the availability of God's presence in their lives. He is reported to have healed lepers and the insane and sent them to the religious authorities to be pronounced ritually clean (Luke 17:11–19). He is reported to have healed many others suffering from a variety of afflictions. Jesus himself interpreted these cures as signs of the presence of God's Kingdom. Since the blind were being made to see, the deaf to hear, the lame to walk, since lepers were being cleansed, and the unclean spirits being cast out of the possessed, the power of God's Kingdom was being made evident to all who had eyes to see (Matthew 11:2–6). His critics, especially some of the Pharisees who opposed him, admitted the miraculous cures but claimed that Jesus was using the power of the Evil One, of Beelzebul or Satan, to accomplish them. Jesus' response was that they were signs of the healing power, of the victory, of God's Kingdom. If they were done by God's power—"by the finger of God" (Luke 11:14–23; cf. Exodus 8:19)—then clearly God was establishing His reign. If they were done by the power of Beelzebul, then since the evil, contrary to its nature, was doing good, the Kingdom of Evil was bringing about its own collapse. Thus, God's rule was being established.

Jesus also saw the simple fact of his proclamation of the presence of God's Kingdom—the mere fact that the good news of God's loving gift was being proclaimed to the poor, to those in need and without hope—as a sign of its presence. He also frequently pronounced forgiveness of sins to individuals (Mark 2:1–12). That sins were being forgiven was seen by him to be a sign of the Kingdom. His opponents took it as such: they blamed him for claiming to do what only God could do and accused him of blasphemy.

Jesus saw his healings, his message of hope to the poor, and his willingness to pronounce forgiveness to sinners, as signs of God's present activity in establishing the Kingdom. Also, many of his acts had clearly symbolic meaning. They could be taken by Jews only as intentional Messianic signs. Although caution should be used in believing some of these to be actual historical acts of Jesus, many contemporary scholars are convinced that there is solid evidence for at least the following signs. Jesus attracted followers, or disciples, from among whom he selected twelve—soon actually called the Twelve—for special training and for leadership (a Messianic sign indicating the coming restoration of Israel through these leaders of its twelve tribes). He apparently sent his disciples out, having empowered them with the Spirit of God, to preach and heal (another sign of Messianic times, that the Spirit of God would be active in people's lives again and that the "lost sheep" of Israel would be sought). He called his disciples and others, who frequently were outcasts, together to eat in a meal of celebration (one of the signs of the New Age was a banquet that those inside the Kingdom would share).

Such symbolism provoked hostility from many religious Jews. Some of the Pharisees appear to have been sympathetic to his mission. However, Jesus attracted strong criticism and opposition from most Pharisees because of his association with sinners (*before* they had proved themselves worthy of God's Kingdom) and because he was thought to relax the commandments of the Torah, especially those regarding Sabbath observance and ritual cleanliness.

Many of the laws concerning cleanliness referred to the distinctions between clean and unclean foods in the Pentateuch and to laws about the ritual cleansing of oneself and of utensils used for preparing and serving food. Jesus, though he did not violate or teach the violation of Pentateuchal laws, did teach that it was inner attitude that mattered to God rather than ritual cleanliness. One could not be defiled by the food one ate, or by omitting ritual. One could only be defiled by one's own personal attitudes, by the thoughts of one's heart (Matthew 23:25–28).

Nor did Jesus teach disregard for the laws about keeping the Sabbath. These laws demanded that no work be performed from sundown Friday until sundown Saturday. There were various exceptions. To save life or prevent serious damage to health or property, work might be done. Also, Pharisaic scribal tradition (in Jesus' day an expert in the interpretation of Jewish laws and Scripture was called a scribe) had created much detailed and specific interpretation as to what counted as work and what counted as justifiable exception. (Was it work, for instance, to clean one's teeth on the Sabbath or could this, under certain conditions, be counted as a necessary function, like eating?)

What Jesus taught and did concerning Sabbath observance had essentially two aspects. First, he by and large disregarded the newer Pharisaic specifications and interpretations of Sabbath requirements, staying with the older, simpler, more open traditions. Sometimes he criticized the Pharisees for their zeal to make clear what the law required, saying that they were loading the people down with unnecessary burdens. Second, he taught that the true keeping of the Sabbath is a matter of one's attitude toward God, oneself, and one's fellow human beings. "The Sabbath is made for man, not man for the Sabbath." Jesus claimed the authority—and was criticized for doing so—to interpret God's intention in giving laws related to the Sabbath and other laws, including those related to marriage and divorce. Also, he was criticized for healing on the Sabbath in nonemergency situations, when the person could just as well have been healed later. His response was that the failure to do good to one's neighbor is not a neutral act when it is a question of sharing the benefits of God's Kingdom; it is a way of doing evil (Mark 3:1–6). Thus the Sabbath is made for doing good. Jesus claimed—another Messianic sign—the authority to interpret what true fulfillment of the law entails (Matthew 12:1–8; Mark 2:27).

Thus, many contemporary scholars believe that Jesus intended his ministry as a proclamation, through signs, of a dawning messianic age. They have debated whether Jesus (1) proclaimed himself to be the Messiah, or (2) believed himself to be the Messiah. Some contemporary theologians have argued that both of these questions are irrelevant from a theological point of view. They are certainly not irrelevant as historical questions. But they are very difficult to answer. The Synoptics, at various points, suggest that Jesus either directly or indirectly claimed to be the Messiah or at least acquiesced when others gave him the title and role of Messiah. The Gospel of John attributes to Jesus not only the Messianic claim, but the claim to be one with God ("I and the Father are one" John 10:30). All of these passages, though, are among those about which New Testament scholars urge caution, since they may be post-Resurrection interpretations read back into Jesus' historical ministry.

At one point in the Gospel of Mark, Jesus is reported as having repudiated the very concept of a Messiah who will be the "son of David"—presumably a military Messiah expected to reestablish the political glories of Israel (Mark 12:35–37). But this does not mean that Jesus rejected the idea of a Messianic Age—we have seen that he proclaimed its dawning presence—or of a Messianic figure, an agent of God who would bring the Kingdom in its fullness. The Synoptic Gospels frequently attribute to Jesus the use of the term "Son of man." The Son of man was a traditional figure of Jewish apocalyptic thought, a heavenly being who would defeat the powers of evil and establish God's reign. Apparently Jesus did speak often of the Son of man in this sense. Scholars are divided as to whether he used the term to refer to himself or to a Messiah for whom he was preparing the way. The Synoptics clearly understand Jesus' use of the term to be a reference to himself.

The "new quest of the historical Jesus" was a movement of New Testament scholars that began in the 1950s. It can best be understood as a movement attempting to renew the use of the New Testament writings as sources of information about the life of Jesus. The "Old Quest" refers to the relatively uncritical use of these writings by scholars in constructing the life or a biography of Jesus. It ended shortly after the beginning of the twentieth century, largely as a result of the critical work of Albert Schweitzer, in almost total skepticism about the ability to know anything about the historical life of Jesus. The New Quest scholars, though maintaining the need for caution in using the gospels—essentially proclamations of faith written in the light of the early Christian understanding of Jesus as the Risen Savior—nevertheless insisted that the gospels provide much more implicit historical data about the pre-Resurrection Jesus than many earlier twentieth-century biblical scholars believed themselves able to insist on.

Many of the new quest scholars argue that even if Jesus did not make direct claims to being the Messiah, the authority he assumed—in his preaching, teaching, healing, forgiving sins, and the importance he attributed to his ministry and message—makes at least an indirect claim to Jesus' Messianic significance. There is solid evidence of his disciples' beliefs and hope that Jesus was the Messiah. There is even evidence that they quarrelled with Jesus over the interpretation of what he should do if he were the Messiah. Often they seem to have tried to shape his acts and attitudes in accordance with what they thought to be appropriately Messianic. There is some evidence that at least two of his disciples had been members of a Zealot organization: Simon, called "the Zealot," and Judas, called "Iscariot." It is possible that these and others became members of Jesus' movement, hoping that he, the Messiah, would lead a victorious Jewish army against the Romans and perhaps against the Sadducees. There is evidence that at various times during his ministry certain of Jesus' followers forsook him when it became clear that he did not intend his movement to become a Zealot revolutionary uprising (John 6:60–69). Judas is reported to have betrayed Jesus to Temple authorities.

Certainly Jesus is pictured as having sympathized with critical attitudes that many in his society had toward rule by Rome, the Sanhedrin, and Herod. However, he taught that the Kingdom would come by God's activity, not by human efforts. He also taught that one should forgive and love one's enemies, return good for evil, and not respond to violence and coercion with violence and angry resistance. In fact, to be righteous according to the law as Jesus interpreted it meant to be as perfect in love as God. God loves and does good to everyone, good and evil alike (Matthew 5:38–48). This attitude set Jesus apart both from Zealots and Essenes (who taught that one should love the children of light and hate the children of darkness). Some recent writers, apparently partly influenced by one aspect of various liberation theologies of the present, have argued that Jesus did indeed lead a Zealot movement against the Romans and the Sadducees, and that at the defeat of this uprising he was executed by the victorious oppressors. Oscar Cullman has argued impressively against such a view.[2] It must be noted that the oppressors of Jesus' day apparently took no comfort from his nonviolent approach, for they viewed his liberation movement as a threat to order and established custom.

One of the most dramatic of the Messianic signs reported of Jesus is the cleansing of the Jerusalem Temple. All of the gospels report this event. The Synoptics place it at the end of his ministry. John's gospel places it, perhaps for symbolic significance, at the beginning.

In the large outer court of the Jerusalem Temple, much activity occurred. Temple worship was oriented to the ritual sacrifice of animals. Animals for sacrifice were kept in the courtyard and sold there to worshippers. There were also money changers in the courtyard, since only the sacred Temple coins could be used for Temple fees and taxes. The courtyard was the only part of the Temple that Gentiles were allowed to enter. A traditional Messianic sign was that with the coming of the Kingdom of God, Gentiles would flock to Jerusalem to worship the true God. In Jesus' day many Gentiles *were* attracted to Judaism; a few became converts, more became God-fearers—persons who remained gentile but worshipped the God of Judaism—and some came to Jerusalem. At the cleansing of the Temple, Jesus and his disciples occupied the outer court of the Temple, driving out the money changers and animal keepers. Jesus is reported to have said in justification of this act:

> Is it not written "my house shall be called a house of prayer for all nations?" But you have made it a den of robbers.
>
> (MARK 11:17 RSV)

Again, many scholars urge caution as to how much information the accounts of the cleansing of the Temple give about the strictly historical career of Jesus. Naturally, the early Christian church would find this a highly appropriate act on Jesus' part, both because of the church's later highly successful mission to Gentiles and its somewhat strained relations to the religious institutions of Judaism. First-century Jews, the Essenes for example, believed that the cleansing of the Temple would be one of the Messiah's most important acts. Malachi 3:1 was widely held to be a Messianic prophecy relating to just such an event. But it seems highly likely that Jesus did cleanse the Temple as reported by the gospels and probably, as the

[2]Oscar Cullman, *Jesus and the Revolutionaries* (New York: Harper & Row, 1970). But compare S. G. F. Brandon, *Jesus and the Zealots* (New York: Charles Scribner's Sons, 1967). Also see William R. Farmer, *Maccabees, Zealots and Josephus* (New York: Columbia University Press, 1957).

Synoptics have it, near the end of his ministry. Such an act would cohere with the other signs of his ministry to which he himself called attention. And Jesus' action in the Temple may reasonably be taken to have been the precipitant, the occasioning cause, of his arrest and crucifixion.

Parables.   One of Jesus' most characteristic methods of proclaiming and interpreting the message of the Kingdom was the use of parables. Literally, a *parable* is a comparison. Often a parable is defined as a very short story that clarifies one major point by comparing an ordinary, everyday event or incident and a more difficult truth or reality.

Jesus told many parables, all concerning the Kingdom of God. All of the gospels contain parables, although they are less frequent and harder to recognize in John than in the Synoptics, and there are fewer of them in Mark than in Luke and Matthew.

Many of the parables concern the importance of recognizing and taking advantage of God's offer of his Kingdom. For instance, one parable in Matthew (13:44) tells of a man who, walking through a field, discovers an enormous treasure. He reburies the treasure and rushes off to buy the field. The point is not that one would be justified in using a deceptive method to acquire property, but that one should act immediately and do everything needful to accept the treasure of God's Kingdom. Another parable in Matthew (13:45–46) concerns a merchant and connoisseur of pearls who owns a marvelous pearl collection. One day he sees a pearl so much superior to any and all he has ever seen that he sells *all* of his other pearls to raise enough money to buy this one.

The parable may be saying that the merchant values the pearl because he believes he will ultimately make a larger financial profit from it than from all of the others he owns combined. This would not change the point of the parable, which concerns the matchless worth of the Kingdom of God to the individual who participates in it. So membership in the Kingdom of God is worth far more than anything and everything else we may have thought of value—belonging to the Kingdom is a value so great to those who possess it that even if they have nothing else, this would be enough.

Some of the parables are intended to show that things appear to be very different to those within the Kingdom than to those outside. Thus in Matthew (20:1–16), workers who have worked all day complain because their employer rewards those who have worked only a short time with as much as he does them. The owner's reply implies that what he is freely giving to some does no injury to the others, since none are getting less than they need or deserve. Thus belonging to God's Kingdom is certainly the gift of God, unearned, and no one should think of herself or himself as being more worthy of God's love, or being worthy of more of God's love, than others are. The love and status that all have who belong to the Kingdom will be more than enough.

One of the most famous parables, the story of the Good Samaritan, occurs only in Luke's Gospel (10:25–37). It is used by Jesus to answer a question asked by a scribe (a lawyer) about what is required if one is to fulfill the commandments of the Torah. The encounter with the scribe and the question about the law occur in Matthew and in Mark as well as in Luke. Although the setting and details differ, in each of the gospels the encounter revolves around the question: Who is righteous in God's sight? In Matthew (22:34–40) a lawyer asks Jesus which is the greatest of the commandments and receives the answer of Jesus that there are two, or that the great commandment has two aspects, wholehearted love of God and love of one's neighbor. Only in Luke is the Good Samaritan story used to give a further answer to the question. In Luke, the lawyer begins the discussion not by asking about which commandment is greatest, but with the question: What shall I do to inherit eternal life? The implication of Jesus' response in each of its gospel settings is that being able to answer *either* question means knowing who belongs to God's Kingdom— that is, who fulfills the commandments. The commandments are to love God with one's whole heart, soul, strength, and mind, and to love one's neighbor as oneself. One who knows God's love—one who belongs to the Kingdom—will be able to love God and neighbor in this way.

In Luke's gospel, the lawyer and Jesus agree that to fulfill these command- ments means participating in God's Kingdom, fulfilling the Law. But the lawyer asks: Who is my neighbor? That is, How can I know whether I have kept this part of the Law or not?

Jesus responds by telling the story of a traveller who is beaten, robbed, and left for dead. He is ignored by a priest and Levite. Keeping the external laws of ritual cleanliness—they would risk being defiled by coming in contact with the dead or dying man—is more important to them than fulfilling God's intention that one should help those in need. The man is, however, helped by a Samaritan. The parable would have been offensive to many of Jesus' listeners. Samaria, the home of the Samaritans, lay on the west bank of the Jordan, separating Judea from Galilee. Normally Jews avoided even traveling through Samaria. Samari- tans were looked upon with hatred and contempt—they were outside the Law, and could not fulfill it because they were religiously unclean. They accepted the Pentateuch, but none of the rest of Jewish Scriptures, worshipped God in their own temple, not the Temple of Jerusalem, and for centuries had been enemies of the Jews. Yet the Samaritan is the one who fulfilled God's commandments. He is the one who loved his neighbor. He is the one seen to be already in the Kingdom.

Other parables, such as the story of the Prodigal Son, which also occurs only in Luke's Gospel (15:11–32), and several shorter ones, comment on God's attitude toward sinners, explain Jesus' concept of his ministry, and contain criticism of the attitudes of some of the religious leaders of Israel. One of the shortest of these (Luke 15:8–10) is the story of a woman who possessed ten coins. She lost one. She looked for it with great zeal, rejoicing when she found it. Thus, God wants to rescue sinners, the outcast, the lost. He does not need to seek those who are already found, like the Pharisees, who *are* already members of his Kingdom if they sincerely accept it. Certainly he loves them too. (Jesus criticized only Pharisees he judged to be insincere, those who put the external keeping of the Law above the inner meaning of it, or who obeyed the external Law for reasons of prestige, social acceptance, of financial or psychological security.) Thus, also, Jesus directed his mission mainly to those who were "lost."

Important collections of Jesus' parables are found in the following Synoptic locations: Mark 4; Matthew 5–7, 13, 21–25; Luke 10–16, 18–19. There are many implicit parables in Jesus' teachings—that is, comparisons so brief that they are not stories but nevertheless have the nature or character of parables. For instance, his saying to his hearers, "You are the salt of the earth, but if salt has lost its savor it is no good and fit only to be thrown out and trampled under foot" (Matthew 5:13). This could easily have been made into a story.

CRUCIFIXION

The gospels give a number of details about the arrest, trial(s), and crucifixion of Jesus. it is clear that many of the Pharisees opposed him, believing that by teaching laxity toward the law he was retarding the coming of God's Kingdom. It is clear that the Sadducees and Herodians perceived his potentially Messianic movement as a threat to the stability of their rule and of their not always harmonious relations with the Romans. Jesus was arrested and given a hearing before the Sanhedrin. It is likely that some of the Pharisees opposed his arrest, and were not informed of the hearings or trial until Jesus' execution was a fait accompli. Apparently, Jesus appeared before the Sanhedrin on charges of blasphemy. It appears that statements Jesus was alleged to have made about the Temple were cited—a prediction of its destruction would have been blasphemous (Mathew 24:2). Possibly some accusations were based on alleged claims of being the Messiah and sayings and actions for which Jesus had claimed direct authorization from God. At any rate, Jesus apparently was found, whether officially or informally, guilty of blasphemy and was sent to the Roman governor with the request that he be found guilty under the Roman law of treason—revolutionary activity or claims—and that he be executed. Much has been written about Jesus' appearance before Pilate, and much still remains cloudy and in doubt about the nature of the hearing and its outcome. What is clear is that Jesus was crucified at the order of the Roman governor and at the hands of the Roman soldiers after having been sent to them by members of the Sanhedrin.

RESURRECTION

Earlier in this chapter mention was made of the accounts of Jesus' Resurrection appearing in the gospels. These accounts are very intricate, weaving together various strands of tradition. What seems most clear is that the disciples, most or all of whom had believed Jesus to be the Messiah, were frightened, shocked, and devastated by his arrest and crucifixion. They probably remained in hiding, fearing arrest as co-consipirators. Later, they were told that some of the women who had been followers of Jesus had learned from a divine source that Jesus had risen from death. Then the risen Jesus began to appear to and among the disciples. The disciple Peter (or Simon) a fisherman who had been leader of the Twelve, apparently was the first to experience an actual appearance of the risen Lord (Luke 24:13–35).[3] Others, usually in groups, also experienced such appearances. One written account by an eyewitness, Paul, is found in the New Testament in I Corinthians, Chapter 15.

Thus the early Christian movement was born of the conviction, attested by experience, that God had raised Jesus from the dead. A contemporary New Testament scholar, Stuart Currie, once remarked that the question, Who must Jesus have been for God to have raised him from the dead? stood at the orgin of all Christian theology. Jesus' original disciples were convinced that they knew at least part of the answer to that question. They had believed before his death that he was the Messiah, the Christ of God, sent to bring in the New Age, to "restore the Kingdom to Israel" (Acts 1:6). Now, on the basis of their Resurrection experiences, they were convinced

[3]See Willi Marxsen, *The Resurrection of Jesus of Nazareth* (Philadelphia: Fortress Press, 1970).

that this was true, and that the New Age was indeed, as Jesus had said, begun. They believed that now it would come, inevitably, in its fullness.

Early Christian tradition, recorded in the first two chapters of the New Testament Book of Acts, reports that Jesus told the disciples to remain in Jerusalem until they received the power of the Spirit of God. The earliest Christian community was made up entirely of Jews. Many of them had been Jesus' disciples throughout his ministry. Others were post-Resurrection converts. They continued to practice Judaism. They worshipped at the Temple. A large group of them lived communally in Jerusalem and presented the message of Jesus as the crucified and risen Messiah to other Jews, teaching that in his life, death, and Resurrection Jesus had fulfilled the Messianic hopes of Judaism, inaugurating the New Age. It was very much against accepted Jewish belief that the Messiah might be rejected, much less crucified (this would have made him ritually unclean, accursed). But by the Resurrection, God had vindicated him, had shown that Jesus was indeed Messiah and Lord. Now God wanted to bring all Jews into the Kingdom by means of Jesus. This was the message of the disciples to their fellow Jews.

The early disciples also believed, at least in theory, that the message of Jesus was relevant to Gentiles too. However, they seem to have had no idea at first of reaching out in mission to non-Jews, either in Palestine or elsewhere. The spread of Christianity to non-Jewish regions and peoples began almost, it seems, by accident. Persecution by Jewish religious authorities of Hellenistic Jewish Christians (beginning with the death of the first Christian martyr, Stephen) drove these Christians out of Jerusalem into Samaria. There they began to make converts. Reports of this activity with its results surprised the Palestinian Christian Jerusalem leadership, who gave it their blessing (Acts 8).

Somewhat later, both Jewish and gentile converts began to be made in the Syrian city of Antioch, one of the largest cities in the Roman world. Here the followers of Jesus were first called Christians. And it was from Antioch that some of the first and most important organized missionary efforts to take the message about Jesus to Hellenistic Jews and Gentiles in the Asian and European parts of the Roman Empire originated.

QUESTIONS

1. Explain and relate the terms *eschatology, apocalypse,* and *apocalyptic thought.*
2. Explain the use of the term *Kingdom of God* in first-century Judaism.
3. Compare and contrast the teachings about the Kingdom of God of the Pharisees, Sadducees, Essenes (Qumran community), Zealots, John the Baptist, and Jesus.
4. Explain the importance of *signs* and *parables* in Jesus' ministry.
5. Explain how their belief in the Resurrection of Jesus affected his disciples.

FURTHER READING

BORNKAMM, GÜNTER. *Jesus of Nazareth.* New York: Harper & Brothers, 1960.
BULTMANN, RUDOLF. *Jesus and the Word.* New York: Charles Scribners' Sons, 1934.
————. *The History of the Synoptic Tradition.* New York: Harper & Row, 1963.

COLWELL, ERNEST CADMAN. *Jesus and the Gospel.* New York: Oxford University Press, 1963.

DIBELIUS, MARTIN. *From Tradition to Gospel.* New York: Charles Scribners' Sons, 1965.

―――. *Jesus.* Philadelphia: Westminster Press, 1949.

FARMER, WILLIAM R., and FARKASFALVY, DENNIS M. *The Formation of the New Testament Canon.* New York: Paulist Press, 1983.

FOLEY, GROVER, trans. *What Can We Know about Jesus? Essays on the New Quest by Ferdinand Hahn, Wenzel Lohff and Günter Bornkamm.* Philadelphia: Fortress Press, 1969.

FLUSSER, DAVID. *Jesus.* New York: Herder and Herder, 1969.

GRANT, FREDERICK C., trans. *Form Criticism.* Chicago: Willett, Clark & Company, 1934. A translation into English of Rudolf Bultmann, *The Study of the Synoptic Gospels,* and Karl Kundsin, *Primitive Christianity in the Light of Gospel Research.*

JEREMIAS, JOACHIM. *Jerusalem in the Time of Jesus.* Philadelphia: Fortress Press, 1968.

―――. *The Parables of Jesus.* Rev. ed. New York: Charles Scribners' Sons, 1963.

―――. *The Prayers of Jesus.* Philadelphia: Fortress Press, 1978.

KECK, LEANDER E. *A Future for the Historical Jesus.* Nashville, Tenn.: Abingdon Press, 1971.

KEE, HOWARD CLARK. *Jesus in History.* 2nd ed. New York: Harcourt, Brace, Jovanovich, 1977.

KELBER, WILLIAM H. *The Oral and the Written Gospel.* Philadelphia: Fortress Press, 1983.

KERMODE, FRANK. *The Genesis of Secrecy: On the Interpretation of Narrative.* Cambridge, Mass.: Harvard University Press, 1979.

LESSING, ERICH. *Jesus: History and Culture of the New Testament—A Pictorial Narration.* New York: Herder and Herder, 1971.

MARXSEN, WILLI. *The Resurrection of Jesus of Nazareth.* Philadelphia: Fortress Press, 1970.

MEYER, BEN F. *The Aims of Jesus.* New York: Oxford University Press, 1979.

MCKNIGHT, EDGAR V. *What Is Form Criticism?* Philadelphia: Fortress Press, 1969.

PERRIN, NORMAN. *The Kingdom of God in the Teaching of Jesus.* Philadelphia: Westminster Press, 1963.

―――. *Rediscovering the Teaching of Jesus.* New York: Harper & Row, 1967.

―――. *What Is Redaction Criticism?* Philadelphia: Fortress Press, 1969.

ROBINSON, JAMES M. *A New Quest of the Historical Jesus.* London: SCM Press, 1959.

ROBINSON, JOHN A. T. *Redating the New Testament.* Philadelphia: Westminster Press, 1976.

SANDERS, E. P. *Jesus and Judaism.* Philadelphia: Fortress Press, 1985.

SANDMEL, SAMUEL. *We Jews and Jesus.* New York: Oxford University Press, 1973.

SCHWEITZER, ALBERT. *Out of My Life and Thought.* New York: Henry Holt and Company, 1933.

————. *The Psychiatric Study of Jesus.* Gloucester, Mass.: Peter Smith, 1975.

————. *The Quest of the Historical Jesus.* New York: Macmillan, 1948.

SHULER, PHILIP L. *A Genre for the Gospels: The Biographical Character of Matthew.* Philadelphia: Fortress Press, 1982.

ZAHRNT, HEINZ. *The Historical Jesus.* New York: Harper & Row, 1963.

CHAPTER THREE

Early Christianity

The emergence of Christianity as a viable, dynamic religion within the cultural context of the Roman Empire required an extended gestation period, yet Christianity ultimately triumphed over all other religions in the European and the Mediterranean cultures.

CHRISTIANITY AND ITS GRECO-ROMAN MILIEU

The Roman Empire

In his fourth-century B.C.E. conquest of much of the known world, Alexander the Great initiated a movement toward political and cultural unity previously unknown in the Western world. This unification of peoples became a fundamental element in the civilization that achieved full fruition in the Roman Empire (31 B.C.E.–400 C.E.). Using his father's consolidation of the Greek city-states into one kingdom as a base, Alexander, a nineteen-year-old student of Aristotle, led his armies east, defeated Persia, and ended its 200-year rule of Mesopotamia and surrounding territories. Ultimately Alexander's armies controlled Greece, Macedonia, Egypt, Palestine, the Mesopotamian Valley civilizations, and portions of India. This startling military achievement, however, was eclipsed by Alexander's vision of a unified Greek culture supplementing and enlivening all the territories under his command. To this end he provided philosophers, teachers, and craftsmen to train all the inhabitants of these lands in Greek culture, philosophy, and language. Divergent political systems, languages, and religions of separate peoples were subordinated to an overarching cultural pattern that for centuries influenced civilizations of the region. Alexander's dream of a united Greek world was cut short by his premature death (323 B.C.E.) and the division of his conquest into three Greek kingdoms (Ptolemaic—Egypt and Africa; Seleucid—Mesopotamia, Palestine, Asia Minor, and India; and Antigonid—Macedonia and Greece). Aspects of the "Hellenizing" of these areas continued well after Rome's conquest of Greece and the eastern world.

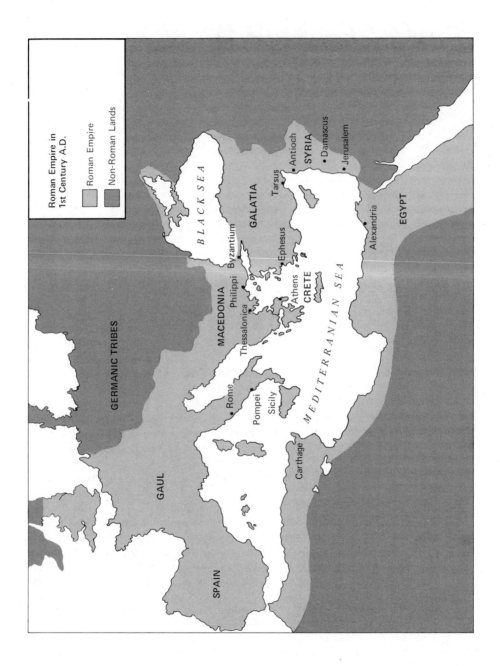

Roman Empire in
1st Century A.D.

Roman Empire
Non-Roman Lands

GERMANIC TRIBES

GAUL

SPAIN

BLACK SEA

Byzantium

GALATIA

Tarsus

Antioch

Damascus

SYRIA

Jerusalem

EGYPT

Alexandria

Ephesus

MACEDONIA

Philippi

Athens

CRETE

Thessalonica

MEDITERRANEAN SEA

Rome

Pompei

Sicily

Carthage

The alliance of the Aetolian League of Greek city-states with Rome in 212 B.C.E. began Rome's eastward expansion, culminating with the defeat of the Ptolemaic Greek kingdom by Julius Caesar in 48 B.C.E. The consolidation of imperial power was completed by Octavian at the battle of Actium in 31 B.C.E., resulting in Rome's rule of most of the territory controlled by Alexander, as well as the western Mediterranean. Rome was to maintain control of this vast empire until the fourth century of the common era.

Alexander's dream of a homogeneous culture, modified by the pragmatism of the Roman emperors, created in the empire a civilization that surpassed any which had preceded it. Land and sea routes built to quickly move army legions and goods facilitated interchange between divergent cultures and peoples. The *Pax Romana* (Peace of Rome) superimposed on those within the empire meant that whole generations of persons were freed from the debilitations of wars that had preceded the empire. Roman law served as a model for local custom and provided an appeals system for Roman citizens, bringing uniformity of law to diverse populations. The use of Greek as the language of commerce, literature, and much of international affairs provided a common means of communication and served as the basis of cultural and intellectual exchange previously unimagined. Migrations of Romans into the territories and of other peoples into Rome itself created a fluid, cosmopolitan culture. Rome's administration of its territories allowed the continuation of national rulers and cultures, as long as they did not threaten Roman sovereignty. Local and international interests could exist side by side. The price paid for these advantages included political subservience, heavy taxation, military rule and the imposition of a rigid social pyramid in which Roman rulers and citizens enjoyed social privileges resting on an often brutal system of slavery.

Changing Understandings in the Empire

In the cultural matrix, traditional patterns of meaning and value were called into question and modified significantly through the long centuries of Greek and Roman rule. Ancient Greek philosophies were based on popular interest in the nature of the universe and the place of humanity in it. The greatest of the philosophers, Plato and Aristotle, offered elaborate constructs that still influence Western thought. During the later Greek Hellenistic period, Platonic ideas came to prominence, even though Alexander had been a student of Aristotle. Plato's concept of an ideal, nonphysical, eternal realm incorporating real values (in contrast to the relative, imperfect values of the physical realm) was to influence much subsequent Greek and Roman thinking. The need for humanity to attune itself to the Good(s) of this ideal realm—justice, truth, beauty, and goodness—lay in the background of Greco-Roman thought. The appeal of these concepts came to renewed prominence in an empire where universal, or international, ideals dominated local cultures. By the time of the Roman Empire, other philosophies had also become popular. Plato's negation of the values found in the physical world did not sufficiently answer the needs of many.

Stoicism.   Stoic thought became the popular philosophy of many leaders in the Roman Empire. Stoicism affirmed the universe to be a harmonious whole in which Divine Fire was the unifying element. This Divine Fire, expressed in *logos*, or reason, was found in all reality. Humanity, in whatever status, slave or master, was an expression of reason. Therefore, all were to live in their predetermined roles carrying out their prescribed duties to the best of their abilities. Virtue was fulfilling one's duty. There was no place in this philosophy for personal immortality. One found meaning in living as reason ordained.

Epicureanism. Epicureanism offered yet another view of the universe. Conceiving of the universe as atoms randomly joined to produce life, Epicurus suggested that there was no immortality and that the gods were not relevant to human existence. He was convinced that humanity's fear of the gods had produced false perceptions and expectations of the universe. Virtue was the eradication of fear and the display of affection for one's fellows. Happiness would be the result of acceptance of life as it is, without illusions, without excessive demands, hopes, ambitions, or fears.

Astrology. Such philosophies fitted well the practical orientation of many in the Roman educated classes. They were not, however, satisfying to many people; and as the empire became cosmopolitan, alternative world views, particularly from the East, gained popularity. There was widespread acceptance in the early empire of Persian forms of astrology, although astrology was certainly not derived solely from Persian sources. Based on the hypothesis that the stars and their motions control the destinies and events of humanity, astrology with its horoscopes and diviners provided a popular frame for understanding and decision making. Underlying Stoicism, Epicureanism, and astrology was the basic belief that the destinies of individuals and nations were controlled by impersonal forces—reason, chance, or fate. The life experienced by many in the Roman Empire made these philosophies appealing.

Roman Religious Patterns

Agriculturally based religions that stressed productivity and survival, although modified as city cultures replaced rural settings, retained a strong influence in the empire. They were supplemented by gods and goddesses identified with particular cities or territories who offered local security, protection, and identity. As the empire transferred local political power to an international entity, local city and agricultural gods and their cults began to lose their appeal, and many persons longed for spiritual sustentation of a more universal nature.

Most of the Greek Olympian pantheon of gods had been, by the time of the empire, identified with the ancient gods of Rome. Serving in some sense the need for more universal religious patterns, these Greek-Roman gods took their place beside local ethnic religions, since Roman policy allowed autonomous religious practices as long as the interests of the empire were not threatened. In this arrangement the worship of Roman gods and goddesses was identified with the state (civic) religion. Every major city had temples dedicated to these deities. Complementing these civic religious figures were the religions of the empire's component ethnic groups. Family and personal spiritual needs were met in both patterns through personal worship of ancient gods and goddesses (including household deities worshipped at family shrines) who served specific needs or functions.

Emperor worship. The Egyptian and eastern Mediterranean pattern of elevating kings to a divine stature, combined with the Roman honoring of heroes, significantly contributed to patterns of emperor worship. Augustus (Octavian), while making no claims of divinity in Rome itself, accepted the accolades of the East proclaiming him a divine deliverer, like Alexander before him. By the time of Christianity's spread (100 C.E.), the cultic patterns of emperor worship were well entrenched. With this development the acceptance of emperor worship became a political expression of loyalty to the empire.

Public worship had as its object the well-being of the state and empire. The emperor, as the most powerful official in the empire, was understood to stand and act as a representative or intermediary for the whole people to insure security, well-being, and prosperity. At death, the spirit (genius) of the departed emperor was believed to become divine and to continue to exert watchful care over the common-wealth. Some of the emperors proclaimed themselves divine while they were still living. Worship of traditional gods continued to serve many of the same functions, but the cult of the empire provided unity on an empire-wide basis, and therefore took on a political as well as religious function.

However, many persons cut off from traditional ties found that the estab-lished civic religions, including emperor worship, did not meet their personal needs. Increasingly, individuals expected more from religion—a source of meaning, guidance, and protection in this life and afterwards—than the state religions could give.

Mystery religions. These needs were met at the common level in many ways. Most popular were a number of religions designated as *mystery religions* by modern scholars. For the most part, these religions were grounded in ancient fertility rites wherein the natural cycle of death and rebirth was reenacted to insure health and prosperity. By the time of the empire they had lost much of their original nature as civic fertility cults. They were transformed into religions that made the mysteries of the universe available to participants. Although numerous, many of them shared several characteristics. Each claimed its adherents, through the acquisition of a secret or mysterious knowledge or rite, would participate in the controlling powers of the universe. Participants were thereby distinguished from their neighbors and elevated above them. One was no longer simply a part of the state or ethnic community. Many of the mysteries claimed that through participating in the rites the participant actually became divine, transcending the limitations of normal life. These religions incorporated elaborate rites of initiation and stringent rules of behavior. Very important was the element of redemption, a guarantee of eternal life. Among such religions were worship of Isis and Osiris, originating in Egypt; Dionysian and Orphic cults from Thrace (modern Bulgaria); the Eleusinian myster-ies from Greece; and the religion of the Great Mother from Asia Minor. Mithraism from Iran normally is considered one of these religions, although it did not share the exact patterns of fertility myth that the others do. While arising in the eastern sections of the empire, these religions spread throughout the Roman Empire during its first centuries.

Isis and Osiris. The worship of Isis and Osiris serves as an example of the mystery religions. This religion was initially related to the agricultural life of the Nile Valley. After centuries of development, the religion became increasingly preoccupied with the mystery of death and became popular throughout much of the cosmopolitan Greco-Roman world. Osiris, a divine king and compassionate ruler of Egypt, enjoyed the companionship and love of his sister and consort, Isis. Killed by his jealous brother, Osiris's body was dismembered and cast into the Nile, which distributed it through the world. Osiris in the state of death became the god of the underworld. In her sorrow and grief, Isis sought the body of Osiris and buried each part as she found it. By her actions, she revived Osiris so that he assumed a dual role as god of the living and the dead. Isis became the agent of life. An initiate into the religion reenacted the suffering and death of Osiris, thereby overcoming death. In Rome, the worship of Isis as agent and symbol of life overshadowed the role of Osiris in the religion.

The worship of Isis and Osiris offered a means of dealing with both life as it was experienced, good and bad, and with death, since the believer was assured of a secure life beyond the present one. The religion was known for its elaborate and rich ceremonies, which provided distinct roles for a devoted, almost monastic, priest as well as the lay adherent and occasional temple worshiper. The attraction of the cult was its provision of a role and place for the individual and its attempt to deal with death, in a culture where public religions seldom promised hope beyond the sustaining of the state and its benefits.

Gnosticism.   Another popular religious alternative in Roman culture was Gnosticism, a complex syncretistic fusion of widely differing religious and philosophical insights with varied cultic practices. Gnostic patterns, of which there were many, existed throughout the empire, often reflecting various Greek philosophies. Gnosticism, influenced by Oriental dualism, separated the universe into a spirit world of light ruled over by a benevolent and loving divine principle and a physical world of darkness created and controlled by the Demiurge, a divine, but evil being, and his representatives. These two worlds were populated and related by a graded hierarchy of beings. Humanity, according to the Gnostics, was one form of these beings, joining the physical evil world with a divine spark or spirit from the world of light. Gnosis (knowledge) of humanity's entrapment in the physical world and the pathways to freedom from it was offered by the religion, often through a savior figure.

CHRISTIANITY AS A ROMAN RELIGION

In the dynamic Greco-Roman world, beauty and brutality lay side by side. Cultural idealism and cruel self-interest fashioned starkly contrasting political and social patterns, while religions appealing to differing needs and interests competed with and complemented one another. Christianity, entering this world, slowly distinguished itself from other patterns of life and cultic community, ultimately becoming attractive enough to be a fashioner of much of the civilization that succeeded Rome. Such a transition involved great struggle and maturation over several centuries.

Persecution of Christians

The initial community of Christians was drawn from the lower economic and social classes. Few Jewish leaders were drawn to the community in Jesus' lifetime, though there were exceptions (John 3:1, 7:50). As the religion moved from Palestine into the Gentile world, the appeal continued to be largely to those of lower social status. Christianity offered to these people an all-powerful God in a world where a myriad of gods vied for attention. It brought salvation to the individual and gave one a place in the community. It also conquered the fear of death, offering hope for eternal life (Romans 8:31–9). An ethic of love based on God's love of all persons, whatever their social status, helped make it an attractive religious alternative.

In a rigidly defined social structure that offered little mobility this aspect of Christianity was particularly appealing to the lower classes. Paul's letter to Philemon, a slaveholder, and the addressing of Luke and Acts to the "most excellent Theophilus" may suggest that by the middle of the first century, Christianity was becoming known among those of status and position. Nevertheless, through the first several decades, Christianity only slowly won to its ranks persons of significant political and social position.

Among Roman officials, Christianity must have closely resembled the mystery religions as it offered individual salvation on the basis of voluntary commitment and initiation into a closed community, which carefully guarded its beliefs and practices. Its separation from Judaism and its position in the empire both legally and socially meant that Christianity enjoyed few, if any, social advantages in its first centuries. Yet it quickly emerged as a religious option in an extremely complex world.

Although Judaism and Christianity took significantly different paths and were separated early, the identification of the two lingered in the understanding of the Roman populace and officials. The position of the Jews deteriorated after the revolts of 66–73 and 132–135 C.E. Jews were looked on with suspicion as revolutionaries whose beliefs and attitudes threatened the state. Christian identification with the Jews meant that some of that same suspicion fell on Christians.

A Martyr's View of Christianity

Fortunately, a unique set of letters from the first years of the second century gives us a fascinating glimpse of one person's experience of Christianity as it matured in the Roman Empire. Picture for a moment a detachment of soldiers making their way on the well-traveled overland route through Cilicia and Asia Minor (present-day Turkey) toward Rome. Chained to one of them is Ignatius of Antioch. We pick up their trek only for a few days between Philadelphia and Troas. At Smyrna and again in Troas, Ignatius asks leave from his guards to receive small groups of persons who bring him messages and greetings from other cities in the area. The centurion in charge of the squad of soldiers grants the request but surely must wonder at the joy and happiness evident in the group. Wasn't his prisoner being taken to Rome to an almost certain death? What is all of this talk of salvation and identification with "Christ" through meeting the lions in the Coliseum? How could that be deliverance? Who were these strange people who were bold enough to appeal to Roman justice when they clearly were unwilling to worship the ancient gods who formed and guided the empire? What did the title "bishop," which they used for his prisoner, mean in their community? Even though this assignment meant that the centurion and his men were able to return home, it was a difficult trip to make. They surely wondered at the excitement and happiness of their prisoner—especially since Ignatius' appeal to Rome was obviously a hopeless one. Death was certain for one refusing to worship the ancient gods and honor the emperor by burning incense in his name. Such rituals affirmed loyalty to the empire. How could anyone refuse this civic duty in the name of loyalty to an obscure crucified Galilean?

Ignatius' letters, written to the churches whose emissaries had visited him on his journey and to others, would perhaps not have satisfied the centurion's curiosity, yet they reveal a young and maturing religious community. In the letters Ignatius emerges as a passionate, real person whose experiences reflect an expanding Christian community in which he had attained, to his seeming surprise, the position of bishop. Clearly Ignatius' understanding of this office differed substantially from that of the Apostle Paul, who saw bishops as collegial workers in the church. For Ignatius, writing some fifty years after Paul, the bishop of a local church had become the sole head of that church. In fact, Ignatius' elevated opinion of the bishop and other officers of the church approached a mystical understanding of their offices:

> Let the bishop preside in God's place, and the presbyters take the place of the apostolic council, and let the deacons (my special favorites) be entrusted with the ministry of Jesus Christ (Magnesians 6:1).[1]

All members of the community were urged to "act in accord with the bishop's mind" and hold him in highest esteem. All bishops were to be obeyed in such manner for "bishops, too, appointed the world over, reflected the mind of Jesus Christ" (Ephesians 3:2). Here we have a religious community where the question of religious authority has been resolved by the assigning to one person final authority—similar to that found in God. Such authority is, however, understood to be dependent on God's grace—Ignatius continually refers to himself as "God-inspired." The office, as one might expect, carried heavy duties, for the bishop was ultimately responsible for the spiritual life of the church.

Other characteristics of these churches are also evident in the letters. Although persecution was a given fact, shown by Ignatius' journey toward the Coliseum, it was within the framework of Roman law and most often localized. Those Christians who came to comfort and support Ignatius in his journey apparently did so without fear of imprisonment or persecution by his guards. In their local area they were not subject to the same persecution under which he was being condemned.[2] Communication between Christians from various locations was open and encouraged. Ignatius is profuse in his thanks to the churches who sent emissaries and urges others to support his home church at Antioch by sending messages and letters (Ephesians 1:1; Trallians 13:1). The interdependence of various local congregations is also witnessed to by Ignatius' repeated call for unity and agreement in belief, worship, and action (Philadelphians 8). While each congregation stands independently from the others, they are inexorably related through their concern for each other, their joint interests (Romans 9:1–3), and the intercommunication of their bishops.

In theological concerns, Ignatius' emphasis on the reality of Christ's Incarnation, Passion, and Resurrection shows a church stressing the salvation themes of the gospel (Smyrnaeans 4:2). Specific reference to Jesus' teaching role is missing from the letters, while his role as savior is a constant theme. What appealed to the Gentiles of the empire appears to be this salvation theme. Paul's emphasis on justification by faith and its dependence on faith as trust is also missing from these letters. Ignatius' image of a "real Christian" is exemplified by his own anticipated martyr-

---

[1]Translations of Ignatius' letters are readily available in a number of sources. The quotations and other references used in this section are drawn from Cyril C. Richardson, *Early Christian Fathers* (Philadelphia: Westminster Press, 1963), pp. 74–120. References are noted by the location of the churches to which Ignatius' letters were written—e.g., Magnesians, Ephesians, Trallians, and so on.

[2]For an extended discussion of the early relationship of Christianity to Rome, see W. H. C. Frend, *Martyrdom and Persecution in the Early Church* (New York: Doubleday, 1967).

dom—one who is convinced of Christ's salvatory role and who is willing to give himself in life and ultimately in death (Romans 3:2). Action—in this case, suffering as did Christ himself—is what counts. Justification is then conviction and willingness to give of oneself. Clearly, some of this attitude and understanding of the faith is dependent upon Ignatius' deep apocalyptic convictions. He is convinced, as most Christians of the time appear to have been, that they were living in the last times (Magnesians 5:1).

The task of distinguishing true Christian belief and patterns from other religious alternatives is a continual concern in Ignatius' letters. Paul's struggle against "Judaizers" continues, perhaps without the same intensity, during Ignatius' time. Such Judaizers urged Gentiles recently converted to the Christian faith to strictly follow Jewish ritual and cultic law (Philadelphians 6:1–3; 8:2–9:2; Magnesians 8:1–10:13). For Ignatius those insisting on Jewish patterns fail to see Jesus as the fulfillment of prophecy and as the divine revelation itself.

While such Judaic patterns were to be resisted, of greater danger, from Ignatius' viewpoint, was the propensity of many in Hellenistic civilizations to see the spirit world as good and the physical world as evil. Gnosticism, which was gaining strength as an alternate religion/philosophy at the time, usually affirmed a savior who had revealed Divine spiritual knowledge of the universal mysteries, thereby providing an escape from the entrapment of the human spirit in an evil physical world. Many Gnostic teachers, recognizing the exemplary knowledge and morality of Jesus, incorporated him into their systems, teaching that he was the divine messenger of saving knowledge. However, since the material world was evil, they taught that Jesus could not have been human, for to be such would mean he was contaminated by the evil physical world. This understanding, while prominent among Gnostics, was also appealing to Christian believers who, from their Greek backgrounds, emphasized the spiritual nature of humanity over its physical reality. For them, like the Gnostics, Jesus was a spiritual entity who only "used" a human body or appeared to be human. Such an understanding, known as docetism, was appealing to many.

This understanding of Jesus was for Ignatius rank heresy. He was so incensed by its presence that he warned against docetic, or gnostic, views throughout his letters (Philadelphians 2:1–3:3; Trallians 6:1–2; Ephesians 18:1–19:3).

> Regarding our Lord, you are absolutely convinced that on the human side he was actually sprung from David's line, Son of God according to God's will and power, actually born of a virgin, baptized by John,... and actually crucified for us in the flesh,... And thus, by his resurrection, he raised a standard to rally his saints and faithful forever—whether Jews or Gentiles—in one body of his Church. For it was for our sakes that he suffered all this, to save us. And he genuinely suffered, as even he genuinely raised himself. It is not as some unbelievers say, that his Passion was a sham (Smyrnaeans 1:1–2).

The attitude toward his own anticipated martyrdom seen in Ignatius' letter to the church at Rome is an early example of a pattern of martyrology that became an important part of second- and third-century Christian life. Ignatius' anxiousness that the church in Rome do nothing to interfere with his sacrifice of his own life to "imitate the Passion of my God" perhaps expresses an extreme position, since the church later discouraged believers from seeking martyrdom; yet those who were martyred came to be revered as the most spiritually mature. They were to be examples for all other believers (Romans 5:1–6:3). For Ignatius and for many within the church of his time, martyrdom was a means of becoming a real disciple, a genuine Christian, a way to "get to God" (Romans).

These letters stress, as does other early Christian literature, the importance of exemplary lives—lives of love, compassion, and forgiveness—which Christians understood to separate them from their neighbors (Smyrnaeans 6:1–7:2; Polycarp 4 and 5). The Eucharist had by this time become the central worship service, and for Ignatius it was a testimony to the humanity of Jesus. Those who denied the human nature of the Christ refused to "admit that the Eucharist is the flesh of our Saviour Jesus Christ" (Smyrnaeans 7:1). It was to be celebrated by the bishop or one authorized by him. Baptisms and love feasts (a common sacred meal) were also worship events and were to be carried out under the authority of the bishop. For Ignatius all aspects of Christian worship and life were structured and focused on purity gained not only in one's personal action but within the framework and supervision of the church. Christianity outside the church and dependent on individual religious experience or conviction, even that of the prophet and martyr, would have been unthinkable.

The image of early Christianity drawn from Ignatius' letters is, of course, only one view. Other Christians left extensive writings elaborating and supplementing the insights and interests found in Ignatius. Many of these show a maturing second- and third-century church marked by occasional intense persecution. As it stabilized in these early centuries, it defined its beliefs over against heretical positions among the faithful, distinguished itself from other religions, developed scriptural canons, and established more universal organizational norms and patterns.[3] In this fluid and occasionally threatening situation, the church continued to expand, finding believers not only among the poor and outcast but among the educated upper classes as well.

CHRISTIANITY AS THE RELIGION OF THE EMPIRE

Imagine the incredulous wonder experienced by Eustathius, bishop of Antioch and one of Ignatius' successors, as he traveled toward Nicaea to attend an empire-wide council of Christian bishops in May 325. He had been invited by the Emperor Constantine himself and was traveling at state expense. The call to the council announced that the bishops were to discuss and finally settle a number of issues that for the past several years had divided Christians.

Much had changed in the two centuries since Ignatius' tenure as Bishop of Antioch. Localized persecution had continued through the second century, yet Christianity found a wider acceptance among persons in all social and economic levels of society. Its attractive teachings concerning salvation as well as the exemplary lives of its adherents appealed to many.

The third century had witnessed major crises in the Roman empire—military pressures from the "barbarians" who surrounded the empire on its frontiers, internal struggles among military and political leaders, corruption of public leaders, and a general moral malaise. Several emperors, to reassert their power and return

[3]The writings of Clement of Rome, Polycarp, Justin Martyr, Irenaeus, Origen, Tertullian, Clement of Alexandria, and others all contribute to a rounded though complex picture of the early church.

the empire to secure prosperity, sought renewal of the ancient Roman religions. Such renewals always meant persecution for Christians. While earlier outbreaks had been localized, these were empire-wide, yet unevenly applied. Nevertheless, by the first decade of the fourth century, Egypt, North Africa, Mesopotamia, and parts of Syria and Asia Minor had so extensively embraced Christianity that policies of discrimination and persecution were not enforceable even by Roman legions. Christianity had become so influential within the empire that it could not be ignored.

The beginning decades of the fourth century were indeed tumultuous for the empire and significantly changed the political and social situation of Christians. In the later years of the previous century, the emperor Diocletian, seeing that he could not efficiently control the empire without aid, established an eastern headquarters in Nicomedia (northwestern Turkey) and appointed Maximian as a subordinate but co-ruler in the West with headquarters at Rome. Each of these rulers took the title "Augustus" and then appointed a "Caesar" as a subordinate to succeed him. So was created in 293 the Tetrarchy—four Roman rulers interconnected by military and political relations as well as by intermarriage of their families. When Diocletian abdicated and retired to private life in 305 (followed by Maximian), the Tetrarchy degenerated into dynastic rivalries that would eventually resolve themselves in the reassertion of rule by one emperor—Constantine.

Before his retirement (303) Diocletian, joined by Maximian, had instituted a great persecution of Christians, trying once and for all to reassert the power and priority of ancient Roman gods. The persecution was intense, with many Christian leaders losing their lives while churches and Scriptures were burned; yet it was still unsuccessful in eradicating Christianity.

The Rise of Constantine

In the dynastic struggle that followed Diocletian's and Maximian's abdications, Constantine, son of the western Caesar, Constantius, rose to preeminent power in his area by the defeat of Maxentius, son of Maximian, in a battle at Rome (312). Constantine, a believer in one supreme god, the "Unconquered Sun," in this battle evidently sought the support not only of the sun god but also of the Christian god. Convinced by his victory, Constantine, who may have had Christian sympathies prior to this event, now began to condemn the repressive religious policies of his predecessors. In the year following his victory (313), Constantine, along with his co-ruler in the east, Licinius, issued the Edict of Milan, an edict of toleration of all religions in the empire: "Since we saw that freedom of worship ought not be denied, but that to each man's judgment and will the right should be given to care for sacred things according to each man's free choice...."[4] The religious freedom granted by the edict meant that Christianity could now be practiced with no interference from the state. Church properties previously confiscated were returned and martyrdom ended: Christianity had entered a new day!

In his reflections as he approached Nicaea, Eustathius must have felt that the changes in the situation of the Christians were so numerous and revolutionary as to be almost incomprehensible. Even though Constantine continued his outward allegiance to the Unconquered Sun until his final military triumph in 324, he clearly grew more appreciative of the Christian God, considering himself from his victory

---

[4]W. H. C. Frend, *The Rise of Christianity* (Philadelphia: Fortress Press, 1984), p. 483.

at Rome a "servant of God." The consequences of this change in imperial attitude were revolutionary. No longer were Christians a persecuted minority; they now enjoyed the favor of the emperor. The rewards of such favor quickly emerged. Constantine during this decade freed the churches in Rome from expensive rents paid on state properties, gave lands to the church, built a large church to honor St. Peter in Rome, and contributed to other churches in Italy. This largesse expanded with time so that the church profited materially from the new relationship to the emperor. Of perhaps more long-lasting consequence was the new status given to the Christian clergy. The bishops were granted immunity from extensive municipal levies and taxes paid by religious and civic leaders. Constantine also gave the clergy, through the church courts, equivalent privileges and responsibilities in certain cases as those carried by magistrates, elevating Christian officials to positions of status and privilege. The transformation such changes brought could hardly have been more surprising for many in the church.

The Council of Arles

In addition to these monumental changes in the life of the church, Constantine entered into church affairs by calling a regional council, or synod, of bishops at Arles. Its purpose was to achieve a settlement of a dispute in North Africa between followers of Donatus, who claimed that bishops must be without blemish (that is, they rejected "traditores," who reportedly had surrendered Scriptures under the persecutions of the previous regimes) and other church leaders who were more lenient toward those who had suffered under persecution. When the judgment of the council failed to convince the Donatists to drop their objections, Constantine attempted unsuccessfully to force their compliance. Clearly the affairs of the church were becoming state issues and important to state policy.

Arius and Arianism

Although amazed at the changes wrought in the church by Constantine, Eustathius could understand the need for a consultation of the bishops. Constantine had only the year before finally succeeded in crushing his imperial rivals and establishing himself as sole emperor. Military victory, however, could not assure acceptance and peace, particularly in view of the bitter political divisions of the past decade. A truly united empire would require peace among its many factions, including its religions. Rivalries among Christians, so recently elevated in Roman culture and scattered through the empire, posed a significant threat to unity and with it to the very fabric of the empire.

The Donatist controversy of the previous decade represented only a limited segment of the church, being largely confined to North Africa. The theological issues constituting the principal agenda of the council to which Eustathius journeyed threatened a much broader section of the church—the more Christianized eastern Mediterranean.

Eustathius must have wondered if it was really possible to settle such issues through a council, since theological issues, previously the concern only of the church, had now taken on state importance. Would the ideas of Arius that were to be discussed at the council be upheld? Clearly he had many supporters in Antioch and throughout the area. Who among the bishops would actually come to the council? What did an ecumenical (universal) council mean for the church in the life of the empire? Surely it signified a new role for the church. If the bishops gathered at the council could really achieve what the emperor hoped, Christianity might well replace the ancient pagan religions that had from the time of Christ been its tenacious rivals.

All of these issues were important and intriguing, but for Eustathius and his peers the council was not principally a political necessity: it was essential to deal with the ideas of Arius. They were relevant to the very essence of the Christian faith. Arius, an Alexandrian presbyter or priest, followed the emphases of earlier teachers, Origen of Alexandria and Lucian of Antioch, by asserting that the divine sovereignty of God did not allow any other being to be of the exact same essence as God. Consequently, while the Word of God (incarnate in Jesus as the Son) shared in a form of the divine essence, Arius believed that the Word was also subject to eternal generation—that it was created out of nothing, like all other creatures. This implied there was a time before the creation of the Word, a time when it was not in existence. Such an understanding of the Son made him divine but not of the same essence as the Father, and in Incarnation this divine Word took the place of the soul in Jesus' human body. Jesus was then a being neither of the same essence of the Father nor of humanity in his Incarnation. This position derived from an emphasis on monotheism that incorporated a Platonic concept of the human body and soul. If this understanding of the Son and his relationship to the Father became the accepted teaching, many bishops and their people would have great difficulties—if Jesus was not divine in the same way as the Father, had the divine truly entered into the

Christ in Chains. Ilgen, Bavaria, eighteenth century.

Incarnation? If his Incarnation made him something other than human, was the salvation offered a salvation for the common man and woman? Arius' position seemed to shift the very nature and meaning of the gospel—even if it solved some difficulties for the intellectual tradition of Greek philosophy raised by believing in an incarnation of a divine being among corrupt humans.

Such was the central issue calling for settlement at the Council of Nicaea. The call also suggested that other schismatic movements would be dealt with, as well as the important question of whether Easter would be observed universally across the church according to the Roman calendar or on differing calendars, as was the case as the council gathered. The meeting was then a most significant occasion ecclesiastically and theologically, in addition to having great political importance.

The Nicene Creed.   Constantine himself opened the proceedings of the some 230 bishops assembled. Their deliberations were open and lively, but with the imperial presence clearly felt. Arius' defense was substantial, appealing to many present. His position was not, however, acceptable to the majority. The council closed by issuing a "creed" carefully crafted to reject his position. It also promulgated anathemas (condemnations, including excommunication) on all who might say that there was a time when the Son was not or that he was of any other substance or essence than that of the Father. The date of Easter was to be set independently of Jewish calculations, a prominent eastern practice. Various schismatical movements were condemned, and requirements for their return to the church were established. Rome, Antioch, and Alexandria, along with Jerusalem, were given special status among Christians; their bishops took on new, unique responsibilities, and their positions now carried new prestige.

In some sense the council reached the apex of change so evident in Christianity during the first quarter of the century. By its combination of political and ecclesiastical interests, it set precedents for church-state relations for centuries to come. With Constantine's participation in its deliberations, the church became inexorably tied to the affairs of state and established patterns of church governance in the Eastern Empire that would last for centuries. Bishops would henceforth be officials of the state, and the church would be dependent on state power; church and state were intertwined, and neither was complete without the other. Because its call had been to all bishops, it was a universal (ecumenical) council that spoke for the whole body of Christians (even though only three representatives from Western bishoprics were present). Its decrees were understood to be binding on all Christians. Using the pattern of consultation so effective for local and territorial issues prior to this time, it established a means for reaching universal agreement on major questions affecting the broad range of Christians. The conciliar pattern was to become a standard form of church organization. Six more ecumenical councils (including representatives from both the East and West) followed its patterns (the last one being held in 787). In promulgating a creed, Nicaea set the parameters for Christian belief and established Christian orthodoxy. Thereafter, to be Christian would mean to agree to test one's belief against a universal standard. With the close of the council, the Christian church entered into new patterns of organization, theological orthodoxy, and state allegiance.

However, Constantine's cherished dream of Roman unity undergirded by Christian agreement proved to be illusive. While the council's decrees promulgated what one could not believe about the Son it did not answer the more subtle question of what was meant by saying that the Son was of the same substance (essence) as the Father. Arius' solution had been rejected but others emerged; the discussion was to go on for another century, only to be settled finally at the Council of Chalcedon in 451. Jesus was declared to be "truly human and truly divine," a statement that still left ample opportunity for varying interpretations. Local beliefs and differences are seldom immediately settled or modified by the actions of councils, and such was to be the case after Nicaea; its creed was slow to achieve universal acceptance. Arius, although banished, continued to be active and his teachings and beliefs were to survive for centuries in some sections of the Eastern church.

Though he did not achieve unity through the council, Constantine did succeed in strengthening his control of the empire. To insure Eastern authority, he launched into a massive reorientation of the empire by transforming Byzantium, an ancient city strategically located in northwestern Asia Minor, into the Eastern imperial capital, a new Rome appropriately named Constantinople. Included in his massive building program was a magnificent church: St. Sophia. This church and its bishop in the coming centuries joined other important churches in Antioch, Jerusalem, and Alexandria, as a preeminent metropolitan see (archbishopric). It quickly became the center of Eastern Christianity.

It was the last decade of the fourth century before Emperor Theodosius decreed Christianity to be the exclusive religion of the empire (392), but the consequences of the changes made in the first quarter clearly anticipated Christianity's emergence as the major Roman religion. From this century, Christianity was to be an integral part of all subsequent Eastern and Western European civilization.

It would be unusual for changes such as occurred among Christians in this century to go unopposed. The move from being a persecuted religion to a position of privilege and honor required compromises that were unacceptable to many; to become part of the state meant to take on some of the state's standards of conduct and value. Christians, whose image of the faith required significant personal suffering, sacrifice, and discipline, found these changes distinctly threatening: without persecution the special role of martyrs, considered by many as exemplary and preeminent spiritual Christians, was lost. As Christianity became the religion of the Roman state, all citizens were assumed to be members of the church, whether or not they exemplified personal commitment or discipline. No longer was personal voluntary commitment a hallmark of faith. For many, these developments compromised the faith and threatened its very fiber.

The Rise of Monasticism

Saint Anthony (251?–356 C.E.), an Egyptian layman, on becoming a Christian sold his properties, giving the proceeds to the poor, and retired to the desert to take up a life of contemplation. There he lived to a very old age (reputedly sustained by dates and honey!) as an exemplary Christian whose spiritual disciplines and abandonment of the world attracted many others to the contemplative life. So began the long heritage of Christian monasticism. In the fourth century many of those disillusioned by the secularization necessitated in making Christianity the official Roman religion turned to monasticism as an alternate pattern of Christian life. Here they could establish patterns of spirituality and discipline that were more demanding than those found in local churches. As martyrdom had been the ideal pattern of Christian life in a previous time, monasticism now took on this role, becoming for the developing church the most respected and revered form of Christianity. Developing rapidly, monasticism's reservoir of talented, disciplined spiritual leaders served the church in innumerable ways. Monasticism's contributions to the life of the church and its resultant influence in both the Eastern and Western churches helped mold a stable Christianity that offered distinctively different patterns of Christian life and service.

If the fourth century closed with the triumphal acceptance of Christianity as the Roman religion, it did not provide the cement that would hold the empire together. Succeeding regimes saw the rapid decline and fall of the empire as emperors were limited in their ability to defend the vast area, racked by internal familial and political disputes and corruption. The western reaches of the empire were overrun by Germanic tribes moving west into Britain and south into Gaul, Italy, and North Africa. Roman civilization, as it had been known earlier, passed from the scene in the West and was severely limited in the East, particularly after the Muslim invasions that began in the seventh century.

The changes and adjustments in Christianity caused by these developments were as dramatic and staggering as those of the fourth century, and we still live with their consequences. Western Roman civilization disintegrated as emperors headquartered in the east could not defend it. As a result the Christian church, the most closely organized, independent Western social structure, rose to a position of social and political preeminence. It was also to produce outstanding Christian leaders such as Ambrose of Milan, Augustine of Hippo in Africa, and, in the next century, Gregory of Rome. St. Augustine's rich thought molded both ecclesiastical and theological life for much of subsequent Western theology. (See Chapters Seven and Eight for more information on St. Augustine and his seminal influence among western Christians.) These developments in the west contributed to a church significantly different from the Christian community that survived in the east. We turn now to examine briefly some general features of these two great branches of Christendom.

EASTERN AND WESTERN PATTERNS
OF CHRISTIAN FAITH

At the height of its power, the Roman Empire imposed significant unity on many divergent people without attempting to eliminate cultural, ethnic, and regional differences among its vast dominions. Distinctions between Persians, Egyptians, Greeks, and Romans themselves, not to mention the numerous other groups within the empire, were vast. Christian groups formed in these cultural and ethnic communities naturally reflected the practices and thoughts of local peoples and thereby incorporated into early Christianity distinctive organizational structures, theologies, and practices.

Considering the two major patterns of Eastern and Western Christianity as they developed after the fourth century, we are, therefore, discussing differences between Greek and Roman cultures that were never eliminated in the Greco-Roman period. The division of the empire into Eastern and Western sections contributed to the reemergence of basic and latent distinctions that characterize these cultures. Roman practicality, seen in thought patterns oriented toward precise definition and efficiency, insisted on clarity of concept, direct expression, and practical application.

On the other hand, Greek interests had always been philosophical; the nature of universal truth in all of its intricacy was more interesting and primary than the practicalities that might arise from such truth. The churches that arose under these differing orientations naturally reflected their foundational systems of thought.

Eastern Mediterranean cultures had been extensively influenced by the Hellenization instituted under Alexander the Great, and it is in these areas that Christianity took on the patterns of Greek thought and practice. These churches have been given in history the general designation "Eastern Orthodox." The term *orthodox* indicates their doctrinal acceptance of the formulations of the first seven ecumenical councils, in contrast to others in their geographical regions that rejected these formulations. Today these churches are found throughout eastern Europe, Greece, and other eastern Mediterranean countries, the Middle East, and the U.S.S.R. Divided into a number of national churches and voluntary organizations, they are unified in their characteristic beliefs and practices.[5]

Western Christianity, on the other hand, for centuries was identified with the church located in Rome. Claiming apostolic foundation and located in the premier city of the empire, this Roman church also understood itself to represent the universal (or catholic) Christian faith; therefore, its usual designation became the Roman Catholic church. Organized on a Western principle of centralization, all other churches in the West were subordinated to Rome. Dominating Western culture from the fourth century until the sixteenth, it continues as the largest unified body of Christian believers. With Eastern Orthodoxy, Roman Catholicism understands the first seven councils to define Christian belief, but it also accepts the decisions of later Western councils that continued to reformulate theology, worship, and organization.

The distinctive characteristics of these two major Christian bodies began in their very earliest establishment and still contribute to the rich mosaic of modern Christian life. Some of the most significant characteristics will show us both the differences and the similarities of the groups.

The Concept of Humanity and Its Salvation

It is not surprising to find that the understanding of humanity and its salvation differs substantially between East and West. Among the Orthodox, humanity is only *fully human,* or complete, when it is in communion with God. The natural state of humanity is to be in God. One is free only when he or she is in communion with God. Humanity, having chosen to reject this full communion, has fallen into slavery to itself and the world. The ultimate result of this rejection is death—an unnatural state. Sin is understood, following the Platonic tradition, as a separation from God in which the image of God becomes unclear, and humanity lives in an unnatural state. Through sin, humanity loses the freedom to be fully human and like God. On these assumptions, the Orthodox understand Jesus' role to be the restoration of humanity's full freedom, the freedom to be in full communion with God. By participating in and then rising from death, Jesus restores the original state of humanity. He deifies humanity by restoring its original communion with God. From

[5]The Church of Constantinople (Istanbul, Turkey), Church of Alexandria, Church of Antioch, Church of Jerusalem, Church of Russia, Church of Georgia, Church of Serbia, Church of Romania, Church of Bulgaria, Church of Cyprus, Church of Greece, Church of Albania, Church of Poland, Church of Czechoslovakia, and Church of America.

this perspective, it is not hard to see that Arius' claims relative to the nature of Jesus were a real threat to Eastern ideas.

Roman theology, taking its imagery from the framework and patterns of Roman law, understood the fall of humanity as the assertion of selfish will against God's intent to create a world of love. Humanity is therefore responsible for its hereditary, sinful condition and cannot be fully human in it. Humanity's rebellion not only doomed individuals to a condition of selfish alienation, but also brought guilt from which there could be no release without punishment or retribution. God's gracious act in sending Jesus was to take upon himself the guilt of humanity, making retribution for sin and restoring the possibility of the unity of love with God, humanity, and the redeemed world. Through God's self-giving, known as his Grace, God's intent in the creation is again possible. Jesus, embodying and exemplifying God's love in his life, death, and resurrection, triumphs over humanity's sin and removes its guilt. The pattern of thought here is juridical: the removal of guilt is central. This has not been all, by any means, that Western Christianity has seen in the Atonement (what God has done in Christ for humanity), but it became the dominant theme. The heavy emphasis on legal and judicial imagery in Western Christianity's interpretation of salvation, nevertheless, differs significantly from the more mystical concept of deification found in the Eastern church. Arius' concern about the nature of the Son carried importance in the West, for it dealt with the nature of the Godhead but did not stir the emotions or interests of the West as it did in the East.

The Sacraments and Worship

The early church borrowed from its Jewish forefathers a number of liturgical patterns and practices, but these were modified in the new cultural settings of the Greco-Roman world. As the church developed its own patterns and emphases, the central day for worship celebration became the first day of the week, Sunday (the day of Jesus' Resurrection)—moving away from the Jewish observation of rest and worship on the seventh, or last, day of the week. Baptism, a Jewish rite of purification and repentance, took on significant new roles as a Christian sacrament through which initiates came into the religion's membership by confessing their sins, proclaiming their faith, and receiving God's grace of mercy and nurture. Like the Jews before them, Christians extensively used written forms of God's Word: the Jewish Scriptures, particularly those understood to be related to the Messiah, soon to be known among Christians as the Old Testament; and Christian writings such as Paul's letters, the gospel records of Jesus' life, message, and death and Resurrection, and other materials written by early leaders that came to be known as the New Testament. A common meal held with worship services evolved into a celebration and remembrance of Jesus' death and Passion known throughout history as the Eucharist (Lord's Supper, Communion). The eucharistic giving of the bread and wine as the body and blood of Jesus became the central element in worship services of the Christian community, making his suffering and sacrifice sacramentally present. Other elements of Christian life took on sacramental form; by the late middle ages both Eastern and Western branches of the church recognized seven sacraments.[6]

[6]Both traditions recognize these seven sacraments: Baptism, Confirmation, Reconciliation (confession and penance), Eucharist, Marriage, Anointing (of the sick), and Ordination (to the ministry).

The need for regularity of pattern and form as well as purity of meaning and intent allowed the clergy to assume a central role in all sacramental acts; eventually, celebration of the sacrament required properly ordained and trained clergy leaders. Elaboration of the worship services and their liturgical embellishment accelerated after Christianity became the Roman religion. Houses for Christian worship evolved from personal homes and public meeting places where fellowship was a central ingredient into elaborate "church" structures specifically designed for worship events—particularly to celebrate sacramental services.

In both the East and West the patterns of worship that developed were similar. They came to dominate the life of the church as Christianity expanded throughout the empire. With all of their similarity, however, there were significant differences in the understanding of the sacraments between East and West. In Eastern Orthodoxy, the sacraments are the means by which restoration of humanity to its Godlike image is available to individuals. Reestablishment of community with God conveyed through the liturgical forms of the sacraments brings humanity to fulfillment and completion. In view of this restoration, Christian experience is most complete when congregations are gathered in worship, particularly in the celebration of the Eucharist. Eucharistic worship is then the most essential Christian act for Eastern Orthodox Christians. Similarly in the West, this sacrament also holds the central place in the worship life of the church, but there are subtle differences in the understanding of the meaning of the sacrament. A Western emphasis on human guilt, present because of humanity's prideful unwillingness to live by God's will, causes Western understanding of Jesus' revelatory role to fall on his sacrificial assumption of this guilt. Jesus takes upon himself humanity's rightful punishment for sin. Each time the Eucharist is celebrated, it becomes a sacrificial act rectifying human guilt. The focus here is on human guilt and its eradication by God's grace, rather than on the deification of humanity, also by Grace, which is the central theme in the Orthodox understanding of the sacrament.

In both churches, the role of worship has been enhanced through the construction of beautiful church buildings and the use of elaborate works of art. For centuries, the most significant art of both regions was incorporated into churches, forming an essential element in worship services and the education of believers. Because the East experienced a strong protest relative to the veneration of statues in worship, Eastern art has concentrated on two-dimensional representations of Jesus and the saints, resulting in a distinctive Byzantine art form, the icon. The extensive use of statues and pictures in the West has continued throughout its history. Art in both sections served an important educational function, with stories from Scripture and church history presented visually in periods of broad-scale illiteracy among believers. Even in modern, visually oriented cultures such use remains important.

In the East, liturgy has normally been in the vernacular languages of the local churches. Several differing but similar liturgies have developed. In the West, the liturgy continued to be celebrated in the Latin language until the Second Vatican Council (1962–1965), giving the liturgy a universal form throughout the church. With Vatican II, the Roman church also embraced vernacular languages and allowed modifications in liturgical patterns.

Ministry

The priesthood.   The emphasis on sacraments and worship in both East and West required that the churches develop a stable, trained, and honored priesthood. Ordination to the priesthood gave the clergy special significance, for in their sacramental functions they became the agents of God's Grace. Similarly, preaching, or proclamation of the gospel, required sound doctrinal grounding and particular abilities; the clergy were therefore understood to need special gifts, training, and personal discipline, all contributing to their distinction from the laity. This distinction of the clergy from lay members of the community did not signify depreciation of lay abilities or responsibilities but rather elevated the clerical image while retaining among the laity an emphasis upon personal faith, individual contact with God, and strictly disciplined spiritual and moral lives.

Patterns of clerical life, however, came to be distinguished among the two Christian branches. In the East, priests and deacons may be married, although they may not contract a marriage after ordination. Bishops may not be married and are drawn from the monasteries, in accordance with a continuing high evaluation of monasticism. In the West, from an early period the church's hierarchy sought to impose celibacy, originally found in monasticism, on all clergy because of the importance and demands of their office (see Paul's admonitions, I Corinthians 7:32ff). This effort was not entirely successful until the medieval period, but continues today within the church.

Bishops and metropolitans.   Founded as it was in the role of leadership, the office of bishop was originally grounded in personal pastoral responsibilities in a local church. Through the centuries, this role remained part of the ideal image of the bishop. A bishop was responsible for the faith of the congregation—not only in its sacramental patterns but also in its spiritual, intellectual, and moral expression. Doctrinal and moral questions were determined by the bishop. As geographical territories were added to the jurisdiction of the bishops, their local image was modified, but the understanding of their role remained the same, even though other functions were added. They became the agents of tradition and succession, since they were responsible for training and ordaining priests. As questions of doctrine, polity, and practice arose, bishops in a particular geographical locality joined with their peers in other churches to form councils and synods. The bishops of provincial towns or capitals who often presided at these synods came to be called *metropolitans* (*archbishops*). These patriarchs held a loose jurisdiction over local churches in their area, even though all bishops were understood to be equals. In the East, the essential nature of these early developments continued, so that while certain churches and their bishops became preeminent, such leadership was understood in a collegial framework. This understanding of the place and position of bishops and patriarchs continues today.

Apostolic succession.   In the West, while the image of the bishop was based on these ancient patterns, the functions of bishops significantly changed. The juridical pattern of thought present in Western theology is evident in its concepts of the priest and the bishop. As early as Irenaeus (ca. 130–202), there emerged the idea of transference of power and true teaching from the apostles of Jesus to their successors, the bishops. Later known as *apostolic succession,* this concept of leadership in the church has several significant features. First, power and authority resided in the office and in the person who occupied the office rather than in the congregation at large. Second, the concept incorporated an emphasis on the passing of truth and authority from one generation to the next, emphasizing the authority both of the transmitting persons and the transmitted tradition.

The Pope and the Papacy.   Complementing these concepts, which took form over the centuries, was the Western church's tendency to pattern its organizational structure on that of the Roman Empire. Officers of the empire held supreme power in office, although they were subservient to superiors and responsible for subordinates. With this hierarchical framework adopted in church organization, the bishop of Rome (the pope) was equivalent in power within the church to the emperor in the empire. Cardinals, archbishops, bishops, and finally priests all held sacramental power and teaching responsibilities appropriate to their positions, each subservient to his superior in the faith. The claim of the Church of Rome to apostolic foundation, as well as its emerging importance in the West, led to the claim that the pope is God's representative on earth with universal dominion over Christian faith. As a consequence of these ideas, clergy have enjoyed, until recent times, almost total authority and control in the church. Vatican II attempted to enlist more participation of the laity in the governance of the church.

The closely disciplined structure of theology and practice inherent in this pattern of authority and tradition focused in the one office of the pope did much to make the Western church one unified body in structure, doctrine, and practice. It also contributed greatly to Western Catholicism's ability to shape European culture during the medieval period.

Eastern and Western Monasticism

While monasticism played a significant role in both the Eastern and Western churches, it developed differences of emphasis, suggesting some of the basic contrasts between these groups. In the East, one joined the monastery to separate oneself from the world and its concerns. The contemplative life of spiritual meditation on God's love was and is a monk's goal. Consequently, while the monasteries have educational functions, particularly among the clergy, they do not have the many service functions that developed around monasticism in the West. Bishops are drawn from the ranks of the monks because of their spiritual fervor and insights—for the spiritual role of the bishop is his most important role in the east. Bishops often depend on their monastic brothers for spiritual sustentation and occasionally for support in other issues, such as the iconoclastic struggle of the eighth and ninth centuries. Monastics may on occasion contribute in social and political situations involving the life of the church, but Eastern monasticism retains its central emphasis on contemplation and separation from the world.

Western monasticism also made contemplation a central point. Nevertheless, other functions came to be attached to the monastery that significantly modified its role within the church. Under barbarian rule (fifth to the eighth centuries), monasteries served as the preservers and depositories of civilization. From this role they became agencies of social conservation. Additional service-oriented responsibilities involved them directly in cultural changes in the West. By their industrious example, they contributed to agricultural reform, cared for the poor and destitute, provided almost all of the education available in the culture, and ultimately not only provided leadership for the church but also offered advisers and counselors to medieval rulers. Medieval monasticism, while still built around spiritual discipline and contemplation, became in the church a locus of missions, education, evangelism, and social service. It also provided teachers for the cathedral schools and early medieval universities. Much of the spread of Western Catholicism as a worldwide church may be credited to these monastic orders, whose members accompanied the western European colonists. The practical service orientation of monasticism reflects the general concern of the Western church with the practical, worldly aspects of Christian life.

Church and State Relations

Concentration on worship and the spiritual life has kept Orthodoxy from having extensive interests in political and social questions. In its early pattern of close affiliation with the secular rulers of the Roman Empire, Orthodoxy generally chose to allow these rulers an important role in church matters. Consequently, state rulers tended to take an active role in church administration and organization. The church became a department of the state, often subservient in secular matters to the emperors and kings. It is not surprising then that among the Orthodox, lay persons may hold significant administrative positions, even becoming leading theologians; in some parts of the church they have traditionally participated in the election of bishops.

These structural patterns served as the foundation on which Orthodoxy's characteristic pattern of church and state was built. Churches are generally state or national churches, except in areas such as the United States, where religious institutions are formed as voluntary associations.

Because of the close association of Orthodoxy with the state, the church's primary role has been to care for the spiritual life of society, serving the state in this manner. With this spiritual orientation and as a state "agency," Orthodoxy has thus seldom questioned the moral, social, or political abuses that may exist in its cultural setting. Seen in this perspective, the role of the Russian Orthodox church in both czarist and communist Russia may be more understandable to Western Christians.

The relationship of church and state in the West has, on the other hand, displayed a much more tumultuous history (see Chapter Four). The claim of the pope to preeminent spiritual power occasionally meant the assertion of political power as well. Ideally, church and state complement each other, but balance of power and influence is always imperfect and fleeting. Generally, the Western church has not been subservient to the state, but has understood its position to be at least equal to that of the state, particularly in moral matters. Therefore, the church has responsibly participated in society in the West, shaping the social, moral and, occasionally, the political norms of the Western states. Often it has served as a critic of culture when society has failed to appropriate or follow its definition of Christian moral norms.

Missions

Under the leadership of the church at Constantinople, the Eastern Roman capital, Orthodoxy not only maintained a viable Christian community and life, it expanded north and east and, even with the diminishing power of the empire, continued to be the major religion of vast territories. Its missionaries were responsible for the Christianizing of much of the Middle East, the Balkans (Rumania and Bulgaria), and, historically most important, Russia. Constantinople, although often threatened, was able to retain its independence until its final capture by the Turks in 1453. Consequently, the church in Constantinople continued to serve as a symbol for Orthodoxy throughout its long history, and even under the Turks it retained its honorific position as the premier church of Eastern Christendom. After the fall of Constantinople, Moscow claimed to carry on Christian leadership as the "third Rome."

The perseverance of the church in the West in a period of crumbling social and political stability gave it a role in the life of Western culture unequaled by any other institution. As a result, medieval Europe was dominated by the church and church interests. Ultimately, Roman Catholicism was successful in converting the Germanic tribes that overran the western Roman territories and, with this accomplishment, expanded into most areas of central and northern Europe, where it had never been accepted during the Roman reign. Middle and eastern Europe subsequently became strong Roman Catholic territories.

Both branches of Christianity were threatened and contained in the southern and eastern Mediterranean by the phenomenal rise of the Islamic faith in the seventh century. The influence of Antioch, Jerusalem, Carthage, and Alexandria was lost as the Muslims limited the scope of Christianity to that of a hereditary, nonevangelistic ethnic religion. The Islamic threat to Western Europe was real as Muslim forces captured much of Spain. They were finally contained in southern France by Charles Martel at the battle of Tours in 732.

Reflection

Christianity's expansion from what was, in the eyes of the Roman emperors, a minor Jewish religious sect to the religion of the late empire and ultimately the religion of the northern Mediterranean world and all Europe is indeed phenomenal. In discussing the early church, we have looked only at a few events that exemplify the story of this expansion. Our review of the continuing development of Eastern and Western Christendom suggests major changes and expanding interconnections between Christianity in its Eastern and Western cultural contexts in the long period following the empire. Space has limited our discussion to highly selected events, issues, and concerns, but it is clear that Christianity cannot be ignored in an adequate understanding of both Eastern and Western European cultures. The story of that relationship in Western Europe continues in our next chapter.

QUESTIONS

1. How was the Christianity that developed in the time of Ignatius and Eustathius influenced by its Greco-Roman setting?

2. What significant changes in the self-understanding of Christianity occurred when it became the official religion of the Roman Empire?

3. Within the Roman Empire at the time of Christianity's formation, what functions did religion fulfill in the society? What were some of the principal religions?

4. What are the principal characteristics of Eastern Christianity?

5. How and why does Western Christian thought and structure differ significantly from that of the Eastern church?

6. What characteristics of monasticism were attractive to the members of the early church? Why was it particularly significant in Western Christianity?

7. Discuss Ignatius' vision of the church as revealed through his letters written to churches in Asia Minor.

8. Discuss the decisions of the Council of Nicaea, showing how they set patterns for later doctrinal and structural development within the church.

FURTHER READING

The following titles are offered as representative works detailing the history of Christianity.

BETTENSON, HENRY. *Documents of the Christian Church.* New York: Oxford University Press, 1963.

CADOUX, C. J. *The Early Church and the World.* Edinburgh: T. & T. Clarke, 1955.

CHADWICK, HENRY. *Early Christian Thought and the Classical Tradition.* New York: Oxford University Press, 1966.

CONZELMANN, HANS. *History of Primitive Christianity.* Nashville, Tenn.: Abingdon Press, 1973.

CORVIN, VIRGINIA. *St. Ignatius and Christianity in Antioch.* New Haven, Conn.: Yale University Press, 1960.

DANIELOU, J., and MARROU, H. *The First Six Hundred Years.* New York: McGraw-Hill Book Company, 1964.

DAVIES, W. D. *Christian Origins and Judaism.* Philadelphia: Westminster Press, 1962.

FREND, W. H. C. *Martyrdom and Persecution in the Early Church.* Garden City, N.Y.: Anchor Books, 1967.

———. *The Rise of Christianity.* Philadelphia: Fortress Press, 1984.

LIETZMANN, HANS. *The Founding of the Church Universal.* Trans. B. L. Woolf. New York: Charles Scribner's Sons, 1938.

MEYERDORFF, JEAN. *The Orthodox Church.* Trans. John Chapin. Nashville, Tenn.: Pantheon Books, 1962.

SCHMEMANN, ALEXANDER. *The Historical Road of Eastern Orthodoxy.* Trans. Lydia W. Kesich. New York: Holt, Rinehart, and Winston, 1963.

VON CAMPENSHAUSEN, HANS. *Men Who Shaped the Western Church.* New York: Harper & Row, 1964.

WALKER, WILLISTON, et al. *A History of the Christian Church.* 5th ed., New York: Charles Scribner's Sons, 1985.

WARE, TIMOTHY. *The Orthodox Church.* Baltimore: Penguin Books, 1951.

CHAPTER FOUR

Models of Western Christianity: Medieval and Reformation

To move from the fourth century to the thirteenth in our story of developing Christianity, is to make a transition similar to a quantum leap in physics: we move from comments concerning a recently legalized religion in the fourth century to discussion of a civilization dominated by an omnipresent and overpowering religious institution in the thirteenth century, the Western medieval Christian church. The intervening centuries are full of incidents that express the intertwining of Christian principles and interests with those of a culture in turmoil. Europe experienced in this long period a number of traumas: first, the loss of the millennium-old Roman civilization; second, relentless maneuvers by tribal leaders and then local kings, dukes, and knights for political control of Europe; and third, the emergence in the late tenth century of a richly successful mercantile and land-based economy. At each juncture in these events the church and its representatives were so integrally involved that by the High Middle Ages to discuss Western civilization is to discuss in some manner the church and the Christian religion it represents. The church was the most prominent and often the most powerful single institution within Western civilization. It spanned all territorial and national boundaries; it was the foundation of the educational system (expanding in the thirteenth century to the university level); its leaders carried rank and prestige rivaling if not superseding that of political leaders; its counsel and decisions—from those of the pope to those of the local priest—affected the lives of all within the society; and its land holdings, including all rights and privileges thereof, were greater than those of any one nation.

THE MEDIEVAL CHURCH AND ITS DOCTRINES

The Holy Roman Empire

The crowning of Charlemagne, king of the Franks, as emperor of the Holy Roman Empire, by Pope Leo on Christmas day, 800, marked the official renewal of a Western empire uniting church and state, even though it was the culmination of a long interdependence of church and state. In a structural pattern articulated as early as the fifth century by Augustine of Hippo in North Africa, the emperor was understood to be divinely appointed to rule in state and political affairs and the pope, also divinely appointed and representing the divine will, to rule in spiritual affairs. Since spiritual life determined one's eternal existence, whether privately or as a political entity, the role of pope was preeminent, although in the physical world the king's power might predominate. Through the ensuing centuries kings and popes would incessantly struggle for real control in both realms, but the wedding of the two powers was never in question.

By the thirteenth century the presence and power of the church had become so universal and pervasive that Pope Innocent III could claim that as the moon received its light from the sun, so the emperor received his power through the intercessions of the pope. In spiritual matters the pope served as shepherd (leader and advocate) of one great flock (all believers); all were under his tutelage, guidance, and, ultimately, his spiritual power. The papacy was therefore preeminent over all spiritual *and* political powers. Clearly in the person of Innocent the papacy reached its zenith of power and prestige. Innocent widely intervened in political affairs across Europe, seeking unity and compatibility in the empire. Through the Fourth Lateran Council (1215), he significantly reformed the church by restoration of clerical and monastic discipline and order and further elevated the place of the eucharistic sacrament by persuading the council to promulgate the doctrine of transubstantiation.

The Doctrine of Transubstantiation

The doctrine of transubstantiation affirmed that, at the words of institution intoned by the priest, the substance of the bread and wine are miraculously transformed into the body and blood of Christ, renewing his sacrifice for humanity. The promulgation of this as a doctrine of the church culminated the historical Western emphasis upon the sacrificial nature of the sacrament. It also guaranteed its central place in the worship and life of the medieval church. It is not surprising, then, to find that the church buildings where such miraculous events took place became the central and most magnificent edifices of the time. Each town and city wanted its churches to honor the mystery of the sacrament. Consequently, magnificent church and cathedral buildings symbolically came to represent the place of Christianity within the society. They were the focus of cultural life, showing the centrality of the faith.

Gothic Architecture

Church buildings in western Europe had traditionally been built in the bulky, substantial Romanesque style of the late empire. A new pattern of architecture, the Gothic, joined these traditional Romanesque patterns, allowing the building of taller, more spacious, and grander buildings. More and larger windows in Gothic buildings allowed light to add its effect to the miraculous events that took place in the cathedrals. In an age when books were few and expensive, and learning was a privilege of an elite class, church buildings, particularly cathedrals, became living books for the vast majority of the people. Incorporated in the windows, tapestries, and statuary of the buildings were biblical stories, stories of the saints, and the faith traditions of particular territories and peoples. One could literally learn the gospel message and the history of the faith through "reading" the buildings themselves. This educational function of the church building took its place as one of its central roles, along with its use as a house of worship and sacrament. Around these great church buildings also grew up market plazas, making the buildings and their courtyards the economic center of town and city life. Slowly cathedral schools, attached to the cathedrals, allowed education to be shared with larger groups in the society.

These developments illustrate how during Innocent's papacy and those that followed, the church had clearly reached the apex of honor, glory, and power, dominating the culture at every level. It is within this setting that we elect to discuss two events, among many, in the life of the church, that were to have far-reaching effects upon subsequent developments in the faith and consequently on Western culture.

THE "LITTLE POOR MAN" AND THE "ANGELIC DOCTOR"

In the following story of Saint Francis the characters used, except for Francis, are fictional but are composite figures illustrating events and changes in twelfth- and thirteenth-century European life that are clearly historical.

St. Francis of Assisi

Friar Richard made his way quickly out of the market plaza skirting the unfinished south wall of the rising cathedral. He had to hurry if he was to arrive at the chapter meeting, where Brother Francis was to report on his latest journey to the East. Richard's thoughts were racing, for his chance encounter with his brother Henri, as always, had caused him to ponder again their many differences of character, understanding, and dedication.

Henri had been most pleased to find Richard in the market, for he had great news he wanted to share with this brother so seldom seen here in Lyon. He wanted to share the news of the family's good fortune. He had only last week completed a pact with Elias, merchant of Pisa, so now they would have an outlet for the works of their craftsmen in Italy and beyond. Their father would have been most pleased. This pact would guarantee the family fortunes, for it promised to double their income, making them one of the chief families of the city. However, what he was so anxious to share with Richard was to tell him of his visit with the bishop only yesterday. He had proposed to the bishop the addition of a chapel to the cathedral honoring their father and mother—an act of gratitude to the Lord for the continuing success of the family fortunes. Such a chapel would not only show their devotion but testify to the position of the family. Perhaps Henri wanted all to recognize that he too, in the way of the time, honored the Lord and faithfully served him as Richard did through his religious vocation.

Richard mused on this news as he moved toward the edge of the city. He was struck again by the reality that as brothers he and Henri lived in very different worlds with distinctive understandings of the gospel. The conversation reminded him of that fateful day some fifteen years earlier when he had gone with some of his young friends to stand at the edge of the plaza and listen to the message of a curious little man called Francis from Assisi in Italy. The crowd that day was not from Richard's community of friends but was made up of the "little" people of the town: servants, street sweeps, carters, and beggars. Many sick people from these groups had also been brought to Francis for his blessing. Francis' message was one of God's love for all people, especially the poor, the disenfranchised, those who had no standing in the society. Richard had been intrigued by this message, which he had not heard at the cathedral or other services of the local church. When he attended sacrament the next day he was greatly surprised to find there Francis along with many of those from the street. They too were to receive the blessing of Jesus' sacrifice.

At the time Richard was intrigued with the idea that Jesus' love extended to these whose position in society, according to the generally accepted perception of the time, testified to their sin and suggested their insolence and immorality. In subsequent conversations Francis had challenged Richard to reconsider his own life-style, to hear this revolutionary interpretation of the gospel—to consider the radical implications of love shared with all. Francis also urged him to simply accompany him for a few months in order to see this love in action. Richard accepted the challenge and ultimately joined the community of brothers, becoming a *friar,* one whose vocation was to serve the needs of anyone, whatever their position, to labor with them, to tend their wounds, to heal their sickness, to give them hope. As he worked with the brothers, he came to understand that the service they rendered was always accompanied by, and often based on, their proclamation, their constant preaching, both within and without the church, of God's saving gift of love in Jesus' sacrifice. To join these lowly servants meant for Richard the renunciation of all family dependencies, subsistence on whatever might be offered by those he minis- tered to, and literally becoming a "poor man," having only "one tunic with a hood and another without a hood, and a cord and trousers."[1]

Henri, like their father and other family members, had accepted Richard's decision to follow this strange monk, Francis. They had been impressed with the sacrifice his life entailed, and in some ways they were pleased and proud to have one of their family in a religious vocation. However, they never actually understood how Richard could find purpose and meaning in a life lived among the poor. Few of their social class could embrace or understand a gospel that demanded poverty and essentially rejected the normal expectation of the material and spiritual rewards that arose from righteous devotion and meritorious service. Henri's response to mercantile success was to build an honorific chapel; but Richard's vow of poverty meant such profit would have been used to assist the poor. Both responses were understood by the thirteenth-century church to be proper service to the Lord, even with their differing motivations and consequences. Henri's righteous gift expressed for the majority a proper response to God's blessing of a righteous life, yet Richard's life of service was a significant counterbalance in a culture threatened by rising materialism within the church. Little wonder then that Richard pondered the nature of the faith and its reflection in his relationship to his brother as he made his way to the chapter meeting.

The Franciscan Order

St. Francis (1181–1226) created the Order of the Friars Minor at least in part as a protest against the insensitivity of this society and its church, where power and position often meant the failure to recognize or minister meaningfully to the vast numbers of poor who formed the labor force and provided the base for the economic

---

[1]*Francis and Clare: The Complete Works,* trans. Regis J. Armstrong and Ignatius C. Brady (New York: Paulist Press, 1982), p. 110.

prosperity of the time. This new monastic brotherhood expressed a renewed interpretation of the gospel as service to those in need. Yet another motivation for forming the order was Francis' response to his own unique religious experience of Christ's presence in his life. Called through a mystical encounter with Jesus, Francis understood he was to "build the church" through testimony to God's love and through service carried out by identification with the poor.

Forming others who joined him into a monastic community, they moved outside the cloister to the streets and byways of the newly arising cities. Their vows of poverty entailed an unwillingness to hold property of any sort. Their decision to live by their own labor or on the alms and offerings of those with whom they ministered brought them the designation as a "mendicant," or begging, order. This new type of monasticism was in direct contrast to the rich, sometimes opulent, holdings of many monastic orders of the time.

The order was further distinguished by its preaching role among those to whom it ministered in service. The Franciscan friars were dedicated to extending the Word of God to those often outside the usual ministrations of the church. Added to this was a missionary concern extending to others who had not heard the word of Jesus' love. Francis even took upon himself an unsuccessful but dramatic mission to the Muslim ruler of Egypt. Francis always understood his mission to be one of the church; all friars were to be obedient servants ministering within the church as one of its branches. Such dedication and service was recognized as a needed reform within the church first by Pope Innocent III and subsequently by Honorius III, who approved the community of friars as a new form of monasticism. The "little poor man" from Assisi had indeed during his own lifetime become recognized as a saint, transforming the meaning of service and love within the church.

St. Thomas Aquinas

As Francis' life was drawing to a close, an Italian nobleman's family celebrated the birth of a son destined to mold the theology of the medieval church into formative patterns still authoritative for the modern Roman Catholic church. Taking the name of his birthplace, Aquino, a small town outside Naples, Thomas Aquinas (1225–1274), was dedicated by his family to the religious life. He entered a local Benedictine monastery as a boy. As a young man, however, he left this monastery to join the Dominican order of friars, formed only a few years earlier.

Dominic, like Francis, as a young cleric recognized a particular need within the church. In his case the need was to counter the heretical teachings of a group called the Albigensians or Cathari (the Pure). This group lived exemplary and dedicated lives of service without the ostentation of the general society. Because they believed that the material world was evil and therefore incompatible with the true world of the spirit, they rejected any worldly temptations and lived austere, disciplined lives, emulating the spiritual idealism occasionally evident in the Scriptures. Their radical rejection of the material world made them essentially dualists and heretical; even though their life-style was very appealing to many in the society—particularly the poor. Dominic, following Francis, chose to live among these poor and to preach to them the orthodox faith of love and service within the material world based on spiritual precepts. Because he and his followers were particularly concerned with a philosophical and theological issue, learning and education were from the beginning expected and highly valued among them.

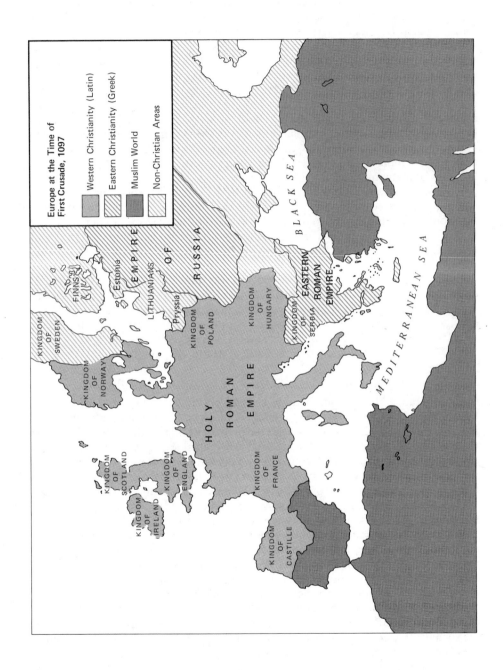

Europe at the Time of
First Crusade, 1097

Western Christianity (Latin)

Eastern Christianity (Greek)

Muslim World

Non-Christian Areas

KINGDOM OF SWEDEN

KINGDOM OF NORWAY

FINNS

Estonia

EMPIRE OF RUSSIA

LITHUANIANS

Prussia

KINGDOM OF POLAND

KINGDOM OF HUNGARY

BLACK SEA

EASTERN ROMAN EMPIRE

KINGDOM OF SERBIA

HOLY ROMAN EMPIRE

KINGDOM OF SCOTLAND

KINGDOM OF ENGLAND

KINGDOM OF IRELAND

KINGDOM OF FRANCE

KINGDOM OF CASTILLE

MEDITERRANEAN SEA

When Aquinas traveled in 1244 to Paris to study in the Dominican cloister at the university, he entered a career of study and teaching that would take him over most of Europe and make him one of the preeminent scholars of his time. His extensive writings were crowned by two works that synthesized medieval philosophy and theology. *Summa Contra Gentiles* was an apology for the Christian faith designed to counter arguments not only of heretics and non-Christians but also of philosophical schools emerging in the universities. Some of these philosophers suggested that human reason did not need revelation or faith as the source of true knowledge. The second work, *Summa Theologiae,* was left unfinished at Aquinas' death. It carried his investigation further and attempted to integrate and combine the truths of reason and faith.

The Crusades

Western philosophy, particularly its theories of knowledge, had been based from the first centuries of the Christian era until the eleventh-century Crusades on Platonic assumptions about how we know. Platonic theories, appropriated as Christian theology when Christianity became a Greco-Roman religion, affirmed that human knowledge depended upon an innate, though imperfect, consciousness of God (the Platonic ideas of Good, Beauty, and Truth). In the revelations of the prophets and ultimately Jesus, humans came to know the true spiritual life that also served as the model for imperfect material life. According to this Platonic tradition, knowledge begins within the soul and is appropriated by an activity of faith that results in knowledge—that is, assent to the truths revealed by God. Knowledge begins and ends in God. This basic image of knowledge had been the pattern throughout the long history of Western theology.

With the eastern contacts brought about by the eleventh and twelfth century's Crusades, however, the traditional concepts of knowledge, art, and human abilities were to change substantially. Organized by the church, the Crusades were to aid the Eastern Christian Empire under attack by Muslim Turks, free the holy lands from Muslim control, and allow renewal of pilgrimage to these lands. The Crusades were briefly successful in this general purpose but had several unanticipated consequences. Although their original motivation was religious, many who participated in them had additional interests. Many noblemen and others saw them as adventurous challenges, and the merchants who helped finance them were interested in expanding markets. In the later case, they were much more successful than one might imagine. The Crusades opened new markets and in return allowed the importation into Western Europe of the vast riches of the East. Consequently, the later Crusades were as much economic in motivation as they were religious. An unexpected result of these new contacts was an intellectual renewal in the West. Greek and Roman art, which had been lost in the West, were reintroduced.

Intellectual Renewal in the West

Among these rediscoveries were the writings and philosophy of Aristotle, long neglected and unknown in the West. This philosophical tradition now became available through contacts with the Eastern civilizations, where it had been preserved by Muslim and Jewish teachers. There was also increasing interest in the works of Muslim and Jewish scholars in Spain and Sicily. These new intellectual resources were very attractive to the philosophical and theological faculties of

European universities, many of which had been founded only a few years before in the thirteenth century. Aristotelian theories of knowledge directly challenged traditional Western Platonic theories, causing the reevaluation and recasting of generally accepted thought, particularly as it concerned human knowledge.

Beginning with an assumption that knowledge arises from the data received through the human senses and is then formulated by reason into specific truths through the mind's ability to generalize from particular instances to universal concepts, Aristotle's theories challenged the Platonic dependence on innate and God-given human knowledge. The acceptance of Aristotelian theories by many philosophers in the West meant that by the thirteenth century some were saying that true knowledge comes only through rational formulations. If these formulations did not agree with Christian assumptions and teachings, believed to come through revelation, reason must be accepted as the true judge. In fact, some came to disregard revelation and innate knowledge as sources of truth in any form. Obviously, such ideas constituted a major threat to traditional Christian theology.

Aquinas' Philosophy

Such was the intellectual scene when Aquinas arrived in Paris. By that time Aristotelian ideas were broadly accepted as leading to knowledge of the world and its phenomena. Clearly, sense experience led to knowledge of the material world, and its truths could be more readily tested by observation. There was much debate and disagreement about the implications of Aristotle's theories, especially as they related to revealed (or innate) knowledge. Aquinas' intellectual energies throughout his life were spent attempting to resolve the differences between the two systems (that of Aristotle's philosophy, based on sense experience and reason, and that of revelation, based on God's self-disclosure and human spiritual experience) by using the contributions of both.

Aquinas' solution was to follow the path laid down by his Dominican teacher, Albert the Great (ca. 1200–1280). Albert had distinguished the fields of philosophy and theology with the affirmation that each contains and pursues truth, but from different perspectives and with differing objectives; therefore they lead to different categories of knowledge. Aquinas, building on this basic idea, asserted that Aristotle had been correct in recognizing that a form of knowledge is gained through our senses and the reasoning process. In fact, a great deal of knowledge can be affirmed in this manner—for Aquinas, and Aristotle, the necessity of a God is clearly evident in the natural order. Order in the universe reasonably suggests an orderer, motion calls for a "first mover," and so on. Beginning with this assumption, Aquinas went so far as to claim that reason leads to the recognition of angels as intermediaries between the spiritual and material worlds.

However, for Aquinas, such truth does not fulfill human need. It is largely descriptive, dealing with the world as we experience it, but does not explain the ultimate nature and purpose of the universe. Aquinas believed that some truth cannot be attained simply through reason. Reason may be able to affirm there is a God, but it does not explain the nature of that God nor give insight into many other questions of vital importance for human life. For Aquinas, answers to these questions can come only by the avenues of revelation used by God through all time. The knowledge of the triune nature of God as Father, Son, and Holy Spirit does not come through reason nor does knowledge of God's merciful nature, as seen in the willingness to suffer for human sin. Knowledge revealed in the Christian religion throughout the centuries differs from that gained through philosophical reason, but it is even more necessary and just as relevant to daily life.

In addition, Aquinas was conscious that few persons have the opportunity or ability to arrive at knowledge through philosophical reasoning. Consequently, the majority of humans would be left without contact with or knowledge of God if these were dependent on reason alone. For Aquinas divine revelation makes it possible for all persons to know God and be recipients of his love and power. Therefore some propositions, such as, "God exists," may be held true by all Christians but arrived at on different grounds; the philosopher holds them to be true on grounds furnished by "unaided" reason, the ordinary believer on grounds of revelation. For Aquinas reason (philosophy) and faith (Christian revelation in the Church) each contribute to knowledge; they are not rivals threatening each other but are cooperatively supportive. Reason and faith can and should be joined together.

Aquinas' solution to the great philosophical and theological problem of the time was to join the contributions of Aristotle to those of Plato (with a long tradition of Christian Platonic interpretations) and baptize both of their teachings as bases of Christian thinking. His achievement, though often questioned in subsequent generations, set the pattern for Catholic theology from his own day until the present. Aquinas was declared the "Angelic Doctor" and a "doctor of the church" (an authorized interpreter of the faith) by Pope Pius V in 1567, and his theological solutions to many questions were made mandatory study for all Roman Catholic students of philosophy and theology in 1880 by Pius XI, although this requirement is no longer imposed.

Francis and his followers ministered to the needs of the poor in a society undergoing vast social and economic changes. In the same time frame, Aquinas, facing change in the very perception of the nature of humanity and the universe, struggled to synthesize traditional Christian faith with an ancient but renewed insight into human reason. Each was to create patterns that became normative for vast sections of Christianity in the next centuries.

CHANGING CULTURAL PATTERNS
AND THE PROTESTANT REFORMATION

The three hundred years between the time of Francis and Aquinas (1200s) and the Protestant Reformation (1500s), like any historical period, experienced significant change, including the gradual modification of numerous social and political institutions. Having become the dominant social structure by the thirteenth century, the church continued its central role in society. Yet its very strength and power opened it (1) to internal dangers of corrupt leaders greedy for control of its wealth and power, (2) to intensified struggles between political leaders and religious leaders for effective control of both church and society, and (3) to the more subtle changes taking place in the philosophical bases of the society, particularly the rising appreciation of human reason and its abilities. Aquinas' synthesis of reason and faith, though widely appreciated, did not suffice for many in the society, and the ensuing centuries saw an expanding role for human capabilities without the traditional subservience to divine guidance or revelation. This attitude came to fruition in the European Renaissance of the High Middle Ages.

The Renaissance

This Renaissance, or "rebirth," reaching full bloom in the fourteenth and fifteenth centuries, expanded the Aristotelian principles of human knowledge so attractive to Aquinas. These new principles of knowledge became the basis of extensive patterns of experimental learning, recovery of ancient art and literature, and, most important of all, a willingness to examine critically everything from the nature of the physical universe to the validity of traditional religion, particularly the power and authority of the church. On the basis of this new knowledge and its freeing effect from the straitjacket of tradition, age-old assumptions were questioned. The nature of the universe itself, the size and form of the earth, the relationship of God to humanity (human free will relative to God's will), and, very importantly, the institutional bases for social, political, and spiritual authority were all reformulated. At the height of the Renaissance, scholars and artists succeeded in modifying for many of the middle-class merchants and intellectuals the traditional evaluation of humanity and its abilities. Generally, they asserted that, rather than being limited by its sinful self-centeredness (the traditional medieval evaluation based on religious definitions), humanity was capable, through free will and the capacities of learning and reason, of unlimited achievement. Humanity's dependence on God was not denied, but a much more optimistic attitude was taken by some toward humanity and its possibilities.

In addition to the contribution of the Renaissance, other cultural changes were threatening the usual structures of society. Feudalism had slowly given way to the nationalistic interests of Europe's various territories. Spain, France, England, and a confederation of German principalities emerged during the period as viable national entities. As these became more self-governing and independent, the traditional political patterns of the Holy Roman Empire were weakened. Expanding vistas, made possible through advances in navigational technology, meant the opening of the Western Hemisphere to discovery and adventure, culminating in the discovery and colonizing of the New World by Portugal and Spain. The development of the printing press made information available to Europeans on an unprecedented scale. Reading and education became possible for all classes. Art and literature no longer focused exclusively on religious subjects as the medieval culture had done. With these changes religion lost some of its luster, particularly among intellectuals, even while it remained a mainstay of culture.

Wycliff and Hus

As culture opened to new forms of thinking and organization, the church experienced increasing attacks on its traditional moral and spiritual leadership of society. As early as the 1370s, John Wycliff (ca. 1330–1384), an English clergyman and scholar, raised questions about the authority of clerics, suggesting that they held their offices as stewards of God. If they were not faithful stewards, they should be removed. Carried to its extreme, this position questioned the traditional authority of the priests and bishops, including that of the pope. Wycliff further assumed that the Scriptures constituted a basic religious authority superior to that of the church and, therefore, should be in the vernacular languages of the people. Acting on this assumption, he translated the Bible into English. Although Wycliff's suggestions were welcomed by some, they were strongly resisted by the church, which posthumously condemned Wycliff as a heretic. John Hus (1372 or 1373–1415), a

Bohemian cleric and professor, applying many of Wycliff's ideas, led a popular revolt against the authority of the church and its moral corruption. Hus lost his life for his beliefs. He was burned at the stake in 1415, condemned by the Council of Constance.

Wycliff and Hus voiced criticisms that were being raised against the backdrop of major scandal within the church. The councils of Pisa and Constance had been called to settle an unprecedented problem within the church— rival popes. Under French influence, the seat of the pope had been removed from Rome to Avignon in 1309 to escape the control of local Roman politicians (who had controlled elections of popes) and to impose French control. Rival popes were chosen in 1378—one Roman and one French. The ensuing struggle for power and the disorganization created by rival authorities were part of the setting for the critiques of Wycliff, Hus, and others. The Council of Constance settled the papal dispute by reestablishing one pope, but it could not quiet the questions that had been raised about authority and about many of the practices within the church.

Martin Luther

The catalyst for permanent modification of medieval Christendom came, nevertheless, from the conviction of an obscure German monk, Martin Luther (1483–1546), that the people of his city were being duped by a commonly exploited money-raising practice within the church. Centuries earlier, Pope Urban, in calling the First Crusade, had pronounced an *indulgence,* which promised that the spiritual Grace accumulated by Jesus and the saints would be extended to Crusaders who "fought for God." Essentially, he promised that their venial (or nonmortal) sins, normally punished in Purgatory, would be forgiven for their extraordinary service to the Lord. Elaborating on this basically Aquinan concept that the church had been given responsibility for the storehouse of Grace attributed to the merits of Jesus and the saints, the church, in the intervening centuries, had extended that Grace on an ever-widening basis through a variety of indulgences. Through this means persons could, first through service and ultimately by purchase, relieve themselves and their loved ones of the usual purgatorial penance for sins. In Luther's time, the idealism of Urban had become basically a commercial exchange. Luther's call for a university debate on the validity of the system, in the form of Ninety-Five Theses tacked to the church door at Wittenburg on October 31, 1517, had consequences that neither he nor anyone else could have imagined. His questions struck a responsive chord, and within three years he had become the center of a full-scale reform movement.

While Luther's initial protest concerned the manner in which indulgences were being sold among the German peasants, it was based on much more profound theological issues. In studying the Scriptures for his lectures at the University of Wittenberg, Luther had become convinced that humanity's relationship to God was not based on the mediated Grace offered by the church through the sacraments, the common assumption of the time, but on personal encounter with God's love and faith in his saving act in Jesus. Luther's understanding of faith moved him away from basic concepts accepted in his day. The medieval Catholic definition of faith reflected the teachings of Thomas Aquinas—faith meant the acceptance of that which one could not know by sensory experience. This included the revealed mysteries taught through the doctrines and traditions of the church. In contrast,

Martin Luther preaching. Detail
from the Cranach Altarpiece.
*(Reprinted through the courtesy of
Lutherhalle Reformationsgeschichtliches
Museum, Lutherstadt Wittenberg,
Germany.)*

Luther, studying Paul and following the lead of Augustine, came to define faith as an inner awareness of, need for, and dependence on God. Faith is trust, as distinguished from intellectual acceptance. This shift from cognitive and rational acceptance to affective and existential trust threatened traditional authority, for it placed individuals in direct contact with God, and removed them from dependence on clerical mediation of God's Grace. It also reemphasized the Paulinian understanding that humanity is not "justified" before God by what it does, but through faith (meaning trust) in God. Justification by faith in contrast to justification by works (participating in the sacraments, penance, and so on) became the clarion call of Protestants.

Because Luther had arrived at his understanding through his personal study of the Scriptures, he insisted that Scriptures were the primary source of contact with God's truth. In the Scriptures, God speaks directly to humanity and through the guidance of the Holy Spirit makes known to the individual his eternal truth. In light of this insight, Luther claimed that the Scriptures were the sole authority in the life and faith of a Christian. In this assertion Luther raised questions about the traditional understanding of humanity's relationship to God, questions about the very basis of medieval Christianity. The effect of Luther's affirmation of scriptural authority was to shift the locus of religious authority from the church and its representatives, the priests, to an individual's faith based on his or her interpretation of Scripture under the guidance of the Holy Spirit. Although Luther, frightened by the excessive claims of some of his followers to spiritual empowerment, did not advocate a totally individual interpretation of the Scriptures, his concept effectively reversed the place and role of tradition (the interpretations and practices of the church as they had developed from the time of Jesus) and the Scriptures among Protestants. Scripture became preeminent over tradition; tradition came to be understood as having only a supplementary authority to Scripture. Perhaps Luther himself did not anticipate that in the Western world the eventual effect of this shift would be to lessen significantly the authority of institutions such as the church and greatly enhance the authority of an individual's personal interpretation of the Scriptures.

Luther's shift in understanding of the place of Scripture had two other important consequences. First, Luther was convinced that Christians should be able to read the Scriptures in their own languages, and he translated the Bible into German. This set the pattern for the vernacular translations of Scripture throughout Protestantism. Secondly, Luther's assumption that anyone could find truth in the Scriptures meant that in place of the old idea of priesthood there emerged a different perception. Since everyone could interpret, there was a "priesthood of all believers" in which all believers were responsible before God for themselves and their neighbors. The degree and quality of one's religious life were not to be identified with particular religious vocations (the priesthood or monasticism). All vocations were to be practiced *religiously*. This second concept did much to blur the distinction between clergy and laity that had been so important in Catholic tradition. Luther's attitude toward the priesthood also recognized the humanity of the priests; he promoted clerical marriage, rejecting the idea that the celibate life is the highest or most Christian form of life. Monasticism, no longer viewed as a higher form of Christian life, was rejected. Priests were urged to marry to experience the fullness of family life and avoid the sexual temptations accompanying celibacy.

The success of Luther's revolt against Roman Catholicism, dependent to a large extent on his political protection by a German prince, Frederick the Wise, led ultimately to the disestablishment of the traditional medieval relationship of church and state. The church in Germany came under the protection of the particular state in which it might be found. This arrangement was made possible by the decision that each German prince should decide whether Protestantism or Catholicism would be the religion of his state. While northern Germany became Protestant, much of southern Germany remained Catholic. The pattern of state churches controlled to some extent by the secular government became normative for a large part of Protestantism. This new arrangement conformed to the rise of nationalism and contributed much to the fragmentation of modern Christian churches.

The establishment of a separate church meant modification of the liturgy and other aspects of church life. Luther understood the sacraments to be an effective means of Grace and insisted upon their central role in the life of the church; he provided for their observance in the vernacular languages to assure meaningful personal participation. However, because for him proclamation of the Word of God was foundational in any meaningful relationship to God, preaching became the focal point of the worship service. He could find only two sacraments—baptism and Eucharist—to be scriptutally based (although he was inclined at times to retain confession and even to consider preaching as a sacrament). Accordingly, he reduced the seven traditional Roman Catholic sacraments to those two.

Differing Interpretations in the Reformation

Luther's place as the front-runner and dominant personality in the early Reformation has never been questioned. It was his forthright defiance of the authority of the papacy and the empire that led to his excommunication and the establishment of an independent German Protestant church. Nevertheless, Luther's reform was accompanied by several independent Protestant movements.

Zwingli.   Ulrich Zwingli (1484–1531), a priest in the Swiss city of Zurich, began an ambitious program of preaching from the Scriptures in 1518. As he worked through the Scriptures, he began to call for reform in the church and its ministry. Zwingli had been trained in the Renaissance tradition with a humanistic education, and many of his innovations reflected its criticisms of the church. Because his criticisms of Roman Christianity were grounded in his reading of the Scriptures, he, like Luther, came to proclaim Scripture as the most important religious authority. When some of his parishioners broke the required Lenten fast, traditionally required of all Christians, Zwingli supported their position, insisting that such fasts should be matters of personal conscience and were not scriptural. Zwingli was subsequently able to persuade the city council, the ruling body in a Swiss city-state (canton), to sponsor a theological disputation on the religious orientation of the city. Although there was no official representative of the Roman hierarchy present, the result of this disputation and another that followed was to establish Protestantism as the religious pattern of Zurich in 1525.

Zwingli does not seem to have been familiar with Luther's works before he began to preach reform; and although he did read several of Luther's treatises, he specifically denied direct dependence on them for his reforms. As Zwingli moved Zurich toward Protestantism, several other Swiss cantons were also taking up the Protestant cause. Johann Oecolampadius (1482–1531) led the city of Basel into Protestantism, following the Zwinglian pattern. The southern German city of Strassburg, guided by Martin Butzer (1491–1551) and others, also followed the patterns set by Zwingli, becoming fully Protestant in 1529.

By the close of the 1520s a distinctively Protestant movement was in place in both Germany and Switzerland. It was marked by significant theological and liturgical patterns: the primacy of scriptural authority, justification by faith, and the centrality of preaching in worship services. Rejected were a number of Roman Catholic practices: the coordinate authority of church tradition with that of scripture, the mass, transubstantiation in the Eucharist, monasticism, and clerical celibacy. In this new Protestantism, laypersons had a much more active role in worship services and church governance. Moral purity and works of charity and love were expected of all believers.

While these patterns made the German and Swiss reformations similar there were important differences. Because the Swiss reform generally occurred in small, localized, and insular city-states, it tended to be more demanding for the local citizens. Strict rules of personal conduct, compulsory church attendance, and the use of expulsion or excommunication were possible in these territories but not in Lutheran German states. There were also more subtle theological differences, the most important of which revolved around the understanding of the sacraments, particularly the Eucharist (the Lord's Supper).

The Colloquy of Marburg.   It was an attempt to solve differences on this question that led to a unique conference in 1529. Because of its consequences for the future of Protestantism, it is useful to look at the event in some detail.

Salvadore Dali, *The Sacrament of the Last Supper.* *(National Gallery of Art, Washington; Chester Dale Collection.)*

Luther had succeeded in establishing his position in Germany on the basis of the protection of Fredrick the Wise. As other northern German states besides Luther's Saxony became Protestant, the question of what pattern of religion would be present in each German territory was intensely debated. In 1526, because neither Protestant or Catholic states were strong enough to force compliance of the others to their own religious persuasion, the princes of the German Empire agreed to a form of religious freedom. Each prince would determine the religious preference of his territory. In 1529, this rather tenuous agreement was rescinded, and clearly the Protestant states faced a renewed political and military threat because of their religious persuasion. During this same period, the Protestant Swiss cantons also found themselves threatened by their Catholic neighbors.

Recognizing the advantage of a united Protestant front in the face of these political difficulties, and knowing that unity was not possible without clarification of theological distinctions between the Protestant communities, Philip, prince of Hesse, a German state bordering Saxony, proposed a colloquy (a dialogue) to be held at Marburg in October 1529. While several topics were open for discussion, the most significant one concerned the differing interpretations given by Luther and Zwingli concerning communion or the Eucharist.

Philip's invitation to Zwingli makes clear his hopes for the conference:

We are presently attempting to call together Luther and Melanchthon, as well as those who share your views concerning the sacrament. Perhaps the gracious and almighty God will bestow his grace so that on the basis of the sacred Scriptures concord can be achieved concerning this article which would enable us to live in common Christian understanding. At this diet [German council of state] the papists attempt to support their false life and morals by insisting that we, who adhere to the pure and clear Word of God, are not of one accord concerning our faith. Thus I graciously request that you will eagerly do your part to bring together in an appointed time and place both you and the Lutherans so that, as I said before, the matter can rightly be brought to a Christian consensus.[2]

Clearly the intent was to gain theological unity that would provide political stability for the Protestant community. On the appointed day Luther, Melanchthon (his close theological ally), Butzer, Zwingli, Oecolampadius, and others opened this significant Protestant council.

How the elements of bread and wine could be understood to be the body and blood of Jesus had been a significant issue of discussion among theologians since the time of Augustine. In the fourteenth century, philosophic thinkers known as Nominalists, as had others before them, questioned the traditional Thomistic definition of transubstantiation. For them there could be no universal substance, only particular substances, so the transforming of the substance of the bread and wine to the substance of Christ's body and blood was not possible. Many Protestant thinkers were influenced by the Nominalists' questions relative to transubstantiation, so it is not surprising to find it receiving renewed scrutiny in Protestant communities.

Luther had asserted from the beginning of his reform that while the Catholic understanding of transubstantiation was faulty in that it incorporated an actual conversion of bread and wine into the body and blood of Christ (leaving only the "accidents," or appearance, of bread and wine), it was correct in insisting upon the "real presence" of the body of Jesus in the sacrament. Arguing from Matthew (26:26–27) and similar scriptural passages, Luther insisted that Jesus' statement "This is my body" meant the real presence of the body and blood in the sacrament. In his understanding, upon the consecration of the elements both the body and blood of Jesus and the bread and wine coexist in full union with one another (a position that came to be known as *consubstantiation*). How this was possible remained a mystery for Luther; yet, even if beyond human comprehension, it was to be accepted on faith.

Zwingli early in his Protestant preaching had adopted an interpretation, first suggested by a Dutch physician, Cornelis Hoen, that declared the bread and wine to be symbolic representations of Jesus' body and blood. The bread and wine were not changed in the Communion but were taken to be symbols of Jesus' sacrifice; symbolically a spiritual presence could be affirmed, but not a bodily presence. This interpretation concentrated on the memorial aspects of the Communion and rejected the idea of Jesus' real presence. Zwingli based his arguments upon John 6 and other passages, where figurative, metaphorical, and symbolic speech was obvious. As the Swiss Reformation developed and expanded, this position became a major distinction of this branch of Protestantism. From 1525, literary works from both Lutheran and Swiss theologians defended their differing interpretations and criticized the opposing views. As they came together at Marburg, their positions were clear and tension was high. Zwingli left Zurich with only a few of the town council knowing of his intended mission and amid rumors that he was fleeing to escape the barbs of his critics. Luther was unwilling to travel in Hesse without the personal protection offered by the guards of Prince Philip.

[2]Hans J. Hillerbrand, *The Reformation* (New York: Harper & Row, 1964), p. 152.

As the discussions opened, it became clear that neither party was likely to compromise. Luther suggested that the Zwinglian group erred in several areas: original sin, justification, and the Trinity, among other issues. Discussion of these matters clarified positions, and the participants came to essential agreement on these points; nevertheless, on the question of Communion there seemed little willingness to compromise. Luther set the tone of the discussion when he dramatically pulled the cloth back from the table around which they sat and wrote "This is my body." Because these were the words of Christ's institution of the supper, he insisted they meant a real presence in the supper. He showed no inclination to back off from this position. Unable to accept this interpretation, the Zwinglian party insisted on their formulation, arguing that the physical body could not be in two places (heaven and earth) at the same time. Unable to resolve their differences, the colloquy closed with a communiqué recognizing that no compromise or joining of the positions was possible. Philip's fond hope of unity was not to come to fruition.[3]

The failure of Protestantism to achieve theological and political unity may have rested at least in part on the differences in the personalities and perspectives of the participants in the council. Scholars have suggested the differing religious experiences and intellectual histories of Luther and Zwingli contributed greatly to their inability to agree. Because Luther's own tortured religious journey made him suspicious of human capabilities, he found relief only in the justification offered in God's Grace through faith. On the other hand, Zwingli, trained in the humanistic tradition, was more willing to give credence to human interpretative powers, so his arguments relative to the supper exemplify a more rationalist approach—i.e., the body cannot be in two places.[4] Other factors obviously were involved in these differences, but clearly Luther and Zwingli represented distinctive approaches to religious faith and life.

The Marburg Colloquy was a foreshadowing of the future of Protestantism. The distinction between the branches of Protestantism at this early date became permanent. Rather than one new form of Christianity contrasting with the Roman tradition, Protestantism was to exhibit many patterns. Its history from that time until the present has been one of continuing separations over the nature and authority of the Scripture, the empowerment of the Holy Spirit, ecclesiastical authority, and a vast array of other issues.

The sixteenth century closed not with two major Western branches of Christianity but with several. One large Christian church, the Roman Catholic, containing within itself a variety of religious traditions, groups, and emphases spread throughout southern Europe and its colonies. Protestantism, in contrast, found its branches in essential agreement in their opposition to much of the Roman tradition but unable to agree among themselves on many other issues. Luther could not have anticipated how his assertion of a personal relationship with God dependent upon scriptural authority rather than the mediation of the priesthood would open the floodgates to the formation of an apparently endless variety of Christian groups in the ensuing centuries.

---

[3]Hillerbrand, op. cit., has gathered not only the record of the colloquy but other accounts of the meeting from a number of sources, including Luther and Zwingli.

[4]See Justo Gonzalez, *The Story of Christianity* (New York: Harper & Row, 1984). II:51.

PATTERNS OF PROTESTANT REFORM

Protestantism's diversity was, however, grounded in cultural and intellectual forces equally as important as the theological differences represented by the arguments of Luther and Zwingli at Marburg. Protestantism arose in several differing communities and peoples of northern Europe, where ethnic and national consciousness had for some time been on the rise. Coupled with the weakening of the Holy Roman Empire's rather tenuous political control, these forces also significantly contributed to diversity in the Protestant world.

The sometimes heady possibilities offered by direct inspiration of the Holy Spirit, the dependence upon individual interpretation of Scriptures, and the excitement of new forms of governance, worship, and ethical practice also made diversity almost inevitable and often very attractive. In many cases, for the first time on a popular level the common people were offered alternatives to the straitjackets of tradition and stultifying authority that had bound their lives and beliefs. Little wonder, then, that Protestantism represented new possibilities. Its diversity was lauded, for it offered an openness and new patterns undreamed of only a few years earlier. The political and spiritual dangers of its deep divisions were soon enough to be evident, but diversity could have hardly been avoided.

The multifaceted nature of modern Protestantism arises out of this complex entanglement of many forces in the sixteenth century. In addition to the Lutheranism discussed earlier, many present-day denominations are rooted in three distinctive Protestant patterns that had emerged by the close of the century.

The Reformed Tradition

As we have seen, the Swiss Reformation began with the work of Zwingli, Oecolampadius, and Butzer, but gained its distinctive character and most lasting influence under the unique ministry of John Calvin at Geneva. Calvin (1509–1564), a Frenchman who fled France after defending Protestant reformers in that nation, brought to Protestantism an incisive mind and distinguished organizational abilities.

For Calvin, the universe and all its blessings, including the gift of salvation through Jesus, was created to glorify God. Therefore all of life was to be dedicated to God. On the basis of this belief, Calvin formulated and systematized existing Protestant theology and included in it a distinctive Christian pattern for the governance of all life, civic and spiritual. Under his leadership and demanding direction, Geneva became a model Protestant state. In theory, if not always in practice, it was ideally ruled by God as revealed in Jesus—a Christian theocracy. As one might assume, its theology and practices were understood by Calvin to be grounded in scriptural patterns. A second-generation reformer, Calvin generally agreed with Luther's and Zwingli's central tenets. He accepted Luther's "justification by faith" as the means by which humanity was to be related to God. Scripture, rather than tradition of the church, was the ultimate authority. Instead of seven sacraments, only two were recognized. Worship was centered around preaching. Calvin's distinction from other reformers came in several of these theological emphases and in his organizational genius as it was applied to ecclesiastical structures.

The magnificence and wonder of God's power expressed in love lie behind Calvin's emphasis on the centrality of God's grace, particularly in light of human sinful pride. Calvin accepted the traditional concept of humanity's sinfulness and, as had Augustine in the early church, taught that fallen humanity's self-centeredness made it impossible for persons to do good simply by their own choice. All good is credited to God. Fallen humanity may do good in the ordinary civic and secular aspects of life but this good is empowered and sustained by God's grace. In their relationship to God, humans can do no "good"—they cannot influence their own salvation. Salvation comes only at the discretion of the Divine: it comes to whom God wills. Humanity cannot will it or achieve it by works or even accept it when it is offered, unless God makes it possible. Because all persons deserve condemnation, God's salvation of even a limited segment of humanity was seen by Calvin to be a joyous and wonderfully merciful act.

To Calvin, it was a great comfort to know that God had elected at least some of humanity to salvation. This doctrine, commonly called *predestination* (see Chapter Seven), wherein some are chosen for salvation and others are not, became a hallmark of the Reformed communities. Calvin believed that the chief end of humanity is to glorify God, and he taught that humanity can best do this through clear obedience of God's will as delineated in Scripture. Since one can only trust in faith that he or she might be one of the elect, all are to live as if they are. Calvin spent much energy defining in a somewhat legal fashion what should constitute a Christian life. He based his ideas on the Scripture, emphasizing the Old Testament as a model for contemporary Christians far more than had Luther or Roman Catholicism.

Calvin also sought to institute what he considered the New Testament pattern of church and civil government in the city of Geneva. A consistory of laypersons and clergy ruled the church, which took upon itself the moral and spiritual supervision of the city. The civil government, divinely ordained as was the church, was to protect and promote the church and enforce its disciplines. Calvin succeeded in establishing close church-state relations, in which the church was very influential if not preeminent. Under this type of rule, the failure of any to conform to the rule of the church not only brought excommunication but could very well bring banishment from the city.

Church organization beyond the local level was provided through synods and presbyteries, whose members included both laypersons and ministers. Ministers were understood to be divinely called to their tasks but were required to receive the approval of the congregation. Using these forms, the church incorporated representational congregational models and the city's governance continued to be based on the republican models of Swiss tradition. Authority lay in the community and its decisions (for church and state decisions). Power resided in the authority of the office established by the community and not the rule of an individual who might hold that office. However, once officers were selected, they were responsible before God for the performance of the office and were expected to bring about compliance with civil and church disciplines in an orderly and fair manner.

In Geneva and the subsequent Reformed churches, patterns of worship were simplified. The sermon, as the proclaimed word, became the central focus of worship services. Extemporaneous prayer often replaced the formal prayers of traditional Roman Catholic liturgy. An emphasis upon personal responsibility before God led to a high evaluation of teaching in the home, the church, and the city, resulting in a well-educated laity and clergy. The insistence on a disciplined Christian life led to pietistic trends wherein vocational activity, recreation, and social life were to glorify God—one did not just attend to God in worship.

When England briefly returned to Catholicism under Queen Mary (reigned 1553–1558), Protestant leaders were exiled and some sought haven in Geneva, where they espoused Calvinistic theology. On their return to England and Scotland, they were anxious to institute many of Calvin's modifications of church polity and practice. Much of the theology was in fact incorporated in Anglicanism, although the polity of Geneva was resisted. Modifications and changes of emphasis and interpretation, particularly in the doctrine of predestination, have occurred since Calvin's time, but basic elements of the Calvinistic reforms are still present in modern Reformed churches such as the Presbyterian church, the Church of Scotland, Dutch Reformed groups, and Congregationalists (now the United Church of Christ). Calvin's theology has also been highly influential among English and American Baptists.

Anglicanism

The Anglicans were the third group representing a distinctive Christian tradition to arise during the Reformation. Although usually considered to be a part of the Protestant community, in fact, Anglicanism is a combination of ancient Catholic patterns of church polity and practice with Protestant theology. Anglicanism draws its name from its historic roots in the Church of England, but modern churches in this tradition are spread worldwide as a result of English colonial expansion. In America this group is represented by the Protestant Episcopal—or simply the Episcopal—church.

The English break with the Church of Rome resulted from religious, political, social, and personal factors. Henry VIII (reigned 1509–1547), king of England and a contemporary of Luther and Calvin, headed a country that had long chafed under the political and economic power of the Holy Roman Empire as well as of the Roman church. The largest landholder in England, the Roman church also had its own court system and generally was not as responsive or amenable to English interests as Englishmen thought it should be. Henry's rejection of the rule of the papacy had the large-scale support of his people, for they saw it as the freeing of England from foreign dominion.

The catalyst for the separation was Henry's desire to father a male heir for the English throne. Since his wife Catherine had not produced a male child, Henry sought the annulment of their marriage. When the pope, under pressure from Holy Roman Emperor Charles V, who was Catherine's nephew, refused, Henry initiated actions that ultimately led to his appointment by Parliament as supreme head of the Church of England. He appointed as archbishop of Canterbury and principal English ecclesiastical officer Thomas Cranmer (1489–1556). Cranmer then granted Henry his annulment. Henry's motivation was both political and personal. So far as the church was concerned, Henry appears to have had little idea that he was bringing major religious change. Under his reforms, episcopal order, liturgy, and practice were to continue in their traditional forms.

However, under the influence of Cranmer and those who followed him, an English Protestant theology rooted in the work of Wycliff and influenced by Luther and Calvin began to develop. Although the English church never lost its interest in Grace manifesting itself in works and their importance for salvation, the role and importance of faith understood in the Lutheran formulation found fertile ground in England. Calvinistic doctrines of God's sovereignty and Grace were attractive. Modifications in worship practices also appeared in the church. The Scriptures were quickly translated into English and placed in each local church. The English church also recognized only the two sacraments accepted by Protestants, but retained a stress on the efficacy of sacramental Grace. Sermons assumed a more central place in the services but did not become the predominant element in worship as they had in continental Protestant theology and practice. The parish system was kept intact, linking the appointment of parish priests and other church officials closely to political preferment. Priests were allowed to marry and monasticism was rejected.

In the course of the English reforms two major groups, or parties, emerged. Traditionalists most closely identified with the ancient Catholic theology, ecclesiology, and patterns of worship, but not advocating Roman control, were identified with the crown and reflected the opinions of the majority of the people. Another smaller but powerful group sought much more sweeping Protestant changes in the English church, with some going so far as to question the episcopal organization and its state support. For their insistence on purifying the church of all "Romish" trappings and patterns, they gained the name of Puritans. The differences between these two major religious groups reflected a deep division in religious understanding and practice in sixteenth-century England. For the Puritans the issues involved more than changes in liturgy and ecclesiology but concerned questions relative to the very nature of faith itself. Taking a more distinctive Protestant position, especially as it was formulated by Calvin, they questioned whether the Church of England did not still embrace a doctrine of justification by works, even if in a modified non-Roman Catholic form.

It was to be the role of Queen Elizabeth I (reigned 1558–1603) and her advisers to achieve compromise between the parties and establish what came to be the lasting character of the English church. In essence it became a *via media* between traditional Catholicism and radical Protestantism. The Thirty-Nine Articles of Religion adopted under Elizabeth, although incorporating ancient doctrinal definitions, also reflected Protestant theological interests and assumptions. The Book of Common Prayer, perfected under Elizabeth, incorporated with modifications the ancient rites of the Catholic church shorn of the elements most offensive to the Protestants (prayers for the dead, and so on). To achieve permanent patterns of conformity, the clergy were required to accept the articles and to use the services of the prayer book in their churches. As a moderate church, the Church of England sought to identify itself with the ancient patristic period, the first four centuries of the Christian era, believing that it was reinstituting the true, original beliefs and practices of primitive Catholicism.

Distinction between the parties continued, however, and erupted again during the Civil War (1640–1660), when Puritan forces achieved temporary control of the country under Oliver Cromwell. However, Puritan divisions among themselves over practice, governance, and attempts to use governmental force to achieve moral discipline ultimately led to their rejection from political power. Accompanying the restoration of the king was a reinstitution of the episcopal Church of England molded after the one formed during Elizabeth's reign. Those Puritans unwilling to conform to this reestablished church were ejected from it. From these "nonconformists" many denominations arose (the English Presbyterians, Congregationalists, Quakers, English Baptists, and others). In the colonization of the seventeenth and eighteenth centuries, many from both the Church of England and Puritan groups emigrated to America and formed the early American churches.

Accompanying the English colonialists, the Anglican church spread through-out the world, and in modern times many independent churches of the Anglican tradition maintain strong fraternal relations with the Church of England. In nations where church and state are separated, as in the present-day United States, Anglican churches have usually combined episcopal forms of church organization with democratic participation of laypersons in the governance of local congregations and the general assemblies of the church.

Radical Reformers

Much of modern Protestantism traces its history to the churches discussed above. Alongside these churches there have existed from the beginning a number of groups that have distinguished themselves by adhering to distinctive doctrines, attitudes, or practices, often supplemented by stringent moral teachings. Because of these distinctive patterns and their tendency to take Protestant insights to their extremes, they have come to be known in history as the *Radical Reformers*. Normally remaining comparatively small, many of these groups have survived, offering in modern Christianity examples of communities distinguished by their dedication to their original beliefs, disciplined, pious life-styles, and service to others.

Anabaptist Groups.   One of the earliest examples of this type of Protestant community began in Zwingli's church at Zurich. Some of his parishioners, led by their reading of the Scripture, came to question whether there was scriptural justification for the practice of infant baptism. They came to the conclusion there was no warrant for such practice. Accompanying this insight was their conviction that baptism should be accepted only by persons mature enough to choose con-sciously to be baptized. Their reading of Scripture also convinced them that the proper mode of baptism was by immersion rather than by the more generally accepted practice of pouring. Since infant baptism was for them wrong and of no effect, in their understanding they themselves were not properly baptized. Acting on these convictions they baptized each other and were soon insisting upon immer-sion as the proper mode of baptism. In the eyes of Zwingli and others, they were by this act denying the efficacy of their original baptism and asserting that in infant baptism the Grace of the Lord was not properly present. The label attached to this group and others of these opinions was that of *Anabaptists,* or "rebaptizers." Since the term itself only applied to a generation of believers who had been baptized as infants, it lost its original meaning in later generations. Persons accepting these beliefs concerning baptism today are usually known simply as "Baptists."

This group and others that followed them, particularly in Holland, were also convinced that the state had no prerogative to determine the religious affiliation or beliefs of its citizens. This contrasted with most of the then-current Protestant thought, which had gained its own independence from Rome by depending on the support of local political units. Most Protestants insisted the state could and should decide which form of Christianity would be practiced in its territory. The An-abaptists essentially called for freedom of religion and separation of church and state. Holding this position, many Anabaptists had little alternative but to separate themselves from society, establishing a number of small independent societies that rejected allegiance to any state. These separated communities understood them-selves to be establishing theocracies (states ruled by God). They established strict life-styles, insisting on simple and unpretentious—spiritual—patterns. Both Protestants and Catholics persecuted them for threatening secular society and undermining the fabric of the traditional political structure with its claim to divinely established authority.

Baptist groups that emerged in succeeding centuries accepted Anabaptist concepts of baptism and religious freedom, but frequently rejected the characteristic separation from society and refusal of political allegiance. Modern Mennonites, Amish, Brethren, and others have carried into modern times the idea of a separated society of Christians ruled by and structured on biblical principles.

The Quakers. Anabaptists represent one type of sectarian group that separated itself from other Christian groups. By the middle of the seventeenth century there were many others. Each group felt itself to be the true embodiment of the faith. In the period surrounding the English Civil War a number of such groups arose. One of the best-known of these was the Quakers, or the Society of Friends. George Fox (1624–1691; see Chapter Eight) distressed by the insincerity of nominal Christians and greatly troubled by their warring with one another, came to a religious experience that changed his concept of Christian expression. Fox taught that each person has a divine "inner light" which, if recognized, leads to spiritual truth—the revelation of Christ and the immediate awareness of his teachings. Truth therefore dwells within oneself. There is no need for church buildings, ministers, or traditional worship services. Sacraments are inward and spiritual, and therefore need no external representation. All human beings before God are equal, so there is no need to recognize class or cultural distinctions. Oaths are unnecessary because each Christian will by nature speak truthfully. Christians will neither go to war nor tolerate social injustice. Christian life empowered by the light will be characterized by good works accompanied by simplicity, purity, and truthfulness.

Fox's teachings gained a substantial following in the troubled times in which he lived, but also prompted persecution, because his movement rejected traditional religious and secular authority. Quaker meetings came to be occasions in which any person who felt led by the Spirit contributed to the service. More formal worship services were eliminated. Monthly meetings provided spiritual instruction, pastoral care throughout the community, and discipline of the members. William Penn brought Fox's teachings to America, establishing Quakerism in Pennsylvania, but allowing all groups to have religious freedom. Though small in numbers, Quakers have contributed ideas, leaders, and support to many causes, working on behalf of peace, race relations, human rights, and social justice.

The Anabaptists and Quakers represent sectarian movements that have spawned many differing groups since the inception of Protestantism. The proliferation of groups seeking change in cultural patterns, claiming particular spiritual inspiration or insight, or making a great variety of other claims has continued, especially in the United States. Although many such groups have been short-lived, others have been attractive to many believers and have flourished. The present diversification of Christian bodies is at least partly rooted in a characteristic Protestant conviction that each individual is capable of knowing spiritual truth and is personally responsible for expressing it. This conviction lies at the core of the Protestant appropriation of the gospel, yet it has sometimes been carried to extremes in Protestant sectarianism, where new denominations or individual churches have separated from their predecessors as the result of minimal differences or nuances of belief or practice.

ROMAN CATHOLIC RESPONSES
TO THE REFORMATION

By the middle decades of the sixteenth century, it had become evident that the domination of Christian tradition, pattern, and governance by the Holy Roman Empire, ruled coordinately by emperor and pope, was at an end. The need for moral and administrative reform within the decadent and corrupt Renaissance papacy had been urged and locally achieved in part by many Catholic contemporaries of Luther such as the Spanish archbishop Francis Ximenes and the Italian friar Girolamo Savonarola. The humanist critiques based on Renaissance scholarship, such as those of the Dutch teacher and writer Erasmus and England's Sir Thomas More, were direct and sometimes startling. Such cries, added to the success of Protestant teachings, all pointed to crisis in the church. By midcentury, the Catholic response began to take several forms, in addition to the political defense of Catholic lands provided by Emperor Charles V and the to-be-expected papal summary rejection of Protestant reforms.

The Council of Trent

Calls for an ecumenical council of the church's bishops had been made by many, including Luther. Protestant establishment of political and religious independence in several northern European countries, plus increasing pressure for genuine reform from within the church, added weight to such calls. After several false starts a general council convened in 1545. Held at Trent, an imperial city in northern Italy, it struggled through many changes in papal and imperial leadership but concluded its work eighteen years later. The council succeeded, even under adverse conditions, in extensively reevaluating the life and work of the church and directly confronted Protestant challenges to traditional theology and practice.

The abuses within the church noted by many revolved around the character and dedication of the clergy and the commercialization of many church rites and offices. The council addressed these issues by eliminating the concurrent appointment of one cleric to several ecclesiastical offices, effectively reducing the dual economic and political benefits of such arrangements. Bishops were also ordered to reside in their sees. Clarification and specific definition of clerical responsibilities, with an insistence on celibacy, solidified discipline among the clergy. Redefinition of appropriate veneration of relics and images and the purpose of indulgences regulated their proliferation and use. Regulated education for the clergy was urged through instructions that required the founding of local diocesan seminaries and a renewed insistence on clerical education. A more unified theology was sought through the suggestion that St. Thomas Aquinas' teachings be normative for the church. To further guarantee unification of theology and insulate Catholic teachers and students from divergent ideas, the Index of prohibited books was expanded to include most Protestant works. These and other reforms clearly signaled a reforming mood within the church. The council participants were especially interested in establishing discipline and eliminating the abuses that had been debilitating to faith and practice among the masses.

The council's response to the specific critiques and charges of Protestant reformers was largely to reject the innovations and retain traditional positions, refining them in the new context of a shattered church. Responding to demands of change in attitude toward and understanding of Scripture, the council reasserted its continued confidence in the authority of tradition *and* Scripture; one could not supersede the other. In scriptural matters, the Latin, or Vulgate, was declared the authoritative biblical translation, in opposition to the Protestant plea for Scripture in the vernacular languages. In addition, the church's role as the sole authoritative interpreting agent of the Scriptures was reaffirmed. The seven traditional sacraments were retained and the sacramental understandings of Luther, Zwingli, and Calvin rejected. Traditional doctrines relative to Original Sin and justification by faith and merit were reiterated. These and other similar affirmations effectively sealed the break with Protestantism, since they conceded little change in traditional doctrine or practice and specifically rejected the innovations of the reformers.

With the decrees of the council, significant reform was possible within the church. Such reform clearly strengthened the Roman Catholic tradition in most nations of southern and western Europe and their colonies, where it remained the dominant Christian tradition. The council's response to Protestantism was molded out of a significant reevaluation and reformulation of traditional dogma and practice. The strength of both modified practice and restored tradition expressed in its decrees was sufficient to define the form and character of Roman Catholicism until modern times.

Revitalized Monasticism

The later sessions of the Council of Trent were significantly influenced by a relatively new Roman Catholic monastic order that had arisen in the midst of the Protestant crisis. Much of the impetus for practical reform of the church came at the urging of representatives of the Society of Jesus (commonly known as the Jesuits). Although the order had not been founded in direct response to the Reformation, it quickly took up the defense of the Catholic faith and aggressively countered the threats to the church represented by Protestant advances.

The founder of the society was a Spanish nobleman, Ignatius of Loyola (1491–1556). Wounded as a young warrior in a battle with France, Loyola was forced into a long convalescence, during which he reexamined his life. The experience convinced him to abandon his military career and turned him toward a spiritual vocation. While his religious struggles convinced him that only the spiritual life led to true fulfillment, he was equally confident that such a life must be completed or affirmed in service. He was, therefore, not attracted to traditional cloistered monasticism, but sought to live out his spiritual convictions through a pilgrimage to Jerusalem, hoping to serve the poor, and as a missionary to the Turks. Thwarted in this endeavor, he returned to Europe determined to seek a theological education, which he pursued at several Spanish universities, completing his work at the University of Paris.

Before his journey to Jerusalem he formulated the basic patterns of his most influential work, *The Spiritual Exercises.* Based on his own mystical experience, this set of spiritual instructions had two foci. First, used personally it was designed to carry an inquirer through four intensive stages of spiritual pilgrimage: examination of conscience, meditation, contemplation, and prayer. These were combined to rid one of self-interest, resulting in the dedication of the self completely to the will of God. Second, used by a community of believers the stages formed the basis of a demanding program of spiritual retreat with the same objective of total dedication to God's will in one's common daily life. The work became the foundation of spiritual renewal and guidance not only for the members of the order but also for the masses evangelized and taught by the Jesuits.

Loyola's dedication and example attracted a number of followers among his fellow students at the University of Paris. In 1534 they formed themselves into a society dedicated to poverty, chastity, missions, education, and the spiritual life. They offered themselves in complete dedication to the pope, as Christ's vicar, and were authorized as a new papal order in 1540. As a vigorous new spiritual community the purpose of the group was manifold: reform of the church by eliminating the gross abuses of the clergy; dedication to evangelical missions, particularly to areas where the gospel had not been preached or taught; service as educators within church schools and the universities; and general service in the administrative affairs of the church. To achieve this, Jesuits presented themselves to the pope as soldiers of God to be used wherever and however the pope might choose. They intended to act in strict obedience to the command of the pope—in sharp contrast to the Protestant objectors to papal authority. Loyola understood that "Man has been created to praise, reverence, and serve God our Lord, and by this means to save his soul."[5] This assumption included belief in free will and the active role of humanity in its own salvation—also a contrast to much of Protestant thought. Confident that persons could be convinced to choose the right path, the Jesuits concentrated on education and missions, rivaling in these areas the leadership of the Franciscans and Dominicans. The society was to enjoy great success in missions throughout the world and to influence greatly the shape of Roman Catholicism from then until the present. In the Jesuits, Loyola's combination of spiritual exercises with their mystical emphasis and complete devotion and service to the church proved a potent impetus to reform and redirection of the church's mission.

Mystical Disciplines

During the closing years of the Council of Trent another response to the need for reform and renewal in the church emerged among Spanish monastics. In a house of Carmelite nuns at Avila a new form of renewal arose in the experience and work of St. Teresa of Jesus. St. Teresa uniquely influenced the subsequent development of Western Christian mysticism and monasticism through her disciplinary reforms and her writings on mystical contemplation. Teresa entered a Carmelite house at an early age but was forty years old when she experienced a conversion to a life of perfection while praying before a statue depicting Christ being scourged. She experienced numerous mystical ecstasies, culminating in—to use her terms—a "spiritual marriage" with God and a vision of Christ. Her own experiences convinced her that the spiritual and vocational discipline of the order was so lax as to be ineffectual. She sought permission to found a sister order, with the intent of returning it to the more strict and ascetic rule that had been present in the earliest formations of the order. Permission was granted and the convent of St. Joseph was founded in Avila in 1562. Dedicated to meditation, contemplation, and intercessory prayer, the new order became known as the Discalced Carmelites (so called for their discipline of wearing sandals in place of shoes). Over the next few years she developed her rule and led her sisters into innovative practices of mystical contem-

---

[5]Ignatius of Loyola, *The Spiritual Exercises*, trans. Anthony Mottola (New York: Doubleday, 1964), p. 47.

plation. The patterns of her reforms spread among male Carmelites under the guidance and influence of her colleague St. John of the Cross. The last few years of St. Teresa's life were spent in vigorous reform of other Carmelite houses and the establishment of new houses (sixteen for women and fourteen for men). Such reforms became an example for other orders, bringing spiritual and disciplinary renewal and vigor into the Roman Catholic monastic movement.

These reforms were highly influential, but perhaps the most significant permanent contributions of St. Teresa came through a series of writings on mysticism that she first developed for her Carmelite sisters and brothers. Undertaken at the insistence of her confessor to record her own experiences and to help clarify and heighten her own discipline, they were shared with others, thereby becoming respected guides to Christian mystical experience. Her spiritual autobiography, *The Life of Teresa of Jesus,* and works such as *The Way of Perfection, Foundations,* and *The Interior Castle* continue to be classics of mystical literature. Teresa's active participation in the reformation of the monastic orders, often against great adversity, while at the same time setting patterns for the most intense contemplation, testified that mystical experience need not be limited to or bound by the cloister.

Teresa's work and example offered yet another response to the needs for reform within the Roman Catholic church during this period. Coupled with the dynamic Jesuit reforms and the modifications promulgated by the Council of Trent, Teresa's contributions form another facet of what in history has often come to be called the Counter-Reformation. While spurred on by the threat of the Reformation, the movement perhaps was not merely an attempt to counter those forces but to enhance renewal already begun in the church. In any case, the last decades of the sixteenth century witnessed the development of a strong, renewed, and disciplined Roman Catholicism prepared to offer its adherents a vigorous alternative to Protestantism. The strength of the renewal is proved in that Roman Catholicism remains today by far the largest Christian body, with a unity and authority often wistfully desired and sought by modern Protestant leaders.

QUESTIONS

1. What were the contributions of the mendicant orders of Francis and Dominic to the life of the church and monasticism?

2. What did Martin Luther mean by the "priesthood of all believers"? How did that belief contrast with traditional Roman Catholic concepts of the priesthood?

3. Explain why Thomas Aquinas' synthesis of Aristotelian and Platonic theories of knowledge was important to the theological life of the church.

4. In what ways did the critiques of the church and its practices made by Wycliff, Hus, and the humanists contribute to the setting for the Reformation?

5. Why may it be said that the Protestant Reformation shifted the basis of authority within Christianity? What became of the new authority in Protestantism?

6. How did the new emphasis on individual interpretation of Scripture and personal experience of religion affect the development of Christianity in the post-Reformation period?

7. The Protestant Reformation turned out to be a very fragmented movement without central unity. Why was this true? What effect did that have on modern Christianity?

8. What were the major branches of the Protestant Reformation? How did they contrast with each other?

9. What were the characteristics of the Anabaptists that separated them from their fellow Protestants? How were they viewed by other Protestants and Roman Catholics?

10. In what ways did Calvin's theories of church and state government contrast with those current in the European culture of his day?

11. What was the Council of Trent and why may it be said that it molded Roman Catholic patterns of theology and practice for subsequent centuries?

12. Comment on the three Roman Catholic responses to the Reformation, showing their distinctive features and their interrelationships to each other.

13. Imagining yourself as either Luther or Zwingli at Marburg, critique the position on the Eucharist offered by your theological opponent.

FURTHER READING

ARMSTRONG, REGIS J. and BRADY, IGNATIUS C. trans. *Francis and Clare: The Complete Works.* New York: Paulist Press, 1982.

AUCLAIR, MARCELLE. *Teresa of Avila.* Trans. Kathleen Pond. New York: Doubleday, 1959.

BAINTON, ROLAND H. *Here I Stand: A Life of Martin Luther.* Nashville, Tenn.: Abingdon Press, 1960.

———. *The Reformation in the Sixteenth Century.* Boston: Beacon Press, 1972.

BOEHMER, HEINRICH. *The Road to Reformation.* Philadelphia: Muhlenberg Press, 1946.

BROMILY, G. W. *Zwingli and Bullinger.* Philadelphia: Westminster Press, 1953.

BURNS, E. M. *The Counter-Reformation.* Princeton, N.J.: Princeton University Press, 1964.

CANNON, W. R. *History of Christianity in the Middle Ages.* New York: Abingdon Press, 1960.

CLEBSCH, WILLIAM A. *England's Earliest Protestants.* New Haven, Conn.: Yale University Press, 1964.

DICKENS, A. C. *The English Reformation.* New York: Schocken Books, 1964.

DILLENBERGER, JOHN, and WELCH, CLAUDE. *Protestant Christianity.* New York: Charles Scribner's Sons, 1964.

FORTINI, ARNALDO. *Francis of Assisi.* Trans. Helen Moak. New York: Crossroad, 1981.

GONZALEZ, JUSTO. *The Story of Christianity.* New York: Harper & Row, 1984.

HALLER, WILLIAM. *The Rise of Puritanism.* New York: Columbia University Press, 1938.

HILLERBRAND, HANS. *The Reformation.* New York: Harper & Row, 1964.

KNOWLES, DAVID. *The Nature of Mysticism.* New York: Hawthorn Books, 1966.

———. *Christian Monasticism.* New York: McGraw-Hill Book Company, 1969.

———. *The Middle Ages.* New York: McGraw-Hill Book Company, 1968.

LITTELL, FRANKLIN. *The Anabaptist View of the Church.* Boston: Star King Press, 1958.

———. *The Origins of Sectarian Protestantism.* New York: Macmillan, 1968.

LUTHER, MARTIN. *Luther's Works.* 55 vols. Eds. J. Pelikan and H. Lehman. St. Louis, Mo.: Concordia Publishing House, 1955.

MANSCHRECK, CLYDE. *A History of Christianity in the World.* Englewood Cliffs, N.J.: Prentice-Hall, 1974.

MCNEILL, J. T. *The History and Character of Calvinism.* New York: Oxford University Press, 1954.

PELIKAN, JAROSLAV JAN. *The Christian Tradition: A History of the Development of Doctrine.* Vol. 1, *The Emergence of Catholic Tradition* [100–600]; Vol. 2, *The Spirit of Eastern Christendom* [600–1700]; Vol. 3, *The Growth of Medieval Theology* [600–1300]; Vol. 4, *The Reformation of Church Dogma* [1300–1700]. Chicago: University of Chicago Press, 1977–1985.

———. *Development of Christian Doctrine; Some Historical Prolegomena.* New Haven: Yale University Press, 1969.

———. *The Excellent Empire: The Fall of Rome and the Triumph of the Church.* San Francisco: Harper & Row, 1987.

RILLIET, JEAN H. *Zwingli: Third Man of the Reformation.* London: Butterworth Press, 1964.

ROUSE, RUTH, and NEILL, STEPHEN. *History of the Ecumenical Movement: 1517–1948.* Philadelphia: Westminster Press, 1952.

SYKES, NORMAN. *The English Religious Tradition.* London: SCM Press, 1953.

SPINKA, MATTHEW. *Advocates of Reform from Wycliff to Erasmus.* Philadelphia: Westminster Press, 1963.

UNDERHILL, EVELYN. *Mysticism.* New York: E. P. Dutton, 1930.

WELCH, CLAUDE. *Protestant Thought in the Nineteenth Century.* New Haven, Conn.: Yale University Press, 1972.

WILLIAMS, GEORGE. *The Radical Reformation.* Philadelphia: Westminster Press, 1962.

WORKMAN, H. B. *The Evolution of the Monastic Ideal.* London: Epworth Press and Methodist Publishing House, 1927.

CHAPTER FIVE

The Foundations of Modern Christianity

The vignettes of Christian tradition we have seen in Chapters Three and Four are intended to give us a feel for the representative experiences and periods of Christian development. Because they are only windows into the vast array of Christian history, they do not attempt to treat the complex intermingling of Christianity with the political, social, and philosophical stories of, first, the Mediterranean world, second, Europe (both Eastern and Western), and finally, modern-day civilizations around the globe. To appreciate the phenomenally varied and rich features of modern Christianity we again look at selected movements and events that have helped mold the character and form of present-day Christianity. Beginning with a distinctive pattern of Christian faith that spans its history, Christian mysticism, we investigate significant developments since the Reformation period from which a vital, energetic Christianity has emerged in our own time.

CHRISTIAN MYSTICISM

Previous chapters reflect many of the forces that have led to diversification in modern Christianity. Yet within many modern forms of Christianity another reality is present that does not depend upon political, ecclesiastical, or theological differences but, in fact, expresses a universal religious characteristic. This is Christian mysticism. Mystical experience has been a part of Christianity from its earliest days, finding expression in many diverse Christian groups, and it still finds strong expression today.

Religion, by its very nature, is concerned with aspects of life that transcend human limitations and comprehension. One of these aspects involves the search for direct personal encounters with God. Since most Christian traditions have stressed personal knowledge of God, it is natural that they have known some aspects of mystical encounter. These have been expressed in many forms, including the sense of awe or sacredness in the sacramental practices of the faithful, the sacred presence felt in buildings and shrines, the awareness of the divine presence in a worship experience, the direct encounter with the Holy Spirit, resulting in "conversion," and many others. In addition to these types of mystical experience, some believers have sought and experienced the religious phenomenon of mystical union with God.

Such experiences are difficult to describe but they assume direct encounter with God and may vary in intensity from simple awareness of being momentarily in God's presence to experiences such as St. Teresa's, which she characterized as a "mystical marriage" with Christ. According to St. Teresa, the relationship was constant, and experiences of contact transcending normal ordinary existence were frequent. For most mystics the test of authenticity of the experience is enhanced consciousness of God's presence in life and the fruits of humility, charity, and service to others.

Eastern Christianity, with its more prominent spirituality, has throughout its history displayed high respect for the full mystical experience. In the West, where the practical and rational approaches to life have dominated, mysticism has been a more unusual phenomenon, but certainly it has been present in many of the variant branches of Western Christianity.

Mystical patterns are found in most religious communities. Christian mysticism is distinguished from other forms of mysticism in two significant ways. Because of its theistic orientation, Christian mysticism has normally rejected pantheistic concepts of the divine. God and the universe are understood by Christianity to be distinct, so in Christian mysticism one is not discovering the divine present in all reality, including the material universe (the pantheistic concept), but rather is in contact with the being that transcends all sense-perceived, discursively known reality, a reality distinct from God's creation. Christian mystics, therefore, do not claim in their union with God to become God or to lose their human nature. While there is union of the wills, two distinct beings remain in the mystical experience. This concept distinguishes Christian mysticism from much religious mystical experience, including that of the Hindu and the Buddhist traditions.

Contrary to common assumptions, Christian mysticism has not been confined to the solitary saints seeking, through ascetic contemplation, individual union with God that distinguishes and separates them from the world. Mystics may (and often do) live quite active lives in the secular world. Mysticism is usually understood to follow a pattern in which the participant moves through purification from the self-interests that tie one to the material world, to illumination in which one is certain in one's own life and being of God's love, and finally to a union of wills so that one's own being is immersed in the indwelling love of God. Union does not occur without discipline and dedication, but neither is it simply a personal achievement. It is a divine gift and carries with it fruits of humility, charity, and loving service and is often accompanied by suffering.

A comprehensive catalogue of Christian mystics and their influence is beyond the scope of this account. Such a list would begin with Paul, the writer of the Gospel of John, St. Augustine, and St. Anthony. St. Francis, Meister Eckhart, and John Tauler offered a mystical response to the medieval involvement of the church in the materialistic grandeur of the age. (As we have seen, one of the responses to the problems addressed by the Protestant Reformation was a renewal within Roman Catholicism of the mystical tradition.) St. Teresa, St. John of the Cross, and St. Ignatius Loyola exemplify this response. Jacob Boehme, George Fox, and William Law are examples of Protestant mystics in the sixteenth and seventeenth centuries. Modern spirituality has experienced a renewal of interest as humanity responds to the extremes of rationalism and secularism. This is supported by the tendency of modern psychology to give credence to the extrasensory, paranormal, and spiritual dimensions of life. Modern mystics influential in Christian life include Catholics Thomas Merton, Henri Nouwen, and Carlo Carretto; Protestants Rufus M. Jones, Evelyn Underhill, Muriel Lester, and Thomas Kelly; and Eastern Orthodox Christians Anthony Bloom and the anonymous author of *The Way of a Pilgrim*.

ASPECTS OF MODERN CHRISTIANITY

The Protestant Reformation opened Western Europe to many innovations in religious thought, organization, and political allegiance that in the ensuing centuries changed the face of Europe and realigned Christianity's relationship to Western culture. Protestant modifications, however, were in actuality only part of a much larger reform taking place within European society.

The legacy of the Renaissance included an intellectual enlightenment, causing historians to refer to the eighteenth century as the Age of Reason. In that century dependence on human reason became so dominant among intellectuals that all thought, including theology, was judged at the bar of its "reasonableness," its validity depending upon whether it could be formulated and proved within the framework of human sensibility. In the same century traditional political alliances, based on the autonomous divine right of kings, disintegrated in the maelstrom of the the American and French revolutions. The Industrial Revolution, fueled by a rising capitalism, transformed the social setting of much of Europe as it shifted economic and political power from a land-based economy to a monetary foundation. Newtonian physics became the basis of a new science intent on practical applications of its insights to manufacturing and agricultural innovations. These in and of themselves were reforming movements with unknown and unanticipated consequences. By the close of the eighteenth century, Europe had experienced a series of revolutions. The Protestant Reformation was, in one sense, a prelude to changes in all areas of life. In this new world, medieval Christian domination of culture was a memory, and even the religious contributions of the Protestant Reformation of the two previous centuries were being modified and expanded to keep the faith relevant for Western societies.

The nineteenth century, heir of these vast changes, in many instances witnessed their maturing into new patterns of thought and life. Newtonian physics allowed technological advances undreamed of: steam engines incorporated into shipping and railroads transformed commerce and made travel available to a much broader section of society; new forms of military combat extended war's possibilities to global dimensions; new building designs, sewage systems, and concentrated industrial complexes allowed cities to replace the town and village as the center of society. The list might go on. The mind-set of observation, theory, and application created new forms of science such as anthropology, psychology, and sociology. Scholars turned their attention and the new methods of inquiry toward prior human experience, and modern historiography was born. Colonialization was renewed with the improvement of navigation and transportation; for the first time in history, European civilization was exported until it truly became global. By the close of Queen Victoria's reign, the English could truthfully claim that "the sun never sets upon the British Empire."

Nineteenth- and twentieth-century Europe also experienced a revolution in the understanding of human life. Humanity came to be seen as self-sufficient and capable of solving the problems of life, given time, discipline, and energy. This attitudinal change was accompanied by a process of secularization in which most of the social functions traditionally related to religion were assumed by the state or other social institutions. For many Europeans, this meant Christian thought and practice were reduced to a secondary, if not irrelevant, position. Individual participation in the outward forms of religion has fallen substantially in the twentieth century. Culturally, however, much of European ethical and moral patterns remains clearly based on Christian principles. Publicly, religion continues to be recognized as significant. A renewal of interest in religious issues has also been underway in recent years. Evangelical Christian groups and groups representing religions other than Christianity have found fertile fields in portions of Europe.

European Protestant theologians led the critical literary study of Scriptures in the nineteenth and twentieth centuries; traditional concepts of faith were examined, using sociological, psychological, and historical tools. Their theological understandings gave a larger role to humanity and its capacities, and contributed to the rise of modern Christian concerns for social, economic, and political justice. To traditionalists, such inquiry often appeared to result in a questioning of basic Christian beliefs and the dilution of distinctive Christian moral and ethical standards.

Developments in European thought and practice have until recent years anticipated changes taking place in the United States. Christian thought has followed the lead of European theologians through much of U.S. history. However, the U.S. setting of Christianity provided a different social climate for its practice. Differences between U.S. and European Christianity have been present from the earliest colonial period. The state churches that existed in the colonial period gradually ceased to exist after the principle of separation of church and state was incorporated into the fabric of American life. Largely Protestant in its early history, U.S. Christianity epitomized the diversity of thought, structure, and practice that evolved during the Reformation. In the United States, the spirit of individualism and the sense of progressive change nurtured a climate in which new Christian denominations continually arose to meet personal, social, and theological needs. Such patterns continue to be a part of the American scene. Although the majority of Christians are found in the ten to fifteen largest denominations, 1988 figures showed at least 250 denominations with more than one or two congregations. If all of the single-congregation churches were added to these figures, the total would amount to several hundred denominations.

The United States has been broadly affected by the same intellectual and cultural changes that have wrought the modern transformation of Europe. American responses have sometimes paralleled those of Europe, but in the area of religion, the differences are obvious. Because religious groups in America are voluntary and aggressively recruit members, U.S. church participation has continued to be substantial. Over 68 percent of adult Americans claim some church affiliation. Public practice of religion remains relatively high despite slackening interest in recent decades. America's mainline denominations are large enough to include within themselves persons of many theological persuasions and practices. As a result, it has sometimes been said that conservatives of one denomination may be closer to conservatives of another denomination than to liberals of their own denomination. The same may be said of liberals. Large denominations tend to include persons of very diverse theological positions and many social and cultural backgrounds. Mainline denominations tend to offer pluralistic ministries to meet the needs of various groups. Smaller denominations are often more unified on theological and social positions and enforce stricter discipline among their members. They often reach elements of society who feel neglected by mainline groups.

While the changing intellectual and theological climate of the nineteenth and twentieth centuries was welcomed by many, especially in the United States, it was also resisted by conservatives in mainline denominations and smaller religious groups. These persons held to their views of biblical infallibility and rejected the optimistic views concerning human abilities taught by liberalism. Such attitudes were incorporated in various movements such as that revolving around the Moody Bible Institute in Chicago. *The Fundamentals,* a twelve-volume publication published privately from 1909 to 1915, stated the case against the innovations in religious teachings. The Five Fundamentals supported by this movement were the verbal inerrancy of Scripture, the deity of Jesus, the virgin birth, substitutionary atonement, and the physical resurrection and bodily return of Christ. While probably not everyone in the movement agreed entirely with the tenets stated in *The Fundamentals,* together they constituted a strong element of resistance to the changes in the churches to accommodate new ideas and trends within the society.

Emphases among conservatives have changed since the beginning of the century, but the general sentiment has remained strong. Often known now by the broad title "evangelicals" and incorporating a greater variety of interests than traditional fundamentalists, the movement has experienced substantial expansion in recent years. Seminaries representing the interests of the movement have become recognized and are generously supported. Radio and television evangelists have created a whole new phenomenon of electronic ministries cutting across traditional denominational lines with a conservative, Bible-centered message. Many have also sought to influence political and moral issues in the nation. Through support of scholarships and endowments, attempts have been made to influence the academic theological community, the traditional stronghold of liberal theological innovations. The liberal-conservative polarity, always present in American religion, does not appear to have lessened, though its forms continue to change.

CHANGE AND ITS EFFECTS

In order to better understand present-day Christianity, we now examine in more detail a few examples of the phenomenal changes that occurred in the late nineteenth and early twentieth centuries. Each of these not only reflects Christianity's responses to humanity's changing understanding of itself and its world but also how each helped mold present-day Christian issues and patterns.

The Bible and Its Interpretations

Innovations in the practical application of rational, objective knowledge to the physical world, which lay at the base of the Industrial Revolution, found their way into all other fields of inquiry during the eighteenth century. Accompanying the colonialism of the period was an intense interest in the flora and fauna of the colonies, observation of their social organizations, interest in their histories, and so on. The results were startling and occasionally demanded major changes in traditional perceptions of the world and the universe.

In the nineteenth century these patterns led to the rethinking of many accepted ideas concerning humanity, its social structures, and the universe itself. Charles Darwin's theory of evolution was based on his biological observations in the islands of the South Seas. His observations would have been impossible without the advances in transportation and scientific methodology of the previous century. Combined with the discoveries in the new fields of geology and archeology, Darwin's theories called for reconsideration of the usual ideas of creation, the age of the universe, and the development of life. Combined with these discoveries, developments in other fields such as history and literature meant an exhilarating outpouring of new information that remolded knowledge.

In Europe and, late in the century, in the United States, traditionally accepted religious understandings experienced the same type of intellectual scrutiny as was being applied to accepted concepts in other fields. Geological and evolutionary theories disturbed many Christians; these theories challenged the usual understanding of the dating of the universe and, in the eyes of many, failed to conform to biblical depictions of creation. Equally important, if less evident to most laypersons, was the work being done in Bible scholarship.

As early as the Renaissance period, scholars interested in antiquity turned their attention to biblical texts, seeking and analyzing their earliest forms. In the intervening centuries this work was extended and expanded; concern for the accuracy and antiquity of the biblical texts became the basis of new examinations and translations of Scripture. Literary criticism and analysis applied to literature of all fields now began to be used in examining Scripture. Historical information and the expanding methods of historical research were applied to biblical history. Archeological attention to the cultures of the biblical era remolded information concerning the religious traditions surrounding early Judaism and Christianity. The result was a wealth of innovative and challenging studies on Christian tradition and particularly on the Bible. One significant pattern of such study serves to illustrate how traditional concepts were changing by the beginning of the twentieth century.

Attention in the nineteenth century focused on the "historical" Jesus and consequently on the New Testament gospels that most explicitly portrayed his life and message. By the eighteenth century, one fundamental problem involved in using the gospels as historical sources had already been noticed by the great German dramatist, critic, controversialist, and scholar G. E. Lessing. The gospels were written years—the earliest possibly thirty to fifty years—after the events they record. They were written not to give biographical information about Jesus for posterity. Rather, the gospels were written to proclaim the early Christian community's (or church's) faith in and about Jesus, their belief that Jesus had come into the world representing God, and that he had come to bring redemption to humanity. The gospels were written to proclaim that Jesus was in some unique way the Son of God and the Savior of the world. Thus, instead of intending to give what a historian would consider biographical or historical information about Jesus, the gospels were written to express and interpret the early church's message about the Christ of its faith. Or as the author (or editors) of the Gospel of John wrote toward the end of that gospel:

> Now Jesus did many other signs in the presence of the disciples, which are not written in this book; but these are written that you may believe that Jesus is the Christ, the son of God, and that believing you may have life in his name.
>
> (JOHN 20:30–31 RSV)

Thus, New Testament scholars as early as the eighteenth century came to believe that the historical materials about Jesus recorded in the gospels had been subjected to arrangement and to theological interpretation in order to serve the church's primary purpose of winning people to the new faith and strengthening them in it. One of the major goals of much nineteenth-century study of the gospels was to strip away or delve beneath the ordering of gospel materials dictated by the church's religious purpose and theological interpretation in the hope of arriving at a solid core of historical data—an outline and explanation of the life of Jesus as it actually occurred and a summary of his teachings.

By the beginning of the twentieth century there had been a proliferation of scholarly and popular "lives of Jesus," many of which had attempted to separate the historical Jesus from the early church's proclamation and interpretation of him. During the first decade of the twentieth century a distinguished German biblical scholar, the many-sided genius (theologian, philosopher, and musician), Albert Schweitzer, wrote a critical study of the lives of Jesus that had appeared in the eighteenth and nineteenth centuries. This book was soon translated into English under the title *The Quest of the Historical Jesus.*[1] In general, Schweitzer argued that none of the lives of Jesus had succeeded in giving an accurate historical picture of Jesus because they had ignored or overlooked the most important background feature of first-century Judaism, its apocalyptic, eschatological beliefs and hopes. In Chapter One we saw that most of the Jewish religious groups and most Jews of the first century C.E. believed that the present age was under the rule of powers of evil. They looked forward to God's inaugurating the New Age, in which his will and kingdom would be established. The Greek term *eschaton* refers to the "last time" or "end time." *Eschatology* literally means "discourse about the last things" and is used, particularly in reference to Judaism and Christianity, to designate beliefs and teachings about the end time, the time of transition from the evil present age to the New Age that God will inaugurate. An *Apocalypse* (literally meaning "revelation") was a type of literary work very common in the times, which, often in highly symbolic form, professed to give information about the coming of the New Age and the defeat of the evil powers that controlled the present age. "Apocalyptic" refers to any message or view characterized by such eschatological themes.

Schweitzer argued that not only were the beliefs of first-century Judaism generally characterized by apocalyptic or eschatological hopes, so was the message of Jesus. Nineteenth-century European scholars, he thought, tended to regard apocalyptic thought as largely incomprehensible or irrelevant. They believed in continuous historical progress under the inspiration of scientific truth and humanitarian ideals. In writing their lives of Jesus, Schweitzer argued, they had left out Jesus' radical apocalypticism—his belief that the old age was soon to be directly overthrown by God with the establishment of a Messianic Kingdom. In doing so,

---

[1]Schweitzer's book appeared in two different German editions, with some changes of emphasis between first and second editions. These changes need not concern us. The important point for our study is the historical impact of Schweitzer's book.

they had made Jesus a nineteenth-century humanitarian. Some of them, critical of Christianity and ignorant of the all-pervasive apocalyptic background of first-century Judaism, had gone so far as to treat Jesus as a kind of madman suffering from various delusions.

Schweitzer's Jesus of history was, then, a radical apocalyptic preacher who had deliberately gone to his death on the cross with the purpose of provoking events that would lead to the coming of the New Age. According to Schweitzer, the New Age had not come as Jesus had thought it would. Therefore, twentieth-century Europeans could not hold the apocalyptic views that Jesus held—they could barely, if at all, understand them. What they could relate to was the radical commitment of Jesus to something, the transcendent claim of the idea of a Kingdom of God, to which Jesus' life had been dedicated. According to Schweitzer, in encountering the historical Jesus, twentieth-century people can find themselves called to a similar total commitment, even though the content of that commitment will be very different from the Kingdom of God envisaged in first-century Jewish apocalyptic thought. Acting on the results of his own inquiries, Schweitzer abandoned his theological professorship, spent several years qualifying for medical degrees, and devoted the rest of his long life to service as a medical missionary in Africa, committing himself to serve on the basis of Jesus' example.

The immediate impact of Schweitzer's work was very great. It was agreed that apocalyptic and eschatological themes dominated first-century Judaism and the message of Jesus. Even more profound was a further result that was not really intended by Schweitzer—namely, New Testament scholars became cautious, even sceptical, about using the gospels as sources of historical knowledge about Jesus. The quest of the historical Jesus was, by and large, abandoned. Schweitzer's historical Jesus seemed as much a figment of his creative imagination to some scholars as did the nineteenth-century portraits of Jesus he had criticized. Some even argued that it is impossible to go behind the "Christ of Faith" of the early church's proclamation to the historical Jesus at all. It was generally conceded that the gospels do not follow a chronology of the life of Jesus, do not allow us to discover exactly when or where his ministry began, how long it lasted, or what its basic phases were.

Modern study of Jesus and the gospels continues to struggle with the issues raised in this lively nineteenth- and early twentieth-century debate concerning the nature of the biblical story and its intent. No modern analysis could fail to deal with the issues and methods that emerged in this and other similar studies.

Personal Religion

Early nineteenth-century Americans who had achieved their independence through great struggle and personal sacrifice often believed in God's role in their good fortune but also reverenced their own capabilities and independence. In that setting a vibrant religion had to affirm both these realities. The Reformation insistence on religion as a personal commitment to God brought about through direct encounter with the Divine that freed one from anxiety while directly molding daily existence fit well in postrevolutionary America. It assumed God's Grace as the primary source of human ability; yet it allowed utter confidence in God-given human capabilities when they had the opportunity and freedom to function. While Protestantism thus seemed especially appropriate for America, it was, over the course of the century, to take on uniquely American forms.

   Charles Finney.   One of these new forms is expressed in the life and work of Charles Finney, the self-educated president of Oberlin College and a significant molder of American revivalism. Finney, born in Connecticut in 1792, was raised in western New York on the edge of the wilderness. According to his autobiography, the settlers in that part of the state had little exposure to religion. Finney received a "common school" education and as a young man taught school in Connecticut and New Jersey before returning to western New York in 1818. Here, while employed in the office of a local lawyer as a student, or apprentice, he became for the first time regularly involved with a settled religious community as he attended Bible study and services in the local Presbyterian church.
   Becoming an avid Bible student, Finney accepted the biblical message of faith but could not affirm a religious experience that gave him peace of soul and mind. Convinced that he had a personal need for "salvation of his soul," he, using the systematic fashion of his law training, set out to "make peace with God." The struggle was great and extended over some time, culminating in several days of intense prayer and personal encounter with God. First, he came to the conviction that he could not "achieve" the relationship.

> Just at this point the whole question of Gospel salvation opened to my mind in a manner most marvelous to me at the time.... Gospel salvation seemed to me to be an offer of something to be accepted: and that it was full and complete; and that all that was necessary on my part, was to get my own consent to give up my sins, and accept Christ. Salvation, it seemed to me, instead of being a thing wrought out, by my own works, was a thing to be found entirely in the Lord Jesus Christ, who presented himself before me as my God and Saviour.

Second, Finney was granted peace in his struggle when he simply accepted God's Grace. His experience culminated in a great sense of spiritual power.

> Without any expectation of it, without ever having the thought in my mind that there was any such thing for me, without any recollection that I had ever heard the thing mentioned by any person in the world, the Holy Spirit descended upon me in a manner that seemed to go through me, body and soul. I could feel the impression, like a wave of electricity, going through and through me. Indeed it seemed to come in waves and waves of liquid love; for I could not express it in any other way.[2]

   Now "converted," Finney was convinced that he should preach, or, as he told a friend he was to represent in court, "I have a retainer from the Lord Jesus Christ to plead his cause, and I cannot plead yours."[3] Finney felt for some time before his personal experience that, of the Christians with whom he studied and worshipped, few expected much of their faith: they prayed repeatedly for an "outpouring of Holy Spirit," a revival, but in fact did not expect it to happen to them. In his judgment, they did not pray in faith. Now from his own experience, he was confident that their difficulty was their failure to expect a personal encounter with God or any real change in their lives. He understood the call of his ministry to preach in such a manner as to bring persons to a lively and vital Christian life.

---

   [2]Charles G. Finney, *Memoirs of Rev. Charles G. Finney* (New York: Fleming Revell, 1876), pp. 14, 20.
   [3]Ibid., p. 24.

Abandoning his law practice, he began study for the ministry with the local Presbyterian preacher, even though he found that he disagreed with him on a number of doctrinal points. The most important was the pastor's insistence upon a limited atonement: the belief that God had determined to save only some persons and all others were lost. For Finney this did not express the gospel as he understood it from his study of Scripture. Although he could not accept this interpretation of atonement, he was ordained by the local presbytery and entered into a preaching career.

Finney's conviction that the faith could and should be a lively and transforming personal reality and his insistence that all persons were included in God's Grace meant that his preaching took a different pattern from the typical doctrinally oriented preaching of the neighborhood that stressed predestinarianism and doctrinal correctness. Before long his preaching became the center of a local revival of personal religious experiences, accompanied by manifestations of the Holy Spirit, healings, and morally reoriented lives. Regional recognition of his ministry was attained through a series of evangelical meetings in northern New York State. He became known for the "protracted meeting," using many of the patterns of frontier camp meetings in towns and cities; an "anxious bench" where kneeling sinners waited for a feeling of God's forgiveness, specific prayers for sinners, and so on. Perhaps as important, he applied the logic of his legal training to his work, insisting that revivals were not dependent upon miracle but on the "right use of constituted means": methodical preparation, a team approach using ministers and laypersons, and careful, systematic execution of the meetings. These methods led large numbers of people to dynamic religious experiences. No longer was it assumed that revivals or awakenings would occur only in an unanticipated outpouring of the Holy Spirit; revivals could be generated through proper planning, prayer, and careful execution. American practicality and ingenuity were being applied to religious meetings.

Incorporated in these meetings was Finney's theological understanding that human freedom meant that sin could be understood as a voluntary act. Holiness was consequently a human possibility, with God's attending Grace, and Finney ultimately embraced a concept of entire sanctification, or Christian perfection. Proclamation of the gospel was designed (1) to make sinners conscious of their sin, (2) to open them to the redemption offered in Jesus, (3) to bring about a conscious, active personal acceptance of this redemption, and (4) to facilitate their entrance into a holy, disciplined life. This theology and these patterns of ministry were taught by Finney when he became professor of theology and then president of Oberlin College in Ohio.

Charles Finney's experience and ministry epitomize several characteristics of nineteenth-century American Protestant religion. Religion, being voluntary, was entered into by personal choice. Significant and vital personal religious experience was to be expected and "conversion" became its symbol. The universality of Grace and freedom of human will to either accept or reject that Grace was assumed. Holiness and righteous living were to be expected of those professing Christian salvation and should distinctively characterize their lives among their neighbors. Central to the whole image was the idea that religion was practical. Revivals depended upon human preparation as well as the blessing of the spirit; scripturally based doctrine should also be reasonable and appealing (a limited atonement did not appear reasonable). Religious experience was expected to have public manifestations, first in conversion and then in changed and holy lives. As important as any other feature was the reality that these images and methods were not limited to one denominational community but by the turn of the twentieth century had become an attractive and expected pattern throughout American Protestantism.

By the close of the nineteenth century many other patterns of religion were also evident in the U.S. population. Roman Catholicism, rapidly expanding with the immigration of the mid- and late nineteenth century, offered other and more traditional European patterns of religious experience. It too, however, took new forms in this country as it assumed its place among other kinds of Christianity. Its adherents, in typical American fashion, sought more personal religious freedom and insisted on a larger share in church governance. America also proved to be a fertile ground for new religions and sects.

Christianity: A World Religion

From its inception, European colonialism served as a vehicle for the spread of Christianity. As priests and missionaries accompanied Columbus to the New World, they participated in other colonial plantations. Advances in the safety and extent of travel added to the interdependence of Europeans with their colonies so that they experienced a first-hand knowledge of the vast cultures of Africa, the Americas, and the Far East. Contact with these cultures included new knowledge of other religions and a growing concern to spread the gospel of Christ around the world. Jesuit and Franciscan missions of the sixteenth and seventeenth centuries were followed by Protestant missions in the eighteenth and nineteenth centuries. America's traditional interrelationship with Europe and its entrance into the world economy during the nineteenth century brought Americans into closer contact with other nations and fostered an interest in missions.

American Christianity was from its beginnings the child of European missions. The Franciscan missions to the Americas planted Christianity there at a very early date. Religious motivations, often based on a genuine sense of specific mission, were foundational in many of the later North American colonies. It was, however, after many years of maturation that American Christians became interested in missions outside their own local communities. Mission consciousness arose with the desire to include Native Americans in the faith, when the earliest missionary society was formed (1798) to evangelize the "heathens" and to ensure that new settlements on the frontier had an opportunity to embrace the faith.

Concern for foreign missions (those outside the United States) is often credited to a much storied "haystack" meeting in 1806 of several students of Williams College, a Congregational school in western Massachusetts. Taking refuge from a summer storm in a haystack, several of the students turned to a discussion of the need to evangelize those in foreign lands who had never heard the word of Christ. Enthusiasm was high, and when the storm was over, Samuel J. Mills, Jr., and others dedicated themselves to preach the gospel in foreign lands. The project was not forgotten; and by 1810, having completed seminary, they had been able to solicit sponsorship of the newly organized American Board of Commissioners for Foreign Missions. In 1812 the first two missionaries set sail for India to carry through the mission envisioned in the haystack. These were the first of thousands of missionaries to take up the task by the close of the century.

The first mission boards were made up of representatives from Congregational churches, but other denominations were quick to follow suit. Among Baptists and other congregationally structured churches, mission boards became significant channels of cooperation between local churches. Around these boards other unifying structures grew rapidly. Coordinating interests beyond the local level and depending upon the dedication of volunteers, often laypersons, these mission boards were precursors of a vast array of voluntary groups organized to pursue particular religious, moral, and political interests. They incorporated particularly American traits: the dependence of the community upon voluntary leadership, confidence that with enough committed persons working together as volunteers almost any goal could be accomplished, and a willingness to give of oneself and one's resources to benefit others. They were also the first groups to foster support of joint interests beyond denominational lines, anticipating important ecumenical interests.

Missionary interests continued to grow throughout the century. In the recovery after the Civil War, missions expanded in every denomination and became more ecumenical. By the close of the century, mission organizations were becoming aware that cooperative efforts across denominational lines were imperative in some mission fields and desirable in most. Volunteer student organizations such as the YMCA in England found quick acceptance in America and became quite strong. Missionary interests were the base of the YMCA organizations as they sought to minister to the large numbers of homeless and poor youth in industrialized cities. In 1888, inspired by the mission interests of Dwight L. Moody and others, the Student Volunteer Movement (SVM) was born. Its principal interests were missions, and thousands of U.S. college students responded to the call by dedicating themselves to missions of all types. John R. Mott's famous book title expressed the desire of the movement: *Evangelization of the World in This Generation.* American citizens' confidence in the future and in their own ability to accomplish the seemingly impossible could hardly be more eloquently stated than in this phrase, which became the motto for the SVM.

CATHOLICISM IN THE NEW AGE

European Roman Catholics (mostly in southern Europe) responded to the Reformation by eliminating many of the abuses objected to by Protestants. However, in defending themselves against some of the innovations of the Protestants, they tended to solidify the traditional teachings and patterns of the church. As a result, the authoritarian episcopal structure separating clergy and laity continued. Theological change was discouraged and the patterns of Christian life dependent on penance and the other sacraments remained in place. This conservative perspective unified the church, which retained a strong influence in the southern European countries. Recently, however, it has experienced increasing disaffection in some strata of society, especially the working classes and intellectuals influenced by modern ideologies such as socialism or anarchism. The changes in European culture detailed above were slower in coming to southern Europe, but did bring forms of modern political and economic change. The Roman church continued to be the state church in most countries, and religious freedom came for many only in the twentieth century.

An essentially conservative perspective made it increasingly difficult for the Roman church to cope with the realities of modern society. Recognizing this, important nineteenth- and twentieth-century leaders, including popes Leo XIII and Pius XI, called for greater social justice and addressed the needs of members of the working class uprooted by economic change and often barred from full participation in society. More recently, responding to the threat of nuclear war, the plight of the poor in the third world, and a need for greater Christian unity, Pope John XXIII called the Second Vatican Council in 1962. John not only invited the bishops of the Roman church but observers and representatives from other Christian communities. By this act he recognized the existence and relevance of other Christian groups—a fact Catholicism had been reluctant to acknowledge. The council took many steps to modify the Roman church. An expanded role was given to the bishops as counselors to the pope. The church was defined as a "pilgrim church" in which both clergy *and* laity have significant roles. Liturgy was allowed in vernacular languages, and modifications created new liturgical patterns. More conciliatory positions were pronounced relative to non-Christian religions, and there emerged a new openness toward ecumenical involvement with other Christian bodies and individuals. Emphasis on Scripture as a coordinate authority with tradition gave it a more central place in worship, private study, and devotion. Such changes in the tradition of the church brought modifications in attitude and practice that perhaps were unanticipated by the council and caused some Catholics to think that the pope and the council had gone too far.

Nevertheless, they clearly made the church more responsive to the needs of modern culture. Also, John XXIII addressed two masterful and revolutionary papal letters—encyclicals—to Catholics and, in the case of the second letter, to all persons of good will throughout the world. *Mater et Magistra* (1961), one of the most electrifying documents to come under a pope's signature, and the equally forceful *Pacem in Terris* (1963) called for worldwide efforts to eliminate human need, achieve social justice, and reverse the threat of war and possible nuclear destruction. Such efforts on behalf of peace, justice, and global understanding have been continued by Pope John's successors, Paul VI and John Paul II.

Although Roman Catholicism entered the Western Hemisphere with the Spanish missionaries and was one of the earliest U.S. religious groups, its strength came with nineteenth-century European migration into the country. In the United States, Catholicism served as a conservative force. It gave many immigrants a feeling of unity and continuity with their origins. In its new cultural setting, however, U.S. Catholicism became progressive, calling for change and modernization within the church. Though questioned by some conservatively oriented Catholics, Vatican II and its modifications have been welcomed by many Americans as a step toward making the church relevant to the times.

This chapter has selectively presented some of the significant changes that have occurred in Christianity over the past two centuries. Other historical incidents, patterns of thought, institutional structures, and examples of change might just as well have illustrated the intensely complex and yet exciting developments that serve as the foundations of modern Christianity. Chapter Nine discusses in further detail some of the issues raised in this chapter.

QUESTIONS

1. How did the eighteenth-century Enlightenment bring another shift in the concept of authority? What has been the effect of that shift?

2. In what ways does the modern setting of Christianity contribute to its diversity? Is this a threat to Christianity or one of its strengths? Explain.

3. What effects have the intellectual changes and scientific developments of the past two centuries had on Christianity in the West?

4. What distinctive characteristics of Protestant American religious experience are typified in the life and ministry of Charles Finney?

5. What do New Testament scholars mean by the term "the historical Jesus"? Explain why many New Testament scholars have made a distinction between the Jesus of history and the Christ of faith.

6. What role did missions play in late nineteenth-century Christianity? What technical and social developments contributed to an emphasis on missions in this period?

7. How has Roman Catholicism responded to the social and intellectual changes in Western culture in the past few centuries?

FURTHER READING

ABBOTT, WALTER, ed. *The Documents of Vatican II*. New York: Herder and Herder, 1966.

AHLSTROM, SYDNEY E. *A Religious History of the American People*. New Haven, Conn.: Yale University Press, 1972.

BORNKAMM, GUNTER. *Jesus of Nazareth*. New York: Harper & Brothers, 1960.

BULTMANN, RUDOLF. *Jesus and the Word*. New York: Charles Scribner's Sons, 1934.

DIBELIUS, MARTIN. *From Tradition to Gospel*. New York: Charles Scribner's Sons, 1965.

———. *Jesus*. Philadelphia: Westminster Press, 1949.

FINNEY, CHARLES G. *Memoirs of Rev. Charles G. Finney*. New York: Fleming Revell, 1876.

GRANT, FREDERICK C., trans. *Form Criticism*. Chicago: Willett, Clark & Company, 1934. A translation into English of Rudolf Bultmann, *The Study of the Synoptic Gospels,* and Karl Kundsin, Primitive Christianity in the Light of Gospel Research.

JEREMIAS, JOACHIM. Jerusalem in the Time of Jesus. Philadelphia: Fortress Press, 1968.

———. The Parables of Jesus. Rev. ed. New York: Charles Scribner's Sons, 1963.

———. The Prayers of Jesus. Philadelphia: Fortress Press, 1978.

NEILL, STEPHEN. A History of Christian Missions. Baltimore: Penguin Books, 1964.

———. Colonialism and Christian Missions. London: Lutterworth Press, 1966.

PERRIN, NORMAN. The Kingdom of God in the Teachings of Jesus. Philadelphia: Westminster Press, 1963.

———. Rediscovering the Teachings of Jesus. New York: Harper & Row, 1967.

———. What Is Redaction Criticism? Philadelphia: Fortress Press, 1969.

ROBINSON, JAMES M. A New Quest of the Historical Jesus. London: SCM Press, 1959.

SCHWEITZER, ALBERT.   Out of My Life and Thought. New York: Henry Holt, 1933.

————.   The Psychiatric Study of Jesus. Gloucester, Mass.: Peter Smith, 1975.

————.   The Quest of the Historical Jesus. New York: Macmillan, 1948.

SHULER, PHILIP L.   A Genre for the Gospels: The Biographical Character of Matthew. Philadelphia: Fortress Press, 1982.

WELCH, CLAUDE.   Protestant Thought in the Nineteenth Century. New Haven, Conn.: Yale University Press, 1972.

CHAPTER SIX

Christian Beliefs

Chapters Three, Four, and Five examined some of the great variety and diversity in the practice of Christianity during several crucial periods of its development. In the present chapter we characterize the basic and underlying unities of Christian belief. This is not an easy task. Some students of Christianity prefer not to speak about Christian belief as a whole but instead about the differing beliefs of various groups of Christians. Variety and diversity have been—and are—as much a feature of Christian belief as are variety of organizational (denominational, churchly, and sectarian) forms and patterns of worship. Differences in beliefs between Christians are seen not just in different historical periods and different Christian groups but in any single (past or present) historical period within the same group or organization. Certainly the reader should be aware that in the following pages, when the authors speak of what Christians believe, or of what a majority of Christians believe, such statements should always be qualified.

Some groups of Christians have held, or do hold, among beliefs they share with many other Christians, beliefs unique to themselves that seem strange to others. Differences of belief will be found even among articles of faith that most representatives of mainline streams (Eastern Orthodox, Catholic, Protestant) of Christianity substantially agree on. Others both within and outside these mainline groups differ in various ways. Even the same belief—for example, the belief in God as Trinity— may seem different among Christian groups, all of whom affirm it, because of their differing contexts or frameworks that involve other beliefs or emphases. The same can be said about any of the world's major religions such as Islam, Buddhism, or Hinduism.

Instead of saying that many Christians believe, and have believed, many things and do not always agree with each other, it is important to see that there is, for Christians, what Kenneth Boulding has called an "image," a basic picture or representation that includes ways Christians typically feel about themselves and others, the world, reality, and truth; how they think about other things; and what they believe. It may well be that in other connections it is important to concentrate on the historical and present differences of belief and practice among Christians. In this chapter we attempt to find an underlying unity by which other unities and differences, as well as possible similarities, among Christians and between Christianity and other religions of the world, can be assessed.

Having said this, we do not mean that no differences in Christian beliefs will be discussed in the following pages. Students of Christian beliefs sometimes distinguish between Christian *dogma* and Christian *theology*. A dogma is a basic belief, usually something that can be expressed in very brief form, such as the Christian belief that God is omniscient and omnipotent (perfectly wise or knowing and all-powerful). Theology attempts to interpret dogma—that is, to explain what it means to say that God is both all-wise and all-powerful—and how that belief can be understood in the context of other Christian beliefs, such as the belief that God is perfectly good and loving. Even within Christian groups where there has been almost complete agreement on dogma, there has often been diversity in theological interpretation. This diversity has sometimes been regretted, but often it has been encouraged and valued. Consequently, even as we discuss those beliefs that unify Christians it will be necessary to note significant differences.

In the following, each section will deal with one or more aspects of Christian dogma. Dogma often raises serious questions that have seemed to many Christians to require theological interpretation. Where such questions have arisen concerning some article of Christian dogma, we will usually indicate a variety of theological interpretations that have been advanced to interpret the Christian belief in question. In this chapter we are interested in presenting what we consider to be the essential unity of Christian beliefs, held in some form by the majority of Christians, as well as some of the varying approaches by different groups of Christians to understand these beliefs theologically. Technically, the term theology refers to the branch of human knowledge that is about God. The term has come to mean that activity of human inquiry that tries to *understand* Christian beliefs—that is, to understand what the beliefs mean and how they can be held to be appropriate and true.

GOD

For *polytheistic* religions there are many gods, and the gods belong to the universe of other beings, including humans and animals. The gods are usually more powerful and more mysterious than other beings. They may even be called immortal, though usually there are stories concerning the origin or birth of various gods. Some gods may even die. Their lives and activities are much like those of humans—they fall in love, become angry with one another, show good will or enmity to humankind. The gods of traditional Japanese religions, the Holy People of North American Indian lore, and the Olympians of classical Greek mythology and cult are examples of this-world gods who are individuals with relatively well-defined personal characteristics within the larger totality of things.

In *pantheistic* religions and philosophies, on the other hand, as in some forms of Hinduism and Chinese Taoism, the Divine is not ultimately individual or personal at all. The Hindu Brahman is a being without *any* characteristics. It is the *one* reality "without a second," without anything else beside it. Brahman is beyond or beneath what we take to be the realities of our experience (which are *not* realities but illusions, unreal or imaginary shadows that derive from and conceal the only true reality). Even the gods of Hindu myth and cultic devotion—the compassionate Vishnu, the dynamic Shiva, the implacable Kali—are only appearances, images, shadows of the one Brahman.

For *deistic* forms of theism—for example, the Islamic religion and eighteenth-century Christian deism—there is an eternal God who created the universe, but stands radically above and (in eighteenth-century European deism, but not in Islam) apart from this creation. In such religions, God is conceived as having only perfect attributes and none of the more human (or anthropomorphic) qualities that the polytheistic deities possess.

In Judaism and Christianity God is conceived of in a strikingly different way from any of these other traditions. God is conceived of, as is Allah of Islam, as being the eternal creator who transcends his creation. Like the gods of Islam or Christian deism, the God of Judaism and Christianity possesses only positive attributes in his perfection. He is also conceived of as being active within the world he has created (the God of Islamic tradition is also conceived of in this way). Finally, however, he is held to have made himself fully present, to have revealed himself, in a decisive sense, completely and perfectly at some point in the created realm. For Judaism, God has embodied his wisdom in the Torah.[1] Christians speak of God as having become incarnate in the world in a human life, in a man named Jesus who lived in first-century Palestine. Christians also believe that after the actual historical period during which Jesus lived in Palestine, having been raised from the dead, he continued and continues to manifest the divine presence, to *be* God Incarnate. They believe that after the Resurrection of Jesus, God's immanent activity in the world, which had in Jewish tradition been referred to as the activity of the Spirit of God, began to be manifested in new ways within the lives of followers of Jesus. It was also manifested by means of the practices, procedures, and traditions of the community—the Christian church—which had come into being to be an extension of the presence and work of the Incarnate God. Thus, of all the major Christian doctrines, that of the Incarnation seems central to the uniqueness of the Christian proclamation. In other religious traditions—for instance, Hinduism and Greek mythology—gods frequently take on, for a time, human form. What Christians have affirmed about the Incarnation of God in Jesus Christ involves a radically different kind of claim.

Certainly some Christians have had differing beliefs about the relation of God to the man Jesus. Some of these will be discussed in this section and also in Chapter Nine. However, it must be affirmed that the majority of Christians of the past and present have professed belief in one God who both transcends the universe that he has created and who sustains it, is immanent in it, who became and remains Incarnate in a series of specific events, and who, by having taken on human nature as the man Jesus, belongs to it.

---

[1]Whether Judaism should be described as incarnational in outlook may be subject to debate. Certainly it is not the intent of the authors to impose an incarnational view like that of Christianity onto Judaism. However, the analogy of the Torah as in some very important sense containing—with inexhaustible depth and richness—or *being* an embodiment of God's wisdom seems importantly analogous to Christianity's understanding of the incarnation of the divine wisdom in the man Jesus. A reviewer of *Exploring Christianity* suggests that the same point should be made concerning Islam's concept of the self-revelation of Allah in the Koran.

The Doctrine of the Trinity

In the early centuries of Christian history there was much controversy about the attempt to interpret what God must be like if all of the things said of him are true. What has come to be called the doctrine of the Trinity emerged during the first 400 years of Christian history as attempts were made to define the limits of what can and should be said about God if his oneness, transcendence, immanence, and incarnateness are to be related without misrepresenting or neglecting any of the four of these attributes. According to orthodox Christian doctrine, God is in essence and nature one, but within his oneness there are three real aspects, or persons. The Greek and Latin terms that were translated by the English term "person" as used in the ancient doctrinal formulations do *not* suggest three separate beings. Our word "aspects," or even "dimensions," possibly conveys more of what was meant than our present use of the term persons. The three aspects (or persons) within the one eternal God were called God the Father, God the Son, and God the Holy Spirit. In orthodox theology, God the Father is associated with that eternal and uncreated source of potency and power, the root of all being. God the Son (or Word or Logos) is associated with the eternal tendency within God to express himself, to create. God the Spirit is associated with the eternal connectedness between these two, the relationship between God as uncreated power and God as creative actuality. Traditionally the attributes of power, wisdom, and love are associated with the three persons of the Trinity, though it is quickly pointed out that these attributes are not separable. That is, God the Father is not just powerful but wise and loving as well; God the Son is not just wise but loving and powerful as well.

Two points about the orthodox concept of the Trinity are important to emphasize. Here the term "orthodox" does not refer exclusively to the Eastern Orthodox Christian tradition but to those Christians who have held theological views agreed on by what we have called mainstream Christianity. First, orthodox theology insists that the distinctions between Father, Son, and Spirit are the *only* real distinctions within God. We may suggest other distinctions, as between his justice and his love, but in fact, his justice *is* his love and vice versa. All his attributes are inseparable. Second, orthodox theologians (e.g., Augustine) insisted that, looked at from the outside, it would be impossible to say that anything we ascribe to God (e.g., creation or redemption) was done by *one* person of the Trinity. God the Trinity always acts as one. The whole of God the Trinity creates, redeems, and so on. To speak of different persons of the Trinity is in effect to emphasize different aspects or dimensions of God's action and being.

Both in the ancient church and in modern times some Christians have strenuously objected to what came to be the accepted, or orthodox, doctrine of the Trinity. Some rejected it outright as a form of polytheism. In modern times the suspicion of an overt or concealed polytheism within trinitarianism was one of the concerns of seventeenth-, eighteenth-, and nineteenth-century Unitarians. Some Unitarians thought of Jesus as being a specially God-inspired man but were unwilling to say that God himself, as the second person of the Trinity, the Divine Logos, or Son of God, had become incarnate in Jesus. In other words, they were willing to call Jesus *a* (or *the*) Son of God, but were not willing to say that the eternal God—that is, God the Eternal Son, or Word—had become and remained incarnate in Jesus.

Others throughout Christian history have *affirmed* a trinitarian theology that was judged inadequate by adherents of the orthodox point of view. Although there are numerous examples of such positions, two major trinitarian views are worthy of special mention. These approaches are sometimes characterized as being either *tritheistic* or *modalistic*. Sometimes they overlap, though they conflict in an important way.

Tritheism. A *tritheistic* approach to the Trinity treats the different aspects of God as three separate, or substantially distinct, individuals. One such school of thought was Arianism. According to Arianism, named for its advocate Arius (250–336 C.E.), Jesus Christ was the first of created beings, a divine being created by, but in some sense distinct from, God. Jesus became an intermediary between the eternal God and the rest of his creation. Arianism was condemned as heretical by the Council of Nicaea in 325 C.E. The phrase in the Nicene Creed, asserting that God the Son "was begotten not made," is a specific repudiation of Arius' views. However, Arianism continued for some time to be a significant rival to the orthodox concept of the relation of God the Father to the Son of God. Today's Jehovah's Witnesses hold a view of the relation of God the Father to Jesus Christ similar to the Arian view. (In a truly tritheistic view the Holy Spirit would be a third divine being, distinct from Father and Son. The center of trinitarian controversy seems to have been the relation of the first to the second person of the Trinity; consequently, the heresies were frequently ditheistic rather than tritheistic.)

Monarchianism, subordinationism, and Sabellianism. The dominant ideas of most tritheistic or ditheistic positions are developed as *monarchianism*—seeing God the Father as the supreme God above the other aspects of the divine nature. The others are conceived of as separate individuals dependent on the Father, who is not dependent on them. *Subordinationism* is a related position that subordinates the Son to the Father and (perhaps) the Spirit to the Son and Father. *Sabellianism* (condemned by the Council of Constantinople in 381 C.E.) was a view that can be characterized as monarchian and subordinationist. In some ways Sabellianism also exemplifies modalism, the other major type of trinitarian heresy.

Modalism. The second major family of heretical positions concerning the Trinity is *modalism*. There are many forms of modalism. For each form, the three aspects of God are seen as not being real distinctions *within* God. For one form of modalism, of which there have been several varieties, there are three successive ways in which God manifests himself in human history. There is the epoch of God the Father, the Creator, and Lawgiver—God as described in the Old Testament. Then there is the Age of the Son, God the Redeemer—the period of the redemptive activity of Jesus Christ described in the gospels. Finally, there is the Age of the Spirit, either inaugurated at Pentecost or at some later point in church history—or just about to be initiated. This is an age in which increasingly the presence and gifts of God are, or will be, made available to believers.

The other major form of modalism has had, as its basis, the belief that in himself God does *not* contain three distinct dimensions or aspects of being, but that the three persons of the Trinity are only concepts by means of which we humans apprehend the various ways in which God appears to us. These varieties of modalism say, then, that the doctrine of the Trinity describes God as he appears to us, or as we think of him, not as he is in himself.

Against both of these positions, the orthodox understanding of God as Trinity insisted that there are three genuine aspects, functions, or dimensions of the true God, mutually interrelated and each always present to the others and involved in all that God does. Thus, God was held by orthodox Christians to be capable of, and to have, genuine community within unity; God is not a solitary individual or isolated ego, substance, or self. To say that the divine being glorifies or enjoys or communicates with himself does not depict God as being either a cosmic narcissist or a collection of independent, separable individuals. We will see later that this way of speaking about God had very great significance for the way in which Christians answered questions concerning who Jesus is and how Jesus, the man from Nazareth, was and is related to God.

Male and female aspects of God. As will be discussed later in Chapter Seven, there always has been much discussion among Christian thinkers about the appropriateness of using finite, or human, language attributes to characterize God. A closely related issue has recently generated controversy. This is the traditionally accepted use of masculine pronouns to refer to God. It cannot be denied that traditional Hebrew thought about God often seems highly patriarchal. But feminine and female aspects were also ascribed to God in Hebrew thought and in the Jewish Scriptures. For example, the scriptural word for "wisdom" in the phrase "wisdom of God" is feminine (see Chapter Seven). Christian Scripture, Christian theological thought, and popular Christian religious language have almost overwhelmingly characterized God, whether in reference to the one divine being or to the three persons of the Trinity, in masculine terms. However, Christian theological thought about God at its most literal has affirmed that (1) God is neither male nor female; (2) God is the source of maleness and femaleness in the created world; (3) God can appropriately be characterized symbolically as being both male and female; and (4) God transcends the distinctions between male and female, masculinity and femininity. How best to speak of God from Christian points of view is one of the major issues of our time (see chapters Seven and Nine). There is some tendency now to guard against sexist practices by speaking of God always as having both male and female characteristics, using both or neither forms of the pronoun. Alternatively, there seem to be tendencies to drop sexual language entirely when speaking of God.

To sum up: Christians believe in a God who is one and eternal, whose goodness and being are perfect and inexhaustible—the source and creator of all that exists. According to Christians, God's goodness and being *are* inexhaustible. Therefore, humans are not capable of complete or adequate definition, description, or comprehension of them. Nevertheless, adequate evidence of God's nature—God's inexhaustible and eternal power, wisdom, and love—is present both in the world God has created (Romans 1:19–21) and in the divine self-disclosure in the life, death and Resurrection of Jesus Christ (John 1:18). All that has ever existed or that will exist has its source in, and is dependent on, God. Yet not any or all of what has existed or will exist can exhaust God's being or power. All that has existed or will exist is made through God's wisdom, yet God's wisdom infinitely transcends all finite reality. God's very nature—the meaning and motive of God's power and wisdom—is love (I John 4:8). This love is without limit (Hosea 11:9).

THE CREATED WORLD

For Hinduism, the natural universe is an illusion. For a religion like the Manichae-ism that St. Augustine embraced before becoming a Christian, the material world, the realm of natural process, is evil—a prison in which the spiritual part of the human soul is imprisoned, longing to be released to the pure spiritual realm beyond the physical universe. In contrast, Christians believe that God has created the universe from God's power, through God's wisdom, by and for God's love (Genesis 1:2–2:3; Proverbs 8:1, 22–31; John 1:1–5). The created world is therefore good (Genesis 1:31), made to achieve and manifest natural perfection in accordance with the potentialities of its created nature. Thus the created universe and all things in it were created in order to share in and manifest God's goodness, love, power, and wisdom. One of the classical confessional statements of Reformed Christianity, the Westminster Shorter Catechism, in answer to the question: "What is man's chief end?" replies "Man's chief end is to glorify God and to enjoy Him forever." In an analogical sense, traditional Christianity has affirmed that this answer might be extended to characterize the purpose and destiny of each thing and of the totality of created things.

EVIL

The Christian affirmation of the goodness of the created world has been the occasion of profound questioning about the origin and purpose of evil in the created world. For religions like Hinduism and Buddhism, evil is ultimately unreal. In Manichae-ism and Zoroastrianism, evil was explained as the result of the activity of a power or principle independent of, and antagonistic to, the good god. For Christianity, nothing exists that is not in some sense created by or dependent on God. This is expressed in the statement that, according to Christianity, God creates *ex nihilo* (from nothing). Also, Christianity affirms that the contrast between good and evil and the existence of evil are not illusory (as Hinduism affirms) and are not (as Buddhism teaches) simply the manifestation of our own imperfect way of looking at things. Rather, evil is a distorted and tragic actualization of good natural capacities and spiritual powers within the universe that God has created. These, as created by God, were and are good and were intended to be used to bring about further good. As misused to produce a distorted goodness, these natural capacities have themselves become distorted and evil.

The existence of evil has been one of the largest stumbling blocks to Christian belief. Two of the most vocal twentieth-century critics of the Christian theistic position, the philosophers Bertrand Russell and Antony Flew, though criticizing all of the traditional arguments given by Christians for believing in God, found the existence of evil the most telling objection to Christian claims that a good, wise, powerful, and loving God created the universe we inhabit. Flew challenged Christians to witness the agonized death from cancer of the throat of a small child while continuing to affirm the reality or goodness of God.

Natural and Moral Evil

Traditionally, at least two kinds of evil have been identified as requiring explanation if the Christian concept of the goodness of God and the creation is to be maintained: natural and moral evil. *Natural evil* refers to calamities and occasions of suffering that befall people and other sentient beings. To many observers or participants, such injury and pain seem disproportionate to any possible good that could result from the events involving them, and the events cannot be explained as resulting from the intentions of intelligent finite beings. Natural evil includes such things as earthquakes, tornadoes, and diseases that cannot be prevented. Why would God have created a universe in which such things happen? If he is all-powerful he presumably could have created a world in which they would not occur. *Moral evil* refers to evil that is deliberately done by, or results from, the actions of rational creatures. It includes crimes, acts of aggression, and acts of injustice or unkindness that cause suffering in others. Why would God endow rational beings with the possibility of having evil intentions, of committing evil actions, of harming themselves and others if God presumably could have created a world in which everyone would always, freely or under compulsion, choose to do good?

A traditional Christian answer to the question of the existence of natural evil has been that the whole created universe and not just its human part has been involved in a catastrophe of cosmic significance—namely, the fall from created goodness known as sin. Paul, in his Letter to the Romans (8:19–23), asserts that the whole creation is longing for its deliverance from bondage to the futility that has befallen it. So even the answer to the question of natural evil would depend on the answers that Christians give to questions about moral evil.

A more recent answer given by, among others, Christian process philosophers and theologians, does not necessarily make sin, or a corruption of nature, the cause of natural evil.[2] In the freedom of the natural order, natural evil is not controlled or willed by God, they assert. The process position maintains genuine freedom at every level of the finite world, though rational and conscious creatures are capable of exercising freedom deliberately and more consistently than those that do not possess conscious rationality. The difference is one of degree. A character in a novel by Aldous Huxley once suggested that rattlesnakes represent a species that long ago went wrong by choosing (however unconsciously) to become predators and to meet the dangers of their environment by secreting and injecting venom. This view would seem to exemplify the process position, giving one form of natural evil at least a partly moral dimension. However, such things as tornadoes would not be examples of moral evil. On the process view, however, they would not result from God's will or God's intention, but simply from the interaction of natural events.

Sin

Traditionally, Christianity has affirmed that humankind was originally good and endowed with the freedom, as a part of its created goodness, to choose between good and evil in achieving self-actualization. Choosing good would lead to genuine fulfillment for the human self and humankind. Choosing evil would lead to negation, frustration, and suffering. A critic like Antony Flew has asked why being

---

[2]*Process philosophy* and *process theology* are terms frequently used to describe the views of thinkers influenced by concepts of the British philosopher Alfred North Whitehead (1861–1947) and of his American interpreter Charles Hartshorne. God is basic to Whitehead's thought, having both eternal and temporal aspects. According to Whitehead, God always is active to bring about the highest possible realization of value in any given situation, but finite realities down to the lowest levels of existence (e.g., subatomic particles) possess genuine degrees of freedom. Thus God influences but does not totally determine or control events.

able to choose what is evil and destructive should be part of a created goodness. The Christian response generally has been that the highest forms of value and fulfillment are to be found in the actualization of individual personality or character and of interpersonal relations involving and expressing love and community. Such actualization entails learning to prefer and affirm the good when there is a genuine possibility that it will not be chosen, and learning to put the welfare of others and of the group ahead of limited selfish interests. Christians have argued that if the highest good an individual can attain is to become a person who freely gives love to God and to fellow human beings, this good can become actual only in genuine choice. Thus, a being who would be good "automatically" would not be good at all. Also, unless persons are vulnerable to injury, pain, and suffering as possible consequences of choice, choice would have no meaning. Everything would be equally good. Thus the *necessity* that natural evil be possible seems implied in the possibility of moral evil, and the *necessity* that moral evil be possible seems implied in the possibility of good.

In the Genesis story of the fall of Adam and Eve (Genesis 2–3), Adam and Eve were given a large degree of free choice about what they *might* do, but were told by God what they *should not* do—they were told not to eat the fruit of one of the trees in the garden they inhabited. Nevertheless, they were not compelled not to eat this fruit—they were not compelled to obey God. In choosing to disobey, they forfeited their original innocence.

It will be noted in Chapter Seven that some Christians have interpreted the narratives of the first few chapters of Genesis literally as describing the events that took place at the creation of the universe, including the parents or ancestors of the human race. Other Christians have understood the stories of creation and the fall to be mythical and symbolic, but nevertheless to reveal important spiritual truths.

The Doctrine of Original Sin. Within the ancient church, interpreters like Origen, St. Augustine, and others treated these stories as containing a large number of symbolic elements. In the modern period, a number of Christians who have understood the Genesis account of Adam and Eve not as literally or historically true have found it of decisive importance in revealing the nature and reality of sinfulness as a common human condition. According to this understanding, sin—Original Sin—is an attitude shared by humans that manifests itself in destructive acts, frequently even in acts that appear to be constructive but are not, since their motivation is distorted by sinful selfishness. In interpreting the Genesis story as an account of Original Sin, the twentieth-century Protestant theologian Reinhold Niebuhr argued that the story does not really intend to tell us about the origin of sin, but about its presence and pervasive power in all humans. Niebuhr was particularly impressed with the human tendency to do apparently unselfish and altruistic deeds that really manifest individual or group selfishness. Thus for Niebuhr, Adam and Eve, rather than being historical individuals, are symbols representing all humanity.

According to traditional Christian concepts of Original Sin, whether or not the Genesis story is interpreted literally, human beings have lost the power to choose good, even though humanity retains moral freedom. External actions and conscious attitudes have been corrupted by a deep preconscious or unconscious selfishness. Original freedom is understood by Christians to mean that humans are created in God's image (Genesis 1:26–30). But original freedom involves the power of humans to separate themselves from God, the source of their lives (and of all life), to separate themselves from their own creative, fulfilling possibilities and from right relation to themselves and other created beings. Christians by and large have affirmed that there was (is) no need for human beings to misuse their freedom and alienate themselves from God, self, other humans and other finite beings. But *exactly this* has happened. The state of separation, of self-destructive estrangement, is real. One aspect of the meaning of Original Sin is the claim that once this estrangement has taken place—once sin has entered human history—there is no way that humankind can recover its lost health, wholeness, or innocence by its own efforts. Based on literal readings of parts of the Genesis account, some of the early church fathers (including Augustine) characterized sin as biologically inherited from Adam and Eve. Some recent Christian thinkers, influenced by contemporary developmental psychologists including Sullivan, Erikson, Fairbairn, or Winnicott, have spoken of the spread of an original attitude of anxiety or mistrust from parent to child by a kind of psychological contagion. Thus, whether the Genesis account is interpreted as literal or as symbolic, Christians who affirm the reality of Original Sin see humanity's fallen state as something with contagious power that has affected all humanity since the beginning of human history.

Predestinarianism. A number of controversial points emerged in Christian theological debates related to the concepts of the fall and Original Sin. Two will be mentioned here. First, if God foreknew humankind would fall, did this mean that humans were never really free? Nothing that is not in some sense already determined can be foreknown. Some Christians, called *predestinarians* (including Augustine), argued that a thing can be foreknown without foreknowledge being its cause. They also argued that sin by fallen humans involves freedom, though fallen humans are not free not to sin. In sinning, humans do what they will. Therefore, they are responsible, even though they could not will to do otherwise. Thus, for Augustine and other predestinarians like Luther and Calvin, God's foreknowledge did not predetermine human sin, but in some sense sin was predetermined or predestined by another aspect of God—his will. Yet though they are predestined to sin, humans nevertheless sin freely, since they follow their own wills in sinning.

Some Christian thinkers, especially contemporary process thinkers, have insisted (in contrast to predestinarian thought) on a radical dimension of freedom in the created world possessed not just by humans but by other finite beings. Thus, for them God does not entirely foreknow the future, much less predetermine it. This, such thinkers have argued, is the only way to affirm a future in which *genuine* freedom can operate.

The majority of Christian thinkers, however, do not accept the extreme predestinarian view of Augustine and the early Protestants. They also do not accept the limited God of process theology. Instead, they have affirmed three beliefs. First, God foreknows the future, but since God's relation to time is not like ours, his foreknowledge does not *determine* future events. Rather, all of our time is eternally present to God. Second, God's providential will does have a determinative effect on what we call future events. This does not nullify but takes account of and makes use of human freedom. Third, all humanity suffers from fallenness and is thus incapable by its own efforts of arriving at goodness. Nevertheless, because of their freedom, humans are responsible for their sinful condition and for their misuse of freedom, which in its fallen state is used to nullify itself.

Pelagianism. A second major controversy related to the doctrine of Original Sin concerns *Pelagianism,* a view espoused by the British monk Pelagius and opposed by Augustine. Pelagius taught that Christ merely assists humans to exercise their innate capacity of free choice, a capacity never fully lost. Thus, each human is capable of exercising freedom to obey or disobey God's commandments.

Augustine opposed this view. Though Christ has made it possible for the guilt of Original Sin to be removed by baptism (or in exceptional cases in other ways), humans are still subject to sin's power; and the final removal of the power of Original Sin is the culmination, rather than the precondition, of the Christian life. According to Augustine and many of the founders and heroic figures of Christian monasticism who influenced him, the Christian life is a pilgrimage largely undertaken to overcome the residue of Original Sin within the Christian. It is through God's Grace at every step of this pilgrimage that the process of transformation will be brought to its completion. Augustine coupled his view of the effects of Original Sin with a rigid predestinarianism, according to which it is completely God's Grace that determines who will and who will not be brought to salvation.

Western Catholic Christianity condemned Pelagianism but did not entirely agree with Augustine. Thomas Aquinas and Western Catholicism generally made room for genuine human cooperation with God's Grace, though that cooperation is made possible through Grace. Early Lutherans and Calvinists tended to follow Augustine's predestinarianism, admitting that predestination and salvation are mysteries of God's Grace that humans cannot entirely grasp. Most recent Protestants have moved to a position indistinguishable from that of Catholicism. Indeed, it is sometimes taken to be an essential part of the Christian understanding of human nature to insist on a degree of genuine freedom in moral choice, in contrast to the determinist views of many secular psychological movements.

The Devil and the Demonic

The New Testament speaks of demonic powers or beings to whom, before the coming and work of Christ, the world had fallen prey. It refers to Beelzebul, or Satan, presumably the lord of the powers of evil. To many Jews and to the Christian author of the New Testament Book of Revelation, the Roman Empire was not merely an evil human organization, it was a supreme manifestation and tool of the demonic kingdom.

Such thought was characteristic of first-century Judaism, though not of the Judaism of earlier Old Testament periods. There is an intelligent being called Satan in the Old Testament Book of Job. *This* Satan is not demonic or evil, but is one of God's servants. Beliefs about the demonic held in Judaism apparently were largely a result of contact with Babylonian and Persian (Iranian) religious thought. By the time of Jesus, such beliefs were widespread. However, the New Testament writers tend to presuppose rather than to expound such beliefs.

Many recent Christians have seen Satan and the other demonic beings as *symbolic personifications* of the evil encountered in human life. But others reject such beliefs as myths that explain away human responsibility for the evil that is perpetrated in human interaction ("The devil made me do it"). Others have seen demonic figures as valuable symbolic expressions of the transhuman causes and consequences of alienation from God, as natural powers perverted or distorted from the creative roles they might have played, as symbolic representation of real though not individual forces or events. Some have found them to be valuable symbolic expressions of the power that evil assumes in corporate human life (as in Nazism or Communism) or in impersonal human organizations (like economic or political institutions) that can oppress people. Thus, the symbols would be valuable corrections of the belief that only *individual* humans can do evil.

Probably the great majority of Christians, however, have understood the devils to refer, literally, to spiritual beings, independent of humanity, that originally were good but through misuse of freedom are now corrupt and destructive. These corrupt beings have been seen not as wholly responsible for the corruption of human goodness, but as contributors to it. The demonic powers have been seen as parasitical on both God's goodness and human freedom.

Christian theological thought that accepts the demonic's literal truth would caution against taking the *human* ways of picturing these forces—the devil and demons—as being accurate representations. Orthodox theologians who take the concept of the devil literally caution that to depict the devil anthropomorphically with sublime grandeur, as in Milton's *Paradise Lost,* or crudely, as in comic strips, is as misleading as the anthropomorphic depictions of God (however valid from an artistic point of view) in Michaelangelo's or William Blake's visual representations of the Divine as a handsome, elderly man. Karl Barth has written a propos of the petition in the prayer that Jesus taught his disciples (see Luke 11:2–4 and Matthew 6:9–13), "Deliver us from the Evil One:"

> In the sixth petition of the Lord's prayer we are not concerned with…minor temptations, which are…relative and bearable.…It is rather a question of the infinite menace of the nothingness that is opposed to God himself.…Our Reformers, Luther as well as Calvin, were acquainted not only with the small temptations but also with the great one. They knew it was with the Devil that they had to deal. For him they had no respect, since he is not respectable. But they knew that he exists.…We perceive and feel his power. To tell the truth, it is only a pseudo power. It is not a real power. The terrible thing about it is that it acts, although this action is unreal.[3]

Thus, even Christians who believe that the devil and the demonic are to be taken as literal concepts warn against taking literally the images and representations humans have used to depict them. They would warn that if evil is truly a disintegrative force, then, rather than being the suave and sophisticated playboy of film and fiction, the devil is simply a boiling ocean of discontent.

This view of the demonic powers, whether taken as literal or symbolic, is entirely consonant with Augustine's understanding, which has largely been accepted by Christian tradition, of evil as not a positive force or power but as absence of, or distance from, the Good (God). Sin is a spiritual being's turning from the true object of its love (God) to a false or (relatively) unreal object. Thus Augustine's view explains both natural and moral evil. Christians making use of the concept of the demonic, either as a literal or a symbolic truth, would also point to the claim, as Mark's gospel shows clearly but elliptically at its beginning, that the powers of evil have in principle and in fact been broken by the redemptive activity of God in Jesus Christ (Mark 1:12–15). Mark's gospel also suggests in a later passage that with the coming of the Messiah and the advent of the Kingdom of God, humans do

[3]Karl Barth, *Prayer According to the Catechisms of the Reformation* (Philadelphia: Westminster Press, 1952), pp. 72–74.

not need to be concerned about the powers of evil external to them as sources of danger. They are to be concerned about the possibilities of evil within their own hearts. This is where the Messiah is to wage his ultimate battle and where his followers must wage theirs (Mark 9:9–13).[4]

The Forms of Estrangement

According to Christian belief, then, freedom is an aspect of the destiny of created spiritual beings. This is part of what it means to say that they are created through God's wisdom and for God's love: They share God's nature and reflect God's creative freedom. But with freedom, created beings possess the power to turn against their created goodness. They have the power to separate themselves from the source of all life, to separate themselves from their creative possibilities and from right (fulfilling, good) relationships to other created beings. God creates free beings. There was and is no need that created beings use their freedom to alienate themselves from God, from self, from other finite beings. Yet Christians believe that freedom actually is, has been, and was misused (I Corinthians 15:21–22; Genesis 3:1–7, 4:3–7; Romans 1:18–32, 5:12–14; James 1:13–15). Christians believe that self-destructive alienation from God, self, and neighbor actually has entered the world, and that, having entered the world, it spreads by a kind of contagion to finite beings before they are able consciously to take precautions against it. Thus, Christians believe that all human beings, when they come to mature self-awareness (Romans 7:15; Luke 15:17), find that they are cut off from God, from right relation to themselves, their fellow humans, and the whole created universe, by a self-rejecting/self-affirming attitude that denies God, neighbor, and self.

Christians have identified two major forms of this self-destructive attitude called sin: willfulness and self-indulgence. In older Christian writings these were often referred to as pride and sloth. Willfulness is the insistence on having one's way even if it means self-destruction. Self-indulgence is self-pity at the results of one's willfulness. Christians believe that all conscious finite beings, when they come to genuine self-awareness, find themselves lost in wrong relation to God and created reality, cut off from geniune life, and, because of willful and self-pitying attitudes, helpless to find true life (Romans 7:21–24).

REDEMPTION AND RECONCILIATION

Christians believe the ultimate answer to the existence of evil, in either its natural or moral form, is to be found in the redemptive activity of God in Jesus Christ. Traditionally, Christians have affirmed that God acts, will act, and once did act in Jesus Christ from the same love, the same wisdom, and the same power manifested in the creation of the world to redeem it and reconcile it to itself and to God. In the life, death, and Resurrection of a human being called Jesus who lived in Palestine in the first century C.E., the fullness of the uncreated wisdom of God—vitalized and

[4]This is, admittedly, a difficult and obscure passage. The interpretation given here rests on the argument that this passage, contrasting God's external protection of Elijah of Old Testament days from the power of his external evil enemies with the complete vulnerability of John the Baptist and the Christ to the power of *their* external enemies, interprets Jesus' entire ministry at midpoint, connecting the beginning and end points—namely, his victory over the demons in Chapter 1 and his struggle with and victory over temptations in Gethsemane, leading to his sacrificial death.

made effective by God's love and power—entered the history of God's created world (John 1:1–5, 9–18; Hebrews 1:1–5; Colossians 1:11–20; Philippians 2:5–10; I Corinthians 1:22–25).

Traditionally, this belief has been referred to as the doctrine of the Incarnation. In the life, death, and Resurrection of Jesus, God took (takes) the willful alienation and suffering of the created world into God's own self and overcomes it. By doing this God made (makes) it possible for all who will receive God's gift of life through faith and repentance to rise from the death of self-destructive alienation to a new life of right relation to God, self, and neighbor.

The name of the Christian doctrine concerning the event of redemption and reconciliation is Atonement. There has never been a fully definitive statement (one that seemed to all Christians to capture fully all that it means) about the Atonement. Some Christians, like St. Anselm of Canterbury, have spoken of the sacrifice of Jesus on the cross as substitutionary. It was satisfaction for the guilt that humankind incurred before the righteous God, a satisfaction provided by God since humanity was (is) incapable of paying it. Others, particularly in the ancient church, have emphasized that in the Atonement God achieves a victory over the powers of evil to which humankind has become subject, thus providing the way by which the captives are set free. Others, like Abelard and Augustine, emphasized the subjective effect on humankind, whose attitudes of willful and self-indulgent selfishness are (were) broken when they see (saw) the sacrificial love of the innocent God-Man given for them on the cross. This concept of Atonement is sometimes called the *moral influence*, or *exemplary, theory.*

It has not been necessary for Christians to choose among these theories, though to many contemporary Christians the satisfaction theory of Anselm seems excessively legalistic, dependent on medieval theories of penal justice and on the medieval hierarchy of relations between nobility, commoners, and serfs. In the past, the moral influence theory has been criticized as being overly subjective. However, Christian thinkers have seen some validity in treating the views as metaphors and utilizing all of them, and others, to characterize the central affirmation that God in Jesus reconciles the world to its creator.

The Person of Christ

Related to the Christian understanding of Incarnation and Atonement were many controversies about the person of Christ. These involved the question of how Jesus is related to God. This issue has been touched on in discussion of the doctrine of the Trinity. Here, it must be said that probably the most tangled of all theological controversies in the ancient church concerned the nature of the personal identity or being of Jesus Christ.

Adoptionism. In some offshoots of Jewish Christianity, Jesus was viewed as a man who, because of his righteousness, was named or designated Messiah and Son of God (usually at his baptism). This view of the relation of the human Jesus to the divine Christ (or Word) is usually called *adoptionism.* It was held by at least one segment of a Jewish Christian group called Ebionites. Their view was described and criticized by the Alexandrian Christian, Origen, and others in the ancient church. The Ebionites emphasized the human nature of Jesus—namely, his having achieved righteousness—as being that which made him able to bring salvation to humanity.

More common were positions emphasizing the divine nature in contrast to the human. The earliest Christian orthodoxy seems to have held God had in some sense united with or taken on human nature by becoming incarnate. Because of this, human nature, without being annulled, was granted the power to triumph over the temptations we experience and conquer the evils we are subject to. Thus salvation was accomplished and became possible for all humans to receive. Some forms of a widespread movement or family of movements called Gnosticism presented variations of, or deviations from, this emphasis.

Gnosticism.   According to Gnosticism, the Christ came in apparent human form to teach the qualified (spiritual) among humanity the way to salvation. Presumably, not all forms of Gnosticism, which was strong in the second and third centuries C.E., were Christian. For those that were, the Christ plays the role of the Divine Enlightener, the Teacher. Already referred to in the New Testament—the Gospel and Epistles of John and certain of Paul's letters seem in part directed against Gnostic emphases—Christian forms of Gnosticism denied the reality or importance of the humanity of Jesus.

For some Gnostics, the human Jesus was only a phantom or an illusion made use of by the Divine Spirit-Christ, who had come to teach the way of escape from the bondage of material existence. For other Gnostics, the Christ was only temporarily united with the human Jesus, departing before the crucifixion. Gnosticism resembles and partly overlaps with Docetic forms of Christianity, which held that to accomplish human salvation, the Christ only *seemed* to become human and suffer and die on the cross. Also, the second-century movement known as Marcionism, begun by Marcion, resembles Gnosticism in seeing the God of the Old Testament as a harsh or even evil being, not the God who sends the Christ into the world to free imprisoned humanity. For Christian forms of Gnosticism and Docetism *only* those humans who are spiritual (in contrast to the majority of humans) will respond to the spiritual Christ who comes disguised as a man.

Monophysites and Nestorians.   Throughout Christian history, many later Christologies (teachings or doctrines about Christ) emphasized the divine at the expense of the human in the person of Jesus Christ. Some of these are discussed in other chapters. For the Monophysites, Jesus Christ was essentially divine in nature. In Jesus Christ there was a human body with a divine soul or spirit. Nestorius (d. 451 C.E.) and the Nestorians affirmed both divine and human natures in Jesus Christ but drew a sharp line separating the two natures. Thus for Nestorius, the Divine Logos did not suffer and die, the man Jesus did.

What was at issue in all the controversies was the question of how the Atonement could take place, unless in some unique and legitimate sense in Jesus Christ there is both full and complete humanity and unique and full self-revelation of God. The position that became known as orthodox, championed by Athanasius (ca. 298–373 C.E.) and by many others, insisted that there must be both and that both natures must be full and complete. On this basis, Nestorianism, Monophysitism, and a host of other positions were condemned. Several ecumenical councils dealt with the Christological conflict. The first Nicene Council's trinitarian formula was related to it. But the formula adopted by the Council of Chalcedon in 451 C.E. probably had the most permanent and decisive influence, though it was rejected by the Monophysites and contested by others for a long time. What Chalcedon affirmed is that

> We all with one accord teach men to acknowledge one and the same Son, our Lord Jesus Christ, at once complete in Godhead and complete in manhood, truly God and truly man, consisting also of a reasonable soul and body, of one substance with us as regards his manhood; like us in all respects, apart from sin; as regards his Godhead, begotten of the Father before the Ages, but yet as regards his manhood begotten, for us men and for our salvation, of Mary the Virgin, the God-bearer; one and the same Christ, Son, Lord, Only-begotten, recognized in two natures, without confusion, without change, without division, without separation; the distinction of natures being in no way annulled by the union, but rather the characteristics of each nature being preserved and coming together to form one person and subsistence, not as part or separated into two persons, but one and the same Son and Only-begotten God the Word, Lord Jesus Christ....[5]

In recent centuries both traditional—conservative or orthodox—and revisionary, or liberal, forms of Christianity have usually affirmed a unique divine and human reality in the one Jesus Christ. Liberal Christians have sometimes charged that more conservative theologians, while paying lip service to the full humanity of Jesus, have tended to let the humanity be swallowed up in the divinity in a kind of modern Docetism or Gnosticism. To conservatives, liberals often have seemed to emphasize humanity at the expense of deity. F. E. D. Schleiermacher (1768–1834), often called the father of Protestant liberalism in Germany, emphasized the deity of Jesus Christ. But like early adoptionism, he also made Jesus' humanity—namely, his perfect consciousness of God (his sense of absolute dependence, trust, and obedience)—the basis of his role as redeemer.

Earlier discussions of Christology, soteriology (the doctrine of salvation), and the Atonement focused on the person and work of Christ. With the rise of the historical caution resulting from the work of Schweitzer and the form critics (see Chapter Five) concerning our ability to discover either a connected account of Jesus' work or a key to his personal attitudes (such as what his consciousness or self-understanding was), some later Christian thinkers shifted from the person and work of Jesus to what God has accomplished in the *event* of Jesus Christ. The theologian and biblical scholar Rudolf Bultmann (1884–1976) spoke of God's action in Jesus as the ultimate event in which we encounter the possibility of salvation, or new life. This possibility comes to us as a demand and opportunity for faith, by which Bultmann meant openness to the future. The openness of faith means that we meet our neighbor with the neighborly love that the gospels show to be both what God demands and what the event of salvation in Jesus Christ makes possible.

Frequently contested, often a source of puzzle and paradox in attempts to talk about who Jesus Christ is and how it is that Christians believe God has acted in him to bring salvation to the world, the Council of Chalecedon's formula, nevertheless, became the major way by which later Christian thinking about Jesus found much of its inspiration and its self-imposed limits.

---

[5]Quoted in Henry Bettenson, ed., *Documents of the Christian Church* (New York: Oxford University Press, 1943), pp. 72–73.

Georges Rouault, *Head of Christ.* Twentieth Century. *(The Chrysler Museum, Norfolk, VA.)*

THE WORK OF THE SPIRIT

Christians believe that because of God's work of Atonement in Jesus Christ, sinful human beings can be reborn to a new life in Christ. The term *born-again* is sometimes used to refer to a dramatic, conscious, emotional experience of change in adults or adolescents stimulated by religious conversion. The term has frequently been used in this way by U.S. evangelical Protestant Christians, who have associated conversion and being "born again" with religious revivalism. However, the concept of being freed from bondage to (original) sin—that is, of being reborn to a new life in Christ—is based on several New Testament passages, particularly on passages found in the Gospel of John, chapters 3 and 4. Most Christian groups believe in the necessity and possibility of new birth, entering a new life in Christ; though for many of the mainstream Christian groups—e.g., Catholics, Lutherans, Episcopalians—the new birth, except in cases of persons converted to Christianity as adults, occurs when the newborn infant is presented by its parents for baptism. Thus, the new birth need not involve a conscious emotional experience on the part of the child. What matters, according to this interpretation of Christian belief and practice, is God's promised willingness to accept the "new" human beings into the family of those who are God's people. At a later date, usually at or near adolescence, after receiving religious instruction, the child, in a ceremony of confirmation, is asked to give personal testimony and commitment to faith.

The beginning of and growth in Christian life for individuals and the continuing life of the Christian community as a whole have always been associated in Christian thought with the work of the third person of the Trinity, the Holy Ghost, or Holy Spirit. As already noted, the Spirit as well as the Son is associated with the work of creation. In Jewish Scripture and tradition the Spirit is the bearer of messages and of power to designated individuals and groups. In the New Testament, the Spirit is at times referred to as the Spirit of Jesus (or of the Lord). The Spirit is given to his apostles as the source of new life. This involves the implanting of Christ in individual believers (Galatians 2:20).

Although there were controversies in the ancient church concerning the work of the Spirit and its relation to the other two persons of the Trinity, by and large these were overshadowed by the controversies concerning the relation of the first and second persons to each other and of the second person of the Trinity (the Word, or Christ) to human nature in Jesus.

One of the most significant of the controversies involving the relation of the Spirit to the Father and the Son contributed to the rupture between Eastern Orthodox and Western Catholic branches of Christianity. (Chapters Three and Five emphasize geographical, cultural, and political sources of the gradual stages leading to the final rupture in 1054 C.E.) As early as the fifth century in some areas of the western Church, the word *filioque* ("and from the son") had been added to the phrase in the Nicene Creed, saying that the Spirit proceeds from the Father. By the ninth century, *filioque* was used throughout the West. The Eastern Church responded indignantly, partly because, according to its beliefs, such a change could not be made without the approval of an ecumenical council involving *all* the bishops of the church, or because something once established by an ecumenical council could not be changed. The outcome was mutual excommunication of Western and Eastern leaders, pope and patriarch. Since that time, Eastern theologians have defended the belief that the Spirit proceeds *from* the Father, whereas Western theologians, Protestant[6] as well as Catholic, have tended to argue that the assertion that the Spirit proceeds from both Father and Son captures the trinitarian position more fully, expressing the community and dynamic sense of God's three-in-oneness and mutuality while fully avoiding tritheism.

COMMUNITY

Christians affirm that God's revelation of God's wisdom, love, and power, God's reconciling gift, was given to specific, actual human beings. The names of many of them are recorded in the pages of the New Testament: Peter, a number of Marys or Miriams, Salome, James, John, Andrew, Philip, Paul (see the gospels and I Corinthians 15).

Christians believe that after his burial, Jesus was raised from the dead by the power of God and actually appeared to many of these people. Jesus' Resurrection and the future gift of God's love, the power and wisdom that come through the Holy Spirit (Acts 2:1–21; I Corinthians 12:12–13), made them into a community. As a result of what they told others about God's self-disclosure in Jesus, many others

---

[6]Karl Barth, for instance, strenuously argued for the *filioque* concept in his massive work *Church Dogmatics*.

became part of this community. The community, the church of Jesus Christ, still exists. Needless to say, it exists in many forms or denominations that have had difficulty recognizing the legitimacy of each other. The members of this community (of these groups) are still proclaiming what they believe to be the good news of God's self-revelation, of the salvation that God brings in Jesus Christ. They affirm that wherever the message is proclaimed, other human beings are being called by the Holy Spirit into the community of redemption and reconciliation. Christians believe that God's reconciliation has actually happened; it is a present possibility for all who will receive the good news of it. They believe that God is still at work bringing God's purposes to fulfillment and completion.

In the New Testament the term *saint* (having the connotation of one who is set apart or holy) is used by Christians to refer to each other. Later the term came to designate Christians of the early and later periods whose lives manifested outstanding holiness. In Western Catholicism and Eastern Orthodoxy, in contrast to most branches of Protestantism, there have flourished many traditions about the saints. A practice of religious devotion, or veneration, directed toward the saints has also flourished. Within Roman Catholicism there are official channels and procedures by means of which deceased Christians may be recognized as saints. The conferral of this status and title is called *canonization*. It is believed that devotion to the saints can enhance one's spiritual growth and be a source of aid in one's life.

The veneration of Mary, the mother of Jesus, has been of special importance, with some differences of emphasis, for both Eastern Orthodoxy and Roman Catholicism. The gospels of Luke and Matthew, which give accounts of the birth of Jesus, refer to Mary as the virgin mother of the Savior. Traditionally, both Eastern Orthodoxy and Western Catholicism have venerated her as "the mother of God." Since very early days of Christian history, Mary has been venerated as the virgin mother of Jesus. Roman Catholicism has argued that she remained throughout her life a virgin, whereas Protestants, traditionally accepting the virgin birth of Jesus, have argued that the gospels support the view that after his birth she lived a normal married life with her husband, bearing the children referred to in the gospels as Jesus' brothers and sisters. In Western Catholicism in the nineteenth century, Mary's Immaculate Conception (her conception and birth in a sinless state, free of the guilt and power of Original Sin) was proclaimed as official dogma. In the twentieth century Pope Pius XII proclaimed as dogma her bodily Assumption into heaven at the culmination of her earthly life.

Protestants have tended to view the saints, including the Virgin Mary, as persons to be admired and imitated, but not to advocate direct acts of devotion toward them. Typically, Protestants have seen the dogmas concerning Mary, and to some extent Catholic devotion to her, as obstacles in the way of Christian unity.

SACRAMENTS

Different numbers of sacraments have been recognized; seven by Eastern Orthodoxy and Roman Catholicism, two by Protestants, none by the Society of Friends (Quakers). All (except the Quakers and possibly a few other groups) have recognized as sacraments baptism, occurring at entry to the Christian life, and Holy Communion (or the Mass), based on New Testament accounts of the last supper Jesus shared with his disciples just before his arrest and crucifixion. Other sacraments recognized by Eastern Orthodox and Roman Catholics include confirmation, marriage, ordination to the priesthood or ministry (these are recognized in religious ceremonies by most Protestant groups but are not held to be sacraments), penance (involving confession of one's sins to and one's absolution by a priestly spiritual advisor), and the anointing of the seriously ill.

Although most Christians see the sacraments as a means of obtaining Grace (and spiritual growth) for partakers of them, there have been widely varying interpretations of their nature. Roman Catholics, Eastern Orthodox worshipers, and some Protestants (Lutherans and some in the Anglican tradition) hold that in the sacraments God's Grace is objectively present, and to such a degree that they have used the term *real presence* to signify its objectivity. Thus, for Roman Catholic belief, during the celebration of Mass the bread and wine become the body and blood of Christ.

Martin Luther stressed the real presence of God in the sacraments to the extent that he was not able to agree with Calvin and other Reformation theologians, who stressed the spiritual rather than physical presence of God in the sacraments. Some Protestants in the Reformed tradition do not go as far as Calvin in stressing even spiritual presence, but see the sacrament of the Lord's Supper as a *memorial,* or commemoration, of Christ's sacrificial death. Baptists tend to avoid use of the word "sacrament," speaking of baptism and the Lord's Supper as *ordinances* instead. For Roman Catholics, the Mass is in an important sense a reenactment, a reoffering of Christ for the sins of the world. Most Protestants avoid the idea of reenactment but see the sacrament as more than a memorial. Though some Protestants use the term *means of Grace* to describe the sacraments, others reject the term as being too close to the Catholic view.

Different views about the significance of ordination to the priesthood or Christian ministry, whether ordination is regarded as a sacrament or not, affect ways in which Christians of different backgrounds have been able to interact with each other. Those Christians accepting the concept of an objective succession of authority and spiritual endowment from the apostles, transmitted by ordination, have frequently been unable to accept the validity of ministerial ordination and orders in groups that do not belong to this line of succession. They have also frequently not been able to accept the validity—apart from certain exceptional cases—of sacraments administered by such ministers. There is a typically objective concept of the priesthood held by Eastern Orthodox worshipers, Roman Catholics, and some Protestants, according to which ordination indelibly confers the status of priest on one who has received it. In contrast, there is an extreme Protestant concept of Christian ministry, according to which the minister is and remains a layperson, perhaps with special educational or personal qualifications, who has been designated either permanently or temporarily to exercise the ministerial office. Most Protestants hold concepts of ordination and of the ministry that fall between these two types.

The sacraments involve physical events and physical acts or elements. The ceremonial acts involved are understood by Roman Catholics as the material or matter of the sacrament. Its form (and that which gives the ceremony efficacious power to be a channel of Grace) depends on the use of the appropriate (definitive) words of institution by one who is entitled to use them.

Many Protestants have defined *sacrament* as "a visible sign of an inward and spiritual grace." One frequently cited Protestant definition or criterion of the true church is "where the Word is rightly preached and the sacraments duly administered."

With all their differences concerning number, mode, and efficacy, Christians believe that the sacraments were instituted by Christ and that participation in them is an important part of Christian life and growth for the individual Christian and the body of Christian believers.

SCRIPTURE

The earliest communication of the message about Jesus was in spoken language. Jesus' teachings, accounts of what he had said and done, and the story of his death and Resurrection, were passed on by the original members of his community. As time passed, written accounts of this teaching and of these traditions began to be made. Letters were written from leaders of the community—from Paul, John, James, and Jude—to groups within the community. Other writings based on the spoken words of and about Jesus that had been handed down by members of the original community, "gospels," also began to appear. These told the story, the good news, of what God had done, of what God was still doing, and of what God intended to do in and through Jesus Christ and the Spirit. As these began to be circulated, they were used in worship and in instruction among groups of the followers of Jesus. Christians soon began to regard some of these writings—which we now call the New Testament—as inspired Scripture, as a record of the events in which God had revealed God's own self. (In Chapter Seven some account is given of different attitudes of Christians toward interpretation of Scripture.)

During the second century C.E., a Christian named Marcion argued that Christians should reject the Jewish Scriptures. He produced a "canon" of Christian Scripture containing his abridged version of Luke's gospel and of some of Paul's letters. Some scholars believe that in reaction to Marcion, the trend toward an orthodox listing, or canon, of Christian Scripture began. From the second century on, there was near agreement by orthodox Christians as to what writings the Christian Scriptures should contain, though there was not unanimity for several centuries.

Christians believe that the record of events given in the Scriptures contains God's self-revelation, since it allows people of all times to participate in the original events of the revelation. That is, Christians believe that the written record can, with the help of God's Holy Spirit, become revelation now. Christians also regard the Jewish Scriptures, which most Christians call the Old Testament, as inspired, as part of God's self-revelation, since the events of God's self-revelation in Christ grow out of the events recorded there, are prepared for and foreshadowed by them. These writings, the Old and New Testaments, are regarded by Christians as a gift of God, through The Holy Spirit, to the church and to the world. (See Appendices I and II for further explanation of biblical writings.)

THE CHRISTIAN LIFE

Christians traditionally have believed that when one enters the Christian community—whether as a baptized infant or as an adult convert—one embarks on a pilgrimage or way of life that ideally involves disciplined growth toward a likeness to Christ. Traditionally, Christian life (based on concepts and terms used in Paul's

Letter to the Romans and on the Gospel and First Epistle of John) has had three stages. First, justification and regeneration, in which one is reborn and freed of the guilt of Original Sin, with the likeness or nature of Christ planted as a seed within. The second stage is sanctification, which is ordinarily understood to be a process. This is seen as a pilgrimage in which God's Grace and one's own self-discipline and devotion nurture the seed of the Christ-nature until it grows to maturity. Lastly, beatitude, blessedness, or entire sanctification is seen as both the culmination of the Christian pilgrimage and its goal. Most Christian groups teach that it is usually achieved after the present life with entrance into the state of eternal blessedness called Heaven.

In New Testament times, growth into saintliness was proclaimed as normative for all Christians. When Christianity became the official religion of the Roman Empire, distinctions began to be made between two classes of Christians, those called to pursue the pilgrimage toward sanctification with intense, complete, and concentrated commitment (largely those who had entered the monastic life) and Christians who attempted to avoid major sin but probably could not achieve sanctification in this life. These would anticipate a period of purgatorial discipline in the next life as preface to entry into the blessedness of knowing and loving God as God is.[7]

With the Reformation, the concept of Purgatory was rejected by Protestants, along with the concept of a higher monastic life aimed at sanctification and a lower secular life aimed at avoidance of sin. Some recent critics of Protestant practice, including some Protestant self-critics, have argued that with the Protestant idea of sanctification's again becoming normative for all Christians, by and large it was equated with moral rectitude or even with conformity to society's codes of ethical virtue, rather than signifying personal closeness to God through love and oneness of will.

Christians believe that through Jesus Christ and the Holy Spirit, created beings can be restored and perfected in genuine life. Beings possessing self-awareness, human beings ("made in the image of God"), acquire through Christ the possibility of a life of consciousness of God's copresence with them, of life in and with God. Christians call this possibility of continuous consciousness of God's reality and presence with them *prayer*. Prayer is both the openness of humans to God and God's openness to them. In prayer, God is self-giving, sharing the divine power, wisdom, and love with the created. Augustine expressed this well in the opening part of his famous *Confessions*, which is itself a sustained and extended work of prayer and meditation. "Lord, Thou hast made us for Thyself, and our hearts are restless till they rest in Thee" (*Confessions* 1,i).

FULFILLMENT: THE NEW AGE

We have seen in Chapters One and Two that for many within first-century Judaism, the expected Kingdom of God was to take place on this earth, perhaps greatly perfected or transformed. Jesus' descriptions of the coming Kingdom do not seem to have been very specific about what it would be like. In fact, his major stress was

---

[7]The concept of Purgatory was discussed in theological works of such early Christian writers as Origen and Cyprian. It became an increasingly important part of Western Catholic belief.

on the availability of the Kingdom *now* as a spiritual possession of those for whom God's will had become the decisive reality of their lives. The earliest Christians apparently expected an imminent return to earth by Jesus with an inauguration of God's Kingdom in its fullness. This expectation characterized both Jewish and gentile Christians.

As Christianity became almost entirely gentile and began to take root as a major institution of the Roman Empire, the concept of the coming of God's Kingdom as a cosmic event involving a renewed or restored earth was postponed indefinitely into the future. Even the term Kingdom of God—so important in the teachings of Jesus—came increasingly to have only a minor or secondary role in Christian proclamation.

What became of increasing concern to many Christians was the destiny of the individual soul after the present life. Hebrew religion had not emphasized the immortality of the soul, a concept belonging to Greek Platonism, the mystery religions, and Gnosticism, but the raising to new life by God of the whole person— the resurrection of the body. Medieval Christianity tended to accept the immortality of the soul, which at death would go to blessedness (Heaven), misery (Hell), or discipline (Purgatory) but which ultimately at the Last Judgment would be reunited with its transformed body for salvation or for eternal punishment. Recently, Catholic theologians have reexamined the concept of Purgatory, a doctrine usually rejected by Protestants.

The majority of Christians no doubt believe in, and the majority of Christian denominations have affirmed, a continuation of individual life beyond this life. Only a small number of Christians have rejected belief in this continuation of subjective life, as opposed to believing only in objective immortality (continued influence). The Christian Scriptures are extremely reticent in their descriptions of the future life (see, however, Paul's letters, especially I Corinthians 15). Popular religion has elaborated greatly on the nature of Heaven and the future life. The religion of the U.S. frontier spoke of a beautiful city with mansions of ivory and streets of gold. Serious theologians, in line with Paul's teaching about the progression of stages of the Christian life, have emphasized the spiritual nature of the new life and stressed that it is probably better not to interpret it as a continuation of the present life but as its transformation and perfection.

Popular religion has also elaborated on the Christian concept of Hell as eternal punishment. Hell has also been given striking treatment in works of literature (e.g., Dante's *Divine Comedy*) and visual art. Some Christian groups—the Universalists, for instance—have rejected the idea of eternal punishment as incompatible with God's love, mercy, and compassion. The Christian Scriptures rarely speak of Hell or eternal punishment. Indeed the concept of eternality associated with it is inferential. When the Scriptures do speak of a time or place or event of judgment involving condemnation and punishment, the language is highly metaphorical. The word often associated with Hell in Jesus' usage referred to a canyon or pit outside the city of Jerusalem that figured in some Jewish apocalyptic literature. Hell was originally, as the contemporary novelist Anthony Burgess has noted, "a rubbish dump outside Jerusalem."[8]

[8]Anthony Burgess, *The Clockwork Testament, or Enderby's End* (New York: Alfred A. Knopf, 1976), p. 4.

Many contemporary Christian denominations are as reticent as the Scriptures, or more so, about eternal punishment. However, it should be said that a consensus found in Christian theological tradition emphasizes that the concept of Hell can be interpreted as affirming God's mercy. If popular images of Hell as a place of physical torture are excluded, the concept is seen to refer to a condition of voluntary, or self-chosen, absence from God. Thus, the concept of Hell refers to God's granting the individual freedom to use the gift of freedom self-destructively, in ways that alienate the individual from God, self, and others. The end result of such a use of freedom would be suicidal. The concept of Hell can be seen as a way of affirming that God allows freedom to be carried to such a limit but still affirms and minimally preserves the individual from absolute self-destruction. One might say that the doctrine of Hell signifies that God chooses to preserve even those who ultimately would negate themselves, others, the whole creation, and God. The term eternal *punishment* is therefore perhaps inappropriate.

Although the continued, or transformed, life of the individual has been an important theme of Christian belief, it has not been thought of as merely an individual concern. That is, the Christian concept of salvation is not individualistic but communal, ultimately involving the whole created universe.

In recent times, Christians have reemphasized the communitarian aspects of the Kingdom. Some adventist sects have revived expectations of the imminent physical return of Christ to the earth. Other Christians have internalized the concepts of the Second Coming, the Last Judgment, and the Kingdom, seeing them as giving symbolic expression to the importance of each moment of life as lived in God's presence. Some Christians, like the theologians of the social gospel, have seen the Kingdom of God as an actual norm to be translated into the structures and processes of present society. During the first years of the twentieth century, Walter Rauschenbusch proclaimed that the family, and the educational, religious, and political institutions of our society were largely Christianized. All that remained was to bring the spheres of economics (through socialism or some adaptation of present economic systems that will emphasize cooperation instead of competitiveness) and of international relations (through effective world government) in line with the already Christianized parts of the social order, thus fulfilling the ideals of the Kingdom of God. Others, like Reinhold Niebuhr, stressed the ideal of the Kingdom as an important instrument of judgment that can bring us to repentance, humility, and action aimed at establishing relative justice, an ultimate goal or norm that is always coming but never is.

Christians affirm that in Jesus Christ God has established the rule of God's love over the universe. God has overcome the evil and alienation that reject God's love. In many ways this rule, the reign of God's love, remains hidden. Christians affirm that it is known in principle to those who are members of God's community, but most Christians have confessed that very often even members of God's community are not as conscious of God's power and wisdom triumphing in love as they could and should be.

To much of the world, the power and wisdom of God's love, its rule and reality, seem unrealistic and unrealizable. But, Christians believe, these will not always be hidden. In Scripture, sermon, and theological work they affirm that God even now is bringing God's purposes to fulfillment. In almost every Christian service of worship they proclaim that God is even now carrying this work to final perfection, to that point in time or beyond time when "the kingdoms of this world" will become "the Kingdom of our Lord, and of His Christ" (Revelation 11:15), to a point in time or beyond when the Lord *shall* reign forever.

Since the earliest days of the Christian community, Christians have believed and asserted that they are living in "the last days" (I John 2:18). For the most part, Christians do not believe this conviction should lead to complacency or arrogant self-assurance on their part. Rather, it is a ground of humility and repentance and a motive for serious efforts to let their lives be dedicated to God's will, whether this means taking the message to others in missionary and evangelistic efforts or working for peace and justice in contemporary society. Christians continue to assert that God is faithful to God's promises (II Peter 3:3–4, 8–10; II Corinthians 1:19–20), that the New Age has already begun, and that the new life in Christ and his spirit is a present reality (II Corinthians 5:17; Luke 17:20–21; Revelation 3:20) whose fulfillment is assured. They see this assurance as more than a word of judgment on the world; they see it as a promise and a demand.

QUESTIONS

1. Compare and contrast the Christian concept of God with those of polytheistic, pantheistic, and deistic religious traditions.

2. How does orthodox Christian trinitarianism differ from and resemble the views that the present book calls tritheistic and modalistic?

3. Discuss what is meant by natural and moral forms of evil and explain why thinkers such as Russell and Flew find the existence of evil a problem for Christian belief.

4. In your view, which form of evil—moral or natural—presents the greatest problem for Christian theism?

5. What do Christians understand by the term Original Sin? Explain the relation of this concept to the Biblical story of Adam and Eve.

6. List and interpret (explain) the different symbolic concepts of the demonic.

7. In what way did the Council of Chalcedon's way of speaking of the divine and human natures of Jesus contrast with other ways (e.g., Ebionite, Gnostic, Monophysite, Nestorian)? What does the present chapter intend when it speaks of Chalcedon's statement as setting self-imposed limits for later Christian attempts to express beliefs about Jesus?

8. Compare and contrast Roman Catholic and Protestant beliefs and practice concerning the sacraments and veneration of the saints and the Virgin Mary.

9. Why did Marcion want to reject the Jewish Scriptures (Old Testament) as canonical for Christians? Why did orthodox Christianity insist on including it?

10. Describe what sanctification means, or has meant, in Christian tradition.

11. Often prayer is thought of as a way in which humans make known their requests to God. Why do you think the Christian concept of prayer is explained in a very different way in the present chapter?

12. Describe how the concept of fulfillment—including beliefs in coming of the
Kingdom, the Second Coming of Christ, and the Last Judgment—has been
interpreted with different emphases during Christian history.

FURTHER READING

AULEN, GUSTAF.   *Christus Victor: An Historical Study of the Three Main Types of
the Idea of the Atonement.* London: S. P. C. K., 1970.

BARTH, KARL.   *Church Dogmatics.* Volume I, Part 1. New York: Charles Scribner's
Sons, 1936.

BETTENSON, HENRY, ed.   *Documents of the Christian Church.* New York: Oxford
University Press, 1947.

BLOOM, ANTHONY.   *God and Man.* New York: Paulist Press, 1971.

BONHOEFFER, DIETRICH.   *Creation and Fall; Temptation: Two Biblical Studies.*
London: SCM Press, 1959.

BOSLOOPER, THOMAS.   *The Virgin Birth.* Philadelphia: Westminster Press, 1962.

CARRETTO, CARLO.   *The God Who Comes.* Maryknoll, N.Y.: Orbis Books, 1974.

CONGAR, YVES.   *Tradition and Traditions.* New York: Macmillan, 1967.

FERGUSON, EVERETT.   *Demonology of the Early Christian World.* New York: Edward
Mellen Press, 1984.

FLEW, ANTONY.   *God and Philosophy.* London: Hutchinson, 1966.

FORSYTH, P. T.   *The Person and Place of Jesus Christ.* Grand Rapids, Mich.: William
B. Eerdmans Publishing Company, n.d.

HARTSHORNE, CHARLES.   *Omnipotence and Other Theological Mistakes.* Albany:
State University of New York Press, 1984.

KALLAS, JAMES G.   *Jesus and the Power of Satan.* Philadelphia: Westminster Press,
1968.

KELBER, WERNER H.   *The Oral and the Written Gospel.* Philadelphia: Fortress Press,
1983.

KNOX, JOHN.   *Jesus: Lord and Christ.* New York: Harper & Brothers, 1958.

KUNG, HANS.   *On Being a Christian.* Garden City, N.Y.: Doubleday, 1976.

LEWIS, C. S.   *The Great Divorce.* New York: Macmillan, 1946.

———.   *The Screwtape Letters* and *Screwtape Proposes a Toast.* New York: Macmillan, 1961.

MELLERT, ROBERT BOROS.   *What Is Process Theology?* New York: Paulist Press,
1976.

NIEBUHR, REINHOLD.   *The Nature and Destiny of Man.* New York: Charles Scribner's
Sons, 1953.

PAGELS, ELAINE.   *The Gnostic Gospels.* New York: Random House, 1979.

PANNENBERG, WOLFHART.   *Jesus—God and Man.* Philadelphia: Westminster Press,
1968.

———.   *Theology and the Kingdom of God.* Philadelphia: Westminster Press, 1969.

RAHNER, KARL.   *The Trinity.* New York: Herder and Herder, 1970.

RAUSCHENBUSCH, WALTER.   *Christianizing the Social Order.* New York: Macmillan, 1912.

RAVEN, CHARLES E.   *The Creator Spirit.* Cambridge, Mass.: Harvard University Press, 1927.

RUSCH, WILLIAM A.   *The Trinitarian Controversy.* Philadelphia: Fortress Press, 1980.

RUSSELL, BERTRAND.   *Why I Am Not a Christian.* New York: Simon & Schuster, 1957.

SEEBURG, REINHOLD.   *Text-Book of the History of Doctrines.* Grand Rapids, Mich.: Baker Book House, 1956.

CHAPTER SEVEN

Faith and Knowledge

Chapter Six presented a number of major Christian beliefs, some that most Christians have affirmed, along with varied interpretations of these beliefs. A question of major importance that arose in discussing those beliefs was: What is the basis of Christian belief? That is, what are the reasons, what is the evidence or support for, the beliefs that Christians hold? Christian theology often refers to this as the question of *authority*. If Christians believe, for instance, that God is both all-powerful and perfectly loving, what is their *authority* for this belief? Or if doubts arise among Christians about what they should believe—what is the truth concerning whether Jesus Christ will literally return to the earth to establish a Kingdom of God, or whether Christians should participate as combatants in wars, or how one becomes and remains a member of the Christian church—how are these doubts to be resolved in ways that remain faithful to standards of honesty and truthfulness and to the identity or authenticity of Christian tradition? These issues—the issues of authority, truth, and integrity as interpreted within Christian tradition—will be discussed in the present chapter.

MONOTHEISTIC FAITH AND THE KNOWLEDGE OF GOD

Behavioral scientists who study religion as a factor in individual and group behavior frequently warn against overemphasizing the belief, or cognitive, side of religion. Although most religious traditions do involve beliefs—for instance, beliefs about the nature of God or the gods, and about the origins of the natural universe and the relation of humans to it and the divine—the belief-claims of a religion may be relatively unimportant in comparison to other aspects of the religion. The way of life it sanctions (moral code) or the cultic and ritual celebrations that make it a focus of group and individual identity are equally important. In a novel that gives a popular but well-informed and accurate fictional portrayal of a Jewish rabbi who uses the methods of Talmudic interpretation to solve crimes, Harry Kemelman has Rabbi David Small say this about the belief side of Judaism:

One immediate difference between Judaism and many other religions is that we're not bound by an official creed. With us, it's largely an accident of birth. If you're born a Jew, you're a Jew at least until you convert to some other religion. An atheist who was born a Jew is therefore a Jew.[1]

Kemelman's character stresses not only that holding specific beliefs is not the criterion of one's being a Jew, though certainly it would be possible to speak about the characteristic belief-claims, or credal content, of Judaism. He emphasizes that, from the point of view of many Jews, living according to the religion's moral and ritual code is a matter of much greater importance than is affirming characteristic Jewish beliefs.

Similar considerations may hold for many Christian groups. However, throughout the history of Christianity and for many Christian groups and denominations, there has been a greater concern about defining and justifying religious beliefs than has been characteristic of most (or perhaps of any) of the other major religious traditions of the world. Characteristically, Christians—especially the leaders of most Christian groups—have held that it is important to know what one is supposed, as a Christian, to believe. Indeed, for many groups it has been held that all adult Christians should understand, if not be able to justify, the basic Christian beliefs.

There are several reasons for the emphasis among Christians on defining, understanding, and justifying Christian beliefs.

1. The early conflict between Christians and Jews concerning the correct interpretation of the Jewish Scriptures caused Christians to seek and emphasize methods for the precise definition and interpretation of scriptural teachings.

2. Christianity arose and spread throughout the non-Jewish parts of the Roman Empire during a period in which many philosophical schools flourished. Some of these schools (Stoicism and Epicureanism, for instance) made dogmatic claims about the truth of their teachings.

Stoicism: Although early Christian teachers and writers found much to admire in the moral code of *Stoicism,* they rejected what they thought of as its crudely materialistic concept of God. The Stoics thought of God as the divine element fire, from which successive universes emerge and to which they return. Stoics believed mature humans were able to grasp the intelligible order of things and the rational moral law that should govern human conduct, because human reason is a spark of the divine reason, or logos. The Stoics emphasized a life founded on acceptance of the divine rationality, dedicated to doing one's duty in all circumstances. They advocated a life of virtuous self-control.

Epicureanism: Christians found little to admire in *Epicurean philosophy.* Epicurus, a Greek philosopher of the fourth century B.C.E., accepted the theory of Democritus that all reality, including the human mind or soul, and even the gods, is composed of atoms. Thus humans and gods were held to be mortal. Epicureanism was a secular approach to life that sought to deliver humanity from religious superstition, including belief in, or fear of, an afterlife.

---

[1]Harry Kemelman, *Tuesday the Rabbi Saw Red* (New York: E. P. Dutton, 1975), p. 50. Used by permission of the publisher.

Other philosophical schools advocated positions of *scepticism,* holding that nothing can be known with certainty. Thus, the need to combat both the dogmatism of philosophical schools that seemed to teach doctrines contrary to the major themes of Christianity and sceptical positions that denied that Christians or others could arrive at a sure grasp of truth contributed to the Christian emphasis on precise definition and justification of belief.

3. In order to justify not merely their religious beliefs and practices but their very legal right to exist as a religious movement within the Roman Empire, Christians also appealed to the arguments and teachings of Greek and Roman philosophers to oppose the polytheistic beliefs of popular Roman, Greek, and Asiatic religious cults of the day. As early as the sixth century B.C.E., Xenophanes and other Greek philosophers had ridiculed the anthropomorphic polytheism of Greek civic and cultic religion. (*Polytheism* is the belief in many gods. *Anthropomorphism* is the tendency to depict gods as being humanlike or in the form of humans.) Xenophanes once said that if horses could talk and had religious beliefs, they would describe the gods as being horselike. Later, Socrates, Plato, and Aristotle condemned popular views of the gods that made them only glorified humans, with human vices magnified (e.g., vindictiveness, spite, jealousy, and sexual promiscuity). Christian preachers and writers used the arguments of Greek philosophical thinkers to support monotheism and to argue for the credibility of Christian claims.

Among the earliest Christian *apologetic writings*—writings that attempted to give a reasoned defense and justification of the Christian religion—are treatises addressed to the Roman emperors Antoninus Pius and Marcus Aurelius (the famed Stoic philosopher) by Justin Martyr, a second-century Christian Platonist. The complex of philosophical doctrines, methods, and attitudes known as *Platonism* seemed to many of the earliest Christian thinkers to be most congenial to the spirit of Christianity. Justin (ca. 100–165 C.E.), before his conversion to Christianity, was a Platonic philosopher. As a young man, he sought philosophic enlightenment from various schools. Stoic materialism repelled him, as did Pythagorean insistence on the study of mathematics as a necessary condition of philosophical insight. An Aristotelian philosopher impressed him as being interested only in the fees he could collect. However, among the Platonists Justin believed that he found true wisdom.

By Justin's time, Platonism had gone through a varied and complex history. Though Plato (ca. 428–348 B.C.E.) believed that ultimate philosophical insight must be born in the process of dialogue and inquiry and cannot be adequately expressed in writing, certain Platonic doctrines formed the basis of the inquiries of his immediate successors in Athens at the Academy, a research center that Plato had founded and directed. Among these doctrines were (1) that reality is ultimately spiritual rather than material; (2) that the material realm is in a state of constant flux, making our knowledge of it at best uncertain; (3) that the true realities are eternal, unchanging forms or patterns, which material realities at best imitate or mirror, or in which they participate; (4) that our minds (reason) can know these forms through intellectual insight or intuition if we rise above attention to sense experience and the distractions of bodily appetite and concentrate on seeking a vision of the ideal, spiritual, and eternal; and (5) that since our minds or souls possess the capacity to rise from the material to the spiritual, we are in fact immortal and in some sense, at least potentially, divine. Plato believed that since through reason or the mind, apart from sense experience, we can know the eternal form or essence of human nature—as well as the natures or essences of other natural kinds, e.g., horses and cows—we can become fully human (i.e., rational, immortal, divine) by governing our spiritual and bodily life in accordance with our knowledge of that essence.

Platonism evolved through a phase of intense interest in abstract, mathematical analysis of philosophical truth into a phase of philosophical scepticism emphasizing the uncertainties of the material realm, and the worthlessness of sense experience as a source of knowledge. In fact, for several centuries, in marked contrast to Plato's optimism about the power of the mind to grasp eternal truth, the Platonic school, opposing Stoic dogmatism, was one of the major sources of sceptical philosophy. However, by Justin's time there had been a revival of a nonsceptical form of Platonism. This revival resulted in the so-called Middle Platonism, which was especially strong during the second century C.E. Middle Platonism was characterized by an emphasis on the reality of the spiritual and the need to cultivate the soul by virtuous living, religious piety, and philosophical inquiry. An emphasis on the divine, or supreme, reality, on God as holy, transcendent, far removed from the material world but approachable through religious reverence, and on moral self-discipline and philosophical quest, made Middle Platonism congenial to Christianity, with its roots in a Jewish monotheism that also emphasized the transcendent remoteness but nearness to human life of the creator. After his conversion to Christianity, Justin continued to profess this philosophy and possibly should be thought of as one of the important second-century Middle Platonists.

4. Later controversies either between Christians and non-Christians—for instance, Muslims of the early Middle Ages who used Greek doctrines and methods of analysis to interpret and state Islamic beliefs—or among Christian groups reinforced and contributed to the Christian tendency to emphasize correct definition, understanding, and interpretation of belief. Many Christian groups have moved closer to each other in their willingness to find agreement in patterns of belief during the past few decades. In earlier centuries some of these groups mutually defined their positions against each other. Catholic belief was defined against Lutheran or Anglican belief, Methodist (Arminian) against Presbyterian or Baptist (Calvinist).

5. Finally, the rise of modern Western scientific theorizing and procedures emphasizing precision and experimental verification has not only presented challenges to Christian belief and raised questions about the compatibility of religious belief with the results, methods, and attitudes—the thought-style— of science, but has contributed to new fashions of thought. The emphasis on objectivity, precision, and verifiability in science has given rise to dichotomies affecting the interpretation of religion that, if they existed at all in earlier societies, were not felt nearly as sharply as they have been in Western societies since the seventeenth century. For instance, the meaning of any religious belief, since the rise of scientific thought, must be assessed by asking whether it is meant literally or symbolically, whether it claims metaphysical, historical, or mythical truth or significance, whether it is to be interpreted in the same way that a specific or factual claim might be treated or in some other way, perhaps in some special religious way.

All of these factors, then, have contributed to the emphasis within varying Christian groups and traditions on the importance of the belief or credal aspect of Christianity—not just the importance of holding certain beliefs, but the importance of being able to define, understand, and justify them. Still, though, Christianity, like Judaism and Middle Platonism, has emphasized God's ultimate transcendence of all finite realities. Thus, one of the major questions for Christian belief has been: How is it possible, or is it possible, for limited, finite human minds to know and understand the infinite, transcendent God? To what extent are human reason and language necessary or useful or adequate in helping us to know God or to understand and communicate religious truth?

DISCLOSURE AND FAITHFULNESS

It is frequently noted that in contrast to theistic Greek philosophers such as Plato and Aristotle, the authors whose writings are found in the Jewish Scriptures did not develop rational proofs for the existence of God or rational analyses of the divine nature. Aristotle, for instance, proves the necessity of God's existence in order to explain how and why the physical universe is kept in motion. By rational analysis, he shows that God must be an eternal, unchanging reality, perfectly actual (i.e., without imperfection, incompleteness, or potential for change) whose nature it is to *think* what is eternal and intelligible (i.e., God eternally thinks his own consciousness). Aristotle's manner of thinking and writing is foreign in tone and substance to the Jewish Scriptures. In them, one finds historical narratives in which the authors hold that God has acted and revealed himself; writings that praise God for his goodness, power, wisdom, and faithfulness as revealed both in his acts and in the natural world that he has created; and a legal and moral code governing human interaction held to be directly revealed by God.

In the Jewish Scriptures, there are frequent assertions that the God worshipped by Jews is a God who has been self-revealing to specific human beings and groups before they knew this God, almost always before they knew God fully. The account in the first few chapters of the Book of Exodus of the freeing of the Hebrew tribes from Egyptian slavery is a good example of the Hebrew attitude. Moses, who is pictured as having fled from Egypt because he has killed an Egyptian taskmaster while trying to rescue a Hebrew from mistreatment, finds refuge with Midianite tribesmen. One day while tending flocks in the vicinity of a holy mountain, he receives a divine summons. The summons is in the form of a bush that is burning without being consumed. Moses, approaching the bush, hears a voice that identifies itself as the God of the fathers of the enslaved Israelites—Abraham, Isaac, and Jacob—and Moses is commanded by the voice to return to Egypt and bring a message to the Israelites that their God—whom they seem to have forgotten—will lead them from Egypt and give them a land of their own. Moses is fearful both that the Israelites will not know who the God of their fathers is and that the Egyptian ruler will not recognize this God's authority or power. However, God promises to vouch for Moses' authority by *signs*. God will reveal God's power, and Moses' role as God's prophet or messenger will be revealed through mighty acts. There follows an account several chapters long of the contest between the Egyptian pharaoh's stubborn will and the power of God as manifested in successively more impressive and frightening displays of power, the culmination of which is the safe passage of the Israelites through the Sea of Reeds as the sea opens for them, only to close on the pharaoh's army, drowning the Egyptians, once the Israelites are safe (Exodus 1–15).

For the Jewish Scriptures, the major problem is not *how* to arrive at knowledge of God through the use of reason; rather, it is how to respond fittingly and appropriately to God's self-disclosure. Pharaoh did not, indeed could not, respond appropriately to God because his heart was hardened. The appropriate response would have been reverence, willingness to act in accordance with God's will, faithfulness in doing this, and gratitude for God's self-disclosure and faithfulness in carrying out the divine purposes. Not only in the early period of Israel's history but throughout the prophetic period, extending into the time of postexilic Judaism, it was expected that God would frequently be self-revealing through specially chosen agents—prophets called to speak for God, priestly figures or seers, people who in special circumstances bore the divine word, and performers of signs that could leave no doubt about the presence and will of God.

However, another avenue beyond that of such special revelations of God's reality and will increasingly came to be emphasized in Jewish belief. Writings in the Jewish Wisdom tradition (Proverbs, Job, Ecclesiastes), the hymns and sacred poetry of Israel (Psalms), and the writings of some of the prophets (e.g., Isaiah 40–55) stress that reflection on natural processes and the experiences of daily life will result in knowledge of God's nature and God's will. According to these writings, the natural order reveals its creator—a powerful God who is just, wise, and faithful to those who respond with faithfulness and with fairness, justice, and mercy toward their fellow humans.

The Twenty-ninth Psalm is a hymn of praise that sees God's dynamic power revealed in the storm. In fact, the Psalms are full of images drawn from the natural realm, evidencing the conviction that God is self-revealing in and through the created order, not only as a God of power and wisdom but as one of supreme kindness, compassion, and faithfulness (Psalms 23, 42). The preservation of the natural order itself—the orderliness of nature, as manifested in the starry heavens and the progress from night to day and from season to season (Psalm 19)—also reveals the Supreme Creator to be careful, caring, and consistent. Many of the Psalms stress God's self-revelation in specific and special historical circumstances of the past (Psalms 44, 77). Frequently these are coupled with prayer to God to reveal the divine power by delivering the people of Israel in present, difficult circumstances, and the faith that this will happen, that God will be faithful to the divine promises.

One note that emerges in later Jewish prophetic, liturgical, and wisdom literature is the emphasis on the transcendent holiness and power of God and the corresponding finitude of human life. The insight into God's transcendent power and holiness is proclaimed as arising through reflection on the intrinsic limitations of finite existence, its transitoriness and fragility, its mortality. This theme is present in Psalms 49 and 90. It is present also, in ways that contrast with each other, in the books of Job and Ecclesiastes. Job, who had complained about God's justice or lack of it, since, he, a righteous man, had experienced terrible and undeserved sufferings, is granted a vision of the transcendent glory of God. Humbled, Job withdraws his complaints and gratefully worships the supremely wise and powerful creator. Though holy and transcendent, God draws close to those who seek God persistently. The author of Ecclesiastes attempts to instill humility and wisdom by showing the intrinsic limitations of human life. In Ecclesiastes, God seems very remote from humans. Nevertheless, through reflection, humans gain insight from God into their lives and the nature of the world they inhabit.

The biblical Book of Proverbs and much of the intertestamental literature of Judaism stress the divine wisdom as the means by which the world has been created and is sustained. It is a reality by which those who respond *wisely* (with insight and faithful obedience) can govern their lives. This leads to a very striking personification of God's wisdom. That is, God's wisdom is treated as if it were a personal being in itself, as in Proverbs 8 (RSV):

> Does not wisdom call,
>> does not understanding raise her voice?
> On the heights beside the way,
>> in the paths she takes her stand;
> beside the gates in front of the town,
>> at the entrance of the portals she cries aloud:
> "To you, O men, I call,
>> and my cry is to the sons of men.
> O simple ones, learn prudence;
>> O foolish men, pay attention.
> Hear, for I will speak noble things,
>> and from my lips will come what is right;
> for my mouth will utter truth;
>> wickedness is an abomination to my lips.
> All the words of my mouth are righteous;
>> there is nothing twisted or crooked in them.
> They are all straight to him who understands
>> and right to those who find knowledge.
> Take my instruction instead of silver,
>> and knowledge rather than choice gold;
> for wisdom is better than jewels,
>> and all that you may desire cannot compare with her.
> I, wisdom, dwell in prudence,
>> and I find knowledge and discretion.
> The fear of the Lord is hatred of evil.
> Pride and arrogance and the way of evil
>> and perverted speech I hate.
> I have counsel and sound wisdom,
>> I have insight, I have strength.
> By me kings reign,
>> and rulers decree what is just;
> by me princes rule,
>> and nobles govern the earth.
> I love those who love me,
>> and those who seek me diligently find me.
> Riches and honor are with me,
>> enduring wealth and prosperity.
> My fruit is better than gold, even fine gold,
>> and my yield than choice silver.
> I walk in the way of righteousness,
>> in the paths of justice,
> endowing with wealth those who love me,
>> and filling their treasuries.

The Lord created me at the beginning of his work,
    the first of his acts of old.
Ages ago I was set up,
    at the first, before the beginning of the earth.
When there were no depths I was brought forth,
    when there were no springs abounding with water.
Before the mountains had been shaped,
    before the hills, I was brought forth;
before he had made the earth with its fields,
    or the first of the dust of the world.
When he established the heavens, I was there,
    when he drew a circle on the face of the deep,
when he made firm the skies above,
    when he established the fountains of the deep,
when he assigned to the sea its limit,
    so that the waters might not transgress his command,
when he marked out the foundations of the earth,
    then I was beside him, like a master workman;
and I was daily his delight,
    rejoicing before him always,
rejoicing in his inhabited world
    and delighting in the sons of men.

And now, my sons, listen to me:
    happy are those who keep my ways.
Hear instruction and be wise,
    and do not neglect it.
Happy is the man who listens to me,
    watching daily at my gates,
    waiting beside my doors.
For he who finds me finds life
    and obtains favor from the Lord;
but he who misses me injures himself;
    all who hate me love death.

Personification of God's wisdom and stress on it as the source and governor of the created world is present in the intertestamental writings: the Wisdom of Jesus the Son of Sirach and the Wisdom of Solomon (Ecclesiasticus). During this period, many of the commentators on the Jewish Scriptures began to stress that God is self-revealing by means of the two sorts of sources mentioned above. First, they saw instances of special revelation in significant historical events and specially called persons. They also saw a more general or universal revelation present in the created universe, to be discerned in the orderly processes of nature and the cause-and-effect laws that can be discerned in human interaction (for instance, that the evildoer will ultimately come to grief, that fools and wicked persons will cause their own undoing, but that the righteous will find strength and ultimate prosperity through their faithfulness and honesty). It came to be emphasized that the culmination of both these forms of revelation is to be found in the Torah, or Pentateuch, the first five books of the Jewish Scriptures. The Torah was given through God's special revelation to Moses. It includes, contains, and in some senses is the special revelation of God's will. It is the code of conduct whose adoption is the appropriate response by God's people to God's mighty acts of salvation, the bond of God's covenant with Israel. Yet increasingly, the Torah (more than the Law but including it) came to be described as the embodiment of God's wisdom itself, the concentrated essence of the wisdom through which the world was created and is sustained. Thus, a bridge was built between the two forms of revelation: special (that given in unique circumstances to specially chosen persons) and general (that available to the insightful and obedient discernment of humanity generally). In the Torah, they are seen to be one and the same.

Thus, the problem of the knowledge of God as interpreted in Judaism does not concern reason's ability to reach beyond itself, as it has so frequently in later Western thought. Rather it is practical in nature. Knowing God is a problem because of human blindness, the refusal to discern what is obvious about the way humans should respond to God—with grateful obedience—and to their fellow humans— with justice, kindness, and compassion. The wise person is the one who is not willfully blind but whose humility and willingness to obey allow discernment of God's law, either as specially given or at work everywhere. Wisdom leading to obedient response culminates in knowledge not only of God's law but in reverent devotion to the lawgiver.

FAITH, REASON, AND REVELATION

The concept of two major sources of knowledge of God, which in reality are one, has frequently been the starting point for Christian thinkers. As we have seen, the two sources, or kinds, of knowledge of God came to be described as general and special revelation. In Christianity as in Judaism, the concept of a general revelation available to all humans reflecting rationally on their experience is based on the belief that God creates and sustains the natural universe by means of God's wisdom, power, and goodness. Thus, the effects and, for some thinkers, the presence of God's wisdom, power and goodness can be discerned in the structure, order, and flow of natural events.

Paul, in his Letter to the Romans, held that non-Jews who worshipped false gods (idols) and behaved immorally were blameworthy, even though they had not received the special revelation from God that Jews had received.

> For what can be known about God is plain to them, because God has shown it to them. Ever since the creation of the world his invisible nature, namely, his eternal power and deity, have been clearly perceived in the things that have been made. So they are without excuse....
>
> (ROMANS 1:19–20 RSV)

The concepts of general and special revelation are usually *connected* in Christian thought by showing that the same divine wisdom that is responsible for creating and sustaining the natural realm is also discernible in the special providential acts of God in human history. Thus, the spirit of God inspires and empowers prophetic leaders, including Moses, Samuel, Elijah, Isaiah, and John the Baptist to carry out God's purposes. In their words and actions, God's wisdom, power, and goodness are apparent. God speaks and acts through them.

The author of the Gospel of John gave the most influential of all Christian formulations of this belief. In the prologue, he affirmed that the wisdom of God that is the source of the entire world was and is also present in the decisive event of

God's special revelation—namely, the person and work of Jesus. Thus, for John's gospel and most subsequent Christian thought, Jesus is more than a prophet inspired and empowered by God, more even than the expected Messiah of Judaism. Jesus is a human being who also is a unique self-disclosure (revelation) of God, one in whose person and work God is fully present:

> In the beginning was the Word and the Word was with God, and the Word was God. He was in the beginning with God; all things were made through him, and without him was not anything made that was made. In him was life, and the life was the light of men....And the Word became flesh and dwelt among us, full of grace and truth; we have beheld his glory, glory as of the only Son from the Father.

> (JOHN 1:1–4, 14 RSV)

The term *word* used in John's gospel is a translation of the Greek *logos,* which had been used to refer to the divine reason, or law, governing the natural order as early as the sixth century B.C.E. by the philosopher Heraclitus. Later, *logos* was used by the Stoics to mean the divine reason. It had been adopted by Jewish thinkers in explaining and interpreting the Jewish concept of the wisdom of God.

The belief that the wisdom of God at work in the whole created realm is uniquely present in the person of Jesus is explicitly expressed in several places in the New Testament, including the Gospel and First Epistle of John, Colossians (1:15–20), Hebrews (2:10), and the Gospel of Matthew.[2]

Because of the connection of special and general revelation—because both ultimately are God's direct or indirect self-disclosure—some Christian thinkers have stressed general revelation as providing a very important preparation for special revelation. Such thinkers have reasoned in this way: It is because *some* knowledge of God is available to us from reasoned reflection on our experience generally that we are able to recognize special disclosures of God's will or of God's self. Even if special revelation goes much farther than the generally available knowledge that we may arrive at about God through reason, if we did not have at least some concept of God, however dim, incomplete, or inadequate, we would not be able to recognize special events or instances of God's self-disclosure. We would not be able to tell the difference between true and false claims to special revelation. Unless we understood, however dimly, *who* God is (in the sense of the passage from Paul's Letter to the Romans), the very idea of a message from God would not occur to us, and the ability to recognize or distinguish true messages from God, or messages from the true God, would be nonexistent. According to Paul, because people had failed to pay attention to what they had been given the power to know about the true God, they became worshippers of false gods.

Justin Martyr has been mentioned as one who found the concepts of Platonic philosophy helpful to his understanding and reception of the Christian message. Justin believed this even though after his conversion to Christianity he criticized some aspects of Platonic philosophy and the philosophical approach to truth apart from Christian revelation.

In general, there have been at least four ways in which Christian thinkers have found the use of reason (related to general revelation) to be of possible value in

---

[2]See M. Jack Suggs, *Wisdom, Christology and Law in Matthew's Gospel* (Cambridge, Mass.: Harvard University Press, 1970).

leading one to the acceptance Christian truth. Some thinkers have advocated more than one of these uses of reason to help persons reach religious knowledge.

Belief in Reason

Some, though not many, Christian thinkers have argued that reason by itself is adequate to the discovery of religious truth. In the twelfth century, at the beginning of the economic and cultural revitalization of Europe, there was a tremendous burst of enthusiasm on the part of some Christian philosophers for the use of methods of logical analysis and proof to explain and establish Christian doctrines—for instance the doctrine of the Trinity—that most have thought of as being far beyond the power of human reason to comprehend. The twelfth-century attempt to use reason as a universally adequate source or criterion of religious truth produced a crisis and was perceived by some Christians as a threat to the integrity of Christian doctrine and the authority of the church.[3] Peter Abelard, perhaps the greatest philosopher and theologian of the early twelfth century, did not go to the extreme of holding that all Christian truth can be established by reason, but his enthusiasm for the use of logical analysis to explicate Christian doctrine led some of his opponents, including the famous mystic St. Bernard of Clairvaux, to charge that Abelard went too far in trying to discover by reason what can only be given by revelation and received and held by faith.

In the eighteenth century, Christian thinkers known as deists (discussed in earlier chapters) wanted to rid Christian teachings of all appeal to the miraculous and supernatural in order to bring harmony between the Christian approach to truth and that of Newtonian science. The deists were willing to make rational reflection on experience the sole source and criterion of religious truth. A deistic thinker such as Thomas Jefferson could argue, for instance, that the message of Jesus was not a supernaturally given special revelation. Rather, it was the purest and most sublime moral philosophy of human history. The eighteenth-century German philosopher Immanuel Kant argued in his *Religion Within the Limits of Reason Alone* for belief in God and a purification of the concept of God based on the knowledge of morality that is innate in the human mind.

Reason Depending on Revelation

The belief that a major part of Christian belief can be arrived at by using reason to reflect on the created world or on reason itself (general revelation) has not been a majority opinion among Christians. Many have believed that rational knowledge leading to insight into the nature of eternal (necessary) truth, the self (or soul), and God may serve a vital function in preparing for the reception and assisting in the understanding of what Christianity teaches about God and our relation to God. Augustine (354–430 C.E.), perhaps the most powerful post–New Testament influence on later Western Christianity, like Justin, found in Platonic philosophy an important preparation for understanding and accepting the Christian message. As a child and young man, Augustine had been exposed to Christian teaching largely through the influence of his mother. For a time he dismissed Christianity, becoming an adherent of Manichaeism, which was one of Christianity's contemporary rivals.

---

[3]M.-D. Chenu, O. P., *Nature, Man and Society in the Twelfth Century* (Chicago: University of Chicago Press, 1968). See especially the first chapter.

Later, becoming disillusioned with Manichaean answers to his religious doubts and moral problems, Augustine began to study Platonic philosophy, most effectively represented in Augustine's time by the Neoplatonic school deriving from Plotinus (205–270 C.E.). As a result of the study of Platonic thought, many of Augustine's religious questions were answered and many of his objections to Christian belief were removed. Particularly, he was impressed with the Neoplatonic treatment of God and the soul as nonmaterial, spiritual realities, and with its teaching of evil as being *not* a reality in itself coeternal with God (as Manichaeism taught) but as the absence of good, as a falling or turning from God.

Plato had taught that all knowledge of true reality, of eternal truths (for instance, the truths of mathematics and the essences or general and specific natures that make plants and animals what they are, their forms) is innate within the soul (or mind). Thus, one should cultivate or "go into" one's soul to find truth, turning from the distractions of sense experience and the realm of material objects. Augustine did not accept the concept of innate knowledge. Instead, he made a subtle modification of Plato's theory of how we acquire knowledge. All true knowledge (such as the truths of mathematics) depends on an illumination of the mind by God—ultimately by that "Light which is the Light of men" mentioned in John's gospel. Thus, even in ordinary knowing we are dependent on a kind of revelation to the mind from and of God. This means that already within us is a kind of implicit *faith*. The innate longing for truth (even about mathematics) and the belief that truth is somewhere to be found, means that we recognize and believe in something higher than the mind—namely, truth. For Augustine, this truth that we all implicitly believe to be a reality either comes from God or is an aspect of God. When we discover truth (or truths), it is because we have implicitly had faith that truth was there to be found, and because God has illuminated our minds so that we can recognize it.

So for Augustine, even general revelation is not something simply put into the world that the mind appropriates. It is an event in which there is active communication by God to the actively receptive human mind. Such implicit faith and the revelation of specific truths about the world may and should impel the mind (or soul) to seek clearer, more explicit knowledge of the source of these truths and of the mind's illumination—namely, God, who is the truth. So a kind of revelation (the presence of implicit faith *and* the illumination of the mind in the discovery of truths) *does* prepare the mind to receive specially revealed, saving truths, for it can bring the mind to knowledge of its own spiritual nature and of its need for a right relation to God. It can bring the individual to recognition that one can find fulfillment only in knowing and loving God. It also can show the mind (or soul or self) that it is helpless in establishing this relation apart from God's Grace. Thus, awareness of how the mind is illumined, even in ordinary knowing, can bring the mind to knowledge of the nature of God as a spiritual being. But this sort of knowing must be completed by illumination concerning the special acts of God's self-disclosure. Augustine remarked that he found much about God the Logos in Platonic philosophy, but did not learn from philosophy that "the Word became flesh and dwelt among us." Augustine learned about God's love of, and saving power toward, lost humankind only through the church's proclamation and the Christian Scriptures attesting to the saving event of Jesus Christ.

A later Christian thinker, Anselm of Canterbury (1033–1109), sometimes called the father of Scholasticism, was also influenced by the Platonic tradition. Anselm was convinced that we have the ability to arrive by rational reflection at a true concept of God based on our own innate awareness of the contrast between our finitude and that which is not finite (God). We thus are aware that God, if God exists, must be the perfect, all-powerful, all-wise, absolutely good being. A perfect being must be free of all limitations. It cannot be dependent on any other being. It follows from this, Anselm believed, that one cannot, without contradiction, think of God as not existing, since the concept of a being that might not exist is not the concept of a perfect being. This line of argument is sometimes called the *ontological* argument for God's existence.

In a sense, for both Augustine and Anselm faith precedes understanding and reasoning about God. In this sense, faith is a sort of deep-level inner awareness of our need for God. We may try to suppress this awareness, but this awareness is always there. It is an implicit faith in the reality of God and a sense of our absolute dependence on God. Reasoning may bring to full clarity what the sense of our finitude means and thus prepare the way for a faith that is an explicit commitment to the God proclaimed in the Christian message. Naturally, this second-level, or explicit, faith, will involve various beliefs about God, but it continues and brings to self-awareness faith of the first level, faith as awareness of our dependence on God.

Reason Supporting Revelation

Still other Christian thinkers have understood human reason to be capable of bringing humans to *inferential* knowledge of God derived from reasoning about the physical universe. (Anselm, Augustine, and many Christian Platonists accepted this use of reason, in addition to reason oriented to the inner realities of the soul.) Christian Platonism, as modified by creative thinkers like Augustine, Anselm, and the Franciscan Bonaventure (1221–1274), was the major philosophical influence on Christian thought from its beginnings until the thirteenth century. At that point, under the influence of such thinkers as Albert the Great (1193?–1280) and Thomas Aquinas (1225–1274), the philosophy of Aristotle became dominant.

Aristotle and Empiricism.   Aristotle, who had been a student, colleague, and friend of Plato, had much in common with him. One of the greatest differences between Platonic and Aristotelian approaches is the theory of knowledge, of how we acquire and validate truth. Aristotle was an empiricist. *Empiricism* is the belief that all human knowledge is derived from sensation. Thus, instead of believing that we use reason to clarify and discover truths innate within the mind (as Plato had taught), Aristotle believed we arrive at truth by extracting information (generalizing) from memory-images that originally come to us by way of the five senses.

Aquinas' Theory of Knowledge.   Partly because of his acceptance of Aristotle's empiricist theory of knowledge, Aquinas drew a sharper line between general and special revelation than the Christian Platonists did. This resulted in his drawing a rather sharp line between the subject matter of rationally acquired knowledge (philosophy and what we would call natural science) and knowledge derived from special revelation (theology). For Aquinas, the human mind is adapted to knowledge of material objects derived from sense experience. Humans are not able to know spiritual entities, the soul or God, fully and directly—intuitively—in the present life. We can, however, through rational reflection on sense experience, arrive at certain knowledge *about* God and the soul. We can know with demonstrative certainty that God exists and that our souls are immortal. We do not have an innate concept of God, and God's existence is not immediately self-evident to us (as Anselm's ontological proof assumed). But we can know God through God's effects. We can infer the existence of God as the supreme, necessary cause of the contingent (and therefore created) world of nature. Otherwise, we would not be able to understand our experience *of* nature.

Aquinas believed that five ways of reasoning lead to knowledge of the existence of God and to an understanding of some of God's attributes. These lines of reasoning, usually called *cosmological proofs* of God's existence, begin with facts of our experience of the physical universe and end with the necessity of concluding that God is their ultimate cause. They concern the existence of motion, causal processes, contingent being, degrees of value, and purposive processes in nonrational nature.

Aquinas and Aristotle believed that the natural order disclosed by rational reflection on sensory experience is characterized by purpose and values. This is certainly true of human life. Human life has goals associated with our natural capacities and tendencies. Through reflection on *human* experience, we can arrive at the content of the *moral* law. Aquinas agreed with the Greek and Roman Stoics in holding a "natural law," or "law of nature," approach to morality. Humans can, through right reasoning concerning natural capacities and needs, arrive at a sound understanding of their rights and duties. He was convinced that all of the Ten Commandments given in the Jewish Scripture (Exodus 20:1–17; Deuteronomy 5:6–21), with the exception of the commandment concerning Sabbath observance, can be discovered by reason. (Some Christians have regarded the Ten Commandments as a foundation not only of Jewish but of Christian morality, indeed as a set of basic moral principles valid for all humanity.)

Why, then, is there need for special revelation? According to Aquinas, it is twofold. Although there is available to humankind natural knowledge concerning God and morality that *might* serve as a basis for understanding and reception of further special revelation and that *might* be used to guide humans in their social interaction, this revelation may not be effective. Not everyone will possess the time, intelligence, or means to arrive at natural knowledge of God or morality. Also, human beings are fallen, sinful, and not naturally good as originally they were created to be. They are inclined to disobey the moral law and to be partial and self-interested in interpreting it. Therefore, God has in various ways provided in special revelatory events much that could have been discovered through reasoning.

The other aspect of specially revealed truth recognized by Aquinas concerns those aspects of God and ourselves that transcend our limited power of knowing by rational reflection on sense experience, but that are related to our need for salvation. These truths cannot be discovered by the use of reason alone, since the human mind in the present life can know material objects directly, but cannot know the essence of God. We cannot even know directly that our minds (or souls) possess an eternal destiny. Nevertheless, certain truths related to God's essential nature—the doctrine of the Trinity, for instance—and God's saving activity—the Incarnation—have been revealed because they bear on our salvation. Much that we need to know for our spiritual welfare about the church, the sacraments, and the Christian life is of this nature. Such truth is not irrational but transcends the capacity of human reason.

Thus, for Aquinas, general and special revelation should work together. General revelation can prepare our minds for understanding and accepting special revelation. Special revelation can reinforce or make us initially aware of the truths of general revelation. By and large, the truths of general revelation will first be acquired as special revelation, taught by the church and accepted and held by faith as the Christian participates in the sacramental life of the church and is obedient to its authority. If acquired through rational reflection, they are no longer held by faith.[4] For Aquinas faith means the intellectual acceptance of a belief not conclusively demonstrated by rational means, held on the basis of the church's authority. Faith is made possible by God's Grace. This use can be contrasted with the concept of faith held by Augustine and Anselm, where the term could signify an innate orientation of the self as a spiritual being to its creator, as well as the more conscious explicit attitude of trust and belief in God as revealed in special events of self-disclosure.

Reason Questioning Itself

A fourth way in which reason has been seen as preparation for the reception of the Christian message involves use of reason to show its own inability to discover truth. During the fourteenth century, many Christian thinkers drew an even sharper line between what can be known by natural reason and what is given in special revelation than Aquinas had done. These thinkers were called *nominalists*. Nominalism is the philosophical view that only individual things exist. There are no general truths or common natures, or essences, of things among the basic components of reality. General truths are only artificially fabricated grouping devices that the mind uses to deal with collections of individual things in a convenient way. Thus we use the concept *dog* to deal with a large number of individuals, similar in important ways, that are really unique.

The term that contrasts with nominalist is *realist*. Realists, of which there have been a great many kinds in philosophical history, believe that general concepts such as *dog* or *human nature* are discovered and not invented. If our concept of *dog* is correct, it corresponds to something objective that dogs have in common. It is this common element, or essence, that *causes* all dogs to resemble each other. For nominalists, dogs simply have been found to resemble each other in various ways. That is why we use the term *dog* to describe them, not because some essence *belongs* to them all in common. For the realist, to know the concept of a thing or species gives us deep and accurate knowledge about it. For the nominalist, a concept is simply a summary of what has been observed in the past. This may not continue to hold in the future. Nominalism tends to go with empiricism. However, Aristotle and Aquinas were empiricists *and* realists, though realists of a different kind than Plato was. If you hear someone say something like: "It is contrary to human nature for a mother to want to give up her baby for adoption," you are probably hearing someone who is a philosophical realist, whether consciously so or not. A nominalist would be more likely to say, "Eighty-one percent of all mothers interviewed say that they would not want to give up their baby for adoption." For the realist, the essence or common nature may simply exist somehow above or apart from the things that manifest it (Plato). It may be a formative power or structure within the particular things that share it (Aristotle). It may be an idea in the mind of God in accordance with which God has created the particular things that belong to common species (Aquinas). For the nominalist it is none of these.

---

[4]See the discussion in Aquinas, *De Veritate*, 14, 9; also Frederick Copleston, S. J., *A History of Philosophy*, Volume 2, Part II (Westminster, Md: Newman Press, 1950), Chapter Thirty-two.

The nominalists were more radical empiricists than Aristotle and Aquinas. For them the generalizations about experience that we arrive at through rational reflection do not disclose the real nature of things. Thus, rational reflection on the mind's contents cannot give certainty. It cannot give us certainty even about the realm of material objects disclosed in sensory experience, much less lead to conclusive proofs of the existence of God, the nature of the self or soul, or the contents of morality. Morality cannot be derived from rational reflection on our capacities and needs. Rather it depends on the arbitrary commandments of God.

William of Ockham.   Possibly the greatest of the medieval nominalists was William of Ockham (1280?–1349). As a Christian theologian, Ockham may be said to have placed even greater stress on special revelation than most of his predecessors had, since he limited the capacity of human reason to arrive at truth. Thus the truths about God and morality that Christianity teaches are to be held by faith (in the sense understood by Aquinas) and acquired through God's Grace as one participates in the sacramental life of the church. The sacraments, as channels of God's Grace, enable the Christian subjectively to have faith in beliefs that are objectively valid, because proclaimed by the church, though they are not rationally provable.

Immanuel Kant.   Like the nominalists, the German philosopher Immanuel Kant (1724–1804) attempted, as he said, to limit the claims of reason to make room for faith. In his *Critique of Pure Reason,* Kant argued that metaphysical and religious beliefs cannot be proved or disproved by theoretical, or scientific, reason, since it is by its nature limited to dealing with questions that can be formulated in terms of observational and experimental procedures and confirmed or rejected accordingly. Kant *did* believe that reason in its moral use is adequate as a basis and criterion of religious belief.

Pascal and Kierkegaard.   More radical had been the seventeenth-century mathematician and scientist Blaise Pascal (1623–1663). In a brilliant work left unfinished at the time of his death but later published as *Les Pensées,* Pascal argued from the finitude of human reason to the need for volitional (willed) commitment to God and a life of faith. In something of the same spirit, the nineteenth-century Danish thinker, Søren Kierkegaard (1813–1855), was convinced that reason is simply not adequate to answer the fundamental questions of life. In a series of highly ingenious writings, Kierkegaard attempted to awaken "the individual" in his readers to the impotence of scientific, philosophical, and socially defined "objective truth" in dealing with questions about the meaning of one's life. Awakened, "the individual" may be prepared to hear the plain Christian message in sermon and Scripture and respond with a leap of faith, a decision to commit one's whole life to the God who became incarnate at an arbitrary place on earth in an arbitrary period of human history.

This fourth use of reason—to show reason's own limits in the hope that this will lead to recognition of the need for the appropriation of (special) revelation by faith—often leads to positions that are highly critical of the use of reason at all as preparation for religious belief or as a source of knowledge about God. Generally, thinkers who reject the use of reason entirely stress the vastness of the contrast between God and finite human reason. They find nothing in common between naturally acquired and specially revealed truth. The rejection of reason has never been a majority position among Christian thinkers, but has had important representatives.

Tertullian, a second-century Christian whose theories concerning the doctrine of the Trinity had a permanent influence on Western Christianity, held that philosophical reasoning is of no value in preparing the mind to understand or accept Christian truth. About some Christian beliefs, such as the Resurrection, Tertullian wrote, "I believe it *because* it is absurd," meaning that the transcendence of rationally based expectations is one criterion of truth about God.

Martin Luther ridiculed attempts of the Christian scholastic theologians to use philosophical reasoning in the interpretation and defense of Christian beliefs. Luther referred to reason as "an evil beast" and "the devil's whore."

Barth and Brunner.   Karl Barth (1886–1968), perhaps the most influential of all twentieth-century Protestant theologians, also stressed the discontinuity between what can be known by human reason and the revealed truths of Christianity. The nominalists had emphasized the inability of reason to know anything with certainty. Thus, natural knowledge cannot provide a starting point for belief concerning God. Barth agreed, saying that God is "Wholly Other" than we are and than the whole realm of what our finite understanding can grasp. Barth also stressed the sinfulness—self-centeredness and selfish distortion—to which all human reasoning is subject. This brings us back to the quotation from Paul's Letter to the Romans with which this section began. Paul stressed the ability of humans to know God through evidences of God's created world. But in the same passage he spoke of an ever-increasing corruption of humanity resulting from human refusal to recognize the true God. Barth, pursuing the theme of the lost capacity of fallen humanity to know God, argued against his former theological collaborator, Emil Brunner. Brunner insisted that even though the corruption of human reason through sin makes it impossible for humans to know God apart from God's special self-revelation, there is a point of contact in human awareness of finitude and need between God's revelation and human reception of it. Barth denied this. There is no connecting link between humans and God, and no basis in human capacities or sense of finitude for knowing God, until God's self-disclosure in Jesus Christ creates the connecting link and gives fallen humans the ability to receive knowledge of God and of their need of God.

Mystics

In contrast to the four ways of understanding reason as preparatory to appropriation of revelation, *and* in contrast to the stress of Christians like Tertullian, Luther, and Barth on holding to Christian truth by simple faith, Christian mystics have stressed the possibility of direct, personal experiential communion with God—which is genuine knowledge *of,* not *about* God. This mystical communion is passively received, given by Grace, and not achieved, though it may be prepared for by moral self-discipline, asceticism, and prayer. Mysticism has some affinity with the Platonic use of reason, since it stresses withdrawing one's attention from the world known in sensory experience and "going into" the soul. In fact, many of the great Christian mystics have held to the Platonic philosophy, though others, like Aquinas, have not. Many mystics argue that such an experience *does* constitute knowledge of God. The question of whether this is a general human capacity possessed by all or a special gift of God's Grace to some Christians may be answered differently. As we have seen, Aquinas and the majority of mystical writers within the Catholic tradition have held that it is a specially conferred Grace, not a possibility, source, or criterion in human nature generally—certainly not in fallen human nature—of the knowledge of God. Many Protestant thinkers, from Luther and Calvin forward to Barth, have been suspicious of mysticism and the claims of mystical theologians. Others, including the Quakers, have recognized the possibilities of mystical experience by emphasizing the presence of the inner light or the Christ within as an aspect of human nature generally and thus potentially as a source of knowledge of God. On the basis of such belief, Rufus M. Jones, a distinguished American Quaker, led a team of Friends to Germany to appeal to Adolf Hitler on behalf of Jews who were being persecuted prior to World War II, hoping that Hitler would respond to "the Christ within" and change his course of action. Some Jews were allowed to leave Germany. The great majority were not.

AUTHORITY

Much that has been said in this chapter leads back to a question that has deeply divided Christians: the question of religious authority. Who—what person, persons, group—or what—words, documents, institutions, experiences—is/are entitled, according to Christian belief, to settle either ultimately or provisionally the question of what is true or false in the area of Christian belief and practice?

The ultimate Christian response to this question has usually been "God." God is the ultimate source of religious authority. The extended discussion of general and special revelation earlier in the chapter is an attempt to explain how many Christians have tried to show how God makes knowledge about God's self available to human groups or individuals. But further attempts at operationalizing this Christian understanding of authority have produced great diversity. Certainly the Scriptures of the Old and New Testaments have been accepted as authoritative by the great majority of Christians. Both Eastern Orthodox and Western Catholic branches of Christianity have emphasized the authority of tradition, along with (and indeed to some extent including) that of the Scriptures. For both, the Scriptures are an inspired crystallization of already existing prophetic (Old Testament) and apostolic (New Testament) traditions. The Scriptures themselves are subject to interpretation in the light of earlier and continuing tradition. For both Eastern Orthodoxy and Western Catholicism, the role of the bishops becomes all-important in interpreting Scripture and tradition. For the Orthodox, the seven ecumenical councils have a decisive position, and in theory the ultimate interpreter of Christian truth would be such ecumenical councils.

For Roman Catholics, the teaching office of the church, expressed either in what has been a universally accepted and proclaimed part of Catholic tradition, or in what the bishops proclaim in ecumenical councils, or what the pope proclaims when speaking ex cathedra, functions in theory to define religious truth authoritatively.

Protestants like Luther and Calvin made Scripture *alone* the source of authoritative interpretation in areas of doctrine and practice. Both argued that interpreters of Scripture should be well-prepared scholars. However, correct interpretations ultimately depended on the illumination of the mind and heart of the Bible scholar by the Holy Spirit. But the Protestant answer that the criterion of religious truth is the Bible as illuminated by the Holy Spirit led to metaquestions concerning criteria of Spirit-illumined Bible interpretation.

Most Protestant groups, including those originating during the Reformation, have adopted credal statements (often including one or more of the historic creeds originating in the ancient and medieval church). They have seen these statements as based on Scripture but also as giving direction to its correct interpretation.

One of the earliest Christian creeds, often called the Apostles' Creed, evolved over several centuries until it reached its "received," or accepted, form around 700 C.E. from a statement that converts to Christianity were asked to repeat, after having gone through a period of instruction in Christian belief, when presenting themselves for baptism. This creed continues to be used by Catholics and by many Protestant groups.

THE APOSTLES' CREED

I believe in God the Father almighty, maker of heaven and earth;

And in Jesus Christ, His only Son, our Lord, who was conceived by the Holy Spirit, born of the Virgin Mary, suffered under Pontius Pilate, was crucified, dead and buried. He descended into Hell. On the third day He rose again from the dead, ascended into Heaven, and sits at the right hand of God the Father almighty. Thence he will come to judge the living and the dead;

I believe in the Holy Spirit, the Holy Catholic Church, the communion of saints, the forgiveness of sins; the resurrection of the body, and the life everlasting. Amen.

After the sixteenth-century split in European Christianity known as the Protestant Reformation, the use of catechisms to instruct church members in dogma and doctrines became very common among Catholics and many Protestant groups. *Catechisms* are summaries of Christian doctrine in a standard question-and-answer format. They are thus suitable for memorization and have been widely used by Catholics and Protestants for teaching children and young people basic Christian beliefs. As mentioned above, in some Protestant groups they have served as authoritative credal statements. The shorter and longer catechisms compiled by Martin Luther may be taken as authoritative statements of Lutheran theology, in Luther's understanding derived from the Bible but also providing keys and criteria for its interpretation. The same is true of catechisms originating among Reformed groups, such as the (Presbyterian) Westminster Shorter Catechism. The Church of England adopted thirty-nine authoritative articles of religion.

Among American Methodists a catechism, containing such questions and answers as the following, was available for use:

Section I   1. (Q) What is Christianity?

(A) Christianity is the religion of God's redeeming love, manifested in the incarnate life, the atoning death, and the glorious resurrection of Jesus Christ, the Founder of the Kingdom of God.

2. (Q) Who is Jesus Christ?

(A) The Son of God and the Son of Mary; very God and very man; and the only Mediator between God and man.[5]

---

[5]*The Standard Catechism* (New York and Nashville, Tenn.: Methodist Book Concern, 1929).

Apparently the Methodist catechism was not used widely for educational purposes and certainly not as an authoritative standard of doctrine or criterion of scriptural interpretation. However, American Methodists do not lack doctrinal standards and criteria. They have twenty-five articles of religion (representing an adaptation made by John Wesley from the Church of England's thirty-nine); some additional articles that emerged in different Wesleyan offshoot groups; some general rules relating to conduct drawn up by Wesley for Methodist societies within the Church of England; and John Wesley's *Standard Sermons,* his *Explanatory Notes on the New Testament,* and the hymns composed by his brother Charles.

In 1972 the United Methodist General Conference, the elected representative body that is solely authorized to take official action on behalf of United Methodists in the United States, while keeping the received Wesleyan standards and offering the "Wesleyan Quadrilateral" of Scripture, tradition, experience, and reason (with Scripture held to be primary) as Methodist doctrinal criteria, seemed to make the whole body of credal and doctrinal statements of the various Christian traditions relevant for making contemporary theological decisions.

However, a more recent General Conference (1988), while keeping most of what its predecessor conference had affirmed, dropped the word "pluralism" as characterizing United Methodism's theological position, reaffirmed the primacy of Scripture, and ended by affirming the denomination's twenty-five articles of religion and Wesley's *Standard Sermons* and *Notes on the New Testament* as its doctrinal standards. Most interpreters saw these actions as a response to feelings among some United Methodists that a more precise (or narrower) way of characterizing the denomination's doctrinal and theological stance was needed.

Some Protestant groups have repudiated credal statements. Influenced by the empiricist psychology of John Locke, and his assumption that the Bible approached without theological preconceptions will yield an overall consistent body of teaching, the Disciples of Christ have long asserted "no creed but Christ." The Churches of Christ, which are historically related to the Disciples, and some Baptist groups have also resisted acknowledging any doctrinal statements or standards except the Christian Scriptures.

Even from the human scholarly point of view, the question of what are the correct methods of biblical interpretation to find the intended meaning of the human author, or the intended message of the God who is believed to have inspired the human author, have been difficult to answer. Early biblical scholars, including the celebrated Origen (185–255 C.E.), argued for different levels of meaning—including literal and various symbolic levels—within the biblical text. Origen argued for faithfulness to the intention of the text but felt that the text sometimes demands symbolic interpretation and almost always has levels of depth and richness of meaning. Protestants by and large have argued for *only* the literal level but have held that even the literal meaning of a text may take highly symbolic forms (as in Genesis, where God is described as walking in the Garden of Eden). The rise of critical-historical approaches to the study of Scripture in the eighteenth and nineteenth centuries (see Chapters Two and Nine) helped, but also further complicated, attempts at interpretation, leading to the recent split between fundamentalists and liberals over the question of how one should approach Scripture. This latter-day controversy is perhaps a further instance of the impact of science on religion, since most biblical scholars have become convinced that they must use the same methods and possess the same objectivity when studying the Bible as scientific historians use in their studies of the past.

Some Protestants have appealed to various kinds of subjective experience—from the inner light of the Quakers to charismatic revelations received by contemporary Pentecostals—as authoritative.

The so-called mainline Protestant denominations and the contemporary Catholic church have accepted the historical-critical approach to the study of the Bible. This approach has involved rejection of traditionally held beliefs about the authorship of some of the biblical books—e.g., that Moses authored the first five books of the Old Testament—and the calling into question of others—e.g., that Matthew, Mark, Luke, and John are known to be the authors of the four gospels. These groups have also rejected any theory of biblical authorship that pictures God as having verbally dictated the Bible to human secretaries. Rather, these Christians understand the authors of the Bible to have been concerned persons of their times who relied on their human skills, reason, and intelligence. Nevertheless, or because of this, the biblical documents are regarded by these Christians as truly expressing, containing, and being the Word of God, a unique, inspired message from God to the world that serves as a part of God's redemptive activity.

One important theme in recent discussions of Christian life has been the emphasis on the essentially narrative character of Christian expression. Some interpreters have held that this insight—that the Christian message or revelation has taken a primarily narrative form—gives new insights into the nature of authority for Christians. A contemporary Christian writer on theology and ethics has noted

> Too often we assume the narrative character of Christian convictions is incidental to those convictions. Both believer and unbeliever are under the impression that narrative is a relatively unimportant moral category. Specifically, we tend to think of "stories" as illustrations of some deeper truth that we can and should learn to articulate in a nonnarrative mode....
>
> I think this is a dire misreading of the narrative character of Christian convictions. My contention is that the narrative mode is neither incidental nor accidental to Christian belief. There is no more fundamental way to talk of God than in a story. The fact that we come to know God through the recounting of the story of Israel and the life of Jesus is decisive for our truthful understanding of the kind of God we worship as well as the world in which we exist. Put directly, the narrative character of our knowledge of God, the self, and the world is a reality-making claim that the world and our existence in it are God's creations; our lives, and indeed, the existence of the universe are but contingent realities....
>
> ...Doctrinally we affirm that God is our creator and/or redeemer, or that God's essential nature is that of a trinitarian relationship. But such emphasis ignores the fact that such "doctrines" are themselves a story, or perhaps better, the outline of the story. Claims such as "God is creator" are simply shorthand ways of reminding us that we believe we are participants in a much more elaborate story, of which God is the author. Doctrines, therefore, are not the upshot of the stories; they are not the meaning or heart of the stories. Rather they are tools (sometimes even misleading tools), meant to help us tell the story better. Because the Christian story is an enacted story, liturgy is probably a much more important resource than are doctrines or creeds for helping us to hear, tell, and live the story of God.

Narrative is not secondary for our knowledge of God, there is no "point" that can be separated from the story. The narratives through which we learn of God *are* the point.[6]

Many have found the emphasis on narratives or stories that cannot be reduced to abstract conceptual language a liberating insight for contemporary Christian understanding. However, some critics have wondered whether the stories themselves do not at least involve or imply collections of propositions about which the hearers have a right to ask the same kinds of questions that have been asked about doctrinal formulations. Among these questions would be: "What do the stories intend to tell us about ourselves, the universe, and God? Are the stories true? How are we to know what the stories mean and whether they are true?" Such critics do not necessarily reject the new emphasis on narrative as the vehicle of Christian truth. They do suggest that the same kinds of questions that arose in earlier discussions of faith and reason continue to arise. However this may be, relatively new movements of theological interpretation bearing such names as process theology, theological hermeneutics, and deconstruction now find their place among more traditionally oriented approaches.

CONFLICTS INVOLVING SCIENCE AND CHRISTIAN BELIEF

This chapter has described efforts by Christian thinkers to deal with the question of how one legitimately can claim to have arrived at knowledge about God. Christians have, as we have seen, attempted to answer this question since the very beginnings of the Christian movement. The question, however, assumed special importance with the rise and triumphs of modern science. Certain aspects of the encounter between the new science and the various branches of Christianity have produced the belief that the methods and results of scientific inquiry contain distinct threats to commonly held Christian beliefs.

One of the most significant early instances is the case of Galileo Galilei (1564–1642). Recent scholarship has shown that the conflict between Galileo and the Inquisition is not as clear-cut an example of the repression of scientific truth by religious authorities as has sometimes been imagined. Galileo, in attempting to establish the truth of the Copernican theory that the sun is at the center of the planetary system and that the earth is one of the planets that revolves about it, had explicitly raised fundamental questions about correct methods of interpreting the Scriptures. Copernicus, a brilliant sixteenth-century Pole—church official, medical doctor, astronomer—had attempted to improve Europe's ability to measure time by suggesting a return to the minority view of the nature of the planetary system held by the ancient Greek astronomer Aristarchus of Samos, who held that the sun (not the earth) is at the center of the universe (and thus at the center of the planetary system). Aristarchus' view had been rejected in antiquity because the contrasting view that the earth is at the center, held by the philosophers Plato and Aristotle and brilliantly supported by the second-century C.E. astronomer and mathematician Ptolemy, had "worked" better in explaining the observed positions of the stars and planets. By the time of Copernicus, the explanations based on Ptolemy seemed to

[6]Stanley Hauerwas, *The Peaceable Kingdom* (Notre Dame, Ind.: University of Notre Dame Press, 1983), pp. 25–26.

work less and less well. Copernicus suggested trying the theory of Aristarchus that put the sun at the center. His views aroused some controversy but were not perceived as a threat to the church. They were attractive to many astronomers and mathematicians.

Two generations later, the Italian mathematician-physicist Galileo Galilei began his defense of the Copernican theory, arguing that the Bible should not be seen as supporting the Ptolemaic position. He was attacked by some theologians and popular preachers of the day. Since he was not a theologian, church officials felt that Galileo was trespassing on their territory. Also, the church had ruled that the Copernican theory could be taught only as a hypothesis, not as established truth. Some theologians and ecclesiastical officials were reluctant to accept Copernican astronomy because it was generally held in medieval times that the Bible teaches that the earth is at the center of the planetary system and that the sun moves around it. Also, Aristotelian philosophy, which held to an earth-centered model, had been successfully integrated into Christian doctrine by such thinkers as Aquinas, John Duns Scotus, and their interpreters.

Not all theologians and religious officials opposed the Copernican theory. Urban VIII, prior to becoming pope, took great interest in the new astronomy and urged Galileo to write about it, cautioning him only to treat Copernicanism not as established truth and to be certain to give a number of "convincing" arguments to support the accepted Ptolemaic (earth-centered) model of the universe. In *Dialogue on the Great World Systems,* Galileo pretended to do this but actually put the pope's convincing arguments into the mouth of the dull-witted, tradition-bound Simplicio, thus seeming to ridicule them. The pope was angry and withdrew his support from Galileo, insisting that he be disciplined.

Apparently a number of other personal and institutional feuds had some bearing on the Inquisition's judgment requiring Galileo to recant his astronomical views and placing restrictions on his future activities. Some scholars have even debated whether falsified evidence—a forged memorandum to the effect that Galileo had earlier been forbidden even to write on Copernicanism—was introduced against him.[7]

However that may be, Galileo *had not* presented in his works and *did not have* decisive evidence to support the Copernican over the Plotemaic system. This was accomplished a generation later by Sir Isaac Newton (1642–1727), who drew on the work of Galileo's contemporary Johann Kepler (1571–1630) (whose work Galileo had apparently overlooked or undervalued). Galileo, one of the greatest experimental and theoretical scientists of all time, has frequently been portrayed as a scientific martyr to repressive religious authority. He was not exactly that, though what the Inquisition did in this instance may have hindered scientific progress in parts of Europe. It did bring discredit to some Christian institutions and their leaders.

The New Science, after receiving its Newtonian form, was largely welcomed by European Christians as providing powerful support for belief in an all-wise, all-powerful God who had created the universe in accordance with the simple yet beautiful laws of nature that Newton had discovered. Deists used Newtonian science as a platform for purging Christian belief of what they considered the fanciful tangle of traditional theological dogma held both by Catholics and by orthodox Protes-

---

[7]For the entire Galileo controversy as well as this point, one should consult the works by Langford, Santillana, and Raven included in the bibliography of the present chapter.

tants. Many Christians, including Joseph Butler (1692–1752), a bishop of the Church of England, argued that the New Science was compatible with traditional belief. Butler, especially in his famous *Analogy of Religion,* attacked deism and defended traditional orthodoxy. In contrast, David Hume (1711–1776), a sceptic, made a devastating attack on the "rational religion" of deism and also ridiculed traditional or orthodox Christian belief, trying to show that the new psychology, with its radically empiricist theory of knowledge, left no room for rational belief in religion *or* in science. According to Hume, there are good subjective (essentially instinctive) grounds for accepting scientific results but not religious beliefs, which he believed to be the result of credulity and superstition, producing intolerance and fanaticism in those who hold them.

Probably of longer-lasting significance for relations between science and Christianity than either the Copernican or the deist controversies was the conflict in England involving Darwinism. Prior to 1859, when Charles Darwin (1809–1882) published *The Origin of Species,* there had been some shocks to the then generally accepted belief that the Book of Genesis teaches that divine creation of the universe happened in six days about 6,000 years ago. Geological evidence indicated that the earth was much older than this and that geological changes have occurred gradually over long periods of time. Darwin's work presented evidence indicating that plant and animal species were not distinct creations that appeared all at once 6,000 years ago, but have evolved over a much longer period of time in accordance with the principle of natural selection. One very controversial part of Darwin's theory held that the human species was not specially created, but has evolved like other species from earlier and simpler forms of life.

Darwinism, thought to be in conflict with a literal interpretation of the Book of Genesis, was also thought to question the accepted religious belief that natural processes and human history are divinely created and guided. However, Darwin's revolutionary theories were soon being championed by representatives of the churches, who argued that there is no fundamental problem if one holds the belief that God created and sustains the universe, but in doing so uses the methods, including the law of natural selection, discovered by science. Influential leaders in the Church of England, including Charles Kingsley (1819–1875), pointed out that even in the ancient church and pre-Christian Rabbinic Judaism the creation accounts in Genesis were not necessarily taken literally and that Christian thinkers such as Augustine had suggested accounts of the creation process not entirely unlike later evolutionary ones.

Perhaps what has usually been perceived by most Christians as the greatest potential threat of the new scientific attitudes is the increasingly successful attempt by scientists to explain natural phenomena as purely mechanical, purposeless processes. Freudian and behavioristic schools of psychology, sociobiology, and recent inquiries into brain functioning have seemed even more threatening than Darwinism, since they have either speculated about or actually created models of human behavior that apparently reduce the human to the interplay of purely natural, random, ultimately chemical and physical, processes.[8] The trend of recent medical practice to treat disturbances previously characterized as *mental* (psychological,

---

[8]One recent, highly controversial, but ingenious argument by a distinguished contemporary biologist for the view that science discloses a universe entirely without purpose and none of whose parts requires the categories of purpose or value for their understanding is Jacques Monod, *Chance and Necessity* (New York: Alfred A. Knopf, 1971).

spiritual), such as depression ("melancholia") and obsessional neuroses, with drugs probably reinforces this belief.

It has frequently been argued that in a mechanistic (deterministic or statistically random) universe, the person—with every significant concept of human freedom, responsibility, value, or dignity—disappears. The philosopher Kant, one of the first to formulate a philosophy of the New Science, argued that it is necessary and legitimate for science to attempt to explain all natural phenomena in terms of mechanical principles, but that a deeper, less abstract level of our experience reveals the realm of morality—of persons, personal freedom, and God. Such scientifically trained religious thinkers as different as the Catholic scientist-priest Pierre Teilhard de Chardin, the Anglican theologian C. E. Raven, and the British mathematician and philosopher A. N. Whitehead have argued that ultimately scientific understanding will suggest—and cannot do without—the category of *purpose* or *value* for its comprehensive interpretation of our experience of nature.

Science has not been without its critics. Some conservative Christians even now argue that a scientific theory such as Darwinism, which is *only* a theory, should not be taught as fact and that the competing theory of the 6,000-year-ago creation derived from a literal interpretation of Genesis should be given equal time in public school science courses. Critics of this and other "scientific creationist" positions argue that the term *theory* in science does not entail lack of confirmation and is not used in this way to contrast with the term *fact*. Instead, a scientific theory is a system of laws and principles used to organize, explain, and predict a potentially unlimited number of facts within a well-defined field of investigation subject to observational and experimental tests. This suggests that it is not accurate to refer to religious beliefs as scientific theories, since what people ordinarily call religious beliefs do not function in this way. They cannot be given limited-frame precision and cannot be tested by using experimental or observational methods. This has been expressed by some writers when they have said that religious beliefs and scientific theories belong to different logical levels or to logically different fields of our language.

A few years ago it was not uncommon to hear it said that scientific statements deal with the *what* (the factual) and religious statements with the *why* (the value) dimensions of our experience. In light of recent studies of the roles of theorizing and experimental testing as they affect acceptance or rejection of scientific theories, this distinction is too simple. J. Bronowski, Thomas Kuhn, and other interpreters of contemporary science have shown that the results of scientific inquiry themselves are embedded in, and presuppose, a value framework. Facts themselves are not absolutes; they are relative to the theoretical frameworks used for establishing and interpreting them. As Kenneth E. Boulding observed:

> Even at the level of simple or supposedly simple sense perception we are increasingly discovering that the message which comes through the senses is itself mediated through a value system. We do not perceive our sense data raw; they are mediated through a highly learned process of interpretation and acceptance....What this means is that...there are no such things as "facts." There are only messages filtered through a changeable value system.[9]

[9]Kenneth E. Boulding, *The Image* (Ann Arbor: University of Michigan Press, 1966), p. 14.

This need not mean that scientific inquiry becomes subjective or arbitrary, though some critics, including Paul Feyerabend, may have suggested as much. In some ways the new understanding of what goes on in scientific theorizing and experimentation has brought scientific thought closer to the moral and religious dimensions of life. But for many thinkers this has served to indicate that great care must be used both *not* to reduce one type of thinking—scientific or religious—to the other, and *not* to draw the conclusion that either invalidates or can replace the other.

RELIGIOUS LANGUAGE: THE PROBLEM OF TALKING ABOUT GOD

Much current inquiry into the question of religious truth (or religious knowledge) has focused on the logic of religious language. The twentieth-century philosopher Ludwig Wittgenstein (1889–1951) cautioned philosophers against looking for an overall theory of the "nature" or "meaning" of language. Rather, he pointed out that there are many different language activities that humans engage in and many different language uses. Context—what Wittgenstein referred to as the "language game"—becomes all-important.

Thus, it may be a fundamental mistake to try to find common standards of meaning and verifiability for scientific and religious statements. This has led many philosophers to explore certain *noncognitive* uses of religious language, in which the speaker does not and perhaps does not *intend* to convey information. Rather, the noncognitive use of language expresses feeling, makes a commitment, helps to cement the bonds of solidarity of a group, or does innumerable other possible things about which it would be ridiculous to suppose that questions of truth or falsity arise, as they would if the language use were assumed to have cognitive content (i.e., to claim to convey information). As has often been pointed out, when a minister says the words in a marriage ceremony, "I now pronounce you united in holy matrimony," or in a baptismal service, "I baptize you in the name of the Father, Son, and Holy Ghost," no one would think that the purpose of the minister's expressions is to give information. Rather, the minister is using language performatively, to accomplish something. Still, the position asserted by some that *all* religious language is noncognitive seems extreme and would not be accepted by most religious persons.

Some present noncognitivist theories of religious language remind one of the view of the seventeenth-century British philosopher Thomas Hobbes (1588–1679). Hobbes held that since God is completely beyond our understanding—even the word *infinite* he held to have no meaning for us—when we speak of God we are not saying anything at all, we are merely expressing feelings and attitudes of reverence. We are praising God rather than characterizing or describing God. In his own time, Hobbes was suspected of being an atheist, but his view has connections both with some of the most recent and some of the oldest Christian understandings about the use of language concerning God.

The so-called negative way of speaking of God, elaborated by Christian mystical writers (greatly influenced by an unknown author long thought to be Paul's convert Dionysius the Areopagite, now usually called Pseudo-Dionysius), consists in successively *denying all* attributes to God. For instance, one denies that God is a material object, since material objects are limited by space and time. Ultimately, one denies *every* distinct possible characteristic as applying to God, since even calling God *wise, good,* or *powerful* limits God by suggesting the way these concepts apply to finite entities. At the end of the negative way, all limitations have been removed from our concept of God. Since this may seem to leave the concept totally empty, many Christian thinkers, though admitting the value of the way of negation, have insisted it should be followed by a positive or affirmative way.

This is possible, according to Thomas Aquinas, because though none of our terms designating finite characteristics apply to God univocally (with the same sense that they have when applied to finite things), they can be used, with caution, *analogically.* Since God is the source of all that exists, then there must be in God as their ground or source something (not necessarily something distinct from God's entire essence) that corresponds (or is analogous to) the positive qualities of finite things. Thus there is an analogy between God's wisdom and human wisdom. So we can legitimately affirm that God is wise, making it clear that God's wisdom is a kind of superwisdom that is not literally or univocally like human wisdom. Some terms would never be applied to God. We would never say that God is evil or that God is foolish or deceitful.

The concept of analogy is not without its difficulties. Some of the greatest Christian thinkers have declined to use the term, preferring the terms *symbol* and *symbolic.* Thus the twentieth-century Protestant theologian Paul Tillich (1886– 1965) asserted that there is *one* literally true statement we can make about God— namely, that God is being-itself (or the power of being of everything that exists). Everything else that we can say about God is a symbolic (presumably nonliteral or metaphorical) statement. For Karl Barth the method of analogy could be used not as a part of our natural reasoning ability, but only on the basis of insights given to faith. Thus, Barth spoke of the "analogy of faith" in contrast to Aquinas' "analogy of being."

As noted earlier, some thinkers have suggested that there are different levels of discourse—scientific, axiological (i.e., dealing with norms, duties, and values), and metaphysical or religious. At each level the use of such terms as *literal, well-defined, precise, verified, acceptable,* and *meaningful* may differ significantly from their uses at the other levels. If some kind of connection between the different levels could be shown, the result might be a usefully modified version of Kantian philosophy, one perhaps resembling the views of the more empiricist-oriented American thinker C. S. Peirce (1839–1914).

Kant held that we must distinguish between the more abstract and the more concrete, comprehensive levels of our involvement in experience. At the theoretical level of scientific inquiry, the human agent abstracts from the more comprehensive dimensions of moral and spiritual involvement and takes the point of view of an abstract subject of knowledge, an observer and cross-examiner of the physical world. The more concrete area of practical involvement is the moral realm. The moral realm is the realm of human interests and values, of duty and obligation. Kant believed the moral realm, the realm of practical reason, to be primary. In an important sense, the theoretical realm, the realm of abstract scientific knowledge, depends on the moral realm, since scientific knowledge is a legitimate human interest, and there are values implicit (truthfulness and objectivity, for instance) in the scientific enterprise, no matter how abstractly detached and impersonal the scientist and science may seem, and at times need, to be. In the moral realm, the primary realm of human involvement, the human agent is disclosed as a colegislator with all other rational beings in a universal community of persons. Membership in this community, which is an intrinsic aspect of our human existence, involves participation in a structure of duties, rights, and unconditional and conditional values. The realization that we participate in the universal moral community provides an opening toward the religious, according to Kant. It leads to rational faith in God as the foundation of the reality and universality of the objective moral order that human reality recognizes as the basis of all valid human values and interests.

Peirce also saw a progression in our experience and knowledge leading from the more abstract elements of pure sense experience through a series of normative intellectual areas (including the sciences) to a comprehensive disclosure of the religious and metaphysical dimensions (including the concept of universal process as guided by and toward *agape,* or divine, self-giving love) that make sense of our experience as a whole. For Kant and Peirce, the universe and human history as a part of it can be conceived as an evolutionary process involving significant degrees of human freedom to affect its destiny but ultimately guided by divine love.

Kant and Peirce both found a fundamental connectedness in our experience (involving *all* human experience) and saw this connectedness as pointing to a divine source or goal. If no connection should be found between the different levels of language use, then we might be left with some version of the Wittgenstein language games approach to the different areas of human discourse. Each area—religion, science, morality—might be seen to have its own rules, its own standards of what is acceptable and what is not, with no need or possibility of being related to other language fields.

In the twentieth century, then, the need of religiously committed persons to understand the ways language is used in science and the ways in which philosophers analyze language is evident. But it is equally evident that users of religious language have contributions to make to scientific and philosophical inquiries into language and the possibilities of its meaningful uses.

Contemporary Christians show few signs of giving up on the effort to deal with the issues that this chapter has presented. Some hold that answers are implicit within traditionally oriented positions (e.g., the Thomistic, Augustinian, Anselmian, Kantian, and so on), though these may be in need of much clarification and reconstruction. Others feel that radically new approaches are needed and imminent.

QUESTIONS

1. What did Christian thinkers of the first few centuries of the Common Era admire in Platonic philosophy?

2. What are the major differences in the approach to knowledge about God taken by a great philosopher like Aristotle and by the authors of the Jewish Scriptures?

3. What do the terms *general* and *special* revelation mean as they are used in the present chapter? Explain the importance attached by Jewish and Christian thinkers to general revelation as a preparation for and criterion of special revelation.

4. Explain—compare and contrast—the four ways in which Christian thinkers have found the use of reason as being of possible value in relation to revealed truth (special revelation).

5. Explain the reasons given by Tertullian, Luther, and Barth for rejecting the use of reason as a basis or preparation for the acceptance or understanding of revealed truth (special revelation).

6. What effect did Aquinas' empiricist theory of knowledge have on his views about what we can come to know about God through the use of natural reasoning?

7. In what ways have catechisms and credal statements been important to some Protestants because of Protestant emphasis on authority of the Bible?

8. What would be the consequence of holding a completely noncognitivist view of religious language? Do most religious persons think that at least some of their religious beliefs contain claims to being true and are therefore cognitive? Discuss and explain.

9. Explain the way of negation and the positive or affirmative way of speaking about God. What is the purpose of each? How does Aquinas' concept of analogy apply to them?

FURTHER READING

AUGUSTINE. *Confessions.* (Available in many translations and editions.)

———. "On the Teacher": in *Augustine: Earlier Writings.* Trans. J. H. S. Burleigh. Volume VI, Library of Christian Classics. Philadelphia: Westminster Press, 1953.

BARRETT, CYRIL, ed. *Wittgenstein: Lectures and Conversations on Aesthetics, Psychology, and Religious Belief.* Berkeley: University of California Press, 1972.

BARTH, KARL. *The Knowledge of God and the Service of God According to the Teaching of the Reformation.* London: Hodder and Stoughton, 1938.

BLACKSTONE, WILLIAM T. *The Problem of Religious Knowledge.* Englewood Cliffs, N.J.: Prentice-Hall, 1963.

BOURKE, VERNON J., ed. *The Pocket Aquinas.* New York: Washington Square Press, 1960.

BRONOWSKI, J. *Science and Human Values.* New York: Harper & Row, 1965.

BUTLER, JOSEPH. *The Analogy of Religion.* (Available in many editions.)

COPLESTON, F. C. *Aquinas.* Baltimore: Penguin Books, 1955.

DILLENBERGER, JOHN. *Protestant Thought and Natural Science.* Nashville, Tenn.: Abingdon Press, 1960.

DUPRÉ, LOUIS. *A Dubious Heritage: Studies in the Philosophy of Religion after Kant.* New York: Paulist Press, 1977.

FERRÉ, FREDERICK. *Basic Modern Philosophy of Religion.* New York: Charles Scribner's Sons, 1967.

FEYERABEND, PAUL. *Against Method.* London: Verso, 1978.

GILKEY, LANGDON. *Naming the Whirlwind: The Renewal of God Language.* Indianapolis, Ind.: Bobbs-Merrill, 1969.

GOLDBERG, MICHAEL. *Theology and Narrative: A Critical Introduction.* Nashville, Tenn.: Abingdon Press, 1982.

HARTSHORNE, CHARLES.   *Anselm's Discovery*. LaSalle, Ill.: Open Court, 1965.

———.   *A Natural Theology for Our Time*. LaSalle, Ill.: Open Court, 1967.

HEIM, KARL.   *Christian Faith and Natural Science*. New York: Harper & Brothers, 1953.

HUME, DAVID.   *An Enquiry Concerning Human Understanding*. (Available in many editions.)

KIERKEGAARD, SØREN.   *On Authority and Revelation*. Princeton, N.J.: Princeton University Press, 1955.

KUHN, THOMAS S.   *The Structure of Scientific Revolutions*. 2nd ed. Chicago: University of Chicago Press, 1970.

LANGFORD, JEROME J.   *Galileo, Science, and the Church*. Rev. ed. Ann Arbor: University of Michigan Press, 1971.

LONERGAN, BERNARD, J. F., S. J.,   *Method in Theology*. New York: Harper & Row, 1979.

———.   *Philosophy of God, and Theology*. Philadelphia: Westminster Press, 1973.

MASCALL, E. L.   *Existence and Analogy*. Hamden, Conn.: Archon Books, 1967.

NIEBUHR, H. RICHARD.   *The Meaning of Revelation*. New York: Macmillian, 1941.

RAVEN, CHARLES E.   *Science, Religion, and the Future*. Cambridge: Cambridge University Press, 1943.

SANTILLANA, GIORGIO DE.   *The Crime of Galileo*. Chicago: University of Chicago Press, 1955.

SMITH, JOHN E.   *The Analogy of Experience*. New York: Harper & Row, 1973.

———.   *Reason and God*. New Haven, Conn.: Yale University Press, 1961.

SWIDLER, LEONARD.   *Consensus in Theology? A Dialogue with Hans Küng and Edward Schillebeeckx*. Westminster: John Knox Press, 1980.

TEILHARD DE CHARDIN, PIERRE.   *Man's Place in Nature*. New York: Harper & Row, 1966.

WHITEHEAD, A. N.   *Science and the Modern World*. New York: Macmillan, 1925.

CHAPTER EIGHT

Representative Christians: Renewing and Sustaining

The adjustments that inevitably come in any community of believers are often responses to social, political, and intellectual modifications in the cultural settings of a religion. However, charismatic individuals, whose personalities and gifts have a significant impact on those around them, have just as often been seen as effecting change or renewal within religious communities. Certainly that has been the case for Christianity. While elsewhere in our discussions we have investigated a number of these leaders, in this chapter we look at the lives of other persons who have uniquely contributed to the understanding, patterns, and expressions of Christianity. Not all of those discussed will be seen by historians as major leaders, but their exemplary lives and gifts have affected the expression of Christianity in their day and often in subsequent generations.

AUGUSTINE

The seminal thought of Augustine (354–430), bishop of Hippo Regius in North Africa, was so profound as to shape the theological and cultural formulations of medieval Christendom, serve as a foundation of Protestant reform thought, and continue as a major touchstone of modern theology. For these contributions he appropriately was declared a "doctor of the church," one of the original four doctors par excellence, by the Roman Catholic Church. Because of some of the unique aspects of his life story, well-documented in his *Confessions* and other writings, his story has become a classic among Christians.

    A native of Tagaste, not far from Hippo, Augustine was nurtured by a Christian mother, Monica, with whom he formed a special bond. Augustine credits his mother with sustaining in him an interest in Christianity and constantly challenging him to be a believer, but he did not enter into the community of the faithful as a child or student. Given a substantial education in Greek and Latin literature in Carthage, Augustine found himself drawn to Latin rhetoric and grammar. As a student, while reading Cicero's "*Hortensius*," he became intrigued with the "love of wisdom," philosophy. Taking up the teaching of rhetoric, he pursued his studies in literature and philosophy. Intrigued by religious questions, Augustine became a Manichaean, a follower of a popular religion of the time. Manichaeanism suggested a solution to the universal question of evil by offering a dualistic scheme whereby the evil present in the world was credited to a primordial battle between light (good) and darkness (evil). Migrating to Rome to teach rhetoric and continue his philosophical studies, Augustine found himself repeatedly driven by philosophical interests to religious issues and concerns and less convinced of the Manichaean answers to these issues, although he had participated in the religion for almost a decade.

During this period he took a mistress, as was often the custom among Roman intellectuals, and fathered a son, Adeodatus. Disillusioned with his situation in Rome and the laxity of his students, he accepted a chair of rhetoric in the Italian city of Milan. By now very skeptical in his philosophical understandings, he gave up his early conviction that philosophy could provide final and complete answers to any question. Exposed to Neoplatonism in this period, his problems with the Manichaean solutions to questions of evil were resolved by the Platonic suggestion that evil is simply the absence of good.

In Milan, at the urging of his mother and attracted by the preaching of Ambrose, the Christian bishop of the city, Augustine returned to attending the church. In private conversations, the bishop was able to respond to Augustine's long-held skepticism concerning Christianity that centered in the action of the God revealed in the Old Testament. Ambrose suggested that these Scriptures might be interpreted allegorically rather than literally. Ambrose, and the Christian tutor, Simplicianus, also opened for Augustine new concepts of Grace and dependence on God. Now intrigued by Christianity, Augustine, meditating in his garden, was led, in his understanding by God speaking through the voice of a child playing nearby, to read a particular passage in Paul's Letter to the Romans (13:13). Taking the passage to speak to his own difficulty in giving up his former life, particularly his mistress, he came to total dependence and faith in Christ. This dynamic experience, known since as an exemplary Christian conversion, led to Augustine's baptism, along with his son, at the hand of Ambrose.[1]

Returning to Africa, Augustine abandoned his scholarly career, dedicating himself to the religious life. With others he formed a lay monastery near Tagaste. In the seacoast city of Hippo, against his will, he was taken by the local people to the bishop to receive ordination in 391. A few years later we find him serving as coadjutor (or associate) bishop to Bishop Valerius of Hippo. Upon Valerius' death in 395, Augustine succeeded to the bishopric and for the next thirty-five years was intimately involved in the life of a local church beset by many difficulties. The period was one of great social and political trauma, with Rome sacked by the Vandals in 410 and the Western Roman Empire in precipitous decline. North African Christianity was still struggling with competing Christian bodies that claimed singular authenticity—schismatic Donatists insisted that Christians who had given up Scriptures to the Roman government under persecution were unfaithful and therefore unworthy to be priests and bishops. Though condemned by the Council of Nicaea in 325, they were still strong competitors for the allegiance of believers

[1]Albert C. Outler, ed. and trans., *Augustine: Confessions and Enchiridion* (Philadelphia: Westminster Press, 1955), Book Eight, Chapter XII.

in Africa. Theological differences among Christians were numerous and as yet often unsettled by the church as a whole.

The challenges of both his own tortuous spiritual journey and the unique crises in the local and universal church of his time provided Augustine with unlimited material for a vast array of writings. In the course of his career, he wrote more than a hundred treatises and books, allowing his fertile and imaginative mind to explore topics of universal concern but generally concentrating on specific issues facing the Christianity of his day. His profound and suggestive commentary on his own crises of faith and belief in these works are the bases of his continuing influence on subsequent Christianity. No systematic theologian, Augustine wrote in the midst of particular crises; consequently, he is often repetitious and occasionally inconsistent. But through all his works shines a profound faith grounded on a unique personal dependence on the guidance and strengthening of God's Grace.

No brief catalogue of his contributions will suffice to show the breadth or depth of his thought, but his influence in Christian theology can be suggested when we note that subsequent thinkers seldom comment on the doctrine of Grace, the relation of church and state, freedom of the human will, or the nature of the sacraments without appropriating or responding to Augustine's formulations. Few Christian theologians had such influence on Christians of all persuasions as Augustine. His most widely known works include the *Confessions, The City of God, On the Trinity,* and *Enchiridion.* Late in life he wrote a work, *The Retractations,* in which he commented on ninety-five of his writings, giving a unique insight into and evaluation of his literary corpus (the Latin root of the title means "to treat again" rather than "retract").

GREGORY I (THE GREAT)

Throughout times of crisis in the history of the church, there seems to emerge an individual who is especially suited to give exemplary leadership (in the annals of the church such persons are usually seen as "raised up" by God). Such a leader was Gregory (540-604). By the late fifth century the glory and power of the Western Roman Empire had disintegrated to a point where social, political, and spiritual stability were rapidly waning. Combining the rare traits of a strong and aggressive leader with the humility and persuasiveness of a spiritual guide, Gregory arose to revitalize the life of the Western Church.

The son of a patrician Roman family, Gregory received an excellent education preparing him for the civil service, which he entered as a young man. Becoming prefect of the city of Rome in 570, he entered into a distinguished career as he supervised the administration of the city, in addition to presiding over the Roman Senate. After serving in these capacities for a relatively short time, Gregory dedicated himself to spiritual endeavors, resigning from his civic service and entering the monastic life. Using his family's properties, he founded a monastery in Rome dedicated to St. Andrew and provided other properties for six monasteries on the family estates in Sicily. His monastic career concentrated on meditation, an austere personal discipline, and study through which he acquired extensive knowledge of the Scriptures and the Latin fathers.

Seeking to use Gregory's administrative experience, the pope called him from the monastic life to serve as one of the seven "regional" deacons of Rome. Soon after his appointment he was sent by the pope as the papal representative to the Byzantine court of the Roman emperor in Constantinople. Here he was exposed to the range of problems facing the empire. The experience convinced him that the western portions of the empire and the church could expect little support or help from the emperor. This period was, therefore, to affect his later attitude and actions greatly when he became the spiritual leader of the West.

Returning to Rome, Gregory became abbot of the monastery he had founded. Serving as a counselor to the pope, Gregory was again to find his genuine desire to follow the monastic life eluding him, for he was elected pope upon the death of Pelagius II. Reluctant to take the office, he assumed its responsibilities at a particularly difficult point. Flooding of the Tiber River, which courses through Rome, had caused a devastating epidemic among the citizens, disrupting the commercial and social life of the city. The political stability of the city was also again threatened by the Germanic Lombards, who had gained control of much of northern and central Italy. Although Gregory sought help from the Byzantine emperor and his representatives at Ravenna, the imperial city in eastern Italy, he did not wait for their response to act. Using his considerable administrative abilities, he rallied the citizens of the city by leading them in a penitential procession, restoring their spiritual confidence and giving them hope while opening the treasuries of the church to relieve their need for food, medicine, and shelter. Rallying the defenders of the city, Gregory personally negotiated with Agilulf, the Lombard chief. An uneasy peace was achieved by Gregory's agreement to pay tribute to Agilulf, since he could not depend upon military help from the Eastern Empire.

Through these actions Gregory reestablished order and stability in the city. Perhaps more important was the significant step he took of leading the church into political affairs when the normal social institutions were incapable of functioning properly. When Gregory's actions were called into question by the imperial court, he rebuffed the emperor, suggesting that he was responsible before God for his "flock" and not dependent upon the emperor. As Gregory strengthened his position in the West, he reasserted the traditional Roman claim that the pope was premier bishop over the universal church. Consequently, he rejected the bishop of Constantinople's use of the title "ecumenical" and received appeals from priests condemned by Constantinople. Nevertheless, Gregory respected the rights of other patriarchs, intervening only where local authority was unable to settle issues and seeking to use his position with humility, claiming that he was the "servant of the servants of God."

His assertion of political power in the West, when necessary, and his claim of universal spiritual jurisdiction served to strengthen immensely the place and the position of the pope and the church in the Western Empire. The precedents set by Gregory were to substantially shape papal authority and influence throughout the medieval ages. Subsequent popes were to appeal frequently to Gregory's actions to support their own entrance into political as well as spiritual affairs.

Gregory's aggressive use of the church's power and authority have made him known throughout history as one of the strongest popes, yet this power was accompanied by a deep spiritual consciousness and genuine humility. Though he himself was from a patrician family and accustomed to wealth, he took seriously the biblical admonitions to garner and use the resources at hand carefully. Consequently, he used the wealth of the church's extensive land holdings throughout the Western Empire for the benefit of those in need. It was from these sources that he had drawn to relieve the people of Rome devastated by pestilence and epidemic. The papal treasury was further used to ransom captives, relieve the poor, and serve the needy.

Gregory's interest in the common man and the parish priest was expressed through other avenues as well. In the midst of an extremely busy administrative life, his interest in worship was expressed in a major reform of the liturgical life of the church. While the *Gregorian Sacramentary* may well have been finally formulated later, his characteristic liturgical concerns are reflected in it, so that it is properly named after him. Anxious that ordinary worshippers participate, Gregory provided for antiphonal patterns to be reinstated in the services. He elevated the place of the homily (sermon) in the service and wrote a number of homilies. He composed some of the prayers that have continued in the liturgy, and his name is attached to one of the most lasting of worship aids—the plainsong, often known as the Gregorian Chant. Writing extensively, his *Pastoral Care* became the medieval guide to the pastoral offices of bishop and priest as shepherds of the faithful; while his *Dialogues,* homilies giving moral instruction and example, served a similar function for the simple and uneducated people. Other works elaborated dogma and gave instruction in morality, spirituality, and mysticism. His moral instructions were frequently cited by those who followed him as teachers and scholars of the church. His elaboration of the doctrines of Heaven, which he asserted may be entered by any saintly soul, and Purgatory, which provided an intermediate state for imperfect Christians whose lives are not free from sin, were encouraging in an age of disintegration and hopelessness. The *Letters* provide an extraordinary record of the period and the forces at work in the sixth-century papacy.

Gregory was able to combine in an unusual manner the interests of the contemplative with the practical acumen of the administrator. He thereby offered to the church both guidance in spiritual development and worship life, while establishing patterns of papal strength that were to be normative for subsequent church history. It is not surprising then that he was pronounced a saint by popular acclamation and canonized immediately after his death. Named as one of the four "great Latin doctors of the church" by Boniface VIII in 1298, Gregory took his place as one of the church's sentinel figures guarding and defining its faith and life.

BONAVENTURE

In the twelfth century, Western Europe began to emerge from a long period of economic and cultural scarcity. The patterns of feudalism began to relax, a class of persons engaged in trade began to appear, cities grew, and with cities came, for the first time in centuries, centers of learning. The first of these were sponsored by the church, attached to cathedrals for the purpose of training theologians. But as Europe emerged from the Dark Ages, from an economic life based on agriculture and warfare, and from almost universal illiteracy, the interest in secular learning also became strong. Such subjects as law, medicine, and literature attracted many to newly thriving cities that had become centers of learning, to cities in Italy and Germany, to Oxford in England, and especially to Paris. By the end of the twelfth century many of the universities of Europe—of great reputation to this day—had, at least in nascent form, been founded (see Chapter Four).

In twelfth-century Europe learning, whether deemed religious or secular, became an adventure. A new world seemed to open up to theologians and philosophers. Long deprived of the major works of the great philosophers of Greece and Rome, dependent for their knowledge of Plato and Aristotle on a few surviving commentaries that blurred the differences in emphasis between these great pioneers of thought, European philosophers of the twelfth century (Peter Abelard [1079–?1144], for instance, and his great teachers and disciples) began to invent their own philosophical tools to explore the doctrines of Christian theology. St. Bernard of Clairvaux (1090–1153) raised his voice in protest against subjecting the mysteries of Christian faith to logical analysis, condemning Abelard's attempt to understand the doctrine of the Trinity by reason. At the critical point, the writings of Aristotle—and commentaries on Aristotle by Jewish and Muslim scholars—were brought to Western Europe from Asia. For the first time in centuries, it was possible to read the works of a systematic writer on philosophy, natural science, politics, and ethics, who began his inquiries from the point of view of human beings and their rational reflections on sense experience. Western philosophy and theology, most influenced by Augustine, had always been Platonic in spirit.

One response to the twelfth-century renaissance of economic and cultural life was the appearance of a new kind of Catholic monasticism: the mendicant orders. St. Dominic (ca. 1170–1221) created his Order of Preachers to combat the new heresies, especially those forming among the rising manufacturing classes of France and Italy, who, becoming Albigensians, or Cathari, were critical of the established church and its priesthood. St. Francis of Assisi (1181 or 1182–1226), out of his intensely mystical experience and his rejection of his father's attempt to steer him into partnership in a successful cloth business, almost inadvertently established the three orders of Franciscans—monks, nuns, and laity—all dedicated to a life of simple piety and poverty. The mendicant orders were so called because they originally supported themselves by begging, since they felt called not to a life of contemplation and manual labor within a monastery but to an active life of preaching in the world. The Dominicans were dedicated to the intellectual task of refuting heresy, the Franciscans to the joyous proclamation of the possibility of living a Christ-filled life of gospel simplicity.

At some time, possibly five years before St. Francis died at the age of forty-four in 1226, Giovanni Fidanza, a physician and member of an Italian noble family, and his wife Ritella, who lived in Bagnorea, not far from Rome, became parents of a son whom they named Giovanni. This Giovanni Fidanza is the man who is often called the second founder of the Franciscan order. He is commonly known as Bonaventure (or Bonaventura)(1217?–1274). He was canonized in 1482.

As a child, Bonaventure became desperately ill. His mother prayed, dedicating him to St. Francis. The child recovered. Bonaventure mentions this event in his biography of St. Francis that the Franciscan order mandated him to write. (Actually he wrote two *Lives* of St. Francis, a "major" and a "minor" one.) He felt that his mother's prayer and his, to him, miraculous recovery bound him in a mystical or spiritual way to the ideals of the saint who had dedicated himself to holy poverty.

By the time Bonaventure entered the Franciscan order in 1243, he had come to a further understanding of his calling. Not only was he to dedicate his life to Christ in accordance with the Franciscan way of complete devotion and poverty of spirit, he was to devote himself to the life of the intellect, to the love of learning, in the Franciscan and Augustinian spirit.

St. Francis had been an unlearned man, barely able to read, yet had rejoiced once at receiving a copy of the New Testament, which he had immediately cut into parts so that they might be circulated among his followers. He had warned about the perils of learning, the dangers of doubt and worldliness that the quest of knowledge posed for simple faith. Yet not long before Bonaventure, a student of philosophy and theology in Paris, entered the Franciscan order, one of the most brilliant philosophers of the first half of the thirteenth century, Alexander of Hales (ca. 1170 or 1185–1245), had become a Franciscan and brought his professorship at the University of Paris to the Order of Friars Minor. Bonaventure understood this as signalling a recapitulation of the history of the early church. Just as Christ's church had begun as a community of unlearned fishermen, before the end of its first generation, it embraced learned philosophers such as St. Paul and Apollos.

Bonaventure became a Franciscan and continued his studies in philosophy and theology, playing an important part in the struggle of the Franciscans and Dominicans to justify the mendicant orders holding chairs in the university. Part of Bonaventure's efforts in this struggle involved his powerful argument for the right of the mendicant orders even to exist against attacks by their opponents in the university. He and Thomas Aquinas, the great Dominican who was in some ways his intellectual antagonist, were at one on this issue. Both were granted delayed doctorates on the same day, October 23, 1257, after the pope ruled that the university must receive the mendicants. The point at issue had been the refusal of the mendicant professors to swear sole allegiance to the university. They had been asked to do this in order to join in a professors' strike protesting brutality against students by the police of Paris. Swearing sole allegiance to the university would have required the mendicants to ignore their vows of obedience to their monastic superiors.

Bonaventure conceived his intellectual task to be the reaffirmation of the Christian Platonism of St. Augustine. Aquinas became the advocate of Aristotle's philosophical approach, arguing that a clear line could be drawn between the realm of philosophy, based on sense experience and reason, and that of theology, whose first principles were derived from revelation. Bonaventure agreed with the distinction between theology and philosophy, but argued that all true philosophy, such as Plato's, recognized the need of a realm of nonmaterial forms or patterns or exemplars that mediated between the world known by the senses and the divine. Aristotle had denied this, separating God, the absent cause of the motion of the material world, from the objects known in sense experience. For Bonaventure and Augustine, all genuine knowing demands an illumination of the soul (or mind) by God. The material world is not a complete realm of knowledge in itself (as Aristotle thought). It is a realm of symbols and images of the divine. Plato was a better philosopher than Aristotle because he recognized the incompleteness of the material world and of our finite knowledge of it. Even so, there were many errors and falsehoods in Plato's philosophy; for, according to Bonaventure, the only true philosophy is one illumined and corrected by the truths of faith and special revelation. The desire for knowledge in order to control the material world is a temptation. The desire for knowledge of the natural world as a world of images of the divine is highly desirable. According to Bonaventure, all humans desire to know and love God. Every creature in the natural world, seen as an image of the divine, is sacred.

Bonaventure could affirm St. Francis' great love of the animals—these are our sisters and brothers.

Historically, Aquinas and his teacher Albert the Great were victorious. By the end of the thirteenth century all of the major philosophers of Europe were Aristotelians, even the great Franciscans Duns Scotus and William of Ockham, who perhaps had some difficulties expressing their Franciscan spiritual concerns in Aristotelian language.

Bonaventure has been called by Etienne Gilson, one of the great twentieth-century historians of medieval philosophy, *the* philosopher of the Christian spiritual (or mystical) life. However, his career as a professor at the University of Paris was cut short when he was thirty-six years old by his election as the seventh minister general of the Franciscan order, a position he occupied for seventeen years.

As minister general, he was required to deal with the increasing controversy within the Franciscan order prompted by the "spiritual" Franciscans, those who wanted to return to the early Franciscan ideal of absolute poverty. The spiritual Franciscans wanted not only to turn their backs on the kind of learning represented by Bonaventure but to reverse the trend of acquisition of monastic property. Bonaventure argued that with St. Francis and eleven disciples the order could subsist by begging, but with hundreds of thousands of Franciscans throughout Europe this would be impossible.

Bonaventure continued to write. His collected works, published in an excellent scholarly edition only about a hundred years ago, comprise nine large, double-columned volumes. Possibly his best-known work is *The Mind's* (or *Soul's*) *Journey into God,* a short work that resulted from Bonaventure's pilgrimage to the top of Mt. Alvernia, where St. Francis, two years before his death, had experienced a vision of Christ and received from a six-winged seraph the stigmata, or wounds, of Christ on his own body. Bonaventure made the pilgrimage shortly after being elected minister general of the Franciscan order. The result of his meditations, *The Mind's Journey into God,* is a masterful expression of his Christian Augustinian-Platonic spirituality.

At one point during his career as general of the Franciscan order, Bonaventure was named archbishop of York by the pope but was able to persuade the pope to change his mind. A later pope, Gregory X, who had been elected when the cardinals had asked Bonaventure to advise them whom to elect, named him cardinal, a position he was told he could not refuse. When the messengers bringing his cardinal's hat arrived at the monastery, they found the minister general of the Franciscan order washing the dinner dishes. During the Council of Lyon in 1274, the preparations for which had been largely delegated to the new cardinal, Bonaventure resigned as general of the Franciscan order. During the council, a major aim of which was to work for the reunion of Western and Eastern Christians, Bonaventure died. His funeral was held with great pomp and ceremony, attended by bishops, cardinals, and the pope. On the way to this same council, Thomas Aquinas, Bonaventure's great colleague, theological and philosophical antagonist, fellow mystic, and—as tradition asserts—friend, died.

GEORGE FOX

By the 1640s religious controversy and religious persecution had reached a point of explosion in England, precipitating civil war. Roman Catholics appealed to the

Bible and tradition. High-church Anglicans and other members of the Church of England loyal to King Charles I appealed to the Bible and tradition. Puritans who wanted to stay within the established church but rid it of what they considered its Catholic remnants—bishops, prayer book, religious images, various kinds of hymns and ways of singing them, restrictions on Bible interpretation by the laity—and Puritans who wanted to separate from the established church appealed to the Bible against tradition. All were filled with passionate intensity. All seemed certain of what true religion and true Christianity were.

In 1643 a young Englishman named George Fox (1624–1691) left his home and his parents because of his uncertainty about what true religion and true Christianity were. Often he had heard ministers, either Puritan or anti-Puritan, speak with certainty, claiming a biblical basis for their positions. He had begun frequently to doubt whether what they were saying was true. Once he heard a Calvinist preacher say that all humans were utterly sinful and only those predestined by God to salvation could be saved. He had doubted this. More and more he felt inclined to dispute what the ministers—later he would call them priests—taught, but he himself was filled with doubts.

He consulted several ministers, both of the established church and among the Dissenters, about his spiritual unrest. One advised him to begin smoking and to sing psalms. Another suggested that he marry. Another advised that he should have himself bled, the standard medical procedure in the seventeenth century (and for another two hundred years) for those suffering from fevers of various kinds. Fox tried having himself bled without result: the physician was not successful in drawing blood from him. He returned home, but his parents were upset when he refused to attend church with them.

George felt that his condition was desperate, that no one could speak to it. As he wrote in his famous *Journal,* one of the spiritual classics:

> I fasted much, walked abroad in solitary places many days, and often took my Bible, and sat in hollow trees and lonesome places till night came on; and frequently in the night walked mournfully about by myself; for I was a man of sorrows in the time of the first workings of the Lord in me....When I had lost all hope,...then, oh, then I heard a voice which said, "There is one, even Christ Jesus, that can speak to thy condition"; and when I heard it, my heart did leap for joy.[2]

It was an inner voice, George was convinced, the voice of Christ within, that spoke to him; and as the voice continued to speak, it began to lead him to an understanding of the truths on which was based the Society of Friends, the society of those who began to join themselves with George Fox in response to his message. For George had become convinced that there was within each human the inner voice, the Christ within, which is the source of all truth.

George Fox's period of seeking lasted for nearly four years. He had been born at Drayton in Leicestershire in 1624. His father was a weaver, a man so devoted to religion that his neighbors had called him "Righteous Christer." George's mother shared her husband's devotion to religion. Both were honest, upright people. Until his period of spiritual unrest, George had never given them, or anyone else, trouble

---

[2]George Fox, *The Journal of George Fox* (New York: Capricorn Books, 1963), pp. 79ff. For additional discussion of the Quakers, see Chapter Five above.

or cause for complaint. After his conversion experience, there were many who complained of him—priests, magistrates, military officers, government officials. Yet his message and his methods were peaceful.

He began traveling about England, telling people about the Christ within, telling them about the way of life that the voice within him was instructing him in: not to use violence, not to take oaths, not to pay the taxes or tithes demanded for support of the established church. (He would no longer refer to church buildings as "churches" but as "steeple-houses," since it was the *people* in whom Christ reigned, not buildings, who were the church.)

Within six years after George's conversion, he had an army of sixty valiant spiritual warriors willing to go throughout England presenting the message. Within two more years there were more than 50,000 Friends. They were called Quakers in ridicule, because George had once cautioned a magistrate that a judge should quake before God.

Quakers were often attacked by mobs of angry citizens. Sometimes the attackers were incited by clergy who resented George Fox's teaching that there should be no professional or paid ministers. Among the Friends, liturgy and ritual were practically abolished: there were no sacraments, no order of worship, no priests. The Friends in meeting would sit in silence until individual members began to share with the group what the Christ was speaking within.

During the Puritan Commonwealth, the exiled sons of Charles I attempted to foment political rebellion. There were assassination plots against Oliver Cromwell, who ruled as lord protector. Public assemblies, including gatherings of dissenting religious groups, were banned. The Quakers refused to halt their meetings, and, brought before magistrates, refused to take oaths in court; and though they promised allegiance to the government and promised to continue to live completely nonviolent, peaceable lives, would not *swear*. Fox pointed out what seemed to him the contradiction of being required to swear an oath on a book that forbade the swearing of oaths.

During the Puritan Commonwealth, George Fox was summoned before Oliver Cromwell. He won Cromwell's admiration and affection, even though the Quakers continued to be persecuted by mobs, ministers, magistrates, and the military. With the Restoration under Charles II, government persecution of the Quakers was, if anything, intensified. Nevertheless, even the king apparently admired Fox.

Quakers had already been imprisoned. Some had died in prison for "causing" the people attacking them to riot. Some had also been imprisoned for refusing to swear an oath of allegiance to Cromwell's government. Under the Restoration, prosecutions for refusing to swear allegiance to the king were frequent. The property of those convicted was subject to seizure by the government.

Margaret Fell, the widow of Thomas Fell, a distinguished jurist, who, during his life, had been able to protect his Quaker wife, was, after her husband's death, brought to trial for continuing to hold Quaker meetings at her estate at Swarthmore. A woman noted for her kindness, beauty, and simplicity, she was sent to prison, where she was held for more than three years. Her property was confiscated because she refused to take an oath of allegiance to the king, although she had promised her allegiance. Earlier, Margaret Fell and her husband had intervened with magistrates and even petitioned the king on behalf of George Fox when he was threatened with violence or imprisonment.

Released from prison, Margaret Fell, already the mother of eight children, married George Fox. Their marriage lasted for twenty-two years, until Fox's death. Even though they were often separated because both travelled on behalf of the message and Fox was frequently in prison, often without heat or food or bedding in conditions of terrible filth, the happiness of their marriage is attested by the affection and warmth of their letters to each other. Fox was beaten many times. His life was threatened by violent mobs and by angry government officials. He always responded with nonviolent good humor, wit, and love, but sometimes with sharp words, warning about the condition of the persecutor's spirit. Believing in the presence of God in his life, he had no fear of violence, pain, or death.

In 1671 Fox sailed to America and traveled extensively, speaking against slavery and in behalf of the Indians. Some British colonists argued that the Indians were not truly human, having no sense of right and wrong. Fox tried to tell the colonists that Christ was truly within each of the Indians, within the colonists, and within all humans. In 1677 he took his message to Holland and Germany.

Quakers took the Bible very seriously: their position on oaths and their refusal to go to war or defend themselves were based on it. Yet George Fox taught that not the Bible but the spirit that gave the Bible, the spirit of the Lord, the voice of the Christ within, is the Christian's true authority. He also had no use for the teachings of many in his time who looked forward to the Second Coming of Christ, since he was convinced that the fullness of Christ can be experienced in one's life in the present. By the time of George Fox's death in 1691—he died after having spoken energetically at a Quaker meeting in London—many had been drawn to his message of the inner witness and a life of peaceful truthfulness and simplicity. He had offered a completely nonviolent spirit of love to all; but he had spoken firmly, sharply, calling persons to account—even magistrates, ministers, the lord protector, and the king—sometimes with the sharpest-edged satire or invective. He spoke, from his concern for them, the truth in love, the spirit's word, to their condition.

ROGER WILLIAMS

By the time Roger Williams was born during the first decade of the seventeenth century, possibly in 1607, England had already experienced more than seventy years of intense religious conflict. This had begun in 1534 when Henry VIII and the British Parliament officially broke with Roman Catholicism and established the Church of England, with the British monarch as its titular head. Under Henry VIII, subjects who wanted to remain loyal to Rome and the pope were persecuted. Even such a loyal subject as Thomas More, on whom Henry often depended for counsel and support, was beheaded at the king's order, though he had promised not to oppose or criticize the king's religious policies in any way but had insisted that he could not as a private citizen endorse them (see Chapter Five).

When Henry's successor, Edward VI, was succeeded by Henry's daughter Mary, those who refused to return to Roman Catholicism were persecuted. Mary's successor, Elizabeth I, reestablished the Church of England, again persecuting those who remained loyal Catholics. During Elizabeth's reign, there began to be an intense struggle between those within the Church of England, the Puritans, who wanted it to become less like the Roman Catholic church and more like Calvinist, or Reformed, Protestantism, and those who wanted to continue forging a distinctive *via media* (intermediate path) or even Anglo-Catholic future for the established church.

When Roger Williams's father brought his family from Wales to London to establish himself as a merchant tailor, James I had succeeded Elizabeth as head of the Church of England, and Archbishop Laud was leading the fight against the Puritans. Puritans had been imprisoned, some had been put to death, many had been sent (or had voluntarily gone) into exile, often to the Protestant parts of Holland or Switzerland. There they imbibed more of the Calvinist influence, which strengthened their resolve to purify the Church of England by doing away with bishops, the mandatory liturgy enshrined in the Book of Common Prayer, works of religious visual art, and other practices that seemed to them too close to Catholic ways.

Increasingly Puritans were designated as Nonconformists, but some of them were becoming Separatists, who wanted to separate from the Church of England. Separatists argued that, since religious commitment is a spiritual matter whose whole validity depends on inner, uncoerced spiritual consent, there should be a *separation* of church and state: the state should not exercise coercion in matters religious, and the church should not seek or expect the state to enforce its claims. This was a new and, to many, a shocking idea. The majority of Puritans, like the majority of high-church Anglicans and Roman Catholics, were convinced that no society could endure in unity and peace without uniformity of religious belief and practice and that it was the duty of the state to enforce such uniformity. Roger Williams was to become one of the most effective and outspoken English advocates for complete liberty of conscience and for preventing the secular state from enforcing religious participation or unity.

As a young boy, Roger Williams became a convert to Puritanism, possibly against the wishes of his parents, even though it was among the middle-class merchants and artisans that Puritanism was showing such rapid growth. As a boy, he assisted in his father's business establishment. While still very young, he learned shorthand and attracted the attention of Sir Edward Coke, one of the most influential jurists of the time and indeed one of the most influential legal scholars of all time. Coke financed Williams's education in the Charter House School, which made it possible for the young Puritan to attend and take a degree from Pembroke College at Cambridge University.

Apparently Coke had hoped Williams would become a lawyer. However, Williams sought and received ordination. For a time he served as chaplain to the family of the prominent Puritan Sir William Masham. Williams was convinced of the correctness of the Puritan position, but he was already winning some of his fellow Puritans to a belief in noncoercion in religious matters. With the increasing persecution of Puritans by church and government officials, Williams decided to emigrate to Massachusetts. Before leaving England, he married Mary Barnard. They sailed from Bristol on December 1, 1630, arriving in Boston at the height of the New England winter.

Roger Williams's reputation of being a pious and godly minister preceded him to the New World, and he was asked to become an official "teacher" in the church of the newly founded colony of Boston. He was shocked, however, to find the Boston Puritans, who themselves had been persecuted as Nonconformists in England, persecuting those who refused or failed to conform to their brand of Christianity. He informed them that he could not accept the position they had offered him: he was a Separatist. For a time he was minister at Salem, which was a Separatist Pilgrim settlement, but was driven from it by the Boston authorities, who brought charges against him. In fact, to escape being banished to England, he left Massachusetts for what is now Rhode Island, making friends with the Narragansett Indians and receiving their permission to settle there.

After some initial uncertainties and difficulties caused by conflicts between the colonists and the Indians, Roger Williams founded a settlement at what was to become Providence. He was soon able to send for his wife and children, who had remained in Salem. Eventually there were six Williams children. Other settlements were made close by. One was called Rhode Island, which eventually became the name of the entire group of settlements.

During his long life, Roger Williams, through the force of his personality and his ideas, assumed a dominant role in the development of Rhode Island. He and the new settlements in Rhode Island were under constant pressure from three sources: First, the Massachusetts Puritans felt that the very existence of Williams's settlements, with their "democratical" government and complete liberty of conscience in religious matters, was a threat to them. When Williams welcomed Quakers and other Nonconformists who had been driven from Boston, the Massachusetts colonists attempted to reorganize the New England settlements so that they could control the Rhode Islanders. In Massachusetts, religious coercion was on the increase, with church attendance enforced by law. Also, most of the Massachusetts colonists disapproved of Williams's friendship with the Indians and his insistence that the Indians agree to the sale of, and be paid for, any land occupied by the settlers. According to the Massachusetts theory, the land belonged to the king of England and had become their property with the charter the king had granted them.

A second source of pressure on Williams was the Indians themselves, who, angered by brutal treatment from the English colonists generally, frequently threatened and, at times, launched war. At one time, Providence was largely destroyed. But the Indians almost unanimously trusted and respected Williams. He was able to bring peace between the different tribes when quarrels arose and also was able to persuade some of the colonists to deal with the Indians fairly and peacefully. At one time, when he was desperately ill, the Indians nursed him to health. On many occasions he used all his persuasive power to prevent settlers and Indians from going to war against each other. Not always successful, he was willing to command his settlements' militias to defend against Indians or hostile colonists.

A third source of pressure on Williams was to be found in Providence and other Rhode Island settlements. At times, democratically elected officials secretly schemed with the Massachusetts colonies to abolish the independence of the Rhode Island settlements. Twice Roger Williams had to return to England: once to get a charter from Parliament for his Providence settlement that would stand up against the claims of the Massachusetts colonies; a second time, to get his charter reaffirmed.

Roger Williams lived until March 1683 and during his long life exerted a decisive influence on the Rhode Island colonies. Even greater, possibly, was his influence on ideas and practices concerning religious freedom and church-government relations in what was to become the United States. He welcomed fifteen

Jewish families to Rhode Island at a time no Jewish immigrants had been allowed into England for 400 years.

Among the Separatists of Roger Williams's day, many came to be called Baptists. Roger Williams is looked upon as one of the founding figures among Baptists in America. Martin Luther had taught the "priesthood of all believers" (see Chapter Four). By this Luther meant that each Christian should be a priest to other Christians. When contemporary Baptists in America use the term "priesthood of all believers," it is more in Williams's sense that they intend it: since spiritual commitment must be uncoerced to be valid, it is the right (as well as the duty) of every human being to seek and arrive at his or her own understanding or insight into religious truth. Luther also taught that religious persuasion should be uncoerced and entirely spiritual, but the Lutheran churches throughout Europe had become state churches. As late as the beginning of the nineteenth century a book by Immanuel Kant, *Religion Within the Limits of Reason Alone,* was censored by the government of East Prussia because it seemed to infringe on Lutheran orthodoxy.

Roger Williams believed and taught these principles, insisting on absolute, uncoerced freedom of conscience for all (including women), even if this led some to profess nonbelief. He did this in a time when such a position was almost unheard of. A generation later in England, John Locke—beginning in 1689 with his *Letters on Toleration,* then in *Two Treatises of Civil Government* (1690), and a little later in *The Reasonableness of Christianity* (1695)—argued for essentially the position that Roger Williams had held. Locke was the most influential English philosopher of his time, perhaps of all time. His background, like Williams, was Puritan and middle class; but, in contrast to Williams, his orientation was largely that of a secular thinker. Locke held that most theological views cannot be given objective proof or disproof; such views are mere opinions and, because they are religiously indifferent, people should be allowed to think what they please about them. The really important beliefs, including belief in God, can be proved, and the state should require them to be held. The remarkable thing about Roger Williams is that he possibly arrived at his beliefs about freedom of conscience, freedom of religion, separation of church and state, and political democracy, which were similar to Locke's beliefs but more radical, from his Christian convictions about the dignity and value of humans based on the nature of authentic faith and therefore of human spirituality.

SUSANNA WESLEY

As self-will is the root of all sin and misery, so whatever cherishes this in children insures their [seeking] after wretchedness and irreligion; whatever checks and mortifies it promotes their future happiness and piety. This is still more evident if we farther consider that religion is nothing else than the doing the will of God, and not our own; that the one grand impediment to our temporal and eternal happiness being this self-will, no indulgence of it can be trivial, no denial unprofitable.... So that the parent who studies to subdue it in his child, works together with God in renewing and saving a soul. The parent who indulges it does devil's work; makes religion impracticable, salvation unattainable, and does all that in him lies to damn his child, soul and body, forever.[3]

[3]Susanna Wesley's letter to her son, July 24, 1732, quoted in Maldwyn Edwards, *Family Circle* (London: Epworth Press, 1949), p. 59.

These words were written by an eighteenth-century parson's wife describing the teaching principles and methods used in her household as she raised her children. John Wesley, founder of Methodism, planning to establish a school for his laypreacher's children, asked his mother to set down the methods and rules under which he had been raised. Susanna obliged, giving us an unusual portrait of both her instruction of her children and of the theological principles that the method incorporated. Family discipline was not simply intended to train well-mannered and productive children; it was an integral part of God's concern for humanity. Indeed, life in all of its details was of God, so instruction on any topic and discipline in all of its forms had as their object awareness of the will of God and inclination toward doing that will.

Reading Susanna's correspondence to her sons John, Charles, and Samuel introduces one to a most unusual woman, whose instruction and advice often reflect the customs of eighteenth-century England but whose religious insights and theological discussion expose an intense faith as well as a productive and creative mind. The example of her Christian life and the power of her thought led her sons to consult her on all topics throughout her long life. John was still adhering to her advice and theological counsel long after he had emerged as an important religious leader in England.

No doubt some of Susanna's pattern for her children had been appropriated in the lively and bustling household of her father, Samuel Annesley. Annesley had been the pastor of a significant London parish, when, with some 2,000 other Nonconformist pastors, he was forced out of the Church of England in 1662. Susanna was born seven years later, when her father's home had become a gathering center for a wide circle of Puritan pastors, leaders, and students. Here as a young girl she met Samuel Wesley, a student at a local Dissenting academy and also the son of a Nonconformist pastor. By the time Samuel and Susanna married, both had abandoned their Nonconformist heritage and returned to the Church of England. Graduating from Oxford, Samuel was ordained a minister in the Church of England. After several smaller appointments, Samuel became the rector of the rural Epworth parish in Lincolnshire. Here Samuel and Susanna were to serve for almost forty years.

Mother of nineteen children (only nine of whom lived to maturity), Susanna carried heavy responsibilities not only in the home but for the management of the family business affairs and, on the occasions when her husband was away, in the parish itself. Because the parish was removed from stable schools, Susanna took upon herself the education of the children. It is this pattern that John remembered and asked her to recount.

For her period, Susanna was well prepared for the task. Although women were not normally educated in anything other than the duties of the household, Susanna was privileged to grow up in a home where learning was a cherished gift and discipline. From an early age she was urged to read, thereby gaining a broad education that included more than a passing acquaintance with philosophy, theology, and the best literature of the age. Her father's library and the household discussions of religion whetted her interest. After marriage, her husband's library was a continuing resource for her own learning. This interest in the intellectual was shared with the children through a strict educational regimen in which each child not only received formalized training but a special hour each week with his or her mother for spiritual formation. Susanna was especially concerned that girls in the household be introduced to a regimen of the mind and not simply their "womanly" duties. She used as the content of her educational enterprises the framework of religious training. This interest led her to prepare "catechetical" manuals on the Apostles' Creed and the Ten Commandments for use of the children, especially after they were scattered from the home as the result of a parsonage fire. Such original works for one's children to use were unusual and give insight into Susanna's constant interest in commitment to, and training for, the Christian life.

Susanna's model for a disciplined spiritual life was shared on a broader basis when, in the absence of her husband on church business, she gathered Epworth parishioners in her kitchen on Sunday evenings. Samuel's extended absence during 1710–11 found Susanna taking a role normally performed by her husband: leading family worship. When asked by a servant if his parents could attend these worship experiences, she opened the doors of the parsonage; and within a few months as many as 200 people were reported to be in attendance. Susanna led in hymn singing, prayer, and then read a sermon, usually from Samuel's large stock. The spirit of the meeting positively affected religious life in the parish, improving personal relations and sustaining spiritual discipline. When questioned about the practice by Samuel, Susanna replied that the curate obtained to fill Samuel's pulpit was dull and did not sufficiently expound the great truths of the gospel. Obviously she understood that she was doing this in the evening meetings. She informed Samuel that she would not cease holding the meetings unless commanded to do so by him as rector and husband. In her opinion, God's spirit was working in the parish through these unusual services and this was justification aplenty. The services were discontinued when Samuel returned to the parish.

Clearly John Wesley's later penchant for disregarding convention in preaching and in the organization of religious societies followed a pattern at least experimented with by his mother when he was a child. The rationale for both mother and son was their clear conviction that if such services enhanced and expanded the spiritual commitment and discipline of believers without interfering with regular church services they were "of God." They asked only that the spiritual results of the services serve as their justification.

The training of her children and her participation in parish leadership suggest that Susanna Wesley's strength of character was always buttressed by a secure and dynamic faith. They also show that an eighteenth-century rural parish wife did not need to be bound by her circumstances when it came to giving testimony to her faith.

ALEXANDER CAMPBELL

The Gospel of John reports that Jesus, not long before his arrest, trial, and crucifixion, prayed for the unity of his followers, asking God concerning his disciples "that they may be one, as we are one" (John 17:11). Throughout Christian history, many Christians have seemed relatively unconcerned at the lack of unity, even at the frequent positive antagonism, between and among diverse groups of Christians. Others have felt anguish at Christian divisions and a powerful longing to establish, or reestablish, unity among the followers of Jesus. In the thirteenth century, Bonaventure worked for reunion between Latin-speaking and Greek-speaking Christians, as did the brilliant fifteenth-century mystical theologian and cardinal Nicholas of Cusa. In the seventeenth and eighteenth centuries, Gottfried Leibniz, one of the most brilliant mathematicians and scientific thinkers of all time, hoped that his writings in philosophy would lay a basis for reunion between Europe's Catholics and Protestants. In the United States during the nineteenth century, many sought a restoration of the primitive unity of Christians against the background of an exploding proliferation of sects and denominations. Alexander Campbell (1788–1866) was one who, driven by a longing for the unity of Christians, labored longest and most energetically to restore what he conceived to be the church's ancient foundations. One result of his work was the growth of two new, original bodies of Christians—very reluctant to call themselves denominations or even to organize beyond the congregationalist level at first. Both churches at present look upon him as one of the fathers in a movement aimed at Christian restoration: these are the Christian Church (Disciples of Christ) and the Churches of Christ.

In many ways, the results of Campbell's work took an almost uniquely American appearance, incorporating, shortly after the Revolution, emphasis on common-sense rationalism, individualism, practicality, pragmatism, and democratic values. These are certainly values that Alexander Campbell cherished and are in large measure characteristic of the groups that today claim him as one of their inspirers.

Campbell was a native of Ireland. In his religious thinking and in his longing for Christian unity, Alexander was greatly influenced by his father, Thomas Campbell, who was for more than forty years his coworker. Thomas Campbell, born in 1763, was the son of a Roman Catholic who had converted to Anglicanism. Thomas, in turn, became a Presbyterian and felt called to the ministry. Presbyterianism in Ireland was under the strong influence of Scottish Presbyterianism. He studied for the ministry at the University of Glasgow. It was not long before the minister Thomas Campbell found himself embroiled in controversies that had been imported into his Irish Presbyterianism by Presbyterian factions in Scotland. In 1805 Thomas tried unsuccessfully to end a split in his Seceder Presbyterian Church (which had itself seceded from the Church of Scotland), in which he belonged to the Old Light faction of the Anti-Burgher party. The tendency of his coreligionists to divide over what he considered matters unessential to the heart of the faith pained him greatly. On this question, he was greatly influenced by the writings of John Locke on religious toleration, as was his son Alexander. In fact, Thomas introduced his son to the writings of Locke, as well as to the study of the biblical languages and other subjects of theological and classical education.

After serving in the ministry and teaching in schools for a number of years in Ireland, Thomas Campbell emigrated, settling in the western part of Pennsylvania in 1807, leaving his family temporarily in Ireland. Before coming to America, his son Alexander was able to study at the University of Glasgow.

In America, Thomas Campbell aligned himself with a Seceder Presbyterian synod but soon found himself heavily criticized because of his increasing insistence that Christianity must be based entirely on the Bible, uninterpreted by creeds or theological doctrinal statements. Eventually he was suspended from ministerial functions in his presbytery. He presented "A Declaration and Address" to the presbytery and synod; and when its principles were rejected, he withdrew from his connection with the American Seceder Presbyterians. He continued to be active in the ministry with a group who called themselves Christians, seeking cooperation with Baptists and other like-minded persons. With them he formed the Christian Association of Washington in Western Pennsylvania.

In the meantime, Campbell's family had come to the United States, and Alexander, feeling the call to preach, sought ordination. He became an effective preacher and found himself in general agreement with his father on basic principles. These were (1) the only standard of essential Christian life and belief is the Bible; (2) Christians should seek unity, avoiding sectarian labels and organizational structures; (3) there is no essential difference between clergy and laity, and church government should be democratic.

Alexander Campbell became convinced that, although the Old Testament should be revered as the record of God's revelation, it is not to be placed on a level of equal authority with the New Testament. This set him at odds with most of the Calvinist-inspired Protestant groups, who had sought a pattern of churchly and civic life in the Old Testament laws given by God through Moses to Israel. Studying the New Testament, Alexander became convinced that infant baptism was unscriptural—he had to decide about this when he and his wife became parents of a daughter—and that the biblical mode of baptism is immersion. As he had been baptized as a child by sprinkling, he, along with his wife and father and mother, had themselves baptized by immersion. Since all of the Christian groups except the Baptists were convinced that both infant baptism and baptism by methods other than immersion were valid and biblical, they were soon strong in their opposition to the Campbells.

Thomas Campbell urged that the message of Christian unity be presented without entering into religious controversy, but Alexander soon became an effective controversialist. He won attention and followers by public debates with Presbyterians, who defended infant baptism. He also debated the "humanist" utopian social reformer Robert Owen, who felt that the times demanded secular social salvation, and a Roman Catholic bishop. Holding strongly to the lay character of the ministry, Campbell worked as a farmer, becoming quite prosperous, on a farm in Virginia given to him by his father-in-law. He was a tireless preacher, lecturer, and teacher, founding a seminary to train the young for Christian citizenship as well as for Christian ministry.

At first the Campbells worked in association with Baptists, but before long it was clear that he and his coreligionists were not Baptists. Sometimes they referred to themselves as Reformers, sometimes as Disciples, Disciples of Christ, or simply as Christians. The movement at first spread slowly from Pennsylvania and Virginia into eastern Ohio, Kentucky, and Indiana. There were great difficulties in developing organizational structures beyond the local congregations, since such associations seemed to involve the danger of the group's being just another sect. Eventually some ministers began to be employed as full-time evangelists and preachers.

Campbell's major principle was expressed in the saying "Where the Bible speaks, we speak; where the Bible is silent we are silent." To him, this meant that Christians should grant freedom of opinion and toleration to other Christians. He refused to rule out the possibility of nonimmersed persons being genuine Christians, though he felt that the Bible clearly called for immersion. Possibly his movement was spread most effectively through the many magazines it spawned. There was a tremendous demand for reading material on the American frontier; frontier people were greatly interested in religious matters, including controversy and debate. Campbell was an effective editor and controversialist, founding *The Christian Baptist,* which was soon superseded—possibly became the name Baptist seemed sectarian—by *The Millennial Harbinger.* Like many others in the mid-Atlantic states and on the frontier at the time, Campbell spoke of the millennium, but he did not emphasize millenarian theology or seek signs of the times. He concentrated on what seemed to him the one essential thing that was demanded for the coming of God's Kingdom: a restoration of the pattern of primitive Christianity in order to achieve Christian unity.

In contrast to such rapidly growing frontier groups as the Methodists and Baptists, who often sought validation of Christian doctrine in highly emotional conversion experiences, Campbell and his followers emphasized a calmly rational approach to Christian belief and commitment. Alexander Campbell shared Henry David Thoreau's and frontier America's passion to seek simplicity, to get to the basics. For Campbell, the creeds and theologies of traditional Christianity, though well intentioned, had obscured the plain and simple teachings of the New Testament. This view he shared with Locke, though Campbell found more in Scripture that was essential than Locke had found. A familiar Disciples' motto became "No creed but Christ." By the late 1820s and early 1830s the movement he led had begun to grow rapidly. The Disciples—sometimes now disparagingly called Campbellites—were able to enter an alliance, not without great tensions, with another group of Christians, inspired by Barton Stone (1772–1844), who had arrived at beliefs similar to those of the Campbells before Thomas and Alexander Campbell had set foot in America. Stone's movement was strong in Kentucky and Tennessee and was spreading into the Midwest. One of the points of tension between the Campbells and Stone involved the name—Stone felt that only "Christian" (not Disciples) should be used.

By the time of the U.S. Civil War, the Christian—or Disciple, Reformer, or Restoration—movement had grown to the point of having nearly 200,000 adherents. Alexander and Thomas Campbell and Barton Stone personally opposed slavery, but Alexander argued for moderate (nonabolitionist) solutions to this problem, lest the nation and the Christian unity movement both be split. The Christians or Disciples were not split by the Civil War but experienced additional strains and tensions as a result of the national struggle. Some Disciples were ardent abolitionists. Some defended slavery. Others were pacifist. Some, including Campbell, were moderates, approving neither slavery nor abolition. All supported their positions by appeal to the New Testament Scriptures. In the year after the war's end, Alexander Campbell died (his father and Stone had preceded him by several years), leaving a distinctively American religious movement with a new generation of leaders, still inspired by a vision of Christian unity based on a return to New Testament patterns of church and individual life. They profited from his example, founding religious papers and journals for popular audiences on farms and in the cities, founding colleges and congregations, appealing especially in the U.S. Midwest and Southwest to Bible-believing Christians to leave their sects and denominations and unite as Christians without creeds or divisions. Such Christians would agree not to insist on any belief or practice not explicitly a part of the universal practice of primitive New Testament Christianity.

FRANCES WILLARD

Nineteenth-century interest in the social aspects of the gospel was not confined to the injustices produced by the industrial and economic changes of the day. Many Americans, particularly Protestants with a Pietistic background, began in the late

1840s to be concerned about open saloons and the disruptions in social and family life caused by alcohol. Several northern and western states passed laws limiting liquor sales, but a real campaign for the abolition of liquor did not emerge until the 1870s. With this campaign, strengthened by the organization of the Prohibition party in 1868 and the Woman's Christian Temperance Union in 1874, came attention not only to alcohol but a number of other social ills of the period. A central leader in the temperance crusade and subsequently in other movements for human (particularly women's) rights was Frances Willard (1839–1898).

Raised in a Methodist home, Frances enjoyed a comfortable childhood, received a respectable education and took her place as a teacher in several academies and normal schools in central Illinois. When the first northwestern women's college (designed to be comparable with men's colleges of the day rather than a normal or preparatory school) was organized as the Evanston College for Ladies in 1871, Willard was chosen as its president. She brought to the position her teaching experience, travel in Europe, and a brief stint as the corresponding secretary of the American Methodist Ladies' Centenary Association (a national group that raised money for Garrett Theological Seminary). Abilities gained in these previous experiences were to be put to immediate use in her position as president, as she was responsible not only for designing the curriculum and administering the college but also for fund raising. In a few years the Ladies' College was incorporated into Northwestern University, also in Evanston (a suburb of Chicago). In this new setting, Willard's role changed, and differences with new university administrators led her to resign the position in 1874.

Forced to take a new direction in her life, Willard, in the fall of that year, accepted an invitation to become the president of the Chicago Women's Christian Temperance Union. In the early 1870s, the temperance cause had reached new heights of recognition in the society. Central to this movement was the organization of women's groups intent on effecting change in liquor laws and practices. The Chicago chapter of the WCTU was a fledgling but quite active part of this movement.

Frances Willard's interest in temperance was of long standing as it was drawn from her Methodist background and other influences. Her work as president of the Ladies' College had allowed some travel that introduced her not only to leaders of women's concerns in education but also with the rising cause of temperance both in Illinois and on the East Coast. The invitation to join the Chicago group in a leadership role was seen by Willard as divinely given guidance about the direction of her life, for now she was presented with an opportunity and challenge to contribute to the larger issues of the society—a desire and calling she had felt for years. The Chicago position entailed a great deal of lecturing, and Frances now found a new outlet for her considerable talents as a speaker. She was challenged with the task of persuading others to give up drink. She did this, as had others, by combining her appeal with the presentation of the gospel as the means for achieving sobriety—she effectively took up the role of preacher. During her first year in Chicago she was active in the organization of the national WCTU, serving as its corresponding secretary, a position that gave her much wider contact and recognition.

In January 1877 Willard joined the national evangelistic team of Dwight L. Moody (1837–1899), American's leading evangelist of the period, while continuing her work as secretary of the WCTU. Although the association with Moody was brief, Willard's talents as a preacher were whetted and she came to a larger understanding of her own commitments. Differences with Moody over her maturing commitment to women's suffrage and her willingness to associate in her temperance campaigns with Unitarians led to her leaving his evangelistic association. The experience, however, helped her solidify and articulate her understanding of women's rights and an ecumenical understanding that embraced all who served God. These became central principles from which she was not to deviate.

By 1879 Frances Willard had become a nationally known figure through her association with Moody and her active participation in the temperance movement, which was becoming a broad movement in the society. Her election as president of the WCTU in that year recognized her unusual talents in the leadership of the movement. She held the position until her death in 1898. Between her elevation to the presidency of WCTU and her death, she became one of the most recognized and influential women in the United States and Europe (through her leadership in the World Woman's Christian Temperance Union.)

While the cause of temperance was undoubtedly the central focus of Willard's public life, it became a vehicle that carried her into leadership roles in a much broader spectrum of social and moral issues and campaigns. Convinced that the home was the special responsibility and sphere of women, she tied her interest in women's suffrage to the concern for temperance. She promoted the right to vote with her interest in the sphere of the home by championing the cause of "home protection." If women were to protect their homes from the evils of alcohol, they should at least have the right to vote on matters pertaining to liquor. It was a small step from that position to demanding the right of full suffrage for women in the society. In a similar manner the 1880s saw the WCTU and other similar organizations take up the banner for a number of other pressing social issues: fair and equal employment practices, free kindergartens for the poor women who must be employed, and a "social purity" platform to control traffic in young prostitutes (a subject long avoided in public discussion because of the general prudishness of the period), separate housing for women prisoners, and general protection of women from sexual abuse and harassment. In these causes, Willard was to play an important leadership role and personally to align herself with even more progressive movements such as the labor movement as it sought to counter the labor abuses of capitalism, Christian socialism as an alternative to *laissez faire* capitalism, and a third political party—the Prohibition party. In each of these, Willard was motivated out of a central concern for a just society in which women could be treated fairly and respectfully.

The Methodist heritage out of which Willard came contributed not only her interest in temperance but her evangelical understanding of the Christian gospel. Throughout her life at its turning points she sought divine guidance through biblical inspiration, a mainstay of evangelical practice. Her oratorical skills were modeled after the preaching styles of the evangelist, and her moral principles were rooted in the piety of Methodism. Her facility at inspiring others to voluntary commitment and responsibility, as well as some of her organizational skills with these groups, had been nurtured in Methodist circles. She was as at home in the temperance camp meeting as in lecture halls of the Eastern elite. However, while her social concern was grounded in her faith, she was ahead of her church in her understanding of the role and place of women. Although duly elected, along with four other women from across the church, by her local conference as a lay delegate to Methodism's General Conference in 1888, Willard and her female colleagues were not seated as official delegates by the conference. Actively supporting temperance, the church continued for some time to oppose women's suffrage, a key issue in its refusal to seat women as delegates at the conference. As with so many of Willard's causes, the changes she sought came to fruition only after her death, but she had been instrumental in laying the foundations on which their ultimate acceptance depended.

Her struggle for recognition in the church prompted Ms. Willard to publish her most ambitious scholarly book, *Woman in the Pulpit*. In the work, Willard used biblical texts, church history, and the egalitarian nature of Jesus' teachings to support a full pastoral role for women within the churches, women's voting rights in the governance of church organizations, and full ordination for women pastors. Clearly ahead of her time in this area, she was simply carrying the principles on which she based most of her social programs into the Christian churches, where women had always contributed significantly to the active life of the gospel.

Ruth Bordin, in recounting the life of Frances Willard, suggests that Frances was successful in her endeavors because she was willing to compromise and reshape programs; she was a consummate politician. Perhaps more important, according to Bordin, Frances genuinely believed in women's special virtues of love and compassion and accepted the understanding of the age that women's particular sphere resided in the concerns and values of family and home. She could always combine this understanding with her own conviction that in order to protect and expand these virtues women must enter into the public arena, where decisions were made that vitally affected the home and women generally. She was successful in her time because she did not find it necessary to abandon the special place and role of women in order to participate in the political process to achieve change.[4]

In spite of the failure to move her church toward acceptance of women's rights and her inability to achieve many of her social programs in her own lifetime, Frances Willard by the time of her death had become a preeminent symbol for women's rights and responsibilities in the society. She was so well known that flags were lowered in Washington, D.C., as well as in Chicago; funeral services were held in several cities; and some 30,000 persons in one day filed pass her bier in Chicago. Her sustained championing throughout her lifetime of often unpopular but morally justifiable causes was founded in her deep faith and conviction that to serve God truly one must "do everything" that one can to attain justice grounded in love.

DOROTHY DAY

Dorothy Day was born in Brooklyn in 1897. The religious background of her parents was Episcopalian but the family did not regularly attend church. As an adult, Dorothy recalled that there was a Bible and a volume of the sermons of John Wesley among the books in their library. She also recalled reading the Bible and some of Augustine's writings and praying by herself. Her father was a sports writer and at times became involved in sports-related business activities. They moved about the country. After her father's employment in San Francisco was interrupted by the earthquake of 1906, they settled in a comfortable middle-class section of Chicago, where Dorothy found herself more and more concerned about the living conditions of the city's poverty-stricken working-class immigrants described in Upton Sinclair's exposé, *The Jungle*.

[4]Ruth Bordin, *Frances Willard: A Biography* (Chapel Hill: University of North Carolina Press, 1986).

By the time Dorothy was a student at the University of Illinois, where she remained for two years, she had become a member of the Socialist party and numbered among her heroes Eugene Debs, the Haymarket Martyrs, and other leaders of the Socialist and radical labor movements. She had also read the classics of British and Russian literature and was deeply influenced by the populist and naturalist strains of realist and modernist writers, many of whom depicted the economic, social, and moral conflicts of contemporary society. She wanted to be a writer. Leaving the university, she began to write for socialist and communist papers. She came to know some of the leading figures among the American avant-garde, playwright Eugene O'Neill, poet Hart Crane, and critic Kenneth Burke, as well as leading writers of the left. She was arrested and jailed for taking part in a demonstration on behalf of woman's suffrage. Later, during the post-World War I Red Scare conducted by the U.S. Department of Justice, she was again imprisoned because of her association with persons in the labor movement. She became a well-known contributor to the communist paper *The Masses* and wrote a novel, *The Eleventh Virgin,* the rights of which she was able to sell to a Hollywood filmmaker. She lived in New Orleans and Mexico and traveled about the United States, holding many different jobs—for instance, as a clerk in a Montgomery Ward store. For a time she studied nursing.

Even during this time of restless travel and activity in and out of the labor movement, when most of her companions were leftist or avant-garde intellectuals, she felt an attraction to the classics of religious spirituality, reading Pascal's *Pensées,* Thomas à Kempis' *Imitation of Christ,* and the writings of Teresa of Avila. In New Orleans, while living in the French Quarter and writing articles on the lives of dance-hall girls, she would find herself attending services at St. Louis Cathedral.

Returning to New York, she fell deeply in love and entered a common law marriage with a biologist, who was, by political conviction, an anarchist. The birth of a daughter Tamar Teresa in 1927 precipitated a deepening of her spiritual concerns. Dorothy did not want her daughter to lead the life she felt she had led, cut off from the spiritual home that she felt the Catholic church gave its members. She began to pray more frequently and more fervently. She took instructions in the Catholic faith and became a convert. This ended her marriage, for her husband, though they loved each other and had been happy together, true to his philosophical convictions, was unwilling to continue the relationship after Dorothy and Tamar entered the church. As she later recalled, she became a Catholic with a sense of deep sorrow but with the sense that this was her deepest need and the deepest need of her daughter.

After her conversion, Dorothy worked for a time as a film writer in Hollywood, lived in Mexico again, then returned with her daughter to New York. As a Catholic, she continued to write, now in Catholic as well as socialist publications, on behalf of justice for the working class. She wrote on behalf of Nicaraguans whom she saw as attempting (unsuccessfully) to throw off a government dominated by a small group of wealthy landowners, kept in power by rich U.S. corporations and their allies in the U.S. government. She was concerned that, as Pope Pius XI had sadly remarked in 1929, the workers of the world seemed lost to the church. She was troubled that because now, during the depths of the worldwide Great Depression, although Catholics were represented in movements on behalf of the poor, the church was not giving leadership. On a hunger march to Washington in 1932, to press for aid to the victims of the Depression, she prayed that she might be given a role, a way in which to work with the poor in service to God.

Not long after this, she was approached by Peter Maurin, a Frenchman who had lived for many years the life of a wanderer and worker—on farms and in factories and mines—in the United States. Born in 1877, Maurin was of French peasant stock, a Catholic who had as a young man worked as a lay brother in the De la Salle Brotherhood, teaching the children of the poor. Later, he became a part of the more radical Sillon movement, an effort of French Catholic young people to bring justice and Christian love to bear on the economic and spiritual life of French workers. This movement had been prompted in part by the encyclical *Rerum novarum* of Pope Leo XIII, who had declared, against the prevailing ethos of capitalism, that "labor is not a commodity," but who had also condemned secularistic and atheistic forms of socialism. The Sillon movement had failed largely because of opposition from conservative French Catholics of the aristocracy and middle classes. Maurin had immigrated to North America, to Canada first and then to the United States, coming to know the condition of urban and agricultural workers intimately. A deeply spiritual man, he had developed a unique style of writing in the genre he christened "easy essays." In these brief essays Maurin concisely and forcefully applied the gospel message of justice, compassion, and love with simple but profound logic. They could be read in a matter of moments, but their direct, gospel style often made their message lodge in the reader's conscience.

Peter Maurin proposed to Dorothy Day that they embark on a cooperative effort to relate the gospel message to working people, to help the poor meet their needs, and to address the moral and spiritual problems of a society in which economic injustice and militarism seemed dominant.

From their meetings was born the Catholic Worker movement. The first issue of *The Catholic Worker,* originally an eight-page tabloid, appeared on May Day in 1933. Soon its circulation had risen to more than 150,000 copies per issue. In New York City's Bowery was established a hospitality house, the House of St. Joseph, where the poor could find companionship, food, and clothing and could be directed to medical care. This was followed by the establishment of other hospitality houses and communal farms—with sometimes thirty or more in existence at once in various parts of the country.

The newspaper became the voice of social and cultural criticism within the U.S. Catholic church and the champion of all sorts of causes. From here, support came for fair wages for cotton pickers in the Depression, the civil-rights movement of Martin Luther King, Jr., the pacifists of World War II, the farm-labor movement of Cesar Chavez, the antiwar protests of Vietnam, and the antinuclear activities of recent years—to name only a few. All of this was done within the church to which Day and *The Catholic Worker* were always loyal, even if they were critical. Day's conviction that there could be no mercy without justice led her constantly to question the injustices within the system of the society and the church of which she was a part. Her deep, almost mystical, faith took some of its inspiration from the Little Flower (about whom she wrote a biography). Thérèse of Lisieux (1873–1897), was a late nineteenth-century French saint (often called the "Little Flower"), whose life of complete obedience in the "little tasks" of convent life and whose patient suffering during a terribly painful terminal illness had profoundly shaped Dorothy Day's understanding of what faith can mean. Her interest was in Thérèse's concern for the little things of life and the "little people" forgotten and abandoned by society.

The social activism of the Catholic Worker movement organized groups throughout the country to carry out lectures, protests, meetings, and retreats, seeking new avenues to deal with social problems. Houses of hospitality provided an opportunity to put belief into action daily by serving meals, dispensing clothing, and caring for the needy.

Dorothy Day's jail experiences were not ended with her days in the feminist and radical labor movements. During the 1950s and 1960s, she and many participants in the Catholic Worker movement were arrested for civil disobedience, protesting America's preparation for nuclear war as evidenced in civil defense drills. Many from the Catholic Worker movement participated in the civil rights and peace and pacifist movements of the 1960s and continue to be active in these causes.

Peter Maurin died in 1949. Dorothy Day, who wrote two moving autobiographical works (*The Long Loneliness* and *From Union Square to Rome*) and a number of reflections on the Catholic Worker movement (including *Loaves and Fishes* and *On Pilgrimage: The Sixties*) and its attempt to work with the poor, the unemployed, the neglected, and oppressed in a modern industrial-technological society, died in 1980. Many, inspired by their example, chose lives of voluntary poverty as part of their vocation or calling from God. A major effect of the Catholic Worker movement she and Peter Maurin started has been its continuing influence on the lives of the many volunteers, Catholic and non-Catholic, who over the years became workers for shorter or longer periods at hospitality houses and farms. While learning about poverty and injustice in modern societies, these volunteers absorbed Dorothy Day's attitude that all humans are poor in their need of love and can be rich in finding God's love in a community where no one puts himself or herself above the poorest of God's children.

MARTIN LUTHER KING, JR.

Among Christian leaders in the United States in the twentieth century, no one stands out more prominently than Martin Luther King, Jr. In the mid-1950s this twenty-six-year-old black Baptist pastor of the Dexter Avenue Baptist Church in Montgomery, Alabama, was abruptly catapulted into the leadership of a boycott by the blacks of the local bus system. Subsequent events were to give him central leadership in a nationwide civil rights movement that ultimately changed the social fabric of American society by ending the policies of racial segregation that had replaced slavery after the Civil War. Because King understood his role as social reformer to be rooted in his Christian faith, the struggle for black equality was nothing more than the message of the gospel—a message of love and justice for all.

Born into the home of a prominent pastor in Atlanta, King was raised among the black elite of the South. Black Christianity with all of its enthusiasm, pietistic morality, and strong organization was the center of black culture, for only there could blacks experience both religious and social life unencumbered by the surrounding white culture. In this setting King was never outside the nurturing web of faith and active Christian life. In his early years he came to appreciate his father's substantial influence in the community, particularly as he observed his father's constant struggle to improve the position of blacks in the larger culture. It was in his seventeenth year while a student at a prestigious black school, Morehouse College, that the younger King answered the call to follow his father into the ministry. Persuaded by a family friend, King's family reluctantly agreed for him to pursue a seminary education in the North: at Crozer Theological Seminary in Chester, Pennsylvania.

The years in seminary introduced Martin to theologians and philosophers who were to have a lasting influence on his intellectual and ethical development and on his faith. Here Walter Rauschenbusch's theories of the social gospel convinced him "that any religion which professes to not be concerned about the social and economic conditions that scar the soul is a spiritually moribund religion."[5] Pacifist thought, particularly as embodied by A. J. Muste, executive secretary of the Fellowship of Reconciliation, attracted him and in the seminary he was also introduced to the ideas of Gandhi's *Satyagraha* (nonviolence) campaign, which had won Indian independence from the British in 1947. Reinhold Niebuhr's writings clarified for him the nature of human evil and the need for divine Grace, as well as helped King understand Christian liberalism's false optimism. Moving to the Boston School of Theology upon completion of his studies at Crozer, King entered into a doctoral program in philosophy. His work with Edgar Brightman and L. Harold DeWolf led him to examine the nature of humanity and God from the personalistic viewpoint. This study also was to have a lasting effect upon his understanding:

> Personalism's insistence that only personality—finite and infinite—is ultimately real strengthened me in two convictions: it gave me a metaphysical basis and philosophical grounding for the idea of a personal God, and it gave me a metaphysical basis for the dignity and worth of all human personality.[6]

Each of these insights was to be called on as King led the subsequent struggle for racial freedom through nonviolent means.

Moving to Dexter Avenue Church immediately after he completed his studies at Boston in 1954, King consciously took up the pastoral role rather than another that equally attracted him: academic teaching. One year later when Mrs. Rosa Parks, a black seamstress, was arrested for refusing to move to the black section of a Montgomery bus, black leaders of the community decided to protest by calling a boycott of the bus lines. Elected as president of the Montgomery Improvement Association organized to coordinate the boycott, King quickly became the recognized leader not only of the local boycott, but of the struggle for equality all across the South. Legal actions stemming from the boycott, which had lasted more than a year, ultimately overturned Alabama's segregationist transportation laws. Central in the struggle was the use of a new methodology of resistance: nonviolent civil disobedience.

Martin Luther King, Jr., took his inspiration for nonviolent protest from the teachings of Jesus, but patterned his method after Gandhi's concepts of *Satyagraha,* which he had been introduced to in seminary. In 1959, after being stabbed in Harlem by a psychotic, he traveled to India to study further the Indian concept of nonviolence and its implementation. An early reading of Thoreau's essay "On Civil Disobedience" had also introduced King to concepts of civil organization and how it may be changed. Now these and Gandhi's ideas had practical application. Out of the crucible of the civil rights conflicts he was to fashion an American form of nonviolent resistance.

[5]David L. Lewis, *King: A Critical Biography* (Baltimore: Praeger Publishers, 1970), p. 29.
[6]Coretta Scott King, *My Life with Martin Luther King, Jr.* (New York: Avon, 1969), p. 104.

Martin Luther King, Jr.   *(Photo reprinted through courtesy of Religious News Service.)*

Like the synthesis in Hegelian philosophy, the principle of nonviolent resistance seeks to reconcile the truths of two opposites—acquiescence and violence—while avoiding the extremes and immoralities of both. The nonviolent resister agrees with the person who acquiesces that one should not be physically aggressive toward his opponent; but he balances the equation by agreeing with the person of violence that evil must be resisted. He avoids the nonresistance of the former and violent resistance of the latter.[7]

To help the black community employ this concept in its situation, he and others organized training sessions on how to react to violent behavior. They were to rigorously stand their ground by disobeying immoral and biased laws while offering love and compassion to any who resisted or challenged them.

From the late 1950s King emerged as a unique leader of a vast and amorphous assault by black persons, and sympathetic whites, upon outmoded and immoral racial laws across the country. He constantly responded to calls to lecture, negotiate, and witness before political bodies, and to lead marches, boycotts, and sit-ins. He was instrumental in forming the Southern Christian Leadership Conference, which became a vehicle for political and protest action. Resigning his pastorate in 1960, he turned his full attention and energies to the movement for civil rights of all persons. Arrested in Birmingham as a result of a protest action, his "Letter from a Birmingham Jail" became a classic appeal to the Christians of the country to reconsider the injustice of segregation practiced at that time. His insistence that blacks needed to be reconciled with whites as much as whites need to be reconciled with blacks did not interest some blacks, who turned to the more aggressive Black Power movement, where the use of violence was condoned and sometimes championed. Among the several books that King wrote supporting and explaining the movement are *Stride Toward Freedom* and *Why We Can't Wait*. In 1968, at a protest event in Memphis, he was cut down by an assassin's bullet.

[7]Martin Luther King, Jr., *Stride Toward Freedom* (New York: Harper & Row, 1958), p. 213.

The efforts of King and others were instrumental in the striking down of traditional segregation laws by the Supreme Court and the Congressional passage of civil rights legislation to safeguard the equality of all. For his work, King received numerous awards, degrees, and honors, capped by the Nobel Peace Prize in 1964. Always the preacher, King made his contribution to the civil rights movement a statement of Christian faith and confidence in the love of God that would ultimately triumph over the pride and egoism of humanity. In his own understanding the boycott that started the movement and the later events that led to phenomenal social change could not be explained: "There is something about the protest that is suprarational; it cannot be explained without a divine dimension....There is a creative power that works to pull down mountains of evil and level hilltops of injustice. God still works through history His wonders to perform."[8]

THOMAS MERTON

Thomas Merton (1915–1968) became—and remains—one of the most influential figures in contemporary Christianity. His father was English, his mother an American. Both were artists who struggled to support themselves by their painting. Tom spent his earliest years in the United States with his parents at the house of his mother's parents near New York City. His grandparents had a strong bias against Roman Catholicism. When Tom was six years old, his mother died of cancer. Merton spent the next several years shunting from place to place, attending a Catholic school in France, living near his father in England, or living with his grandparents in America. When he was fifteen, his grandfather established a trust fund for him that guaranteed his financial independence. Shortly afterwards, he endured a difficult time during which his father was dying of a brain tumor. His parents had never manifested interest in religion; but while he was dying, Merton's father showed a strong sympathy for Catholicism.

After his father's death, Merton traveled in Europe, and under his guardian's influence, read the most advanced modernist works of literature, including the novels of D. H. Lawrence, who glorified a return to a primitive sexuality. Visiting Rome, Merton was impressed by the spiritual content of works of art he had intended to appreciate only for their formal and stylistic merits. At one point he felt a strong sense of the spiritual presence of his deceased father. Enrolled as a student in Cambridge University, he was impressed by the vision of spiritual harmony presented in Dante's *Divine Comedy* but neglected his classes and spent much of his time drinking and in sexual exploits. A woman became pregnant; and when this became known to Tom's guardian, he forced Tom to leave Cambridge in disgrace. Tom was surprised and humiliated. He had thought his life-style was the same as his guardian's. Later, when the woman and their child were killed during the German bombing of London, Tom experienced a deep sense of guilt at having abandoned them.

He went to the United States and enrolled in Columbia University, where he studied literature, wanting to become a great poet and novelist. Looking into the mirror, he tried to see a physical resemblance between himself and William Shakespeare. Like many young people, he became a communist, joining the party in 1935 and, disillusioned, leaving it in the same year.

[8]Ibid., pp. 69–70.

Studying literature with Mark Van Doren and medieval Catholic philosophy with Daniel Walsh, he became attracted to Catholicism. The book *Ends and Means* by the novelist Aldous Huxley introduced him to religious mysticism. The English poet William Blake, certainly not a Catholic but an intensely spiritual writer, influenced him, as did the Jesuit poet Gerard Manley Hopkins, who joined traditional Catholic theology to a revolutionary method of poetic metrics and versification. Tom wrote a master's thesis on Blake's symbolism and for a time taught in Columbia's Extension Department.

Merton was baptized a Catholic in 1938, with three of his Jewish friends standing by to give spiritual support. He had, during his time at Columbia, been introduced to Eastern mysticism by a Hindu practitioner.

He worked with a Catholic group in Harlem helping the poor. He applied for admission to the Franciscan order but was rejected when he told the story of his Cambridge life. For a while he taught English at a Franciscan school, St Bonaventure's College. His readings in Huxley and others had made him a pacifist. Having made retreats at two Cistercian monasteries, he entered the Cistercian (Trappist) monastery of Gethsemani in Kentucky on December 10, 1941. He was twenty-seven. Although he had wanted to be a great writer, he renounced this ambition when he became Ludovicus, or Louis, a Trappist monk, committing himself to the vows of poverty, chastity, obedience, and silence. After his ordination to the priesthood he became known as Father Louis, though he published under the name "Thomas Merton" and in later years often signed his correspondence "Tom."

The life of a Trappist monk in 1941 was highly structured. The day was divided into periods of group worship, work, meditation, and rest. But Merton was soon given the responsibility of writing. At first he was assigned the task of writing works dealing with Cistercian monastic life, including lives and studies of earlier Cistercian heroes. In 1948, however, was published the—heavily censored—account of his early life, conversion, and entry into monasticism, *The Seven Storey Mountain*. Merton had originally included in this work the story of the sexual affair that had led to the conception and birth of his illegitimate child. The monastery's censor had crossed this out. "But St. Augustine in his *Confessions* told of his love affair and his illegitimate son," Merton protested. "You are not St. Augustine," the censor had replied.

The Seven Storey Mountain became an immediate best-seller, appealing to many in the late 1940s, Catholic and Protestant, who were seeking deeper spiritual meaning. Applicants for the monasteries multiplied. From then on, Merton had celebrity status. But his life was not an untroubled one. There were genuine conflicts with his abbot of eighteen years, whose decisions he was resigned to accept because of his vow of obedience. He was required to write, but his writings were subjected to censorship. He also felt called to a life of greater solitude, free of the rigid routine of monastery life. It was a long time before his abbot was willing to grant this.

After his conversion, he was at first very hostile to non-Catholic forms of Christianity. As he continued to develop, he opened more and more not only to non-Catholic Christianity but to the other great religions of the world. He became one of the great interpreters of Christian and world mysticism, heavily influenced by Teresa of Avila and John of the Cross but also by Hindu, Buddhist, and Muslim mystical writers.

For many years he was master of the novices in his monastery, in charge of instructing new monks in theology, the Bible, Christian devotion, and the ways of monastic life. His talks to novices were characterized by spontaneous good humor and a command of biblical and theological knowledge enlivened by wit and humanity. One of his novices was the Nicaraguan Ernesto Cardenal, who, returning to Nicaragua to found a spiritual community and prevented from doing so by the U.S.-supported government, became active, as poet, priest, and government official, in the Sandinista cause, which he interpreted as God's cause in behalf of God's oppressed poor.

During the 1960s, though a monk confined to his monastery, Merton became deeply involved in attempts to apply Christian love to the problems of society, becoming through his writings active in the civil rights movement and in anti-Vietnam War protest. He received and counselled civil rights and peace activists at his hermitage at the monastery. By this time he had convinced his monastic superiors that the structured monastic life may be only a way station to the life of "transcultural maturity" that is the goal of Christian experience for all. He sought to continue his relationship with the monastic community but to live a life of freedom in Christ for his spiritual development and writing.

Merton became both a critic of what he considered institutional deadness and a supporter of the reform being carried out in the Catholic church during the Second Vatican Council. By circular letters sent to correspondents all over the world as well as by his published writings, he made known his criticisms of the Catholic church and Catholic monasticism for the shallowness and authoritarianism that he perceived in existing habits. He also stressed his belief in the possibilities of renewal. He made known his view that the Vietnam War was the stupidest event in U.S. history, as well as his hope that Americans would make their country a force for peace, nonviolent love, and healing in the world.

There were rumors that Merton was going to leave the Catholic church or at least the monastic life. There were rumors that he was going to become a Buddhist. His letters and journals show that these rumors were ill founded. His deepest commitment was to a life that would eventuate in oneness with God; he understood his vows as a Cistercian monk to be an integral condition of achieving this goal. Because of his writings, the many writings by friends, acquaintances, and monastic colleagues, and authorized and unauthorized biographies, probably as much is known about Merton's life as about any figure in world religious history.

Toward the end of his life he was in much demand among Catholic monastics and others to speak about the spiritual life. In 1968 he went to Asia to study his order's monasteries there, to participate in conferences on Christian and other forms of monasticism, to encounter religious authorities on the spiritual life (including the Dalai Lama), to learn more of Hindu and Buddhist spirituality. It was in Bangkok, exactly twenty-seven years to the day after entering the monastic life, after having given a talk in which he dealt sympathetically not only with Eastern forms of spirituality but with the possibilities of spirituality in Marxism, that he died. A Mass was celebrated for him in the Kentucky monastery, in conjunction with sacramental recognition of the life and work of another Christian, the Swiss theologian Karl Barth, perhaps the greatest Protestant theologian of the twentieth century, who also died on December 10, 1968.

Many of Merton's ideas of monastic reform, giving greater freedom to monks and nuns in their attempts to grow into "transcultural maturity" in Christ, have been accepted by his and other monastic orders. Other monks and nuns have followed Merton's example in speaking on controversial social and political issues.

As a writer, Thomas Merton was poet, theologian, moralist, and witness. As a poet, he became convinced that language must be pulverized, smashed, reduced to its roots, to express authentic experience in a time when most people hate and hide from truth and reality. His later poems, especially the long poems "Cables to the Ace" and "The Geography of Lograire," attempt this. Influenced by the modernist poets of France, Russia, Latin America, and the United States, he thought that to avoid the deadening effect of literary fashions and academic criticism, poets should write antipoems. As a theologian, he integrated into his vision of Christian experience the thought of the great Catholic mystical writers, including Teresa and John of the Cross, but especially those, such as Bernard of Clairvaux, of the Cistercian tradition and also the earliest Christian hermit monastics, the desert fathers. As a moralist, he insisted that God is always for peace and mercy as against violence and power, always for justice and compassion toward the poor. As a witness, he expressed what it means to have a thoroughly modern life, indeed a privileged life, but to experience a need for that which, demanding poverty of spirit and perhaps physical poverty, will fulfill a hunger for the eternal.

MOTHER TERESA OF CALCUTTA

Modern modes of communication, transportation, and organization have made possible the phenomenal worldwide growth of a Roman Catholic religious order founded only in 1948: the Missionaries of Charity. Whereas worldwide expansion would, in previous generations, have taken long years, this order has covered the world in just four decades. As the soul of the movement, Mother Teresa of Calcutta (1910–), stands as a demure dynamo of spiritual power: one who has recaptured for current times the Christian compassion for the plight of the hungry, the poor, the sick, the dying, and the destitute.

Born in Skopje in present-day Yugoslavia of Albanian parents, Agnes Gonxha Bejaxhiu was raised in a pious, disciplined Catholic household in an area of mixed nationalities and religions. At the age of eighteen, Agnes joined the Sisters of Loreto to become a missionary. The order, founded on the rules of the *Spiritual Exercises* of Ignatius Loyola, was basically an Irish teaching order. Taking the name of Teresa after Teresa of Avila and the Little Flower, the nineteenth-century French saint Thérèse of Lisieux, Agnes was assigned to Darjeeling and then to Calcutta in India.

Here, for some twenty years, she taught the daughters of India's middle and upper castes, ultimately becoming the headmistress of the convent school. However, her convent was located next to Moti Jheel, a *baitas,* or shantytown, where many lived in squalor. The plight of the people of this slum attracted Teresa's compassion, and in August 1948 she requested permission from her mother superior to live outside the convent in the slum to minister to the needs she saw there. When the Vatican granted the request, she left the security of the convent, first taking medical training from an order of U.S. missionary sisters and then returning to Moti Jheel. With no precedent or guidance, she simply took her skills and love to the streets, first living with the Little Sisters of the Poor and later accepting the generosity of a local Catholic family, who provided her (and her helpers) lodging. Wearing a simple white sari with a blue band and a cross as her habit, she took on the form and the appearance of an Indian woman simply serving those around her.

Within a few months, several of the girls she taught at the Loreto convent joined her in the streets. Insisting that they finish their schooling, Teresa extended their learning by teaching them to minister to the sick and dying. In October 1950, the congregation of the Missionaries of Charity received approval from the pope and was constituted as a religious order of the church. Some twelve young women, along with Teresa, constituted the new order, but the expansion was steady and varied. The Missionaries of Charity now has several hundred houses, clinics, and schools and more than 2,000 nuns. Joined by a smaller group of Missionary Brothers of Charity (founded in 1963) and the International Association of Coworkers of Mother Teresa, the work has expanded to be one of the most dynamic of Christian communities at the present time.

Living under strict devotional rules, the order is dedicated to the service of others, based on Jesus' statement that as one feeds, clothes, and cares for others one is caring for Jesus himself. The words of one of the coworkers explains the motivation for service: "When I cleanse the wounds of the poor, I am cleaning the wounds of Christ."[9] Service, therefore, for the order is based not on social or personal need but genuine religious love. The community's day begins and ends with prayer, combines work with meditation, and includes the celebration of the Eucharist. Mother Teresa insists that it is the sacrament that empowers service:

> That is why we need the Eucharist, we need Jesus—to deepen our faith. If we can see Jesus in the appearance of bread, we can see Him in the broken bodies of the poor. That is why we need that oneness with Christ, why we need deep faith in Christ. It is very beautiful. When we have that deepening of contact with Christ and can accept Him fully, we can touch the broken bodies. We put into practice straight away. You need the poor to touch Him. You feed yourself in the Eucharist, and after you are fed you want to use that energy, to give it out.[10]

Often refusing gifts that would elevate the sisters above those whom they serve (for example, washing machines), the order sees poverty as both spiritually and physically necessary. Poverty provides the freedom and detachment to serve at any place and in any situation, for one is not bound by expectations or rewards. Perhaps as important is the realization by the recipient of this love that the service is given by one who also has nothing and expects nothing but only gives. Although service may take any form and is molded to fit the needs of the societies in which the order serves, in India service has centered on four major areas: care for the dying in houses for the dying (the first of which was established in a house originally designed for pilgrims to a shrine of the Hindu goddess Kali), care for the newborn in homes for children (often cast away by their families), care for lepers in special colonies, and feeding the hungry. Each of these ministries arose to meet a need present in the social situation of the area. Ministering is done without inquiry into the religious faith or allegiance of the needy; the message of the gospel is in its witness of love.

Mother Teresa's spirit has been molded by years of giving herself completely and fully. As she began the ministry in total trust and with no means of support, she continues to admonish the sisters of the order to trust: "God will provide." She, and

---

[9]Desmond Doig, *Mother Teresa: Her People and Her Work* (New York: Harper & Row, 1976), p. 145.

[10]Ibid., p. 165.

Mother Teresa.   *(Photo used by permission of Religious News Service.)*

now the order, lives with the complete confidence that if they are willing to give in total trust they will indeed be provided for through God's love. This faith is welded to an indomitable spirit and aggressive energy. The sisters (and brothers) have established ministries where few would be willing to venture and where the possibilities are extremely bleak.

Recognizing that rules are necessary, the order is well structured; but Mother Teresa's practicality and desire to serve allow her to bend and set aside rules where helpful. Willingness to serve simply without unnecessary concern for the future occasionally may lead to impetuousness; yet Teresa's insights, assertive action, and willingness to venture into services unanticipated or undreamed of by others have produced profound personal changes and social services few could have anticipated or envisioned. Perhaps the clue to the accomplishments of the order is found in Mother Teresa's understanding of the human will. For her, humanity's freedom of the will is the center of one's being. One chooses to live and act through this will. Therefore, one must choose to love God; even Jesus himself cannot force one to choose—each of us *allows* Jesus and his love into our hearts. In Teresa's understanding, what the sisters and brothers of the order have done is to allow God's will to replace their own wills, to place themselves totally in God's hands. Then, they are able to do as God wills: to love and serve without thought of self.

Mother Teresa has often been called a modern-day St. Francis, and certainly she emulates his insights and service. Beginning her day by repeating his oft-quoted prayer to be an instrument of God's love, her insistence on poverty for the order witnesses powerfully in the materialistic world of today, as did Francis's own rejection of wealth. Like Francis, she or her helpers may be found at any point of crisis in the world today: she has traveled to Beirut to minister to the displaced and hurt caught in the Israeli-PLO conflict. While she travels the world ministering to the needy and seeing to the affairs of her order, her mission remains the slums of Calcutta, where she returns as often as possible. She has been honored with numerous awards, doctorates, and the Nobel Peace Prize in 1979. An internationally known figure, Mother Teresa insists that the publicity that has come to her work in the past decade is God's means of making the world conscious of the poor and needy; publicity is not something she deserves or seeks—it is the poor who are being honored. Her resolution is to speak to humanity's inhumanity to itself—which she calls lack of love—by ministering to the needs of the body of Christ as it appears in the hungry, sick, and dying.

DOM HELDER CAMARA

One of the most difficult situations for Christian leaders throughout history has been found in Christian majority settings in which society or the state seem to perpetuate situations of injustice that go directly against Christian teachings. The medieval church claimed the right to intervene to correct injustice or misbehavior on the part of governments and ruling groups that threatened the spiritual well-being of the populace. Even as late as the 1950s, the Vatican intervened to help drive from power the Argentine dictator Juan Peron.

The church's intervention in political and socioeconomic morality has been an uncertain prospect, however; not sure of success, the church has often feared creating a backlash of sentiment and antichurch repression. Probably the most difficult situations have been those in which not specific actions of single individuals but an entire social and economic system seems to be creating great spiritual harm to the members of a society. Such has been the case in some third-world countries of the twentieth century.

Modern economists have suggested that contemporary third-world countries differ among themselves as to the causes of poverty and the difficulties in achieving balanced economic development. Some countries are poor because they lack natural resources. Others are poor because they lack an institutional—educational, economic, political, cultural—infrastructure that might enable the inhabitants to work together constructively to attack the problems of poverty and population growth. Others are unable to provide an economic life above levels of dire poverty for many inhabitants because of a political-social structure that perpetuates wealth and prestige for a few. This has been the case in many Latin American countries. In these countries, especially after World War II, many leaders in the Catholic church have attempted to work for economic change, motivated by the belief that Christian teachings demand justice and concern for the poor.

Some Christians, including priests and nuns, driven to a point of desperation, have embraced Marxist revolutionary ideas, methods, and causes (see Chapter Nine). Many others have sought to work nonviolently, developing specifically Christian approaches to the problems of poverty caused by social injustice in Christian societies. Among these, Dom Helder Camara, archbishop of Olinda and

Recife in northwest Brazil, is one who became a symbol of Christian concern and compassion, freedom, and love.

Helder Pessoa Camara was born in 1909 in the port city of Fortaleza in northern Brazil. His mother was a devout Catholic. He later said that he learned from his father, a religious skeptic, that it is possible to be good without being religious. As a theological student, Camara was impressed by a visit to the seminary of a dynamic and self-denying priest, Father Cicero, who was regarded by the ecclesiastical establishment as something of a rabble-rouser, but by the peasants as a saint because of his concern for them. In the early days of his priesthood, Camara believed that communism was the biggest threat to his people. For a time he supported the fascist "Green Shirts." Long before his elevation to the episcopacy, he had decided that communism was not the real threat; rather, it was attitudes of greed and the economic structure of a society that failed to help the poor.

Helder Camara served for a number of years as bishop of the *favelas,* the slums of Rio de Janeiro. Here he became interested in the plight of the poor, focusing on an economic system that allowed little upward movement and often produced a basic servitude of the masses to the interests of a relatively few wealthy landowners and merchants. Camara became convinced that the system was not merely one of Brazil's making but the result of an international system that exploited the third-world countries for the benefit of Western capitalism.

Nevertheless, he was convinced that the selfishness and indifference of his country's economic and political ruling classes were a major source of the problem. He believed that in third-world countries where there was sufficient capital and many resources, investment only resulted in projects that depleted the economic resources, further enriching the country's elites and foreign corporations at the expense of balanced growth. His interest in redistributing the wealth of the land led him to work for social and economic reforms. He became an active organizer of a movement called Action, Justice, Peace, seeking reforms in all sections of the society but with particular emphasis on land reform and the improvement of the wages of the poor. Although basically socialist in his concepts, he sought new models that would not be patterned after Western or Marxist types of socialism. Convinced that the methods of transformation must be nonviolent, he nevertheless had sympathy for those who had lost hope in the possibility of peaceful change.

A Roman Catholic loyal to his church and its hierarchy, Helder Camara believed that at times it was necessary to criticize aspects of the church's role and position in Latin American society, since the church at times has supported and benefited from its alliance with the ruling classes. Symbolic of his position was his refusal to live in an Episcopal Palace. He chose instead to live among his people, experiencing and enjoying direct contact with them. He decided early not to cut himself off from dialogue with all factions in the church and in society, seeking to make the church a mediator and servant among the people.

Having emerged as an authentic voice expressing third-world needs, Helder Camara became a symbol of liberation theology, which focuses on reformulating the Christian message in ways that are not tied to Western modes of thought—theological as well as political and economic—that have dominated European Christianity for centuries. Liberation theologians have shared his intense concern for justice and freedom for the poor (see Chapter Nine). Although he chose to write little, concentrating instead on organization and action to bring change to Brazil, the intensely personal, devotional, and spiritual quality of his writings has won Dom Helder Camara a large readership in Europe and North America. Retirement from his episcopal office did not lessen Helder Camara's importance as a symbol of Christian presence in ministry to those in the contemporary world who suffer from economic structures and imbalances that produce poverty.

FURTHER READING

No list of questions is included for this chapter. The individual biographical sketches readily lend themselves to further research and comparative study. The following list of bibliographical suggestions gives a minimum group of a small number of the most useful sources for each of the exemplary Christians discussed in this chapter. In most instances, we have limited ourselves to listing three sources, often of a varied nature.

AUGUSTINE

BROWN, PETER. *Augustine of Hippo.* Berkeley: University of California Press, 1967.

BATTENHOUSE, ROY, ed. *A Companion to the Study of St. Augustine.* New York: Oxford University Press, 1954.

OUTLER, ALBERT, trans. and ed. *Augustine: Confessions and Enchiridion.* Philadelphia: Westminster Press, 1955.

GREGORY I

BARRACLOUGH, GEOFFREY. *The Medieval Papacy.* New York: Harcourt, Brace and World, 1968.

DUDDEN, F. H. *Gregory the Great.* Oxford, Eng.: Oxford University Press, 1905.

BONAVENTURE

BONAVENTURE. *The Soul's Journey into God, The Tree of Life, The Life of St. Francis.* New York: Paulist Press, 1978.

GILSON, ELIENNE. *The Philosophy of Bonaventure.* Paterson, N.J.: St. Anthony Guild Press, 1965.

GEORGE FOX

BEST, MARY AGNES. *Rebel Saints.* Freeport, N.Y.: Books for Libraries Press, 1968.

FOX, GEORGE. *The Journal of George Fox.* New York: Capricorn Books, 1963.

ROGER WILLIAMS

BAINTON, ROLAND HERBERT. *The Travail of Religious Liberty.* Philadelphia: Westminster Press, 1951, Ch. 8.

SCHEVILL, JAMES.   *The Bloody Tenet.* In *Religious Drama: I,* ed. Marvin Halverson. New York: Meridian Books, 1957.

MILLER, PERRY.   *Errand into the Wilderness.* Cambridge, Mass.: Harvard University Press, 1964.

SUSANNA WESLEY

EDWARDS, MALDWYN.   *Family Circle.* London: Epworth Press, 1949.

HARMON, REBECCA L.   *Susanna: Mother of the Wesleys.* Nashville, Tenn.: Abingdon Press, 1968.

ALEXANDER CAMPBELL

Abilene Christian University Center for Restoration Studies.   *Light from Above: The Life of Alexander Campbell.* Nashville: Gospel Advocate Co., 1988. Videocassette (67 minutes).

RICHARDSON, ROBERT.   *Memoirs of Alexander Campbell.* Philadelphia: Lippincott, 1868–70.

TUCKER, WILLIAM E., and MCALLISTER, LESTER G.   *Journey in Faith.* Saint Louis: Bethany Press, 1975.

FRANCES WILLARD

GORDON, ANNA A.   *The Beautiful Life of Frances E. Willard.* Chicago: Woman's Temperance Publishing Association, 1898.

BORDIN, RUTH.   *Frances Willard: A Biography.* Chapel Hill: University of North Carolina Press, 1986.

DOROTHY DAY

DAY, DOROTHY.   *The Long Loneliness.* New York: Curtis Books, 1952.

———.   *Loaves and Fishes.* New York: Curtis Books, 1963.

MILLER, WILLIAM D.   *Dorothy Day: A Biography.* San Francisco: Harper & Row, 1982.

MARTIN LUTHER KING, JR.

LEWIS, DAVID L.   *King: A Critical Biography.* Baltimore: Praeger Publishers, 1970.

KING, CORETTA SCOTT.   *My Life with Martin Luther King, Jr.* New York: Avon, 1969.

KING, MARTIN LUTHER, JR.   *Stride Toward Freedom.* New York: Harper & Row, 1958.

THOMAS MERTON

MOTT, MICHAEL.   *The Seven Mountains of Thomas Merton.* Boston: Houghton Mifflin, 1984.

PENNINGTON, M. BASIL, O.C.S.O. *Thomas Merton: Brother Monk*. San Francisco: Harper & Row, 1987.

MOTHER TERESA

DOIG, DESMOND. *Mother Teresa: Her People and Her Work*. New York: Harper & Row, 1976.

MOTHER TERESA. *The Love of Christ: Spiritual Counsels*. New York: Harper & Row, 1982.

———. *Heart of Joy: The Transforming Power of Self-Giving*. Ann Arbor, Mich.: Servant Publications, 1987.

MUGGERIDGE, MALCOLM. *Something Beautiful for God: Mother Teresa of Calcutta*. New York: Harper & Row, 1971.

HELDER CAMARA

CAMARA, DOM HELDER. *The Church and Colonialism*. Denville, N.J.: Dimension Books, 1969.

———. *Revolution Through Peace*. New York: Harper & Row, 1971.

CHAPTER NINE

Christianity and Contemporary Issues

Not too many years ago, one frequently heard predictions of the end of the influence or even existence of religion in the modern world. Some felt that the spread of scientific values and the apparent victory of scientific modes of thinking in the conflicts between science and religion (see Chapter Seven) had resulted in the discrediting of religious beliefs and institutions. Others argued that with the increasing ability of humanity to control its destiny through technology—to deal with age-old problems of disease and poverty in practical ways—religious questions about the meaning of life would no longer be of interest to anyone but the emotionally maladjusted. In a novel by Anthony Burgess, for instance, the socially nonconforming poet F. X. Enderby is reconditioned in order to be cured of the compulsion to write poetry. Enderby is retrained for a socially useful role—that of bartender. The irony is that since the early nineteenth century, with the romantic and modernist schools of poetry, poetry was viewed by some poets and readers to be a substitute for religion, a means of expression of the spiritually transcendent. Enderby's late twentieth-century society is depicted by Burgess as believing itself to have no need of spiritual transcendence. Unfortunately, or fortunately, the reconditioning fails, and Enderby ends as he had begun—a person who is a frequent source of annoyance and dismay to the plastic or clockwork society.[1]

Predictions of the end of religion or of religious influence in contemporary society have not been borne out, though it does seem that many aspects of major religious institutions are changing. By means of these changes, religion seems to be not only surviving but in some parts of the world gathering strength (though frequently some of the changes are sources of concern to religious leaders and their followers). Both sets of phenomena—the persistence of religion and the changes that are affecting religious traditions and organizational patterns—can be seen most clearly if one considers Christianity in the contemporary world. This is true probably because of its size—Christianity is by far the largest of the world's

---

[1]See Anthony Burgess, *Enderby* (New York: W. W. Norton and Company, 1963 and 1968).

religions—and because Christianity is found in all types of societies, from the most modern to more traditionally oriented ones.

In the United States, religious affiliation is at an all-time high, and the great majority of those belonging to religious organizations are adherents either of the Roman Catholic or of one of the mainline Protestant denominations. Even among those who have no formal ties to a religious organization, an overwhelming number profess beliefs, such as a belief in God and in an afterlife, drawn from the Judeo-Christian framework. Many express preference for one or another of the major Christian denominations. This is established by numerous opinion surveys. In some ways, in-depth studies reveal a stronger, if more varied, persistence of religious attitudes than the simpler opinion surveys do. At the same time, the United States is becoming an increasingly pluralistic society. Until the middle of the twentieth century, mainline Protestants perceived the United States as a predominantly Protestant country. By the 1970s, it had become clear that Roman Catholicism is as large a part of U.S. Christianity as Protestantism, being much larger in membership than any of the Protestant denominations and having in many ways moved to the center of American life. Also, many non-Christian religions—including Islam, Buddhism, and Hinduism—though numerically much smaller than the Christian denominations, have achieved an increasingly public presence.

In Europe, the traditional bastion of Christendom for a millennium, sociological research shows a vastly different picture. There is no doubt that during the past two centuries there has been a significant decline in religious participation, even by those who are nominally adherent to Christian denominations. In some traditionally Protestant areas—such as England and Scandinavia—where large numbers of the population are automatically considered members of the established church, perhaps less than 10 percent of the nominal members are participants in the actual life of the church to which they belong. In England many of the larger "free" churches, such as Methodism, have experienced dramatic declines in membership and participation. Catholicism has also experienced declining participation and institutional loyalty in most European countries, though much less than that of the extreme Protestant cases. Nevertheless, even in these cases, sociological research suggests that many nominal adherents who never or almost never participate in religious organizations continue to define themselves and their lives in terms of inherited religious beliefs—sometimes given highly subjective and individualistic redefinition. Such evidence indicates that even the secularized European is more attached to, and probably more susceptible to, the claims of the Christian religion than official participation figures suggest.

Even more surprising has been the persistence of the Christian religion and of Christian institutions in Marxist countries, where for years there were government-directed attempts to liquidate religious influence. It may be easy to explain the enthusiastic participation of the majority of Poles in Catholic Christianity, given the unpopularity of the communist regime, the prior commitment of Poles to the Catholic Church, and the identification of Polish Catholicism with Polish nationality.

However, the persistence of Christian participation in the U.S.S.R. itself was to many both surprising and significant. After 1917, the communist government placed severe restrictions on the practice and propagation of religion. It tightly controlled the Russian Orthodox church, limiting the number of churches, clergy, and the amount of theological training that clergy were allowed to receive. During the Second World War, some concessions were made by the government to the church in order to secure support for the defense of the U.S.S.R. against German invaders. By the early 1960s, the U.S.S.R. was expressing dismay that after forty-five years of trying to educate the Russian populace away from religious adherence, and after offering incentives and penalties—opportunities for education and advancement in social and economic status having been largely closed to religious adherents—at least half the population of the country continued to have their children baptized. At that time, further severe restrictions on the teaching of religion were placed both on the church and on parents. Nevertheless, participation in the Orthodox church persists in the U.S.S.R. and there is a flourishing Baptist movement. Despite the government's persecution, sectarian groups of Pentecostals, Adventists, and Jehovah's Witnesses also have persisted. Even more remarkable, possibly, is the recent change in attitude toward religion that has accompanied the "opening" of Russian society under the leadership of Mikhail Gorbachev. Gorbachev not only suggested a need for communists to reexamine the traditional policy of hostility to religion, suggesting that it may have been a mistake, but urged governments in the Eastern European communist countries to be more accommodating to the churches. In 1988, the government of the U.S.S.R. joined the Russian Orthodox church in celebrating 1,000 years of Christianity in Russia.

In China also, where only a small minority of the population has ever professed Christianity, enthusiastic, flourishing groups of Christians emerged from the underground after the relaxation of nearly thirty years of government control and repression. Allowed contact with Christians in other parts of the world, their first request was for help in securing Bibles and other Christian publications in Chinese.

In Latin America, Christianity at present faces both great challenges and great difficulties. Traditionally Roman Catholic, most Latin American countries have experienced shortages of priests—to the point that some adherents in interior parts of the countries rarely have contact with the official church. The church has also been confronted with the political and economic conflicts these third-world countries experience. Traditionally, the church has been perceived as supporting the status quo and the small ruling class that many in the population see as having blocked the needs of the majority for justice and opportunity. In recent years, some Catholic leaders in these countries—bishops, priests, and nuns—have taken strong positions against the status quo. Some have called for nonviolent efforts to bring social change. Some have been willing to collaborate with Marxist revolutionaries, and a few have been killed while engaged in revolutionary action. Others have been assassinated merely for speaking out, or for working on behalf of social justice. By and large, Latin American countries remain solidly Catholic, though there has been significant Protestant growth, especially among Pentecostal sects, in recent years.

In parts of the world that are predominantly non-Christian, Christianity has made surprising gains. For a decade and a half after the conclusion of the Second World War, it was frequently suggested that much of the non-Christian world of Asia and Africa was likely to be closed to Christianity. Partly, such predictions were based on traditional associations of Christian missionary efforts with European colonialism.[2] After achieving independence, for instance, India imposed severe

---

[2]The disruptive effects of some Christian missionary activity on a traditionally oriented tribal society and its entanglement with European colonialism are excellently portrayed in the novels of the Nigerian writer Chinua Achebe. See especially *Things Fall Apart* (Greenwich, Conn.: Fawcett Publications, 1959).

restrictions on Christian missionary activity. One of the results of such acts was a greatly accelerated movement toward independence of the native Christian churches, so that they are no longer seen as subservient to Western missionaries, Western control, or Western leadership. In most cases, this has greatly strengthened these groups, both Protestant and Catholic, and has made them largely responsible for evangelistic and missionary efforts in their own and other third-world countries.

Thirty years ago, some Western Christian leaders predicted that most of Africa would soon be closed to Christian evangelism, especially because of the large number of conversions from indigenous tribal religions to the Islamic faith. But within the last twenty years there have been large numbers of conversions to Christianity, sometimes involving entire tribes. Some areas of Africa now represent extremely rapid growth areas for Christian denominations. The greatest growth is occurring where native leadership is strongest.[3]

From all indications, then, the twentieth century is not likely to be a period in which the Christian religion declined in numbers or in influence. However, it may be true that the nature of Christianity's influence and even of its presence in twentieth-century societies has been greatly affected by major changes in modern societies and in the world at large.

RELIGION IN MODERN SOCIETIES

There can be no doubt that underlying economic, technological, social, and political changes in Europe between the thirteenth and sixteenth centuries did much both to cause the breakup of Western Christianity into a number of national churches and separatist sects and to determine the form that these emerging religious organizations took. Such innovations as gunpowder (leading to more powerful weaponry), the magnetic compass, and the printing press stimulated the development of national consciousness and of the national state. It was the emergence of greater national consciousness, greater literacy, a middle class engaging in manufacture and trade, and governments committed to expanding their territories that made a place for the newer forms of church organization (in contrast to the universal but diverse and flexible Catholicism of the Middle Ages). The nation-state tended to be intolerant, exclusive, power-seeking, and concerned about its identity and survival. The national church attempted to express and justify the relative completeness and independence of its nation-state. The sect attempted to provide spiritual room or breathing space *outside* the monolithic structure and order of the nation-state for those who felt only marginal ties of loyalty to it but who were nevertheless physically and culturally surrounded by an absolutist society and government (Leviathan, as the seventeenth-century British political philosopher Thomas Hobbes called it). Even Roman Catholicism took on a new shape after the Council of Trent. Some regions (like France) functioned almost independently of Rome at times. Overall, though, the Western Catholic church became, like a vast national church, more monolithic, less diverse, and less flexible.

[3]To take just one example: In August 1982, Bishop Leslie Newbigin, serving in the Church of England after years of leadership in the Church of South India, told a conference on global missions in Ohio, "For the first time the church's mission has a home based in every part of the globe and is growing out of each place." He cited the three-million-member Kimbanguist Church, based in Zaire, one of the most rapidly growing in the world, as one that has never been dependent on foreign missionary leadership.

During the twentieth century, a significant countertrend has set in. A plethora of new nation-states, formerly subservient to European colonization, has emerged. These states, belonging to the third world, have some of the same concerns for identity and independence that characterized those of seventeenth-, eighteenth-, and nineteenth-century Europe. Yet they are by and large plagued by poverty and dependent on the first and second worlds for technology and economic assistance. The nation-states of Europe have, meanwhile, changed from world-controlling empires to participants with other nations in order to secure a future free of the threats to economic, political, and environmental security that the twentieth century has spawned.

The two superpowers, the United States and the U.S.S.R., were never nation-states in the classic European sense. Each, relatively isolated geographically until the rise of twentieth-century modes of transportation, "contains multitudes"—a great diversity of diverse religious, ethnic, and cultural (and in the U.S.S.R., national) groups. These internal differences are frequently sources of tension, as in present conflicts in the U.S.S.R. between Christian Armenians and their Muslim neighbors, or the desire for greater if not absolute independence by the Baltic Latvians and Estonians. Controversies have also arisen in the United States concerning the status of English and other languages such as Spanish, Chinese, and Vietnamese. Externally, each of the superpowers in the twentieth century has been driven by a need not to have the rest of the world closed to it and not to be "encircled" by hostile nations. Each has at times accused the other of a kind of paranoia, the United States believing that Russia exaggerated the fear of the possibility of a Muslim extremist government in Afghanistan that might generate unrest among the Muslim population of the U.S.S.R., the Russians saying much the same about U.S. fears of Marxist governments or movements in Cuba, Nicaragua, and El Salvador.

In the twentieth century, technology (possibilities of almost instantaneous communication and transportation of messages and destructive weaponry) and economic organizations (such as the multinational corporations that can exert more power than some governments) have brought a world into being in which "humankind is the unit of cooperation."[4] This concept was explored and developed by the World Council of Churches during the 1940s and '50s. The related concept of "the responsible society" was intended to provide a norm for all societies in the present world context. According to the World Council's definition, a responsible society is a society

> where freedom is the freedom of men who acknowledge responsibility to justice and public order, and where those who hold political authority or economic power are responsible for its exercise to God and the people whose welfare is affected by it.[5]

During the 1960s and '70s the same organization came increasingly to see that where "mankind is the unit of cooperation" much of the interaction may take the form of exploitation (of the economically and politically vulnerable third-world countries by their wealthier, more powerful partners). Also, one aspect of

---

[4]This concept, originally phrased "mankind is the unit of cooperation," was developed by a meeting of the International Missionary Council held in India in 1938.

[5]Walter G. Muelder, *Foundations of the Responsible Society* (New York: Abingdon Press, 1959), p. 19.

"humankind as the unit of cooperation" has been the threat of the whole world falling victim to a self-produced nuclear holocaust.

During the late 1960s and early 1970s some American political analysts were predicting a trend toward world decentralization, with the great powers retreating into their continental "spheres of influence" and avoiding world entanglements. These predictions were diagnosed by other analysts as having resulted from disillusionment at unsuccessful U.S. attempts to influence events in Southeast Asia and at U.S. dependence on Middle Eastern oil.

The dynamics of twentieth-century economics and technology seem to militate against decentralization. If anything, the difficulties the superpowers have had in exerting influence within their spheres of influence (the United States in Latin America; the U.S.S.R. in Eastern Europe and Afghanistan) and the volatile internal social mixtures within each of the superpowers and their spheres would seem to support rather than negate trends toward greater international interaction.

Americans may be initially at a loss—but should not be surprised—to hear Japanese and Polish country-and-western bands and their vocalists singing about jambalaya and crawfish pie or about a cotton patch down in Louisiana. The process of internationalization of all aspects of life is not likely to stop unless a world catastrophe occurs.

If the twentieth century is seeing the emergence of a truly world society, then one would expect Christian religious groups and organizations to mirror this process. And this is exactly what is happening. The Roman Catholic church now is a truly international church in a way that it has never been before. Its bishops come from practically all parts of the world. Statements and appearances of its popes, even in non-Catholic and non-Christian countries, are events of first importance. Its leadership is truly international. Priests, theologians, and administrators may shuttle from Dallas or Calcutta to Rome and back just as executives of the multinational corporations do.

Protestant and Eastern Orthodox groups, especially through cooperative efforts like the World Council of Churches, have established international presences and have achieved international consciousness. Even denominations like the Southern Baptists and Churches of Christ in the United States, which do not ordinarily participate in ecumenical organizations, send missionaries to far-flung parts of the world and see their internationally known leaders by way of satellite transmission taking part in world affairs, as in a recently highly publicized mission of Dr. Billy Graham, in the interest of world peace, to Russia.

CHARACTERISTICS OF MODERNIZATION AND RELIGIOUS RESPONSE

Equally important as the internationalization of most of the Christian denominations have been the effects of modernization on them internally and in relation to other Christian groups.

Anthropologists explain many of the characteristics of human societies by using a continuum that extends from the simplest to the most complex societies. Such a continuum may begin with hunting and gathering societies and move through nonspecialized agricultural, specialized agricultural, nonspecialized industrial, to the highly specialized industrial societies found in contemporary Europe, the United

States, the U.S.S.R., and Japan. The more complex the society, the more highly specialized are its social and vocational roles. In a hunting and gathering society there is almost no specialization in economic or social roles. There is little or no specialized knowledge. By the time an agricultural society emerges, there is a far greater degree of specialization. Usually there will be a priesthood (specialists in religious knowledge), a military caste (specialists in war and in ruling), a class of artisans (specialists in making and building), and the great majority of the population, which has no specialized knowledge or skills. Specialization in the economic and social roles of men and women will have begun to develop. Also, the more complex the society, the larger the population tends to become—to the point where population size becomes socially and economically dysfunctional and threatens social stability.

The continuation of these trends explains much about life, including religious life, in today's specialized industrial societies. Technological innovations, such as automation, have done much to eliminate the need for a large pool of unskilled laborers. Training for most occupations and professions requires a high degree of specialized training. Paradoxically, however, since many occupations and skills soon become outmoded, a high degree of flexibility is also increasingly built into such training. In a sense, specialized industrial societies require more and more in the way of development of metaskills and metaeducation. Almost mirroring the interchangeability of unskilled workers in nonspecialized industrial societies, the highly skilled workers and professionals of specialized industrial societies become more and more interchangeable. With the weakening of the nuclear family, such interchangeability also becomes characteristic of domestic and family roles. In less complex societies, the religious experts possessed almost a monopoly on learning and specialized skills. In modern societies, secular knowledge and skills have eclipsed the religious, leading in some ways to a democratization of religion, since the lay adherents of a religion may be better educated and more literate than its "religious specialists." Thus, skills other than specialized theological or doctrinal knowledge are looked for in religious leaders. They may be skilled at managing organizations or at giving psychological counseling to individuals or families.

Sociologists have noted a number of characteristics of complex modern societies in contrast to those of simpler, traditionally oriented ones. Characteristics of modern societies may be listed as (1) urbanization, (2) atomization, (3) rationalization, (4) differentiation, (5) privatization, and (6) institutionalization of innovative attitudes.

Urbanization.   *Urbanization* refers to the fact that in modernized societies the great majority of the population will not be engaged in agricultural (primary) economic production but in industrial (secondary) production and in service (tertiary) occupations. The freeing of the majority of the population to engage in production beyond the needs of simple survival has been the key to the economic expansion of industrial societies.

Urbanization has not been without its negative consequences. In industrializing societies, it has disrupted traditional family relations and cultural patterns. Also, the interaction of highly industrialized societies with simpler societies has led to some enormous contemporary problems (e.g., the growth of population well past the danger point in third-world countries, largely caused by new medical technology developed in industrialized societies and applied in the simpler ones). More than a billion of the world's population is now estimated to live in dire poverty, often in starvation or near starvation. The enormous population growth of the twentieth century and the related problem of world hunger are largely results of interaction between the rich nations and the poor.

Atomization. *Atomization* refers to the tendency of traditional family, clan, and kinship patterns to break down in modernized societies. Families no longer work as single economic units. Family units tend to become *nuclear families*—parents (or a single parent) and children. Large families are no longer economically functional. In the most modernized societies, the nuclear family, stripped of the traditional support of the extended family, appears to be extremely vulnerable to social pressures and instability. The psychological and social effects of reduction to the nuclear family cannot as yet be gauged. In some ways, with high divorce rates and the tendency of parents to remarry and assume responsibility for multiple sets of children, there may be a trend for a new kind of extended family to develop.

Rationalization. *Rationalization* refers to the fact that in highly modernized societies the activities, especially economic but also political and cultural, of individuals, groups, and organizations tend to be coordinated by semiautomatic mechanisms (the market, planning by governmental agencies, the communications network, and so on). Information communicated by a government agency in one part of the world concerning the health effects of tobacco use may have a disastrous effect on the economy of a tobacco-producing area. Satellite communication or the world record industry may cause musicians in Japan or Poland to adopt a new musical style. Such effects need not be intended by their originating groups but are highly influential in determining social patterns.

Differentiation. *Differentiation* refers to the tendency of organizations in complex societies to become more highly specialized. Think of the trends in medicine and in industrial and service occupations in twentieth-century America. The sociologist Talcott Parsons pointed out the drastic effect of differentiation on Western religious organizations and institutions. According to Parsons, much recent talk about secularization in modernized societies stems from the fact that many of the traditional social functions—education, health and welfare, charity, even entertainment—formerly performed by Christian churches have been taken over by government at various levels. This fact possibly as much as any other has led to a *perception* (whether justified or not) of a declining role or influence of religion in society.

Privatization. *Privatization* refers to a tendency in modern societies for the areas of subjective involvement of individuals to be rather sharply separated from those of public (political and occupational) activity. A person may be an engineer, a lawyer, or a mechanic, but the area of life in which he or she finds subjective satisfaction may be the activity of an amateur actor, yachtsman, or football fan. Entertainment, as an escape from the pressure or the boring routine of work, assumes major importance in the lives of some individuals; it is perhaps the major industry of society. Activities such as presidential election campaigns are presented in the guise of entertainment, with the competition between candidates in projecting an "image" highlighted.

The sociologist Thomas Luckmann has argued that, increasingly in modern-ized societies, religion for many individuals has come to belong to the private, subjective sphere of life rather than to the public realm. To the extent that this may be true, it goes against much of the recent effort of Christian denominations, Catholic and Protestant, to be socially relevant and to apply the Christian message to the needs of society. (See earlier chapters for discussion of the social gospel ideal of twentieth-century Protestantism and the social involvement of twentieth-century Catholics expressed in papal encyclicals and liberation theology.)

Luckmann's position has been described as follows:

> In relatively simple societies the sacred...cosmos permeates social institutions such as labor and kinship. The religious representations serve to legitimate action in all areas of life and are mediated through all institutions in the society. But more complex societies tend to develop specialized institutions to maintain and transmit the sacred cosmos.[6]

As noted above, Luckmann believes that the phenomenon of privatization (a consequence of rationalization and differentiation) is leading to a new role for religion, or a new form of religion, in modern industrialized societies. In earlier stages of society, religious ideas and feelings gave an overall meaning to life. Religious organizations gave their blessing to the state, work, education, and family life. In modern societies, each of these areas of life—even marriage and the family—has tended to be separated from its earlier religious ties. Each has become rational in relation to the functional requirements of the particular institution or area of life.[7]

The Protestant Reformers interpreted one's work as the major way by which the individual responded to God's call to serve neighbors. In modern societies, work may be seen either as a boring economic necessity or as a way to climb the social ladder. The same applies to education. It formerly was seen as a way of fitting oneself to serve God. Now it is generally presented to young children as a necessity if they are to do well economically and socially. Work and education are presented as requirements that society imposes on the individual with little concern for his or her interests and choices.

In this situation, according to Luckmann, the unique or subjective character-istics of the individual are of no importance to the organization or social institution; and the individual, though perhaps occupied for many hours a day and dependent for a livelihood on participation in the organization (e.g., the company for which the individual works) invests little or no subjective interest in it, except as the individual may use it as a vehicle to rise economically and socially. In Western society, individuals are expected to show little loyalty to the organizations that employ them, and organizations little toward their employees or to the communities in which they reside. This lack of personal investment of meaning may apply not only to the political sphere, to one's occupation, but to one's family life and roles as well. This may mean that the individual, though conforming to the political, economic, and social demands of society, will find the meaning of life elsewhere. The result, according to Luckmann, may be that

---

[6]Emily C. Hewitt, Lawrence H. Mamiya, and Michael C. Mason, *Models of Secularization in Contemporary Sociological Theory* (New York: Studies in Education, 1972), Publication No. 1, p. 23.

[7]See Thomas Luckmann, *The Invisible Religion* (New York: Macmillan, 1967), pp. 195–96.

the large primary institutions of modern society—notably, government, business, and industry—operate according to their own "functional" and "rational" norms and are not guided by religious sanctions. Such institutions are meaningless to the people who work within them.[8]

In other words, they are subjectively meaningless, though objectively they require large amounts of the individual's time and energy. Thus the man may do his duty as breadwinner and father, but find his real satisfaction in watching the Dallas Cowboys on Sunday-afternoon television. Or a young woman may be a straight-A student in college, but find holiday trips to the ocean or skiing trips to the mountains the really important events in her life.

Until very recently in European societies and even in parts of the United States, religious participation was socially required, sometimes by law. In modern societies then, according to Luckmann, *religion* becomes privatized—a largely personal, subjective affair. Individuals are not subject, unless they choose to be, to institutional religious control or guidance. For some, religion itself, as traditionally defined, becomes meaningless. Others will be affected by deep anxiety at the apparent loss of the controls that traditional values and norms have exercised on society and seek through participation in sectarian or cultic movements to find something in their personal lives to take the place of the lost center of meaning. Still others will seek through political and communications activities to restore the directing role of religious values to the society. Some will seek to make the religious organization more relevant to the society, to meet the needs of individuals adrift in the secular sea or to forge a new way of interaction between religious values and secular institutions. For still others, religion may be a very important, indeed the most important, dimension of life, but confined to the private sphere—a subjective task, a lifelong quest for inner meaning, for self-discovery.

Institutionalization of innovative attitudes. *Institutionalization of innovative attitudes* designates the deliberate, formalized, and institutionalized expectation and promotion of change—a prochange orientation—throughout contemporary societies. This promotes in every social institution an openness to diversity. However, it may also encourage the planned obsolescence not only of products and fashions but of beliefs, attitudes, ideas, organizations, communities, and persons. These all become expendable due to the rational needs of the social and economic system. Ideas go out of fashion because a new generation must write its Ph.D. theses, invalidating old concepts to make room for new ones. Persons still capable of years of productive work are retired to make room for new generations of climbers on the rungs of corporate ladders.

RELIGIOUS ORGANIZATIONAL STRUCTURE IN MODERN SOCIETIES

Given the preceding discussion, it seems reasonable to suggest that the different Christian organizations—churches, denominations, sects, and cults—will offer a

[8]Hewitt et al., p. 14.

full range of options for individual adherents. However, it also is reasonable to believe that the great majority of Christian churches and groups in modern societies will tend to approximate the *denominational* type.

The *church* type of religious organization is one which for all practical purposes includes the whole society. One is born into it. It usually makes a clear distinction between clergy and laity, between the realms of the sacred and the secular. It *is* the custodian of the religious institutions of the society. There will be two set standards of behavior for the society—one for the full-time religious and another for the secular. But control will be exerted over all. The secular government is the church's ally in enforcing religious and moral conformity.

In contrast, the *sect* type of religious organization is one in which membership is voluntary. In important ways, it calls on its members to withdraw from significant parts of the society, seeking to separate the holy people from the corrupt and worldly. In theory, all adult members are sanctified or saintly; perhaps they are priests or clergy. Though membership is voluntary, strict control is exerted over individual members or they are expelled.[9] The tendency of the sect is to become an isolated, separated community (like the Amish in the American Midwest); or to attempt to become a church through the conversion of the whole society (early Christianity in the Roman Empire); or to move toward denominational status (Methodists and Baptists in the United States).

The *denomination* is an organization characteristic of modernized or modernizing pluralistic societies. In some ways it is churchlike, stressing nurture and education rather than adult conversion. Membership in it is voluntary, but may be a result of family tradition, personal convenience, or habit. It exerts much less control over the behavior and consciences of its members than either the church or the sect. In fact, it is sometimes characterized as a focus of secondary rather than primary loyalty. To the extent that this is true, it does not necessarily follow that the members of the denomination do not make a primary religious commitment. It may simply be the case that they have become relatively autonomous religiously—with their subjective religious attitudes having primary significance in their lives but their denomination producing an important objective vehicle for their expression, fulfillment, or personal growth.

Thus if it is true that the so-called mainline religious organizations, including even the Roman Catholic church, in contemporary advanced societies tend to approximate the denominational pattern, this does not mean that the importance of their role in individual and social life is diminished, only that it has changed. We may expect to see in modern pluralistic societies a continued subjective intensity and individualism in which the participation of individuals in religion is enabled and balanced by religious organizations serving as carriers, interpreters, and modifiers of objective religious tradition. It is entirely possible that for both individuals and organizations the interchangeability of individuals and the sharp separation between the private and public spheres of meaning will prove untenable. Individual and group life may ultimately become too precarious in privatized societies to be tolerated by individuals seeking wholeness in individual life and as persons-in-community.

---

[9]The term cult is usually used to refer to a small group dominated by the personality and teachings of a powerful individual. After a generation or two the cult usually dies out or develops into a sect or denomination.

CONTEMPORARY ISSUES
AND CHRISTIAN RESPONSE

Christianity and the Values of Society

In the context of the preceding discussion, one of the major issues faced by Christian churches is how to relate to the societies in which they find themselves located. Two contrasting dangers for religious organizations in contemporary societies present themselves. One was noted by Dietrich Bonhoeffer, the German Protestant pastor, while in prison because of his resistance to the Hitler government's attempt to take over the German Protestant church by subordinating it to Nazi ideology. Bonhoeffer noted that when humanity's major struggle was against *nature*, the church had a large field of activity, since the church could step in with its answer—God—everywhere human ability to control life broke down. In modern times, however, humanity has become increasingly able through social and political organization and science and technology to deal with the problems that earlier were left to religion. So the church has been pushed to the margins of society, dealing only with the leftover ultimate questions (e.g., death, guilt, and so on).[10] Bonhoeffer felt that the church should seek its place at the center of society. It should become involved in the secular, since it is the secular that largely shapes and affects the lives of people now, and Christ above all was and is "the man for others." Note the ambiguous possibility here: the church might seek to remake the secular in accordance with some set of religious values, or it might attempt to interpret the meaning of secular involvement for its adherents and society—to witness and serve rather than direct and shape. The second possibility is the way advocated by Bonhoeffer.

If Bonhoeffer saw the danger of an increasingly marginal role in society for Christian organizations, Martin Luther King, Jr., frequently expressed the fear that the churches too often are only vehicles for perpetuating and reinforcing the accepted values of the society—they are thermometers instead of thermostats. In fact, Bonhoeffer's and King's diagnoses probably accurately describe the fundamental temptation of the characteristic types of religious organizations of their own societies—the established church in Bonhoeffer's Germany and the denomination in King's America. As King saw, the church in the United States is likely to become simply another civic organization or service group under constant necessity to demonstrate its social usefulness and progressive spirit.

Christians and the State

Historically, Christians have taken a wide range of positions concerning the relation of Christianity to the political and governing institutions of society, the state. Even in the New Testament, differences of attitude are expressed. The Old Testament concept of the Jewish state as a theocracy, governed by a king and by priests who are God's servants responsible for the well-being of God's holy people, is not repudiated; but when the Christian movement originated, Judaism was ruled by gentile Rome and the theocracy was an ideal, that of the coming but not yet present Kingdom of God (see Chapter Two). Luke-Acts treats Rome as a largely beneficent, possibly divinely ordained source of law by means of which early

---

[10]Dietrich Bonhoeffer, *Letters and Papers from Prison*, enlarged edition (New York: Macmillan, 1972).

Christianity could spread throughout the world in a legally protected, orderly manner. The author of the Book of Revelation, writing after some Roman persecution of the early church had occurred, treats Rome—the city, its emperors, its government—as an agent and tool of Satan.

Medieval Western Christianity saw church and state as two divinely ordained societies, separate but not wholly so. Since both were aimed at providing for the good of human society, the spiritually superior church had the right at times to intervene, giving direction or correction to the state when it failed in its God-given duties. During the Protestant Reformation, Lutheranism saw church and state as being separate, though both had God-ordained tasks, that of the state being to use the instruments of evil (violence) to restrain human sinfulness. The role of the church was to be wholly spiritual, correcting the state only through prayer and preaching. Christian princes might, when necessary, reform both church and state. Calvinism, seeing church and state as far more separated than Catholicism or Lutheranism did, nevertheless made their relation one of dynamic interaction, since those who were secular magistrates were also Christian laity, the people of God. Secular governments in Calvinist areas often served to enforce rules of public and personal morality, including church attendance. The Anabaptists by and large felt that Christians should spiritually, and sometimes physically, withdraw from participation in the state, since it was, as Luther had taught, a power using evil means to restrain evil; but as Luther had *not* taught, the state was itself evil with no rightful jurisdiction over Christians (see Chapters Four and Five).

Christians in the present have often agonized over the relation of Christians to the state, as this has involved both personal and institutional life. In countries where Christians have been a minority, Christians attempting to bear witness to their gospel have at times encountered persecution when they understood their witness to involve speaking against government policies. Toyohiko Kagawa (1888–1960), a Japanese Presbyterian minister who spent much of his life ministering spiritually and physically to the poor in Japanese slums, was imprisoned during the Second World War because of his pacifism expressed in the founding of an antiwar league.

In Nazi Germany, traditionally a Christian country, Hitler attempted to take over the state-established Protestant church, insisting it assert that his National Socialist movement was the fullest modern expression of Christianity and that all church members of Jewish descent be expelled. Many German Christians went along with this, but a large group of them refused to do so. Among these, the theologian Karl Barth (1886–1968) was expelled to his native Switzerland, and Martin Niemöller who, in rejecting the Nazi claim that Hitler was the absolute leader, or Führer, of every German, affirmed: "God is my Führer!"

A younger leader in the "Confessing Church" that opposed the Hitler takeover of German Protestantism was Dietrich Bonhoeffer (1906–1945). Bonhoeffer, a Lutheran minister, son of a distinguished psychotherapist, had become a believer in pacifism and nonviolence through the example of the Hindu leader Mohandas Gandhi. Nevertheless, Bonhoeffer decided that Hitler's attempt to take control of the church must be resisted. Before the Second World War, he headed an underground theological seminary to train ministers for the Confessing Church. After its discovery and closing by the Nazi government, Bonhoeffer traveled to America, where he could have remained throughout the war. However, he felt it was his duty as a Christian to be with those in Germany carrying on the struggle against Hitler's totalitarianism; during the war, he was associated with a group of military officers, acting largely from similar Christian motivations, who attempted to assassinate Hitler in order to bring the war to end. Although not actually involved in the assassination attempt—Bonhoeffer had already been imprisoned—and even though the government was not aware of his involvement with this group, he was executed at the age of thirty-nine just before he would have been liberated by American troops. His death was intended to assure that he would not be one who would survive to shape a post–Nazi Germany.

Difficulties of Christians living under Marxist regimes have already been cited. Russian Nobel Laureate novelist Alexander Solzhenitsyn (1918–), who had been a Marxist but was converted to Christianity as a result of his experiences while imprisoned in a labor camp during the resumption of Stalin's policy of internal terrorism, took the view that true Christians could in no way cooperate with a Marxist government and must oppose it in all ways possible. On the other hand, Joseph Hromadka (1899–1968), a Czechoslovakian theologian who had studied and taught at Princeton Theological Seminary (Presbyterian) in the United States, after returning to Czechoslovakia taught that Christians should cooperate with a Marxist regime to the extent that it was trying to improve the lot of its people, holding that Christians cannot be committed a priori to any type of economic or political system. Hromadka chided Americans for overlooking the injustices of capitalism and neglecting the opportunities of socialism to move toward greater human freedom. Solzhenitsyn chided Americans both for their secular materialism and for believing that any form of Marxism could be anything but antihuman.

Christians in third-world countries with Christian populations but ruled by political oligarchies controlled by the wealthy classes have experienced great difficulties. In Latin America some Catholic priests and religious leaders have cooperated with Marxist revolutionaries against what they perceived to be unjust regimes. In Colombia, the priest Camilo Torres was killed by government forces while engaged in revolution. In Nicaragua Ernesto Cardenal was active in the Sandinista revolution and after its victory served in the revolutionary government. In Brazil, Dom Helder Camara sought by nonviolence and spiritual influence to bring change for the poor (see Chapter Eight).

In the United States, probably more than in any other country, a different kind of problem arises. The great majority of the population are professed Christians of one denomination or another. Many social forces, expressed in a more and more strict interpretation of the U.S. Constitution's prohibition of the power of Congress to make laws respecting the establishment of religion, have caused the removal of many ceremonial expressions of religion from public life that once were thought to be acceptable. These include prescribed prayers in public schools, prescribed readings from the Bible, displays of manger scenes on government property, and so on. Some American Christians feel that such changes have made the American state hostile to religion. Others argue that it is in the best interest of both churches and society for the state to be religiously neutral. There has also been increased government action, including court rulings, to guarantee freedom of religious expression. This has been applied to non-Christian as well as to unpopular Christian groups. Sometimes it has been argued that the only way that the right to free religious expression for all can be guaranteed is by neutrality of the state toward religious institutions and groups. But a consistent implementation of such a policy might remove even more vestiges of publicly supported religion—for instance, government-supported chaplains in the armed services, even perhaps the oath taken in some courts or swearings-in of government officials, "So help me God," and the slogan, "In God We Trust," on coins. In modern and postmodern pluralist societies there may be no combination of attitudes toward church and state relations that will satisfy a majority of Christians.

Christianity and Social Evil: The Holocaust

Modern Christians at times find themselves faced with social evils that are the direct consequence of their own historical prejudices and biases, which do not conform to traditional teachings of Christian love. The conflict of Jew and Christian in the Middle Ages was typified by the Spanish Inquisition and the official stance of Western Christianity that Jews (who were frequently blamed for the death of Jesus) were "deicides"—killers of God. Jews had little hope of escaping latent and active anti-Semitism. Nevertheless, reflecting the attitudes the Enlightenment fostered, Jews, particularly in Western Europe, became convinced that if they lived actively as citizens contributing to their societies, acceptance would be inevitable and anti-Semitic prejudice would die. In much of Europe this was not the case. The late nineteenth century brought renewed anti-Semitic outbursts in France and Germany.

Also in the nineteenth century, Russian Judaism was accused by the Russian Orthodox Church of undermining the church and the established order of the tsar, since church and state were one. Although not responsible for the initiation of charges of the "blood-libel," a superstitious belief held by some Christians that Jews practiced ritual murder, Russia proved fertile ground for such accusations.

At the beginning of the twentieth century, Jews throughout Europe were subject to racial prejudice and in Eastern Europe to persecution. Enjoying relative economic independence and freedom in the West, they found that the old anti-Semitic prejudices had been aggravated by the new social mobility and visibility of Jews prominent in the arts and professions. In the aftermath of the First World War, Germany's economy and its traditional political life were devastated. The rise of National Socialism under Hitler was a response to the disappointed hopes and fears of many in the new, disturbing situation. In his program for German recovery, Hitler incorporated racist myths according to which Jews were a threat to the pure Aryan Germans. Given latent and frequently overt anti-Semitism, it was not difficult for Hitler to make the Jews scapegoats for all of Germany's problems. Restrictions on the Jews began in 1935 with the promulgation of laws that limited Jewish participation in society. These were followed by the destruction of synagogues in 1938, the opening of concentration camps in 1939, and finally a program of systematic extermination. These policies were applied to all captured countries so that much of the Jewish population of Europe was destroyed; some 6 million Jews had lost their lives by the end of the war.

The effect of the Holocaust on Jews and on Jewish-Christian relations has been more far-reaching than many Christians realize. Recognition of worldwide interdependence of Jews has resulted in significant emphasis on unity and the defining of Jewish identity. It has also brought a resurgence of interest in and study of ancient religious and cultural identity. The creation of a Jewish state was certainly augmented by the Holocaust. In recent years, literary treatments of the Holocaust in novels, plays, and films have been numerous.

The works of Elie Wiesel and other Jewish writers have raised questions about why the Holocaust happened and how its having happened can be appropriated by Jews—and Christians—in terms of their attitudes toward each other and their beliefs about God. Questions about the meaning of evil and its relation to God—and whether in the light of the Holocaust Jews and Christians can continue to believe in a God who is good, powerful, and loving—have been explored by Jewish theologians, particularly Richard Rubenstein.

Christian thinkers have also sought to understand the Holocaust. They have been particularly concerned about what the Holocaust says about the meaning of human life and the relation of human beings and groups to one another. They have been concerned about the involvement of Christians in the horror, as well as the lack of protest by Christians who knew of the events, or should have known, while they were taking place.

Ecumenical Relations

One pressing issue for contemporary Christian organizations concerns their relations with each other. There has probably never been as much cooperation and good feeling between the different Christian denominations as there is now. Very large steps have been taken between the Roman Catholic church and the Church of England and between the Roman Catholic and European Lutheran churches toward doctrinal and practical agreement. There have been mergers between many of the Protestant denominations—in Canada and in India, for instance. In the United States, major progress toward union or unification of more than ten mainline Protestant denominations in a Consultation on Church Union was made during the 1960s before negotiations came to a temporary deadlock.

In spite of this ecumenical interest, it seems likely that the future of the majority of Christians, for the present, will be denominational. In contrast to sects or churches, denominations do not define themselves as antagonistic to each other. Their tendency is to approximate each other, to become similar, and yet to provide enough diversity to attract a maximum number of adherents. This does not mean that cultic and sectarian groups will not have significant influence in contemporary society. Sectarian groups (perhaps in unorthodox forms) may indeed exert a large influence on the denominations. Yet it is clear that the majority of persons in contemporary society will not be attracted to cults (like the Unification Church) or to sects. Historically, sectarian movements have frequently brought renewal to the Christian movement as a whole. The various monastic renewal movements within Roman Catholicism functioned as sectarian groups that stayed within the church (see chapters Three, Four, and Five), thus providing new options of participation. Even within a single denomination, congregations of various types (e.g., from high church to low) will attract a larger and more diverse membership than will uniform or interchangeable units.

Another important issue concerns the relation of Christian to non-Christian religions, especially in those parts of the world where non-Christian religions predominate. Perhaps its claim to exclusiveness—to exclusive access to God—has been one of Christianity's traditional strengths. Yet many contemporary Christians (e.g., Thomas Merton) have seen great strength, truth, and beauty in the religious traditions of Buddhism, Taoism, and Hinduism without necessarily sacrificing claims to the uniqueness of Christianity. Will contemporary Christianity be strengthened or weakened by an attitude of openness toward and cooperation with the other world religions?

Judaism and Christianity:
Their Continuing Uneasy Kinship

Throughout Christian history, relationships of Christians to Jews have been marked by tension. Animosity often has run deep, for they were grounded in differences of faith, in variant understandings and treatments of common Scriptures, and in differing interpretations of the will of a commonly acknowledged God. Obvious contrasts in life-style and patterns of worship compounded tensions between the two religious communities. From an early time, Judaism was the minority group.

Christian ambivalence toward Jews and their religion arose early, as indicated by Paul's comments in the Letter to the Romans, Chapter 11. There, the Jews are seen as disobedient to God's commandments. This disobedience is not seen by Paul as having had totally negative results. According to him, it resulted in the possibility of non-Jews being included in God's plan for the Jews. Paul sees the Jews as incorrect in their beliefs and attitudes, yet he insists that they are God's chosen people and will be brought back to their privileged position in and through Christ. Such a position laid the groundwork for Christian endeavors through the centuries to convince the Jews of the falsity of their beliefs and their need to accept Christ. Such endeavors, no matter how well meant Christians may have believed them to be, frequently intensified antagonism and increased Judaism's sense of being a persecuted minority.

Misunderstanding and mistrust between Jews and Christians from this source has been especially significant in the United States. Much of American Protestant Christianity, stressing personal religious experience, came to accept a conversionist attitude toward religion. Such an understanding has placed great emphasis on the initiation into the Christian life as an experience requiring conversion, or "new birth." This understanding assumes that prior to conversion, one's religious convictions and experience are inadequate and incorrect. It also assumes that it is the duty of converted Christians to seek to lead others, including adherents of non-Christian religions, to such a conversion experience, and that non-Christians should welcome such evangelistic efforts to unite them to Christ. Jews are likely to reject these assumptions, feeling that their religion is quite adequate and seeing no need to change. In fact, their religious perception is very different from that of conversionist Christianity. For Jews, religion is a part of the givenness of life. Typically, Jews do not expect or want non-Jews to convert to Judaism. They expect persons to live faithfully within their inherited religious milieu. Failure of religious life means failure to live with moral and spiritual sincerity, observing precepts and laws that may require renewed commitment but not conversion. Jews do not share the Christian belief that Christianity is the completion or fulfillment of their religion. Many zealous Christians have found this fact hard to understand.

The twentieth century brought efforts by many Christians and Jews to eliminate prejudice and anti-Semitic practices. In the United States, the National Conference of Christians and Jews was founded in 1928 to promote mutual understanding and cooperation. While there was no concentrated Christian effort to protest Germany's progressively more and more virulent anti-Jewish policies between the world wars, some Christians spoke out against them. Groups such as the Quakers attempted to intervene, to exert direct moral influence on the German government on behalf of Jews. The Quakers and others facilitated escape from Germany and resettlement in other countries for Jewish refugees. In the aftermath of the Holocaust, the world Council of Churches denounced anti-Semitism. In 1965 the Second Vatican Council of the Roman Catholic Church promulgated a far-reaching schema on the Jews and other non-Christian religions. In it, the view of the Jews as perpetrators of deicide was rejected. Jewish organizations such as B'nai B'rith have worked since the nineteenth century to spread information among Christians about Judaism and to defend Jews from prejudice and falsehood.

Since World War II, the study of Judaism by Christian scholars has greatly expanded, leading to numerous attempts to promote understanding and rapprochement. American colleges and universities, some sponsored by Christian denominations, have included the study of Judaism and have employed Jewish scholars in their departments of religious studies. Such inclusion has been possible because Judaism is seen not only as one of the major world religions but as an American religious tradition with the same status as other religious alternatives. Christianity and Judaism seem as inextricably joined to each other now as they were in the past, in ways that perhaps go far beyond what most Christians who live in Christian majority settings realize. Openness and joint interest, particularly in the face of the threat to both religious traditions by attitudes of increasing secularism, have not totally eased the tensions in Christian and Jewish relations. Karl Barth, perhaps the greatest Protestant theologian of the twentieth century, denounced anti-Semitism as a terrible crime and saw the continued existence of the Jews as a sign of God's faithfulness to his promises. Nevertheless, Barth seemed to think that a major task for Christian self-understanding is the continued theological rethinking by Christians of the relation of Christianity to Judaism.

Ethnic, Cultural, and Racial Differences

Not only are attitudes toward other religions and cultures a crucial issue for contemporary Christianity, attitudes toward ethnic, cultural, and racial differences *within* the Christian world are still of decisive significance. Most of the mainline Christian groups now admit that in much of the past there was too ready an identification of European or American cultural values with the values of Christianity. Now it is largely agreed that the gospel can find its setting in a large variety of cultural contexts (how one covers one's torso, or whether one has tea at four P.M. is of little significance for the gospel). It is still a major agenda item for Christian religious groups in the twentieth century to see what this will mean for doctrinal expression, organizational structures, liturgical practices, and codes of morals and etiquette.

As for the question of race, in theory this may have been solved by Paul when he wrote in his Letter to the Galatians:

> There is neither Jew nor Greek, there is neither male nor female, for you are all one in Jesus Christ.

(GALATIANS 3:28 RSV)

In practice it has not been solved. The U.S. denominations contributed significantly to the struggle for civil rights by black Americans during the 1960s. Yet U.S. churches still are largely segregated, and many black Americans believe that the civil rights struggle died prematurely during the 1970s. A theology of racial differences was elaborated largely in the modern period to justify first slavery, then unequal treatment of blacks. Such a theology is still used to justify the racist society of South Africa, in spite of heroic protests by black and white Christians.[11]

Racial discrimination in South Africa, upheld by the legal system, the police, and the military, and justified by some Christians (while opposed by others), has become a focus of worldwide protest but shows no sign of weakening.

The Meaning of Being Human

Perhaps the major complex of religious and moral issues in contemporary societies is centered on the question of what it means to be human. As Bonhoeffer noted, humans are no longer constrained by nature in many ways that obtained in the past. Technology has opened vast possibilities for changing or redefining the meaning and limits of human existence.

Ecology.   One important task undertaken by Christian theologians has been a rethinking of the very concept of nature. This has included new attention to a Christian understanding of the natural environment that humans share with each other and with nonhuman forms of life. Since the rise of modern science and technology, humans in industrializing societies have tended to take an exploitative view of the environment and the nonhuman world, often justifying this view by elements of the biblical tradition (Genesis 1–3, for example) that set humans above the rest of the created world.

With new perceptions of the dangers both for human life and for the other species that unrestrained technological exploitation of the environment has brought, many Christians are beginning to look at other elements within the Christian traditions: The view that humans have a duty to protect and care for the created world and the sense of kinship of humans, exemplified in such Christians as St. Francis of Assisi, with nonhuman forms of life. The Protestant theologian James Gustafson has recently engaged in a major effort of theological rethinking embracing these issues.

In recent years, there has been a small but growing movement among some Christians toward vegetarianism. Sometimes this is an expression of kinship with nonhuman forms of life. More frequently, perhaps, it is a response to the problem of world hunger, expressing the belief that it is wrong to spend the world's resources in the rather uneconomical production of meat while millions of fellow humans are starving.

Work.   The meaning of work (occupation or vocation) is changing rapidly and radically in contemporary society. In the past, work was variously characterized by Christians as a penalty imposed on humanity for Adam's sin or as an opportunity to serve God and neighbor through practical action. More recent secular prophets such as Marx and Freud have looked at work as fulfilling innate human needs for creative expression, either when it is freed of the fetishistic demands of capitalist economics (Marx), which place the functioning of the impersonal system above the

---

[11]See Alan Paton, *Too Late the Phalarope* (New York: Charles Scribner's Sons, 1953).

needs of living human beings; or when it is freed of neurotic fantasy elements (Freud), which distort the realities of the present in terms of unconscious conflicts carried over from the past. One of the problems that contemporary religious thought must engage is that of the meaning of human work as an aspect of human activity generally. The idea of status seeking by climbing socially prescribed occupational or career ladders would seem to be as vulnerable to Christian as to Marxist or Freudian critiques.

Medicine, technology, and bioethics.　A host of issues cluster around new medical technologies that allow new ways of terminating, prolonging, and even creating human life. In vitro fertilization, surrogate mother- and fatherhood, and genetic engineering involve practices that many Christians, including official agencies speaking for some denominations, have found in tension with, or contrary to, accepted Christian teaching. During the past few years, the issue of abortion has become one of the most explosive and divisive on the contemporary American scene. Traditionally oriented Catholics and Protestants have argued that abortion is equivalent to murder, since the fetus from the moment of conception is a unique human being endowed by the creator with full human dignity and significance. Other Christians have argued in the name of autonomy and of the communal shaping of personality that women have a nearly absolute right to the control of their own bodies. Also, the fetus does not become distinctively human except through the process of socialization, they argue. Perhaps the majority of U.S. Protestants and some Catholics have tended to take an intermediate position, being opposed to abortion in most cases but willing to grant it in others—in cases of pregnancy resulting from rape, danger to the life of the mother, or serious malformation of the fetus. Since the 1973 Supreme Court ruling that struck down existing state laws forbidding it, abortion has become a major method of birth control in the United States. A vigorous, often religiously motivated single-cause antiabortion movement has exerted political power in an attempt to reverse this trend. There have been many attempts to use philosophical and theological analysis to clarify the issue, but positions on both sides of the question seem to have hardened.

Sexuality, marriage, the family.　The issue of abortion raises profoundly the question of the nature and significance of human life. So do the related technologically created possibilities of pregnancy by artificial insemination and in vitro fertilization. It is clear that technology has produced the need for a radical rethinking in religious circles of the meaning of human sexuality, marriage, parenting, and the family. To mention the first of these, note that traditionally the Christian churches have regarded marriage as a sacrament or quasi-sacrament and have opposed divorce. The Catholic church has held firmly to this position, though it recently has shown increased willingness to grant annulments of marriages. Many Protestant groups have greatly relaxed their positions in this respect, by and large accepting, without always recognizing, divorce, and granting remarriage at will.

Traditional Christian attitudes toward human sexuality have been mixed, seeing sex as a part of the natural goodness of the created order but also at times associating it with the fall and Original Sin. For centuries, the highest form of Christian life was understood by many Christians to be the celibate life. Many traditional Christian attitudes toward sex and sexuality, including attitudes toward homosexuality, are being reexamined in the light both of scholarly interpretations of biblical texts and of data from the behavioral sciences.

The position of women.   Questions concerning human sexuality, marriage, and the family lead ultimately to questions concerning the position and rights of women. It frequently has been claimed that the position of women—in contrast to their position in the Roman Republic and Empire—was significantly elevated in Christian teaching and practice. One text cited is Paul's saying that in Christ "there is neither male nor female."

Paul also held an elevated view of male responsibility in the marriage relationship and in religious roles (I Corinthians 14:33–35). He is often given a major share of responsibility for the traditional Christian attitude supporting male dominance in family, church, and society. However, in what seems to be a crucial, if difficult, passage, Paul admits a mutuality between the two sexes, according to which neither is dominant, God is (I Corinthians 11:2–16). It cannot be denied that attitudes supporting male dominance developed early in Christian thought and practice:

> With the rise of asceticism as a major factor in the life of the church, the conservative view of the role and status of women became more pronounced. From the standpoint of the ascetic, who had withdrawn to the desert to flee the wickedness of the world, women became sources of temptation; after all, Eve had been the one responsible for Adam's fall, for the entry of evil into the world. Women were blamed by such writers as John Chrysostom and Ambrose for being immature and ignorant, conditions which, where they existed, are easily explained by the educational neglect of and social discrimination against women characteristic of the period. Clement of Alexandria, however, argued that by nature there was (and ought to be) complete equality between the sexes. (He did believe that there should be some differences in vocation.) It would be fair to say that the social position of women in the Roman Empire remained largely unaffected by the spread of Christianity. This is seen in the minimal role allowed to women in the institutional life of the church. In the Eastern part of the Empire (and perhaps also in the West) there was a regular *ordination* of deaconesses. Deaconesses were allowed, however, to minister *only* to women, and they were not allowed to perform ecclesiastical functions thought to be proper to the male, such as teaching or praying aloud in worship services or approaching the altar. This is in stark contrast to the practice of many of the heretical sects of the period, such as Montanism, in which women were allowed more active roles. With the onset of feudalism, women lost many of the rights they had had in the urban setting of the Roman Empire.[12]

In recent years, the Roman Catholic church has done much to recognize and augment the role of women in the church, such as designating outstanding women saints of the past (Teresa of Avila and Catherine of Siena) as doctors of the church. However, recent popes have continued to affirm that there can be no reconsideration of the traditional denial of the status of priesthood to women. Some Protestant groups, such as the United Methodist church, have recently allowed full rights of the ordination to ministry to women. In some United Methodist seminaries, as many as 30 percent of preministerial students are women. Other groups—for instance, the Episcopal church—have found the ordination of women a point of bitter controversy, embraced enthusiastically by some but opposed by others. Certain theologically conservative Protestant groups, especially Pentecostals, have always allowed full rights of ordination to

[12]Robert C. Monk et al., *Exploring Religious Meaning,* 3rd ed. (Englewood Cliffs, N.J.: Prentice-Hall, 1987), p. 230.

women. Others, like the Southern Baptists, though ultimately congregationally controlled (i.e., each congregation is free to adopt its own policy), have been largely negative toward the ordination of women.

In addition to the question of the role of women in religious organizations, the churches increasingly will have to confront the larger question of the significance of the largely economically motivated emancipation of women in modern societies. Although many Christians have supported women's equality on the basis of their understanding of the gospel, they have perhaps not yet fully examined to what extent the economic basis of the movement masks new forms of the exploitation of women, thus giving some justification to conservative critics of the feminist movement, who have argued that women possess more rights and better protection where there are unequal roles and treatment. To take just one example, many have seen athletics in the United States—from public schools to universities to professional sports—as frequently being based on the exploitation of athletes; the institutions involved have felt little enthusiasm for the recent drive to incorporate full-scale programs of women's athletics into the existing systems.

World Order, Justice, and Peace

Political and economic justice. Another cluster of problems centers around issues of justice, order, and peace in the contemporary international system. Leaders in the World Council of Churches (Protestant and Eastern Orthodox) and many Roman Catholic thinkers became sensitized during the past three decades to the growing disparity between the standards of living in advanced industrial societies and those in the third world. They were inclined to sympathize with third-world voices, even Marxist ones, who blamed the industrialized societies for their exploitation and neglect of the third world. This has led to some negative reaction against the World Council in the Western countries, especially the United States, and against Catholic and Protestant leaders by ruling groups in certain countries, especially in Latin America. Critics have charged those sympathetic to third-world liberation movements with being gullible tools of cynical Marxist revolutionaries. Other, more sympathetic voices, have charged that the Western capitalist countries misperceive the world when they see it as dominated by a capitalist-Marxist conflict, since the real issue is that of the exploitation and neglect of the poor by the rich. These voices argue that to interpret revolutionary struggles in such places as Nicaragua and El Salvador as primarily conflicts between international Marxism and the free world is naive, misleading, and potentially disastrous. The diverse movement called liberation theology—emphasizing the need of oppressed majorities and minorities for liberation from political and economic exploitation—has been the most vital theological movement of the past two decades.

Nuclear war. Another major problem concerning international order is the threat of nuclear war. Roland Bainton has pointed out that traditionally there have been three Christian positions about war. One has been the pacifist position of such groups as the Society of Friends, the Church of the Brethren, the Mennonites, and of such individuals as Leo Tolstoy, Muriel Lester, and Martin Luther King, Jr.

The second position has been that of adherence to the criteria of justified war, criteria that must be met before a war can be begun or waged.[13] According to such theorists as Augustine or Aquinas, these criteria are universally recognized among civilized nations and are known by natural reason. They include protecting civilian populations from direct attack, being certain that the damage inflicted by waging the war is less than the harm of not waging it, aiming at a better condition for all affected as a result of the war, and having a reasonable expectation that the aims of the war will be achieved.

A third position, that of the crusade, was introduced to account for *some* wars (especially those of the Old Testament Israelites against the heathen Canaanites) waged at the direct command of God. In the present international context, some Christians have argued that a militant crusade against godless communism, even if it resulted in the destruction of all life on earth, would be justified. More have asked whether, given the threat of total annihilation that nuclear war poses, the criteria of justified war could ever be satisfied in international conflicts involving even the threat, much less the use, of nuclear weapons.

During the 1980s, governing bodies and leaders of major Christian organizations within and without the United States issued statements questioning whether nuclear war, even in response to a nuclear attack by an enemy, could ever be morally engaged in. Two thoughtful and lengthy pastoral statements—one by the American bishops of the Roman Catholic church, the other by the bishops of the United Methodist church—called into question the acceptability of a nuclear deterrence strategy and urged Christians to become actively involved in peacemaking at all levels—international, national, local, and family—as an alternative to the stance of deterrence and reliance on military means of defense.

Theological Questioning

Contemporary societies provide a large arena for theological rethinking. Three major areas of contemporary inquiry are the identity and significance of Jesus Christ, new approaches to theology, and the varieties of uses of the Bible in Christian thought and life.

Understanding Jesus and the Christ event.   In earlier chapters, it has been noted that the present century has been one of major theological rethinking among Protestants and Catholics. The process continues. In Chapter Six, the concept of the Incarnation held by conservatives was described as saying that God took on human nature in Jesus Christ. For liberal Christians, this doctrine might be described by saying that Jesus expressed God fully. In Chapter Six, the traditional, or orthodox, view was described as holding that in the man Jesus (not to be thought of as existing prior to or independent of the Incarnation) God expressed or revealed himself fully. A recent, worldwide debate has raised questions about whether the traditional language of Incarnation, and of the Trinity, of three persons within one nature, or of two natures within one person, is at all adequate anymore.[14] Essentially this

---

[13]For a brief discussion of the just war theory, see Monk, et al., pp. 248–51.

[14]See John Hick, ed., *The Myth of God Incarnate* (Philadelphia: Westminster Press, 1977). Also Michael Green, ed., *The Truth of God Incarnate* (London: Hodder & Stoughton, 1977); and Michael Goulder, ed., *Incarnation and Myth: The Debate Continued* (Grand Rapids, Mich.: William B. Eerdman's Publishing Company, 1979).

debate stems from the larger question of whether traditional orthodox theology, by adopting categories of Greek philosophy to interpret what happened in Jesus Christ, does not falsify the essential event of the gospel proclamation. The idea that the use of Greek philosophical concepts (substance, nature, and so on) in some ways distorted the Christian message has frequently been expressed—by such persons as Rudolf Bultmann, Reinhold Niebuhr, Leslie Dewart, and others. Their position, however, has frequently been contested.

Also, the idea that the Christian message was originally proclaimed in a language heavily dependent on myth and mythological concepts and that such myth-impregnated thought forms make the gospel unintelligible to people in scientifically dominated societies has been advocated by Bultmann and others. This issue also has been variously discussed, with some theological conservatives denying that the Christian language uses myth and thinkers like Tillich, Niebuhr, and Jaspers arguing that myth is indispensible for the communication of religious truth. Such debates have called into question traditional trinitarian and incarnational concepts. Many have rushed to defend these concepts, impressed with the resilience and durability of the language and concepts of orthodoxy.

The debates are not yet finished. They have encompassed a broad range of topics. Catholic and Protestant theologians are currently reexamining the nature of the church. One issue that has received much attention is the contrast between the church as an institutional structure and as a community (people of God). Catholic theologians, especially, have reexamined the significance of tradition, the nature of authority as related to ecclesiastical offices, and the relation of Christianity to non-Christian religions.

Theology as practiced within the Christian churches and academic communities at present is a sign of the continuing vitality of Christian belief and commitment. It is also at times a source of intense controversy. The fact that religious studies and sometimes theology have a setting in contemporary secular academic contexts is itself a source of diversity and at times of controversy. There continues to be pressure on theologians to conform in their theological conclusions both to the expectations for commitment of traditional religious communities and authorities as well as to the critical standards of the secular academy.

Liberation theology. As noted previously, the attempt by Christian denominational leaders and theologians to think through the political and economic implications of the gospel, particularly as related to the third-world experience of oppressor and injustice, has given rise to liberation theology. Particularly strong in Latin America and arising from both Catholic and Protestant sources, this movement has been varied and influential. Within the economically powerful northern industrial societies, it is usually studied in theological seminaries. It has been welcomed by some as restoring a genuine, frequently lost dimension of Christianity's proclamation of God's will for all of life. Others have charged it with substituting popular political slogans for the gospel and of being uncritical in support of left-wing, including Marxist, movements.

Black theology. A response by black Christians to continuing racist patterns of oppression and injustice in church and society, and to the religious justification of such patterns, has been the attempt to reflect on and draw strength from the black experience of oppression, endurance, hope, and struggle. This has resulted in black theology, one of the many variant forms of contemporary liberation thought. Most black theologians encourage members of other oppressed ethnic, cultural, racial, or sexual groups to join the attempt to find new relevance in the gospel by reflecting on their experience in similar ways.

Feminist theology. Much has been written in earlier sections on perceptions of the need to examine and recast many traditional patterns based on male-dominated or patriarchal patterns imposed on earlier expressions of Christianity. Feminist theology, which can be considered a form of liberation thought, attempts to do this. It is an activity carried on by women who believe that such rethinking is necessary before any in society can become truly free. It shows great variety, taking more moderate to more radical forms.

The new evangelical theology. As mentioned in Chapter Five, postfundamentalist conservative or evangelical theology, especially in the United States, has shown increasing vitality. A broad-ranging debate concerning the Bible has recently emerged among American evangelical thinkers. Theologians like Jack B. Rogers and Donald McKim have raised questions concerning the traditional conservative concept of biblical inerrancy, while wanting to maintain a distinctive evangelical attitude toward Scripture. Another characteristic note among present neoevangelicals is an increased willingness to make political judgments and to become involved in political protest or activism. These can extend from individuals or groups supporting the Moral Majority and right-wing causes to others like Jim Wallis and his coworkers, publishers of *Sojourners* magazine, who, from a radically evangelical biblical perspective, support nuclear pacifism and identification with the poor of the third world.

Rereading the Bible. Possibly the most exciting challenge in present-day Christianity is found in efforts to come to terms with the Christian Scriptures as the primary source of Christian life and thought. In the late seventeenth and eighteenth centuries, partly owing to the Enlightenment, partly as an attempt by Christians to extend the internal and external evangelization that resulted from the Reformation, Counter-Reformation, Pietism, and Evangelical Awakening, the historical-critical approach to the study of the Bible emerged.

The Bible began to be studied with all the tools of historical scholarship at the same time that these tools were being developed to study other works of ancient literature—for instance, the poems of Homer. Historical study of the Old Testament called into question traditional beliefs about authorship (for instance, that Moses had authored the Pentateuch) and suggested that many of the early parts of the Bible, traditionally taken to be historical (for example, the stories of the creation, and flood, and the patriarchs), involved the use of myths and legends to express religious understanding.

The New Testament also was subjected to critical analysis, sometimes in the interest of a faith seeking greater understanding, sometimes by critics who were hostile to official theological interpretations of the person, life, and teachings of Jesus and wanted to restore what they considered the original purity of his message. (In Chapter Five a detailed discussion of the rise of the historical-critical approach to the study of the Bible in the nineteenth century, culminating in the work of Albert Schweitzer, was given.)

Schweitzer's work initiated what has been by now almost a century of intensive scholarly efforts to recover the history of the writing of the New Testament gospels and of the development of its underlying oral and written sources. Prominent among these scholarly efforts have been the development of form criticism (tracing the history of oral tradition underlying the New Testament text); editorial, or redaction, criticism (discovering the unique literary and theological contributions of the authors of the gospels); genre criticism (assessing the influence of Hellenistic literary models on the New Testament writers); and canon criticism (understanding the process by which some early Christian writings were accepted as Scripture while others were not).

As the historical study of the Bible developed, it was often perceived negatively by some Christians. In the late nineteenth and early twentieth centuries, Catholic scholars were told by the Vatican not to accept many of its assumptions. Protestant fundamentalism was in large part an outgrowth of the rejection of the historical-critical methods and results. However, by the 1960s, almost all denominational branches of Christian scholarship had accepted at least the methods and some of the results of the historical-critical approach. After the Second Vatican Council, Catholic scholars enthusiastically embraced it. Even conservative Protestants give weight and credence to it; many have been recognized as outstanding contributors utilizing its methods. This is not to say that the historical-critical method of Bible study is no longer controversial. In the United States, Southern Baptists have been locked in controversy over whether the Bible is to be held literally and verbally "inerrant."

It can be said, however, that the majority of Christians now recognize a wide variety of materials within the Bible: laws, poetry, history, myth, legend, proverbs, moral teachings, exhortation, parables, visionary prophecy. These materials were written under a wide variety of historical circumstances and for a variety of purposes. In the same way, Christians have, over the centuries, read and reread the Bible in a wide variety of contexts, in many diverse ways, and for many reasons. It is often said that the Bible can only be reread because it comes in a variety of translations and earlier readings. Some contemporary interpreters believe that the greatest challenge to contemporary Christians is—given the help that historical-critical and literary scholarship provides—to learn to reread the Bible in ways that do not separate its historical human character from the possibility of its being a primary vehicle or voice of God's revelation.

THEOLOGY AND CHARISMATIC RENEWAL

One of the most dramatic recent developments in world Christianity has been the rise and spread of charismatic movements. These may be regarded as a rebirth rather than an entirely new development, since, as Ronald Knox pointed out in a classic study, charismatic phenomena have been present in many settings during Christian history. Knox's treatment of charismatic groups and individuals in past Christian history, written from the traditional Catholic standpoint, is not entirely unsympathetic.[15] He saw charismatic phenomena occurring ordinarily among groups of Christians subject to persecution (sometimes from other Christians) or alienated from Christian majorities considered by the charismatics to have become secularized, spiritually dead, or lukewarm.

[15]Ronald A. Knox, *Enthusiasm: A Chapter in the History of Religion with Special Reference to the XVII and XVIII Centuries* (New York: Oxford University Press, 1950).

The rise of the modern charismatic movement in the United States was initially Protestant in provenance, with new denominations, often called (generically) Pentecostal, such as the Assemblies of God. These Christians frequently had seceded from established Protestant denominations, particularly those in which a strong emphasis on highly emotional or experimental religion and a separation from worldly practices such as wearing jewelry and fashionable, expensive clothes or attending the theater, had been replaced by middle-class respectability. The emphasis of the Pentecostals was on ecstatic religious experience, involving three of the "gifts of the spirit" dealt with by Paul in his First Letter to the Corinthians, chapters 12–14 —namely, speaking in tongues (glossolalia), the ability to heal by spiritual means, and prophetic utterance. To charismatics, those Christians who have been baptized into the holy spirit have reached a higher level of Christian life than Christians who have merely experienced conversion. With spirit baptism come the gifts of the spirit. Some Christian mystics, such as St. John of the Cross, considered ecstatic experience as a possible or even normal stage on the way to the goal of Christian spirituality—the unitative experience of oneness in God's love—for some Christians. Paul in I Corinthians said that the spiritual gifts were good but recommended that not all Christians should seek all of them—the only gifts of the spirit to be sought by all being faith, hope, and love, and, possibly, the gift of prophetic utterance.

American Pentecostalism initially spread among persons in the lower economic classes, particularly among ethnic minorities or immigrants in cities. After the Second World War, however, there was a second rebirth of charismatic Christianity, this time in the established churches, especially Episcopalian, Presbyterian, and Lutheran, and, a little later, among Methodists and Roman Catholics. In these so-called mainline denominations its appeal was often to the wealthy and to middle-class Christians who had become disillusioned with the "spiritual temperature" of ordinary Christian experience, or who felt an emptiness in their spiritual lives.

In some of the established churches the charismatic movement produced controversy, with charismatics seeming to accuse noncharismatics of not being fully Christian and noncharismatics accusing charismatics of being spiritually arrogant or mentally unbalanced. Some denominations, such as the Southern Baptists, took a hard line toward the movement, expelling congregations that had become charismatic. Others tried to make room for what seemed to be the new vitality of those who were experiencing a new intensity of devotion, commitment, and feeling in the Christian life. Charismatic experience, though at times an object of controversy, seemed to provide genuine elements of renewal among clergy, laity, and some of the religious (monks and nuns) among American Catholics.

On the world scene, charismatic Christianity has spread rapidly and extensively during the twentieth century. This has been true in Asia and Africa but most notably in Latin America, where Protestant Pentecostalism has made great inroads on what has been traditionally Roman Catholic territory. The spread of charismatic Christianity has no doubt been stimulated by television evangelists with worldwide audiences.

To noncharismatics, Christian or otherwise, charismatic and fundamentalist approaches to Christianity are often thought to be the same. There is some reason in this, since both charismatics and fundamentalists tend to be theologically conservative, often sharing the fundamentalist belief in a literalistic approach to the Bible. But many charismatics do not hold the fundamentalist view of Scripture. And many fundamentalists are entirely negative toward the ecstatic experience of speaking in tongues and prophetic utterance, holding these to have ended with the first generation of Christians. According to them, this direct manifestation of the holy spirit in the Christian life was no longer needed once the New Testament Scriptures had been produced.

Some conservative Christians in the American fundamentalist tradition consider speaking in tongues to be a manifestation of demonic spirits. On the other hand, the behavioral scientist Felicitas Goodman considers it to be a learned, semivoluntary change in brain function. To the charismatic Christian, speaking in tongues is a direct manifestation of the spirit of God praying and praising through the believer in divine or angelic speech. But the significance of charismatic Christianity, with its claims to immediacy of the divine in present experience and its emphasis on the ecstatic, is much greater than the question of glossolalia.

Some exponents of contemporary Christianity regard Pentecostalism and charismatic movements as the major phenomena of twentieth-century Christianity. Others regard them to be a lesser but nevertheless important source of much-needed spiritual vitality. To some, they are mainly a distraction from the more pressing facts of contemporary Christian life: the need to interpret the Christian message in the context of late-twentieth-century physics and biology, and the need to confront the world's oppressed and oppressors with the challenge of human liberation. Be this as it may, the need to interpret charismatic Christian experience is a major challenge to contemporary Christian theology.[16]

POPULAR CHRISTIANITY

Doctrine, organizational structure, and forms of worship do not merely separate differing Christian groups from each other. These elements often serve to create, strengthen, and transmit unity from community to community and from generation to generation. Perhaps even more important than these formal aspects of Christian tradition as sources of unity and meaning for groups and individuals have been the elements of popular religion. These are aspects of religious feeling and practice that sometimes go unnoticed in studies of religious history. Popular religion often provides a focus for family, congregational, and community-wide participation in religious groups and tradition. *Popular religion* designates those patterns of religious participation—beliefs and customs—not articulated at levels of abstract intellectualism. These include practices that appeal to the uneducated and the educated, to young and old alike.

Like most other religious traditions, Christianity observes a number of holidays commemorating events important to its history. For Christianity many of these holidays are based on biblical or ecclesiastical happenings. Their observance may be prescribed in the liturgical calendars of the different Christian denominations. Christmas and Easter, commemorating the birth and Resurrection of Jesus, respectively, probably are the two most widely celebrated of Christian holiday periods. Aspects of these holidays that may make the largest impact on participants frequently are those that have grown up spontaneously in popular tradition or even those that have been commercially promoted by secular interests. Santa Claus and

---

[16]For further discussion of this topic and a variety of points of view, consult the Further Reading section of this chapter for works by Ronald Knox, Felicitas Goodman, and H. Newton Maloney and A. Adams Lovekin.

the exchange of gifts and Christmas cards, going caroling, going to parties, perhaps an annual school Christmas pageant, or the community-sponsored performance of an oratorio such as Handel's *Messiah* have come to symbolize Christmas for many individuals.

Various informally developed customs associated with the sacraments or with quasi-sacramental practices—marriages in Protestantism or wakes before funerals—may create bonds of unity and a sense of community among adherents. A Wednesday night church supper, regular participation at a church-sponsored bingo night, or the church's softball team may be a primary focus of religious identification and loyalty.

If one understands only the official theology and polity of a denomination, it is difficult to see which aspects of religious meaning are most alive to its adherents. In the Middle Ages in Europe, the importance of seeing and receiving benefit from various religious relics, alleged or genuine, became very great. Enough fragments of Christ's cross were supposed to have been in Europe to provide materials for several large buildings. These and a multitude of other relics, including branches from the burning bush associated with Moses' call, became objects of pilgrimage to many of the faithful. The Crusades provided a rich body of fact and legend that appealed to popular imagination. Miracle and mystery plays, dramatizations of the biblical stories by the guilds and crafts utilizing amateur talent, created comradeship. They were also educational devices for whole towns and villages.

The revivals and camp meetings of frontier America were not only an important method of denominational recruitment but occasions for recreation, socializing, and finding marriage partners. Twentieth-century television evangelists make use of the most sophisticated methods of programming and public-relations techniques, copying the style, and at times employing the same performers, as those appearing on popular variety shows.

Stories of contemporary appearances of Christ, the Virgin Mary, and other saints, often with special messages of encouragement for groups or individuals, have in most periods of Christian history generated fervor and devotion. During the past century reports of such appearances in Portugal (the Miracle of Fatima) and France (at Lourdes) have received acceptance and approval by the Roman Catholic hierarchy. Lourdes has become an important site of pilgrimage, with many accounts of miraculous healings.

Apocalyptic speculations associated with signs of the end of the world or the transition from one spiritual age to another have also had large appeal. In the Middle Ages, the speculations of the monk Joachim of Flora generated enthusiasm and scattered movements that became embroiled in conflict with the leadership of Catholicism. During the past two centuries, apocalyptic speculation has flourished among some Protestant groups and their offshoots. Often Christian apocalypticism is based on some synthesis of various biblical sources: the Old Testament books of Ezekiel and Daniel, and the New Testament Revelation and Paul's letters to the Thessalonians. Millennialism, a belief in the imminent return of Christ to earth to rescue the faithful—the Rapture—before the final battle with the forces of Satan—Armageddon—spread in nineteenth-century America and still lives among Seventh Day Adventists, many Pentecostalists, Baptists, and others. During the early 1970s several U.S. sects became convinced that Christ would return to earth in the year 1975. There were reports of preliminary appearances alleged already to have happened. Reports of these appearances were spread by word of mouth. At various times throughout Christian history, including the present, small or large groups have sold their possessions, abandoned secular occupations, and withdrawn to remote sites to await the visible return of Christ.

Often denominational leaders, sensitive to the moods, anxieties, and aspirations of the rank and file of their organizations and communities, have been able to make use of popular forms of cultural expression and symbols of cultural quest to give powerful new expression to the content of Christian faith. Some of the medieval popes, as well as popular saints like Francis and Clare of Assisi, and, in our times, Thérèse of Lisieux, utilized forms of popular culture to revitalize Christian expression. Martin Luther and John and Charles Wesley also did this, especially as they developed new forms of Christian congregrational music and new forms of sermon and popular religious literature.

Sometimes Christian leaders are appalled at the forms that popular devotion and enthusiasm take, fearing the dangers of superstition and crude distortion that these can give to the content of Christian faith and life. Oftentimes, leaders are alarmed at the vast potential for exploitation of the gullible faithful by calculating charlatans. In contemporary America, there have been active magazine and radio campaigns to sell various guaranteed miraculous healing devices, including prayer cloths, drops of water from the Jordan River, and autographed pictures of Jesus Christ. Of greater concern have been the money-raising projects of some televangelists of the "electronic church"—several of whom have been embroiled in scandals involving charges of sexual misconduct, misappropriation of funds, and tax evasion during the late 1980s.

Despite the risk of superficiality and exploitation, popular forms of religious expression are indispensable keys to the understanding of what being an adherent to a particular denomination in a particular setting means. Popular religion indeed often tells us better than anything else what being a Christian means and has meant to the majority of Christians across the centuries.

Contemporary Forms of Witness, Life, and Expression

If the sociological theory developed in earlier pages of this chapter is accurate, we may anticipate a wide variety of forms of Christian witness and life-style in contemporary societies. Many of these are illustrated in Chapter Eight. Two not discussed there that show contrasting extremes of Christian expression, life-style, and witness will be briefly examined here.

Simone Weil. Simone Weil was a Frenchwoman who came to maturity between the two world wars. She was of Jewish background, a brilliant student of mathematics, literature, and philosophy. She was a fellow student of Simone de Beauvoir and Jean-Paul Sartre, developers of the philosophy of atheistic existentalism. She became convinced of the truth of the Christian gospel, though she was attracted to such nonorthodox expressions of it as the Albigensian radical separation of spirit and body. Her closest advisor was a Catholic priest. Nevertheless, she refused baptism, believing that God had called her to be a Christian outside the established church. She was concerned about the lot of French working people and worked in a factory, refusing the advantages and comforts that her middle-class background could have given her. When Germany defeated France during the Second World War, she went to England to work with the Free French resistance.

Refusing to eat more than she believed the population of occupied France received, she died, partly as a result of malnutrition, during the war. Highly individualistic and deeply Christian, though unbound either by traditional orthodoxy or church structures, her deeply mystical writings have influenced many. She was impressed with the uprooting of people in the contemporary world and believed that people could find roots only by turning to God. For her, the religious life was one of suffering and inner purification, involving sharing the lot of the world's poor.

Billy Graham.   Billy Graham, an American, was born just a few years after Simone Weil. He came to maturity in roughly the same time period, but in a vastly different social and cultural setting. An American Southerner and a Baptist ministerial student, according to his biographers he made a deliberate decision to turn his back on the historical-critical approach to the Bible. He accepted, in American fundamentalist fashion, the literal inerrancy of the Scriptures. In the late 1940s he came to national, then world, prominence. He had adopted the methods of his great nineteenth- and twentieth-century predecessors—Protestant evangelists who held revivals in major metropolitan centers of the United States and Europe, using tents or municipal auditoriums. Billy Graham used the devices of revivalism in the United States and Europe, especially England, holding campaigns that lasted in some cases for several weeks. To the traditional revivalist methods he added radio and television, becoming one of the pioneers of the electronic church. He differed from many evangelists of the electronic church in that he insisted on the cooperation of (mainly) evangelical Protestant denominations in sponsoring his appearances and gave a strict account of the contributions he received and the uses to which they were put. He urged converts to affiliate with a local church and denomination of the individual's choice. He promoted ecumenical cooperation among the various evangelical denominations.

His message was apocalyptic and simple. He stressed the imminent literal Second Coming of Christ and the sinfulness of the contemporary world. He proclaimed that humanity was living in the last days, using the threat of nuclear war, the breakup of the family, and rising crime rates as evidence of this. Graham was criticized for the simplicity and lack of social relevance of his message by such a spokesman of twentieth-century Christianity as Reinhold Niebuhr. Nevertheless, during the course of his ministry, Billy Graham began to speak out in support of civil rights for American ethnic groups. This stand was almost unheard of at the time among prominent white Southern Protestant fundamentalists. More recently, he has taken a strong and controversial stand in support of nuclear disarmament, alienating some of his traditional followers. Up to date in terms of programming and organization, striking those who hear him as eminently sincere and committed, Dr. Graham is perhaps the best-known figure of contemporary world Protestantism, although he belongs to a denomination, the Southern Baptists, some of whose representatives refuse the designation Protestant.

Both individuals, Simone Weil and Billy Graham—one apparently free of tradition, the other seemingly tradition bound—incorporated elements of Christian religious tradition, while rejecting others, in their approach to Christian life and witness. Each, however, was willing to incorporate new insights, in some ways to develop and others to transform earlier positions in the attempt to express what it means to be Christians in unique cultural settings.

What of the individual Christian in the contemporary world? We can expect that the majority of individual Christians will be tolerant of Christians in other denominations, and even within their own denominations, who hold significantly different religious positions from their own, though on some issues, more frequently moral and political than doctrinal or liturgical, there will be tension and conflict. Individual Christians will be interested in their own ethnic and denominational roots, to the extent of wanting to internalize them—wanting to become true Catholics, Presbyterians, Baptists, Disciples, or Nazarenes. But they will be relatively autonomous or individualistic in doing this—wanting to become Catholics, Presbyterians, Baptists, Disciples, or Nazarenes of their own kind. Perhaps the major task of Christian groups in modern societies will be to assist them in doing this rather than to indoctrinate or mobilize them to fulfill organizationally defined goals.

QUESTIONS

1. How has the concept of Christian missions changed since the Second World War?
2. How do the differences between simple and complex societies and the characteristics of modernized societies affect religion and religious organizations in the modern world?
3. Explain the differences between church, sect, and denomination as types of religious organizations.
4. How are changing attitudes about the role of women in society affecting religious organizations and attitudes?
5. How are the two aspects of international relations discussed in this chapter interrelated?
6. What questions about major traditional Christian theological beliefs and practices have been raised by the Holocaust and by Christian-Jewish relations generally?
7. What are the major sources and emphases of liberation theology, black theology, and feminist theology?
8. What is popular Christianity? Give some examples of popular Christianity from past and present societies, explaining why leaders of Christian denominations may both approve and disapprove of popular religion.
9. How has the historical-critical and literary approach to the study of the Bible affected the way Christians understand and reread the Bible?

FURTHER READING

ABRECHT, PAUL, ed. *Faith, Science and the Future.* Geneva: World Council of Churches, 1978; Philadelphia: Fortress Press, 1979.

BAINTON, ROLAND C. *Christian Attitudes Toward War and Peace.* Nashville, Tenn.: Abingdon Press, 1960.

BELLAH, ROBERT N. ET AL. *Habits of the Heart.* New York: Harper & Row, 1985.

BERRY, WENDELL. *The Gift of Good Land.* San Francisco: North Point Press, 1981.

BOSWELL, JOHN.   *Christianity, Social Tolerance, and Homosexuality.* New York: Oxford University Press, 1980.

BOULDING, KENNETH E.   *The Meaning of the 20th Century.* New York: Harper & Row, 1964.

CLARK, ELIZABETH and RICHARDSON, HERBERT.   *Women and Religion: A Feminist Sourcebook of Christian Thought.* New York: Harper & Row, 1977.

DEWART, LESLIE.   *The Future of Belief: Theism in a World Come of Age.* New York: Herder and Herder, 1966.

FRADY, MARSHALL.   *Billy Graham.* Boston: Little, Brown, 1979.

GOODMAN, FELICITAS D.   *Speaking in Tongues: A Cross-cultural Study of Glossolalia.* Chicago: University of Chicago Press, 1972.

GRAHAM, DOM AELRED.   *Conversations: Christian and Buddhist.* New York: Harcourt Brace Jovanovich, 1968.

GREELEY, ANDREW M.   *Unsecular Man: The Persistence of Religion.* New York: Schocken Books, 1972.

GUSTAFSON, JAMES M.   *Ethics from a Theocentric Perspective: Theology and Ethics.* Vol. I. Chicago: University of Chicago Press, 1981.

KATOPPO, MARIANNE.   *Compassionate and Free: An Asian Woman's Theology.* Geneva: World Council of Churches, 1979; Maryknoll, N.Y.: Orbis Books, 1980.

KNOX, RONALD A.   *Enthusiasm: A Chapter in the History of Religion with Special Reference to the XVII and XVIII Centuries.* New York: Oxford University Press, 1950.

KÜNG, HANS.   *Does God Exist?* Garden City, N.Y.: Doubleday, 1980.

————.   *On Being a Christian.* Garden City, N.Y.: Doubleday, 1976.

LONG, EUGENE THOMAS.   *Jaspers and Bultmann: A Dialogue Between Philosophy and Theology in the Existentialist Tradition.* Durham, N.C.: Duke University Press, 1968.

MALONY, H. NEWTON, and LOVEKIN, A. ADAMS.   *Glossolalia: Behavioral Science Perspectives on Speaking in Tongues.* New York: Oxford University Press, 1985.

MCCURLEY, FOSTER R.   *Ancient Myths and Biblical Faith.* Philadelphia: Fortress Press, 1983.

MCFAGUE, SALLY.   *Models of God: Theology for an Ecological, Nuclear Age.* Philadelphia: Fortress Press, 1987.

MOLLENKOTT, VIRGINIA RAMEY.   *Women, Men, and the Bible.* Nashville, Tenn.: Abingdon Press, 1977.

MOLTMANN, JÜRGEN.   *Experiences of God.* Philadelphia: Fortress Press, 1980.

MONK, ROBERT C., et al.   *Exploring Religious Meaning.* 2nd ed. Englewood Cliffs, N.J.: Prentice-Hall, 1980.

NATIONAL CONFERENCE OF CATHOLIC BISHOPS.   "The Challenge of Peace: God's Promise and Our Response." A pastoral letter on war and peace. Washington, D.C.: United States Catholic Conference, May 3, 1983.

THE NATIONAL CONFERENCE OF CATHOLIC BISHOPS.   "Economic Justice for All: Pastoral Letter on Catholic Social Teaching and the U.S. Economy." Washington, D.C.: United States Catholic Conference, 1986.

NIEBUHR, H. RICHARD. *Christ and Culture.* New York: Harper & Row, 1951.

OGDEN, SCHUBERT M. *The Point of Christology.* New York: Harper & Row, 1982.

OTWELL, JOHN H. *And Sarah Laughed: The Status of Women in the Old Testament.* Philadelphia: Westminster Press, 1977.

PARSONS, TALCOTT. *Sociological Theory and Modern Society.* New York: Free Press, 1967.

PÉTREMENT, SIMONE. *Simone Weil.* New York: Random House, Inc., 1976.

RICHARDSON, HERBERT. *Nun, Witch, Playmate.* New York: Harper & Row, 1971.

ROGERS, JACK B., and MCKIM, DONALD K. *The Authority and Interpretation of the Bible.* San Francisco: Harper & Row, 1979.

ROOF, WADE CLARK, and WILLIAM MCKINNEY. *American Mainline Religion.* New Brunswick, N.J.: Rutgers University Press, 1987.

RUETHER, ROSEMARY. *Sexism and God Talk: Toward a Feminist Theology.* Boston: Beacon Press, 1985.

SCHALLER, LYLE E. *Understanding Tomorrow.* Nashville, Tenn.: Abingdon Press, 1976.

SCHELL, JONATHAN. *The Fate of the Earth.* New York: Alfred A. Knopf, 1982.

SCHILLEBEECKX, EDWARD. *Jesus: An Experiment in Christology.* London: William Collins' Sons, 1979.

SHANNON, THOMAS A., ed. *War or Peace?* Maryknoll, N.Y.: Orbis Books, 1980.

STROBER, GERALD S. *Graham: A Day in Billy's Life.* Garden City, N.Y.: Doubleday, 1976.

UNITED METHODIST COUNCIL OF BISHOPS. "In Defense of Creation: The Nuclear Crisis and a Just Peace." Foundation document. Nashville, Tenn: Graded Press, 1986.

WARD, HILEY H. *Religion 2101 A.D.* Garden City, N.Y.: Doubleday, 1975.

WEIL, SIMONE. *Waiting for God.* New York: G. P. Putnam's Sons, 1951.

Appendices

APPENDIX I: JEWISH AND CHRISTIAN CATEGORIZATION OF JEWISH SCRIPTURES

Note: In most instances the Christian arrangement follows that of the Septuagint (the Jewish translation of the Hebrew Scriptures into Greek made ca. 300–100 B.C.E..), with some differences in names of books.

Hebrew Bible (Masoretic Text)	*Christian Old Testament*
I. The Torah	**I. The Pentateuch**

The Five Books of Moses

Genesis
Exodus
Leviticus
Numbers
Deuteronomy

II. The Prophets	**II. Historical Books**
Former Prophets	Joshua
Joshua	Judges
Judges	Ruth
I–II Samuel	I–II Samuel
I–II Kings	I–II Kings
Later Prophets	I–II Chronicles
Isaiah	Ezra (or I Esdras)
Jeremiah	Nehemiah (or II Esdras)
Ezekiel	*Tobit
	*Judith
The Twelve	Esther (with * additions)
Hosea, Joel, Amos,	*I–II Maccabees
Obadiah, Jonah, Micah,	III-IV Maccabees (never
Nahum, Habakkuk, Zephaniah,	recognized as canonical
Haggai, Zechariah, Malachi	by Christians)

Hebrew Bible (cont'd.)	*Christian Old Testament (cont'd.)*
(Masoretic Text)	

III. Writings

Psalms (Songs of Praise)
Job
Proverbs

The Festal Scrolls

Ruth
Song of Songs
Ecclesiastes
Lamentations
Esther
Daniel
Ezra–Nehemiah
I–II Chronicles

III. Poetry and Wisdom

Job
Psalms
Ecclesiastes
Song of Solomon (Song of
    Songs)
*The Wisdom of Solomon
*Ecclesiasticus (Wisdom
    of Jesus ben Sirach)

IV. The Prophets

Isaiah
Jeremiah
Lamentations
*Baruch
*Epistle of Jeremiah
Ezekiel
Daniel (with *additions)
Hosea, Joel, Amos, Obadiah,
Jonah, Micah, Nahum
Habakkuk, Zephaniah, Haggai,
Zechariah, Malachi

*These books, included in the Catholic Scriptures as indicated, are included in the Protestant intertestamental Apocrypha and are not recognized by Protestants as canonical (see Chapter Four). Also included in the Protestant Apocrypha, and since the sixteenth century printed in the Catholic Vulgate as appendices to the New Testament, are works entitled I and II Esdras (by Protestants) and (by Catholics) III and IV Esdras. Some other works, not listed here, are included in the Protestant Apocrypha. There is great variation in spelling of the names of many of the biblical and apocryphal books as listed in Roman Catholic and Protestant versions.

APPENDIX II: WHAT IS THE NEW TESTAMENT?

The New Testament is a collection of writings that originated in the early Christian church. None of these writing is lengthy. Most, perhaps all, of them originated during the first eighty years of the Christian movement. They were circulated among the various Christian congregations of the ancient world and ultimately became part of the New Testament canon because of their nearly universal use and recognition as Scripture, or inspired writings, among Christians.

Gospels

Collections of stories about Jesus and his teachings with interpretations of them by the early Christian community (including the author of each gospel). Although the gospels form a unique literary genre, they differ among themselves by resembling different literary genres current in the ancient world. Each gives a connected account of the ministry, crucifixion, and Resurrection of Jesus.

Matthew
Mark   *Synoptic*
Luke   *Gospels*

John

History

An account in two parts, by the same author, of the significance of the ministry of Jesus and beginning and expansion of the Christian movement against the background of world history. Though "Luke" is placed with the gospels, it is the first part of a work to some extent modeled on Greek and Roman historical writings.

(Luke)–Acts

Letters

Communications from Christian leaders to Christian congregations or (more rarely) to an individual Christian dealing with specific problems involving belief or conduct. Usually—Paul's Letter to the Romans is an exception—these are genuine letters dealing with one or more specific, practical problems. Romans, which also deals with a number of specific issues, gives a systematic, connected account of Paul's teaching about God's redemptive act in human history.

Letters by Paul	Letters attributed to Paul*	Letters not originating from Paul or his circle
I Thessalonians	Ephesians	I Peter
II Thessalonians	I Timothy	II Peter
		Jude
I Corinthians†	II Timothy	II John
II Corinthians†	Titus	III John

Letters by Paul (*cont'd.*)	Letters attributed to Paul*(*cont'd.*)	Letters not originating from Paul or his circle (*cont'd*)
Galatians‡		
Philippians‡		
Philemon‡		
Romans		
Colossians		

Theological and Homiletical Treatises

These are writings, inspirational and homiletical—sermonic—in nature. Though each is called a letter, and to some extent is, formally, they are more like devotional essays or meditations (I John and James) or even treatises (Hebrews) than like the other New Testament letters.

Hebrews
James
I John

Apocalyptic Writings

There is one fully developed Christian Apocalypse in the New Testament. (I Thessalonians, II Peter, Jude, and the Synoptic Gospels contain apocalyptic elements). This is the Book of Revelation, or the Revelation to John. Most scholars believe that it was written during a period of intense persecution of Christians by the Roman government, perhaps the first (under the emperor Nero) or second (under Domitian) persecution, which provided a severe shock to the fledgling Christian movement. Using all the symbols of popular apocalyptic writing, Revelation seeks to urge Christians to remain loyal to their faith, promising that God will soon vindicate them by overthrowing the demonic powers that control the Roman Empire. Although affirming its spiritual validity for present-day Christians, most scholars believe that interpretations which tie Revelation to specific twentieth-century and future events and dates fundamentally misinterpret it.

Revelation

*Letters thought by many scholars to have originated from a later "Pauline" circle.

†I and II Corinthians viewed as a unit seems to contain more than two related letters not necessarily now in the sequence of their original composition.

‡These contain important autobiographical materials.

Index

Israelites, as chosen people, 2, 3; covenant with God, 3, 4, 5

Jacob, 2
Jehovah's Witnesses, 105
Jerome, St., 11
Jerusalem: as center of religious pilgrimage, 19–20; as City of God, 4; destruction of after war with Rome, 9; Hell, literary location, 123; Judeans return to after post-exilic period, 4; Sadducees in, 6; Sanhedrin, 19; Temples, 4, 6, 7, 9, 19: cleansing of by Jesus, 26–27
Jesuits; *See* Society of Jesus
Jesus Christ, 146, 173, 213, 218, 224; birth accounts of in Gospels, 17–19; Christological conflict, 115, 116; cleansing of Jerusalem Temple, 26–27; crucifixion, 8, 16, 19, 29; disciples, 7, 8, 15, 19, 23–24, 29, 30; Gnostic view of, 115; "historical" Jesus, 16–17; human nature of, 218; identification of as Messiah, 8; incarnation, 103, 114; in Jewish community, 7–9; in the wilderness, 15; John the Baptist and, 15, 19, 20–22; life, accounts of in Gospels, 15, 17; Messiah, 14, 16, 17, 18, 25, 29, 30; ministry, 15, 19–28; nature of, 118; parables, use of, 27–28; person of, 114; repudiation of messiah called "son of David," 25; resurrection, 16, 17, 19, 29–30, 113, 118–19, 121; revelation or self-disclosure of God, 118–19, 121, 137; role in Eastern Orthodoxy, 49; role of atonement in Western Christianity, 50; rumor of return in 1975, 224; Schweitzer, Albert, view of, 92–93; "Son of God,", 14, 15, 16
Jews, derivation of name, 5
Joachim of Flora, 224
Job, 133
John of the Cross, St., 83, 87, 186, 222
John Paul II, Pope, 98
John the Baptist, 15, 19, 20–22, 136; identification with Elijah, 15, 22; proclamation of, 22–24
John XXIII, Pope, 98; *Mater et Magistra, Pacem in Terris,* 98
Jones, Rufus M., 88
Joseph, 8
Josephus, 6, 17
Judaism: apocalyptic beliefs, early, 20, 92; beliefs, 207; and Christianity, historical relationship, 1–13; concept of God, 103; derivation of name, 5; Elijah, forerunner of the Messiah, 14, 15; first-century characteristics, 111; Hebrews, development of beliefs and practices, 2–5, 8; Jesus in Jewish community, 7, 8; Jewish Christianity, 8–9; Jewish religious parties, 5–7; Messiah, belief in, 6–7; New Age, belief in, 2, 7; post-Jerusalem community, 9–10; rabbinic Judaism, 9; Roman rule of Judah, 5–6; Russian, 210; spirit, concept of, 118; Talmudic interpretations, 128–29; Torah, 103; war against Romans, 9; *See also* Scriptures, Hebrew
Judas "Iscariot," 25
Justin, 130, 131, 137, 138

Kagawa, Toyohiko, 208
Kant, Immanuel, 154, 171;*Critique of Pure Reason,* 143; *Religion Within the Limits of Reason,* 138
Kelly, Thomas, 88
Kemelman, Harry, 128–29

Kepler, Johann, 150
Ketubin, 11
Kierkegaard, Søren, 143
King, Jr., Martin Luther, 182–85, 207, 217; *Stride Toward Freedom,* 184; *Why We Can't Wait,* 184
Kingdom of God, 15, 16, 22–23, 27–28, 122–23, 124, 146, 207; John the Baptist's proclamation, 20–22; as message of Jesus, 15, 22–23, 24; Toyohiko Kagawa and Kingdom-of-God movement, 208
Kingsley, Charles, 151
Knowledge of God, belief systems: Christianity, 132, 136–45; Judaism, 132–36
Knox, Ronald, 221
Kuhn, Thomas, 152

Language, religious, 153–55; masculine pronoun, use of in reference to God, 106
Last Judgment, 124
Law, William, 87
Leibniz, Gottfried, 173–74
Leo III, Pope, 57
Leo XIII, 97; *Rerum novarum,* encyclical, 181
Lessing, G. E., 91
Lester, Muriel, 88
Liberation theology, 192, 217, 219
Licinius, 43
Life of Theresa of Jesus, The, 83
Locke, John, 147, 171, 174
Lourdes, 224
Loyola, Ignatius, 81–82, 87, 188; *Spiritual Exercises, The,* 81
Luckmann, Thomas, 204
Ludovicus (Thomas Merton), 186
Luther, Martin, 67–70, 72–73, 110, 120, 144, 145, 146, 171; excommunication, 69–70; indulgences, system, 67; Ninety-Five Theses, 67
Lutheranism, 67–73, 146, 208

Maccabees, 4, 5, 6
Manichaeism, 107, 138, 159
Marcionism, 115, 121
Martyr, Justin, *Dialogue with Trypho,* 11–12
Martyrdom, 39–42, 43
Marx, Karl, 214
Mary, Virgin, 18, 224; veneration, 119
Mater et Magistra, 98
Mattathias, 5
Maurin, Peter, 181
McKim, Donald, 220
Melanchthon, 71–72
Mennonites, 79, 217
Merton, Thomas, 88, 185–88, 211; *Seven Story Mountain, The,* 186
Messiah, expectations of, 2, 4, 7–8, 14, 15; Essenes, 7; identification of Jesus as, 8, 14, 16, 17, 18; Messiah of Israel and Messiah of Aaron, 7; Messianic signs, 22, 24–27, 30; Pharisees, 6; prophet, appearance of, 25; Sadducees, 6; "Son of David," 25; "Son of Man," 25; Zealots, 6
Methodism, 146–47, 172, 176, 177, 178, 197, 206, 216, 222; American, 147; suffrage, opposition to, 179; temperance stand, 177; Willard, Frances, 176–179
Metropolitans (archbishops), 52
Middle Ages, Catholicism in, 199
Millennialism, 224
Mills, Samuel J., 96